WHAT is your PERSPECTIVE OF TRUTH?

CARL L. JONES

Gotham Books
30 N Gould St.
Ste. 20820, Sheridan, WY 82801
https://gothambooksinc.com/
Phone: 1 (307) 464-7800

Published by Gotham Books (date published June 2022)

ISBN: 978-1-956349-44-3 (sc)
ISBN: 978-1-956349-45-0 (e)

Any people depicted in stock imagery provided by iStock are models, and
such images are being used for illustrative purposes only.

certain stock imagery © iStock.

Because of the dynamic nature of the Internet, any web addresses or links contained in this book may have changed
since publication and may no longer be valid. The views expressed in this work are solely those of the author and
do not necessarily reflect the views of the publisher, and the publisher hereby disclaims any responsibility for them.

This is a work of fiction. The characters, incidents, and dialogues are products of
the author's imagination and are not to be construed as real. Any resemblance to
actual events, entities, or persons, living dead, is entirely coincidental.

CONTENTS

INFORMATION

ACKNOWLEDGEMENT

⸻

I acknowledge MY **ADONAI YAHUSHA HAMASHIACH**, MY **SAVIOR**, for ALL the things HE has done in my life. Without HIM, it would be impossible to do anything. HE is on the throne, and I do worship HIM for all things. HE is the Head of my life, and everything I am is because of HIS sufferings, HIS death, and HIS resurrection. I thank THE FATHER (YAH) for allowing HIS SON to come down from Heaven and offering HIS SON for our ransom from sin (eternal death, separation from HIM) so that we may live with HIM forever and forever. Amein Amein Amein. HalleluJAH! I would love to thank my ADONAI YAHUSHA HAMASHIACH for saving my pitiful and dreadful soul. And the Muslims served the same Deity. They referred to HIM as Allah. If you look at the word HalleluJAH the first portion of it you will see in the Hallelujah Halle and if you spell that backward you will have Ellah and in Spanish the letter e has a sound thereby, we have Allah, but they believe that the SON of YAH was a good man. I would like to PRAISE MY GOD for giving me the common sense of what HE has and done in giving me the ability to write these words in this book in which many will not see, but are HOPELESSNESS lost in this matrix of a man playing with our minds body and soul. I acknowledge THE RUACH HA'QODESH for leading me to write this information and I ACKNOWLEDGE YAHUAH THE FATHER for what HE has done for me and giving me what HE wanted me to know and so I pass it on.

HALAL: to praise, to shine, to boast, to rave, to celebrate, to be clamorously foolish. **YADAH:** the extended hands, to throw out the hands, therefore to worship with extehands, to lift the hands.

TOWDAH: an extension of the hands in adoration, to avow your acceptance, It is used for thanking GOD for things not yet received as well as things already at hand.

SHABACH: to shout, to address in a loud tone, to command, to triumph.

BARAK: to kneel down to bless GOD as an act of adoration, to salute.

ZAMAR: to pluck the strings of an instrument, to sing, to praise a musical word which is largely involved with joyful expressions of music with musical instruments.

TEHILLAH: The singing of **Hallal** to sing or to laud is perceived to involve music, especially hymns of the Spirit or praise.

FOREWORD

---✧---

**PROVERBS 16:3 "The lot is cast into the lap, but the
whole disposing thereof is of YAHUAH."**

The Cepher Bible converts the name from English to THE ORIGINAL **HEBREW**
names. The Hebrews are people that are called" The **My People in The Bible"**
and they have more melanin in their skin tone which makes them darker than the
ones we saw in the movie "The Ten Commandments." You see we have been deceived by
them in charge of this disinformation and brainwashing of a group of people who are The
Heart of YAH. Yes, I said The Heart of YAH because HE sent HIS SON to save The Lost
Sheep of Israel **Mattithyahu 10:5-6, 15:24.** I prayed for this and was led by THE RUACH
HA'QODESH to write this book. Avraham our forefather is a Hebrew and everyone born
under him are The Hebrews and not so-called whites because there are no white people or
black people in the world. This information of black and white is set up by man. What we
have in this world are NATIONS and not races. We have been labeled black and white but
that is hyperbolism. We have people who have very little melanin (so-called white) and those
with more melanin in their skin tone than others, but this was done by who? YAHUAH
period! It is HE that is the determining factor for all things and many don't believe there is
A CREATOR. You see my skin tone is brown and not black because there are people from
India darker than me and they are not called black and there are people much lighter than me
and they are called black and we are not black but our skin tone is determined by the amount
of melanin we have in our DNA (Deoxyribonucleic acid). Maybe we are called black because
they KNOW something? Because in The Bible you will not see black or white nations. These
nations have names and are NOT described by a color or race period. Many believe the sun is

the center of the universe and that the earth rotates around the sun, but it is just the opposite and that the sun is not 93,000,000 million miles away from earth and we believe this **crap or dung or manure**. The earth does not move; it is stationary. The sun rises in the east and sets in the west and this was confirmed by YAH and the sun and moon are placed in the expanse or firmament, but man has tried to unconfirm this truth by giving us lies upon lies. And stay away from and beware of **LIARS** because liars lie.

Dear reader, I tried in my writings to put the names from their English to their Hebrew names. You see Jesus (YAHUSHA), Jacob, (Ya`aqov) John (Yahuchanon), Miriam (Miryam), Mary (Miryam), Joseph (Yoceph), Abram (Avram), etc were not white or black because they were HEBREW people of color. You see there is no white race or black race. The people that label themselves as white are in reality have a very low percentage of melanin in their DNA. Our skin tone, eyes color, and hair color are determined by the amount of MELANIN in our DNA. Melanin is a natural skin pigment. These special skin cells called melanocytes make melanin. Everyone has the same number of melanocytes, but some people make more melanin than others. You see it is ELOHIYM that has determined who you are. So don't get angry just accept who you are **because there is NOT anything you could have determined who you are**, but be grateful who you are period because we will be judged by HIM who has made us. HE has made us all THE GREAT I AM **EHAYAH ASHER EHAYAH**. You see, the race is not in The Bible, but the word nation is in The Bible. You see, we have been labeled as black and the majority of our color is **BROWN** and not black. You see, some of the people of India are darker than us and **they are not called black.** We have been made blind by the one who publishes this information to keep up hate because we all came from one man that YAHUAH made from the dust of the earth. YAHUAH has made all we see. So, if you become angry, get angry at YAHUAH because I am just the messenger. These men and women the nation of Israel was Hebrew and so thereby they had Hebrew names and KJV destroyed that emphasis by replacing their names with some type of English name. For instance, John is called the baptizer, but in Hebrew, it would be Yahuchanon the immerser. You see this information comes from The Cepher Bible which translates the names back to their original name and not to some English name. And this is one of the reasons I invested my money into The Cepher Bible and it had other books the KJV left out that were in 1611 KJV. The modern-day KJV left out those books to hide the truth.

This book can be shocking, debated, criticized by some and to others, it may not be, but study. This book will be very controversial because it will be in direct contradiction of what you have been taught all of your life, but please do not disregard this information but investigate this information because YAH said to His People they are destroyed because they rejected the information that were given them by YAH. You have the wonderful choice to accept this information to research or you can stay in your stupor or status quo just like the people in the movie called "The Matrix". In the movie, they didn't realize what had happened, but they were blinded by a lie. And only a few selected **souls knew the truth.** I have heard **Hosea 4:6** all my life but part of that verse opened my EYES. It says" **My people are destroyed** for **THE** lack of knowledge: because **you** have **rejected THE KNOWLEDGE"** and verse **14 e** says "therefore the people that do not understand shall fall". All I ask of you to do is just think and **READ & STUDY** to see if we have been **TOLD THE TRUTH**. Just like the movie "The Matrix", you can take the blue pill and stay asleep or you can take the red pill and wake up. The choice is yours. The only thing I can do is open the door to your mind and see if things we have been told are true. Because of this information, I will die for because the world system wants you to stay blind and not see the truth. **WAKE-UP!**

WHEN WE DON'T HAVE ALL OF THE CORRECT OR RIGHT INFORMATION, THIS CAN LEAD or CAUSES GREAT CONFUSION.

YAH is fed up with all these lies our pastors/teachers have passed on to those generations they have taught lies to.

We believe ELOHIYM or we can continue with the precept of a simple-minded man having concoction. We can believe the ONE that made man. ELOHIYM is the maker of man. Man has gone astray and is <u>way</u> off course for his life. He can continue to sprout disbelief in ELOHIYM Words just like Nimrod. ELOHIYM Words bring life. ELOHIYM can bring honey and water from a rock and man cannot. Man is so simple and refuses to take ELOHIYM at HIS Word for what it is. It is the truth as **John 17:17** says. Life seems unattainable, but faith in ELOHIYM is life. Open your eyes and satanism (and the people in the church help the world to celebrate this day even though YAH has nothing to do with it). We have allowed witchcraft in our houses through the media of television shows like Bewitched, Aladdin, Harry Potter, and the list goes on. They have gently tricked us or deceived us to not be so alarmed about **witchcraft**. We Have been lulled into accepting witchcraft that it is ok, but witchcraft in any form is wrong for believers to be aligned to or associate with in no matter what form or fashion. It was the death penalty in the Old Testament. Easter has its bunny, which can't lay eggs. This is celebrating the goddess ashtoreth which is a pagan god. We have been led to believe in these evil forces by men of no good who are bastards to the word of YAH. We have men leading us into literal darkness. I believe YAHUSHA came as a baby, lived as a man among us sinless, died on a cross, was placed in a tomb and arose from the tomb after three nights and three days, stayed on this earth another forty days talking to his followers, went into heaven and now we are awaiting for HIS return. Why because HE loves Israel and I am of the Hebrews/Israelites. MESSIAH/YAHUSHA is the first part of the GODHEAD and the second a Hebrew man.

believe what is before you before it's too late. Believe GOD The Maker and The Creator of all you see.

The Messiah was not born in December. All lamb is born in the springtime. The MESSIAH was **THE PASSOVER'S LAMB for the world that THE FATHER commends!** The MESSIAH did not die on a Good Friday. That information is totally wrong and erroneous to believe because The Word of YAH says something completely different. Halloween has to do with witches. How many of us know that the KKK is a Christian group? The KKK get their uniforms from Catholicism. Roman Catholicism breaks the commandment of graven images. The statue of the so-called Messiah and the statue of the so-called Mary. These are graven images in which the second commandment says not to do, but they refused to follow that commandment.

If you want to be made aware of this presence of darkness then read YAH's word that this world has hidden and be enlightened with the truthful eyes or you can REMAIN in your blindness. Therefore study, watch and pray because we are in the last days on this planet called earth. Some say that The Creator did not send HIS Son to the cross. So, did He come into this world? How did He leave this earth? Did He die? And how are you saved from your sins though your cleanness when your cleanness is like filthy rags? Oh, foolish Galatians, you are still in your sins far from the peace of GOD as Pa'al said. For THE MESSIAH died and arose again so that ALL may come to HIM in peace and not in condemnation and ruin. This is just like the information when Yitschaq willingly was going to allow his father Avraham to sacrifice him on the altar. Yitschaq was carrying the wood (the cross). There are two people with Yitschaq, Avraham traveled three nights and three days and they rode an ass and satan tried to dwarfed or derail this plan. For there will be a new heaven and new earth says The GREAT I AM THAT I AM. Amein. The reason I wrote this book is to clarify one thing only. We all have been misguided by some preacher, teacher, apostle, clergy member, minister, scribe, religious leader, or whatever else they preferred to be called. We have been taught all our lives that YAHUSHA died on a Friday and rose early Sunday morning. I have been working on this for a number of years, and there is **NO** way, according to the WORD of ELOHIYM, that YAHUSHA died at 3:00 p.m. on Friday and rose Sunday morning. This does not agree at all with what the biblical text says and if any preacher says it does, he cannot read or interpret the WORD from the (KJV) King James Version correctly. Even **Hosea** disagrees with what the preacher preaches **6:1-2.**

I am sorry to have destroyed your faith in your minister, but we should have never placed our faith in a man anyway, for the BIBLE states to have faith in ELOHIYM only. We don't put faith, reliability, or trust in an individual anyway. How foolish are we? ELOHIYM is immutable on these two things: HE cannot lie and HIS promises will become true. YAHUSHA stated that all it takes to move a mountain is faith the size of a grain of a mustard seed. Some people believe that YAHUSHA HE meant things in our life, but I believe that YAHUHA was looking at a mountain range when HE spoke those words. Have your ministers moved any mountains lately? You will notice in my book that certain words that are capitalized aren't in my books. That's because all are gods that we have made them and no god can stand before my ELOHIYM this is not a typographical error, but it was intentional. Intentionally done to get us to rethink our mind from this broken (satan-led) society. This society's thinking has been soiled by men led by satan. The days of the week and planets are referring to other Elohiym (gods in English). Why is this important because of the way our thinking has been formatted? We have been programmed to accept not the truth but lies on top of lies until the truth has been deleted from society or memory and we believe the truth is now a lie. We have been programmed to accept not the truth, but lies. When the truth is presented to us, we think that it is a lie, because of the way we have been taught all our lives. An example would be like this. A man asked his wife "Why did she cut off the turkey tail?" And the wife said," I don't know." She said, "Let me ask my mother." And the mother said," I don't know." And she said, "Let me ask my mother." And that mother answered," Because the turkey wouldn't fit in the pan and we cut the tail off." So, everyone was just following an example but didn't know the true reason why. So it is in our society that we do the same thing because of things that happened years ago and we don't know why.

Why did all of this occur? We are living in the matrix (this world of sin controlled by the god of this world) until we are awakened. Awakened by the **TRUTH**. I have been awakened by the truth of ELOHIYM'S Word and not by the false teaching of man and satan. satan desires to replace the TRUE ELOHIYM, but his plan has failed miserably. I asked YAH why HE allowed the deceiver to do what he did? Who knows more than ELOHIYM or man? You have the choice to believe YAH. How did all of this blindness occur? I have asked YAH different questions and HE led me to study HIS WORD because what I was reading and understanding was not coming out of men's mouths was completely different than HIS Word. HIS Words and man's mouth cause me to have conflicts. When there is conflict, the conflict has to be resolved. If conflict is NOT resolved that causes division and division has to be resolved if not then death (separation). There is a saying: sticks and stones may break my bones, but words will never hurt. I totally disagree with this statement. I have considered this statement as a lie because words do hurt and words can cause generations to be lost forever and family and friendship can be destroyed because of words but words can also heal. Sometimes we harbor words in our memory forever. Two sisters came to a disagreement so many years ago and now they can't remember how the incident started. So our words can hurt. Our words are destructive. The bible says we have power in the tongue. It is not talking about the tongue, but the words dwelling in our heart, conscience, our mind, and soul. You are what is in your soul. Keep hearing good and you are most likely to do good. If you hear bad you are most likely to do bad. So the statement stick and stones may break my bone, but words will never hurt is so not true. Would rather hear "Baby I love you sooooo very much today" or would you rather hear Baby "I can't stand you" or "Baby I'm going to kiss you gently and softly on your lips every day" or "Look man I am going to run over your dead body over and over again." Which of these words are helpful or which would put a smile on your face? So then can words hurt? These very words will cost me my life here on this earth, but I no longer care for life here on this earth, but I am not talking about committing suicide, but making a comparison between this life and my eternal life with THE MESSIAH in which I am headed too. There is no comparison between life here on this earth and to be with my MASHIACH, but my eternal life with my HA'MASHIACH in heaven and also on the new earth. For as the Apostle Pa'al said "It is far better with YAHUSHA HA'MASHIACH than here on this earth. There is no comparison. When you arrive there, you first notice how great the air is that you are breathing. Look at your vacuum cleaner and you will notice all the dirt you are breathing NOW, but not in heaven the air is so very pure. I will be with ADONAI YAHUSHA HA'MASHIACH which is far so much better than being here on this earth with those that are misleading us away from YAHUAH'S Truths. You may wonder who I am talking about when you see YAHUAH. YAHUAH is THE FATHER, YAHUSHA THE SON, and RAUCH HA'QODESH The HOLY SPIRIT. All of this information has been hidden from our eyes [The true Israelites/Hebrews]. Many thought that The Hebrews/Israelites were in Israel, but that is so NOT true. Our fore parents were kidnapped from the land of Eden brought to the Americas and the islands sold into slavery as the Bible said. The first group of Israelites were not in slavery for 400 years in Egypt, but were slaved for only about 215 years because there were not 400 years between Yoceph's death and Mosheh's birth, so, thereby **Genesis 15:13-14** was not fulfilled until recently. Our fore parents were kidnapped and came to the Americas in august 1619 so add 400 to that and we have the year 2019 now is 400 years and now are awaiting the Exodus. Oh, yea and you (white evangelical Christian) thought Israel was across the seas, and we here in the Americas and the islands the one you have labeled as black, African American, colored, or ni_ _ _ _s. Oh yeah, surprise! We who ELOHIYM has created with **melanin** in our **DNA** are the true nation of Israel from our father Ya'aqov. People may ask "Does that make any difference?" Would you like TRUTH or lie in your life? Amein. The reason I am so passionate about it is that pastors will be stuck on the name Jesus and THE SON OF YAH was born into a Hebrew family and not Greece's family. THE SON OF GOD nationality is Hebrew so HE was born and given a Hebrew name. You see Jesus Christ is a Grecian name and not a Hebrew name. Plus, I gave this pastor some information and he just shrugged it off. He just explained it off. He did not stop but simply explained it off. He wanted to remain in the folly and he took the blue pill. When someone doesn't want to listen, you can't do anything for them but to PRAY. Many of you are reading this right now. I know this information is controversial because we have all grown up in this matrix with conceded information of what we have been taught all our right lives and when someone contradicts that information we reject it, but please don't be like the people in the Bible that is to say My people are destroyed for a lack of knowledge because they have rejected the knowledge. **Believe this the sun is not the center of the universe as we have been told by the matrix because we see the sun as that little ball in the sky that circle earth and not the earth circling the sun because the earth is stationary it does not move, but the matrix says the exact opposite and WE HAVE BEEN LIED too.**

All media information [books, pictures, movies, television shows, and historian experts] has distorted the truth by making all characters in biblical television and movies non-melanin. The ones that own the media are non-melanin people who have tried to succeed to destroy all information that does look like them and to whitewash history. Unless we examine what is out there, we won't discover it. A friend of mine once said, "that truth is easy to find, but to accept it is very difficult." We won't read because it is old information, but to know history you have to read history. I know Christians/Believers who have been in the church (the called-out ones) for more than forty years who have NOT read the bible from Genesis to Revelation. What reason will you give for yourself when you see YAHUSHA on that day? What reason will I give on account of myself? What excuse am I going to give to HIM? He will look me dead in my eyes and what reasons am I going to give? He loves you anyway.

This scene was not in the Ten Commandments movie. Moses in the book of Exodus placed his hand in his bosom and took it out and it turned white like leprosy. And he placed his hand back into his bosom and took it out and it changed to his other flesh. Why wasn't this in the Ten Commandments movie? Miryam in the **12th chapter of Numbers** was turned white as leprosy for a week. Yoceph standing before his brother, but all his brothers saw were just Egyptians, but Yoceph recognized his brothers. Do non-melanin people think that everyone looks like them? Pa'al in the book of Acts was thought to be an Egyptian. **Genesis 25:25** gave a description of Esau, but not Ya'aqov aka Jacob. Why not give a description of Ya'aqov? Because Ya'aqov looked like his parents but not Esau. Ya'aqov is the color of his parents. Jacob is an English name, but his Hebrew name is Ya'aqov because he is Hebrew, not English. The moviemakers were trying to get Julie Roberts to play Harriet Tubman. The producers said, "They won't remember that because it happened so many years ago." This is the same reason they the ones in charge of the media] have exploited the bible with lies in these movies. A non-melanin person **CANNOT** become more non-melanin! Can he? The Hebrew/Israelites are people of various colors because of melanin. Did you read this statement? The reason I say "are" instead of "was" is because we are still alive today. We are your coworkers, neighbors, teammates, relatives, and friends. And the curses and blessings that applied to our forefathers still applied today. We are in the Americas continents, Australia, Jamaica, Bermuda, Puerto Rico, Cuba, and the British Isles. The great deception by the non-melanin man. It is like a painting that has been covered up with a fake image and then someone sees the flaws and discovers the truth. A painting worth millions of dollars. This is how it was done. I discovered the truth by studying The Word of YAH and listening. You have to study and listen to The RUACH HA'QODESH. We are never led wrong by The Author of HIS Word. We have been misled by man because salvation belongs to the people of YAH. **Psalm 77:15** says YOU[YAHUAH] have with your arm redeemed <u>your</u> people, the sons of Ya'aqov and Yoceph. Ya'aqov has translated into English meaning, Jacob. Yoceph was translated into English meaning Joseph. In the 1611 KJV, there were no j in that version. The letter j was not formed until 1633. Every name in the 1611 KJV started with the letter i instead of a j. So, the name in which the whole world was saved was called in the 1611 KJV was Iesus which is close to the Grecian supreme god Zeus. **HOW MANY OF YOU KNEW THIS?** So, **Acts 4:10-12** is a flawed verse because it gives the wrong name! How then can we be saved by Iesus when that is **NOT THE SON OF YAH's name? The SON OF YAH came into this earth through Hebrew parents not Grecian or English parents, but Hebrew parents.** Please let this sink in, but we can only be responsible for what we know and nothing else. Do your own studying as the bible says **2 Timothy 2:15**. If I went to France would my name change? What this has done is to destroy a people's mind, heart, and culture who are the true and real sons of Ya'aqov. Do you remember the television miniseries ``Roots' and the character played by Lamar Burton? The slavemaster had Kinte Kunta tied to a pole and had him whipped until he said the name English name, Toby. **<u>THIS IS HOW IMPORTANT NAMES AND LANGUAGES ARE!</u>** This was intentionally done to blind The True People of YAH. I know certain people are not going to accept this because it destroys their unrighteous thinking and concept of what the truth is. A friend of mine once said that *"truth is easy to find, but to accept the truth is difficult."* Many of you reading this will either accept or reject or further study but as the bible says **thou hast rejected knowledge**. The truth has been hidden from our eyes for hundreds of years. Guess what, I am in THE FATHER'S Hands THE CREATOR. I shall not fear what man may do to me because at the end of this life we must all face YAHUSHA in judgment. We are "The My People in the Bible". **Proverbs 21;31 Proverbs 29;25 Proverbs 30;5.**

Thank you for purchasing this book for whatever reason to criticize or to learn the end of this earth is coming but it is my hope that you may learn what was given to me that I pass it on to you so that we all may learn and you be the judge if this is true. Who is right, the preacher or ELOHIYM? **Isaiah 29:12-13** states, "Ye will be taught the precept of a man because he is unlearned. Open my words and learn from me, for you are without excuse, for my word is before your eyes."

We are the people in the bible. Thereby, we are the nation of Israel lost in the Americas. The curses and blessings are passed on unto us, the true people of YAH. YAH states in the **tenth chapter of Yahuchanon (John)**, "HE (YAHUSHA) and other sheep I have which are not of the <u>fold</u> them also, I must bring, and there shall be one-fold and one shepherd." Who is the first fold? Who is YAHUSHA talking to? He was talking to Israel or Yashar'el. YAHUAH loves Ya'aqov. He has chosen Ya'aqov. **Yesha`yahu (Isaiah) 42:6** says He called us into righteousness. **Yesha`yahu 43:4** He loves us. **Yesha`yahu 41:8** says we are HIS servants; He has chosen the seed of Avraham's Ya'aqov. Yesha`yahu **41:10** says "Fear not, for I AM with you." We have been chosen. When The MESSIAH comes back, it is for the nation of Yashar'el only and not for the church. The word church actually means the called-out ones who have been adopted into the nation of Yashar'el. The church is the other fold that is mentioned in the tenth chapter of Yahuchanon. The church will never no not ever replace Yashar'el. Why? Because YAH loves Yashar'el (**Malachi 1:2 Romans 9:13**). And Yashar'el is in actuality a spiritual awakening because there be physical Yashar'el that will be left to condemnation because of unbelief in what THE MESSIAH did on the cross and the resurrection from the tomb. There will be plenty of Yashar'el separated from The FATHER because of their unbelief in THE MESSIAH finished work. Trying to declare their own way to salvation in which there is not but **ONE WAY TO THE FATHER** and that is through the death burial and resurrection of our savior **ADONAI YAHUSHA(this name mean THE FATHER'S SALVATION) HA'MASHIACH (this name mean The ANOINTED ONE)**. So, we have **The Father Salvation for the Anointed Ones**. And those that are trying to create your own way to salvation, baby you are SO VERY MUCH CONFUSED. **TAKE THE FATHER'S PLAN that HE has already CREATED** and not your way, please. Then how else do you come into salvation? Did He come to this earth? Did He not live among us? Did He not die? How did He die? Oh, why did HE die? Oh, you fool believe what is before you because you are in your unrighteous works? You can't be righteous because your righteousness is as a filthy rag in the eyesight of GOD, accept what He has done freely given without cost because this earth will end and where will you be without HIS works and resurrection ole fool?

The church will not ever take preeminence over Yashar'el. The church (the called-out ones) is the other fold, and there shall be one-fold and one shepherd. I am no longer calling myself a Christian, but I am now calling myself a Hebrew. I no longer believe in Christmas, Halloween, New Year's Day (because The Hebrew calendar starts in the spring and not in winter), good Friday, and easter. MESSIAH did **NOT** die on a good Friday. Some people may say I am crazy, but I am in the right mindset. These are ALL pagan holidays that have NOTHING to do with Yashar'el. YAH said Holy Days, but a man declares holidays.

We can believe anything we want, but you'd better believe what ELOHIYM said instead of what a mere man says. **Yesha`yahu 29:12-13** says *"And the book is delivered to him that is not learned, saying, Read this, I pray thee, and he saith, I am not learned. Wherefore ADONAI said, Forasmuch as this people draw near me with their lips do honor me but have removed their heart far from me, and their fear toward me is taught by the precept of men."*

So, preachers today are supposed to be learned men (going to theology schools), yet they teach the precept of the non-melanin theology schools, which won't recognize who the true Yashar'el are. These men are teaching what they have learned from another man and NOT what ELOHIYM says. The words have been changed from the original language. GOD was not Lord because that is an England title of nobility because it is still used today. THE FATHER name is YAH pronounced as in the word **HalleluJAH [Psalm 68:4]**. ELOHIYM said don't take away from my words, but that has occurred and those who did this will and are being punished. These men are headed to destruction. This Bible is about The Hebrew GOD and the people in the book of The Old Testament are Hebrew people, not jews because that word jews is only 388 years old, but we are **The Hebrew People** as Pa'al. The Hebrew People are **"THE MY PEOPLE" in The Bible**. Many preachers TODAY will deny this truth, but GOD is unchangeable. **THE TRUTH HAS BEEN HIDDEN FROM OUR EYES. Do you believe this? Genesis 14:13, 39:14, 40:15, 41:12, 43:32, Exodus 1:15, 2:6, 2:11, 2:13, 3:18, 5:3, 7:16, 9:1, 10:13, 21:1, 1 Samuel 13:3, 13:7, 13:19, 14:11, 14:21, 29:3, Acts 21:38, 2 Corinthians 11:22** and **Philippians 3:5** For GOD'S people are **destroyed** for a lack of knowledge because they have rejected knowledge. MESSIAH sees ALL the destruction of HIS people and HE will uncover the crookedness of all evildoers. Who are GOD'S people? **Psalm 77:15** *"You have with your arm redeemed your people, the sons of Ya'aqov and Yoceph."* Celah. **Psalm 105:6** *"O ye seed of Avraham HIS servant, ye children of Ya'aqov HIS chosen."* **Psalm 147:19** *He shows his word unto Ya'aqov, HIS statues, and HIS judgments unto Yashar'el.* Wisdom 16:20 *Instead, whereof you fed your people with angels' food.* Wisdom 18:13 *For whereas they would not believe anything by reason of the enhancements; upon* *the destruction of the firstborn, they acknowledged these PEOPLE to be sons of ELOHIYM.* The New Testament was translated from Greek, not Hebrew and The MESSIAH is not Greek so thereby HIS name **CAN'T BE GREEK.** HIS mother was not English, but she is HEBREW so her name **CAN'T BE the English version of Mary, but Miryam (Hebrew).** These men are CALLED by the WRONG name. They in the New Testament Can't be called James, Peter, or John because these are English names and not Hebrew names. **What we want is THE TRUTH and nothing but the truth. My people are destroyed because 1) A lack of knowledge 2) because they REJECT KNOWLEDGE. I have always heard the first part of HOSEA or HUSHA 4:6, but the full verse brings everything into the knowledge of the truth.** MESSIAH is on His way back to set the record straight and to give out rewards to the broken heart. Man can continue his way, but MESSIAH will pardon who HE will for MESSIAH loves Ya'aqov and his descendants. All records will be made right. Don't be weary but be strong and endure. For MESSIAH Hands are everlasting seek me and My way for I, THE MESSIAH will return soon and very soon. Seek truth for those that have The Words you will have no excuse A.S.K. Ask to keep at it, seek to keep at it, and Knock keep at it. And you will see The MESSIAH in peace. Be not deceived by the precept of man. Study GOD'S WORD and The COMFORTER will always be with you! Amein.

Non-melanin people history teaches about the Jewish holocaust that happen in the 1940's but these same writers **REFUSED** to recognized the first holocaust (the slave trade on those filthy slave ships, slaves chained together, unable to go to the potty, but having their bowel movement and pissing on themselves) that happened in the 1600's 1700's 1800's 1900's and is still happening today, police officer killing us in the streets and getting away within in the court system, lynching us and barbequing us on pole and setting around joking. The United States Senate passed an anti-Asian bill, but NOTHING for people of melanated skin tone people. Our foreparents were kidnapped from the land of Eden placed on those nasty filthy slave ships starting in 1619. They were chained together unable to defecate and piss except on themselves. The dead were thrown overboard alongside the living to sharks awaiting a meal. The women were menstrual on themselves. Where do you think they USED the bathroom on these filthy disease ships? Can you imagine the smell of these ships? And millions of our foreparents died on these Atlantic trips. This is why I say The Holocaust was NOT in the 1940's (the so-called jews), but it was way before of those who have been labeled as black, but the 1940's are impostors for we who are melanated are **THE TRUE SONS AND**

DAUGHTERS OF YAH, but those who publish books refused to identify the RIGHT people as **THE TRUE MY PEOPLE** in The Bible that is read each and everyday that are supposed to be teachers of YAH's Word. These men are teaching what they have learned from another man and not what ELOHIYM says. Why are we treated as such because some of the people from India are darker than me and I am labeled as black, but in reality, my skin tone is brown.

The majority of the names have been changed from the original language and we've got generations of people lost with NO idea of what is happening in this world. Just lost and maybe this book will enlighten some people's thinking because there is a computer saying g.i.g.o. (garbage in garbage out). So, we have people that are fed garbage and their thinking becomes garbage or trash. And the TRASH is stinking because it is full of junk and has no nutritional value at all. When things are whitewashed or lied too, this creates problems with our thinking and culture and our ways of life.

The meaning of the word Hebrew has been described as the door to the house of knowledge. Door to the house of the first. Or doors to the house of the beginning. What is Hebrewism? The MESSIAH or YAHUSHA HA'MASHIACH who died and arose again for the forgiveness of all sins. We are forever forgiven for past, present, and future sins. We are no longer required to bring any type of clean animal (without blemish) to sacrifice to die for our sins. Why? Because YAHUSHA was the perfect lamb of YAHUAH (THE FATHER). He is the only begotten SON to THE FATHER (THE LAMB OF ELOHIYM for the sin of the word). He died and rose from the tomb after three nights and three days, as the scriptures say, and not two nights and one day. We believe the word of YAH, and we are the (meaning of *the* is: used, especially before a noun, with a **SPECIFYING or particularizing effect**) "my" (meaning of *my* a form of the **POSSESSIVE case of I**) people of the bible who have melanin in our skin tone (except the Chamites). We are the direct descendants of Avraham (Abraham), Yitschaq (Issac), Ya'aqov (Jacob), Mosheh (Moses), Daniyel (Daniel), Yesha`yahu (Isaiah), Shalomah (Solomon), Kepha (Peter), Mattithyahu (Matthew), Yahuchanon (John), and Pa'a l(Paul). We are the "my" people of the bible period. HalleluJah! The bible states, With the lack of knowledge, my people are led into destruction, yet this GOD loves Ya'aqov and this GOD hates Esau (**Malachi 1:2-3; Romans 9:13**). Do you see why we have been deceived by those who translated THE WORDS OF YAH.

We are a people whose language and identity were stolen or taken away. We are a people who were kidnapped into darkness, but YAH is now awakening HIS people by removing the slumber from our eyes and unstopping the deafness of our ears. We are HIS people. **Yesha`yahu 49:3** says, "You are my servant, Yashar'el, in whom I will be glorified." Kunta Kinte was tied to a pole and whipped until he said his English name Toby in the TV miniseries *Roots*. In the year 1619, our foreparents endured those filthy, brutal, embarrassing, and nasty slave ships and we are still enduring the treatment of less than a man and the wrath of those that write misleading material in those so-called history books.

The return of The MESSIAH is real soon! The world has been conditioned not to believe HE is returning. The world has been conditioned to accept The Mark of the beast. What is The Mark? Could be a chip or a tattoo. It is an allegiance and loyalty to the man of sin. It is something that you will get accustomed to. Something that seems so incidental that you will most likely accept it as a positive tool to be used in everyday life. It will be a part of your everyday life but will have eternal separation from THE CREATOR. Whether you can remove this Mark is another question? It will be a part of your life. Have you ever lost your cell phone? How was your life? I imagine the Mark will be the same way. You may ask "What's wrong with being chipped?" Anything chipped can be almost located anywhere in this world. Anything chipped can be programmed. Anything chipped can malfunction. What happens when the system goes awry? And by the way, who made those chips anyway? Will you accept the chip to keep your head attached to your body? ADONAI YAHUSHA HA'MASHIACH is on HIS way back. You see we have been duped, deceived, constructed, tricked, beguiled, seduced, or bamboozled to believe things to be fact because someone has published materials and has alphabets behind their name and to THE CREATOR it doesn't carry enough weight because the alphabet was given by another man and not by THE CREATOR. And is it TRUTH, what they have published? What is the truth? **Yahuchanon 17:17** declares "Thy word is truth." If it doesn't meet GOD's standard then is it true? It comes from the blind leading the blind. Were they (the PhDs) at the beginning? No. They got their information from another corrupt person. Which makes no sense according to THE WORD OF GOD in which they do not believe. Just because they have all these accolades of man and alphabets behind their name is it true, what they have written or said? We have been engraved, immured, or embedded with false misleading misrepresented lies by people with the help of satan. What has happened, liars have published materials and lies mixed up with truth make things cloudy murky and the truth is hidden from the light. And our heart and mind are enclosed with darkness. The truth has become a lie and the reality that we live in has become warped when the truth becomes warped and when truth appears we feel it is not the truth, but lies and the lies appear to be the truth in our functioning reality. And our understanding soul, mind, and heart have all been deceived by a lie. And we can no longer believe the TRUTH is the TRUTH but our belief is a lie. Did THE MESSIAH die on a Friday? We have been told this is true, but **Matthew 12:40** says something completely and totally different. What you don't want is liars publishing materials, but this has already occurred. The reason why is because liars lie. This will lead many away from THE TRUTH and these lies become truth and we will believe these lies as true, but lies can be judged by GOD Words.

Many believe the sun is 93,000,000 million miles away from the earth (then how big is the sun), but in fact, the sun was placed in the firmament (the arch of the sky) as the moon as Genesis says. So, thereby the **sun is NOT 93,000,000 million miles from earth and it is NOT THE CENTER OF THE UNIVERSE. Just look into the sky, the firmament or the expanse!** In the book of Enoch, the sun and the moon are the same sizes **Enoch 78:3** and **72:47.** In fact, the sun and moon are the same dimensions. You can see this if your pupils are dark enough. This is why we can see and have Solar and Lunar eclipses. They are the same size. Our eyes and mind have been closed off from THE CREATOR by the lies of man. We recklessly go forth from The CREATOR'S viewpoint to the viewpoint of a simple-minded man. Because liars can have all these accolades, but if that person doesn't have THE TRUTH of GOD'S STANDARD that person doesn't mean anything to GOD. Lies will be written to eschew the truth of THE CREATOR'S Word. These lies have been published for so very long and now we feel they are true because they are published and we feel they are true, but we won't believe the truth because we have believed the lie to be the truth and our eyes and mind and heart are **CLOSED** to the truth. We think THE TRUTH is then a lie which in reality The Truth is The Truth, but the lie has become our truth. So, a report published by a stupid man has become the truth. This lie has become truth for us in our understanding, soul, mind, and heart. Have you seen the movie *The Matrix? Those people **thought** they were living in the truth, but the truth was so far away from them.* Are you awake yet? Wake up, people. Please wake up. You see we have been **LIED** too. And we feed on these lies everyday, but men want to keep you in their hands to assuage you from THE TRUTH. **_Why is there modified cornstarch_**? And we eat it everyday. Why modified cornstarch? What is the reason?

All these lies of men! Seedless grapes and watermelons, that was never meant to be, but the man went against YAH'S Rule and made it be. WE HAVE BEEN DECEIVED BY LIARS, but this earth is on its way out and there will be new heavens and a new earth. **Revelation 21:1, Yesha'yahu 65:17.** And YAHUAH will tabernacle with men and they **SHALL be** HIS People **Revelation 21:3. And ALL who denied HIM will forever regret that decision for your eternal destination will totally be disastrous with darkness, pain, regret, and no rest FOREVER and you will forever hear the piercing and shrilling noise wanting rest, but that has now passed and you will forever be forgotten Revelation 21:4-5.**

The church feels it has replaced Yashar'el, but this is so far from THE TRUTH. It has relied on the KJV for so very long not understanding how things are so flipped NOW. The word Christian is in the KJV and it appears three times. **Acts 26:28** was converted from the word Netseriy which is The MESSIAH adopted hometown. **Acts 11:26** it was converted from the word Mashiachiym which means anointed one and **1 Peter 4:16** It was converted from the word Mashiachiy which means anointed ones. So, as you can see is this true are you a Christians because THE SON OF YAH was not Grecians, but Hebrew, and this name Jesus was not Jesus in the 1611 KJV, but Iesus and the word Christ is also Grecian which mean anointed one, but in Hebrew it is Messiah. What do you think? Are you a Christian? A lot of pastors remind me of Nat Turner who was reading from a slave bible to keep the slaves in line, but Nat was awakened by YAH and he discovered what was right.

The MESSIAH loves Yashar'el because HE said He **ONLY** came for **"THE LOST SHEEP OF YASHAR'EL." Matthew 10:6** and **15:24.** ELOHIYM had to get his first wife back but because of the law [in which HE Created], this prevented HIM from doing so. So, HE had to die and transform himself into another man because this would have defiled the land and HIS word, and thereby, He transformed Himself into another man. This would prevent heaven and earth from disappearing because HE states in HIS Word that heaven and earth would pass away if HIS Word is not fulfilled. In the third chapter of the 8th verse of Yirmeyahu, He divorced Yashar'el. And He had to get His wife back but because of **Deuteronomy 24:1,** He would have broken His law that He established. So, He had to become a new man. This is the one reason that after the resurrection He was **NOT** recognized, by those who knew Him before His death and after His resurrection, they didn't recognize Him because He has transformed Himself into another man. So, the church will not no not ever replace Yashar'el because the church is a part of Yashar'el, but many in the church will reject this information, but in the BIBLE that they preach and teach from because they (the church leaders) have the Pharisees mentality (they have been engraved to believe like their teachers) of the scriptures not accounting to THE WHOLE WORDS of the Bible. Just like the Pharisees and Sadducees of the old way of stinking thinking and I feel for their stinking thinking and not their message from YAHUAH because in the eleventh chapter of Romans it states that ALL of Yashar'el shall be saved. The true name of THE SON OF GOD is not Jesus as it has been engraved for us to believe or think, but HIS true Hebrew name is YAHUSHA HA'MASHIACH and these preachers know it. **Why they** (preachers stewards' teachers of today) **REFUSED to use HIS true HEBREW name BLOW ME AWAY.** I was surprised by an ex-pastor of mine saying that name, but he never no never expressed that name to me while I was under his teaching. Maybe because of fright, but this was done on a one-on-one. **PASTORS YOU WILL BE HELD ACCOUNTABLE FOR NOT INFORMING YOUR FOLD (YAH" S FLOCK). You see you are just a steward of what is not yours and you will be held in accountability on judgment day for not informing people of what you know. THE MESSIAH** nationality is Hebrew and not Grecian because Jesus Christ is a Grecian/English name and it is NOT Hebrew it is like a person that was born in China and had Chinese parents calling herself Maria Gonzalez which is a Spanish orient name. This would not be logical at all. Do you see where I am coming from? Does this make any difference? I would say yes because TRUTH MATTER. Do you like being lied to? But according to the one that published the material it is right. So, thereby our children are led by stinking funk up thinking of satan teacher's philosophies. Let's put the correct perspective on what we should learn. Does this make any sense to you?

Preachers, you are leaving GOD's people in darkness (lack of light, no knowledge, blindness) and it is your responsibility to bring people out of darkness and NOT to let them wander in darkness, but that will be on you one day to report to judgment and the question will be why did you do what you did? What will be your response? The word of YAH will make you free. Why did you not set the people's minds free from this present darkness, that you knew and you (the steward the preacher of today) would NOT give this information out. Freely given and freely give out this information. Why! Why! Why! All you had to do was release the information that was given to you by THE RUACH HA'QODESH and now you (the steward) are standing before ME with your mouth wide open and you can't respond, can you?

So, THE MESSIAH had to die because the first husband could not remarry the first wife again no not ever because it would defile the land. So, when The Messiah died, He became a new man and this is the reason the disciplines did not recognize Him. This is the reason the disciplines and this includes the women did not recognize Him because His glory had changed and He became a new man.

So, The Messiah is coming for Yashar'el only. This includes those that have been engrafted into the body by believing He died and rose again. Remember the exodus included strangers also and not just Yashar`e'liy

In the 1611 KJV, there are no words with the letter "j" in that bible at all. All the words start with the letter "i". So, why did we come with the letter j in today's KJV? In the 1611 KJV, the majority of names were changed to some type of English name. In the 1611 KJV the name that started with an I Iesus Iacob Iames Iohn Iudah Issac and so on, but in the 1633 KJV we have names such as Jesus Jacob James John Judah, but Issac was left allow, why because it would look strange "Jssac". Why did all of this occur by a man putting a backward hook-on j on the letter i. You added an alphabet and my name changed? WOW! And preachers know this, or they should, but they fail, fail, fail to inform THE CREATOR 'S congregations because preachers are just stewards that THE CREATOR has placed YOU over HIS Flock, but you fail to guide HIS FLOCK in the right direction, but we will be rewarded according to the standard what THE MESSIAH judged us to be rewarded according to our stewardship.

The letter" j" was not formed until 1633. A person put a backward hook on the letter i and made a j. The name Jesus is closely associated with the Grecian supreme god Zeus. This name Jesus was transliterated (misrepresent) the greek god Zeus. The SON of ELOHIYM'S name in Hebrew is YAHUSHA. YAHUSHA is a combination of two names. The two names are YAHUAH and YESHUAH. So, we have YAHUAH'S SALVATION. It means THE FATHER'S SALVATION. THE FATHER's name is YAHUAH and the word Salvation in Hebrew is Yeshuah.

The name Jesus is only 388 years old, but He THE SON came into this world over 388 years ago. Does this make sense? Yes, or no? We are being misled by the god(s) of this world (who are the adversaries) of THE CREATOR. And man is in kahoots and complete compliance with the god of this world. Who is the god of this world? It is the house of satan.

Christ is a Greek term meaning anointed one, but in The Old Testament, it was MESSIAH. MESSIAH is the Hebrew word for the anointed one.

The word jew is only 388 years old because the letter j was not formed until 1633. It was the original Yahudah. He is a great-grandson of Avraham. Avraham is a Hebrew **Genesis 14:13.** Yahudah is a son of Ya`aqov. Ya`aqov name was changed to Yashar'el. He had twelve sons and one daughter and these twelve sons of Yashar'el formed the twelve tribes of Yashar'el and his grandfather is Avraham which is **OUR forefather.** And GOD told Avram that his seeds would be in a strange land and be afflicted and suffer (not sojourning) for four hundred years in that land, but we have been deceived or taught into thinking that the first group of Israelites were in Egypt and suffered for 400 years. The majority of preachers are brainwashed into thinking that Yashar'el spent 400 years in Egypt, but The Israelites were not in Slavery for 400 years and so pastors/teachers pass this wrong and misleading information to the world today and we foolishly believe these misaligned pastors/teachers of GOD's Word. Yashar'el did not go into slavery until after Yoceph's death. **Exodus 1:8** *"Now there arose up a new king over Egypt, which knew not Yoceph.* **Exodus 1:11-12** states," *Therefore they did set over them taskmasters to afflict them with their burdens. And they built for Pharaoh treasure cities, Pithom and Raamses. But the more they __afflicted__ them, the more they multiplied and grew. And they were grieved because of the children of Yashar'el."* There are not 400 years between Yoceph's death and the Exodus of Mosheh. Two sources 1) Matthew McGee states Yoceph's death was in 1640 BC and Moseh's Birth 1576 BC and when you subtract that we have 84 years. 84+[80 (Mosheh time in and out of Egypt)] = 164 years.

2) Dan Roth states Yoceph's Death in 1672 BC and Mosheh's birth in 1608 BC and when you subtract that we have 64 years. Add 64 + [80 (Mosheh time in and out of Egypt)] = 144 years of Yashar'el's slavery in Egypt. And secondly, Levi died in Egypt and his son was Kohath and his son was Amram and his son was Mosheh. So, there are not 400 years between Levi and Mosheh. 400 years have happened here in spiritual Egypt, the Americas. The first slave entered here in the year 1619 and it ended in 2019 just a couple of years ago and THE GOD states HE will punish that nation and not nations. So now we are waiting for THE EXODUS as The GREAT I AM STATED in **Genesis 15:14** *"And also that __nation__ whom they serve, will I judge: and afterward shall they __come out__ with great substance.* The United States is under judgment. Look how much debt it is in. The United States is in debt of $36,000,000,000,000 trillion dollars (federal reserve's notes, which is not real money; The constitution states that all debt shall be paid by silver and gold and not paper money; (the only value is that we have placed that value on paper dollars). This will never no not

ever be paid off, but I have heard it may be on the higher side, someone stated it is more like 60,000,000,000,000 trillion dollars. If you took all the money of the richest people in the USA that money would not make a dent in that type of debt and besides that, reserve notes are not even constitutional. Have you read the constitution of The United States? I am afraid the majority of Americans don't even have a copy of the constitution and it is not studied in school. We are just given the highlights and to fend for ourselves. There should be a course in high school in which we should study the constitution and dwell on what it means to see even if we are even living under the constitution.

The KJV left out words that are in The Septuagint and the Cepher Bible has in them. The KJV says **DON'T TAKE THE WORD OF ONE WITNESS BUT TWO OR THREE WITNESSES.** People have taken the authority of one witness and have shoveled that one witness information down into our naive and erroneous thinking and that one witness is so wrong, but I have two witnesses which show that one witness was incorrect and not giving the correct information.

Exodus 12:40 in **_The KJV_** says "Now the sojourning of the children of Israel, who dwelt in Egypt, was four hundred and thirty years.

Exodus 12:40 in **_The Septuagint Bible_** says" And the sojourning of the children of Israel, while they sojourned in the land of Egypt and the land of Chanaan, was four hundred and thirty years.

Exodus 12:40 in **_The Cepher Bible_** "Now the sojourning of the children of Yashar'el, who dwelt in the land of Mitsrayim, and in the land of Ken`an, they and their fathers were four hundred and thirty years.

So, as you can read as we so richly, reverence and endear to the KJV, but it has LEFT **OUT WORDS,** which changes the dynamic and meaning and concept of any sentence, statement, paragraph, or book.

Is there a difference between affliction and sojourning? **Affliction**: to distress so severely as to cause persistent suffering or anguish. **Sojourn**: To stay as a temporary resident. So, is affliction and sojourn the SAME? Yes, or no?

The Israelites **were** in slavery for less than four hundred years because they did not go into slavery until after Yoceph's death. The work of Josephus states the Israelites were in slavery for about 215 years, so thereby **Genesis 15:13-14** was not fulfilled until August of 2019. The first slaves were brought into America in the year 1619 this strange land. The Americas was a strange land (spiritual Egypt). Many preachers believe and think non-melanated people are the Israelites, but that is so terribly wrong also. Non-melanated people never were in slavery for 400 years and this is so far from the truth because they **_CANNOT_** become more non-melanated because the true Israelites are in the Americas with melanin in their DNA. As YAH told our forefather Avraham" I will bless them that bless you and curse them that curse you and these BLESSING and CURSES are TRANSFERRED to his true seeds of Avraham.

The calendar is all screwed up because the Gregorian calendar starts in winter and ends in winter, but YAH told Mosheh in Exodus this is the first month for you which started with the cycle of the new moon. So we have spring, summer, fall, and winter. Whereas the Gregorian calendar starts with winter, spring, summer, fall, and winter. Does this make sense? We have been indoctrinated, embedded, and engraved to believe a certain way for so long. You can't find Sunday, monday, tuesday, wednesday, thursday, friday, or saturday in the word of YAH because it was not important to place ungodly names on HIS creation.

The continent Africa name came from a Roman general named Scipio Africanus. Man has tried to supersede the word of ELOHIYM. The Moors called Africa Alkebulan which means "The garden of Eden" or the mother of mankind. ELOHIYM called it Eden as He said in Genesis 2:8 "He planted a garden eastward in Eden."

The earth does **NOT** rotate around the sun. The sun rotates around the earth. If you don't believe me, read in the book of **Joshua 10:10-14** Joshua said "sun, stand still" and the moon did not move and he did say earth standstill. YAHUAH hearkened unto the voice of a man. In other words, YAHUAH had the sun and the moon not to move. So, as you can read the sun stood still and did not move. The earth does not move. The earth is in a fixed position in the universe. So, all these years teachers, scientists, and professors have all fed us **LIES and we won't question them because we have been trained not to question authority.** We are trapped in the web of lies.

So, as we read you call yourself an African-American and guess what you're NOT. You are from Eden as well as your foreparents Avram and Sarai.

The MESSIAH was **NOT** born in December but in the springtime. The conception took place in the Hebrew calendar in the sixth month **Luke 1:26**. This month falls in the summer time which was like July/August. And you go back three months and we have the springtime like May/June on our calendar. This was the month of Sivan. Many people put up Christmas trees, which is against The WORD (but many Christians celebrate this pagan holiday and have no guilt or shame just going along with this-worldly and pagan holiday of mixing paganism and Christianity with THE MESSIAH's birth. **Jeremiah (Yirmeyahu) 10:3-4** The reason I spelled it Christmas is that this is how it is **PRONOUNCED** without the t and the t is silenced. This t is not pronounced and you are leaving the cross out and HE THE SON came to die for the sin of the world to reconcile man back to ELOHIYM. So, put away your pagan and false idols and holidays that are supposed to represent THE SAVIOR OF THIS CREATION. He was not born on December 25. So, retain that money and save on buying gifts that have NOTHING to do with HIS BIRTH. I had a sixth-grade teacher in 1965 and he and yes, he asked us to draw pictures for Christmas and we all drew about presents and trees, but nothing about the true meaning. Needless to say, he was so disappointed about that that he expressed that to us and we went back and made the correction, but if that was done today that teacher would have been persecuted and fired for trying to help to conform our stinky thinking about a holiday that has NOTHING and I mean NOTHING to do about us and gifts. Our thinking can be so FOUL as individuals and we need pastors and teachers to put our thinking on the RIGHT tracks. And this is the action that pastors are to do, but many pastors today just are not doing as instructed by The RUACH HA'QODESH. Many are NOT telling the truth and the sheeples are not taking time to study so we have many pastors who are doing as they were chosen not to do. Many are called, but few are chosen.

THE MESSIAH IS ON HIS WAY BACK FOR THE NATION OF ISRAEL ONLY FOR THOSE THAT BELIEVED HE DIED AND ROSE AGAIN FROM THE TOMB AND WE WILL FOREVER HAVE EVERLASTING LIFE WITH THE FATHER AND THE SON AND THE RUACH HA'QODESH FOREVER SO SAY THE GREAT IAMTHATIAM EHAYAH ASHER EHAYAH AMEIN.

All I required of you was to speak truth to My People in darkness. You (stewards) sickened ME and now your rewards have been taken away from you because of your inept attitudes and ways. So, now you see your mistakes. I sent and brought you witnesses, but you (stewards) refused my witnesses and relied on the septic thinking of the Pharisees. I was NOT pleased with your ways.

The name Jesus is very close to the Greek god Zeus. So, Acts 4:10 says in the KJV "Be it known unto you all, the people of Israel, that by THE NAME of JESUS CHRIST of Nazareth whom ye crucified, Whom GOD raised from the dead even by HIM doth this man stand here before you whole"

The Cepher Bible says **Acts 4:10** "Be it known unto you all the people of Yashar'el, that by the name of YAHUSHA HA'MASHIACH of Natsareth, whom ye crucified whom YAH raised from the dead, even by HIM does this man stand here before you whole ."

Many have revered the KJV, but I have found TRUTH because THE WORD came to save The Hebrews first and then to other nations. THE SON of YAH came through Hebrew parents. The KJV converted the majority of people's names in the KJV from Hebrew to English. Why? Several reasons, but that is another issue. So, I have presented to you the same verse from two different bibles, so what is the SON OF ELOHIYM name because Acts 4:12 states **THERE IS ONLY ONE NAME THAT SALVATION COMES THROUGH Jesus or YAHUSHA? Can you be saved by more than one name?** You chose one, but I chose HIS TRUE Hebrew name ADONAI YAHUSHA HA'MASHIACH MY DELIVERER AND SAVIOR AMEIN.

The psychology of this world is like this. We the people that came to the Americas and are told we are black, but in reality, we are many hues of color from light as those that are called white to the color of Hershey chocolate bar. Is a Hershey bar black or very dark brown? Our skin tone and hair eyes color are all DETERMINED by the amount of melanin in our D.N.A. [Deoxyribonucleic Acid] In the United States I have been labeled or grouped under black racial profile, even though you look at my skin tone it is BROWN and not black. My grandson's skin tone is lighter and people would say he is black, but he is much lighter than me. I have more melanin in my DNA than he does, but people say he is black also. Why? But I go by the nationality of Hebrew because Hebrew people are ALL different shades of color. Oftentimes the simplest words are overLOOKED in **The Bible,(THE WORD OF YAH)** but we **CAN'T** just overlook these words because YAH said even the title can't be overlooked because if so heaven and earth would pass away! We have to have a passion for the word. Amein.

Why does OMB directive 15 list the mid-eastern as white and there are people from India whose skin tone is darker than mine who are not listed as black? So, OMB needs to remove this designation of black and white because it is intoxicated and totally WRONG because those listed as whites are not WHITE and those listed as black are not BLACK because those who are labeled as black are so many hues of color because of the melanin in our skin tone, but people are tunneled vision and don't see TRUTH because I AM NOT

BLACK as you can see, but of THE HEBREW NATION OF THE LAND OF EDEN FROM THE NATION YASHAR'EL.

In this book, you will find names different because the people I'm referring to are not English, but Hebrews and Hebrews are not English or Grecian's, so Hebrews WOULD NOT have English names or Grecian's names, but HEBREW names, so virtually every name in the Bible are INCORRECT. It would be like a person born to Chinese parents born in China, but having a Spanish name. Does this make sense? The names that I typed in this book are Hebrew names for the most part. We have been engraved into thinking of Jesus, Peter, James, etc, but these are English names and not Hebrew names. Does it make any difference? If your name is Curtis, would you answer Carl? If your name is Mary, would you answer to Brenda? Then why in the world would you change my name into some type of English name when I am Hebrew. Look at the mini tv series "*Root* ". Why would they change Kinta's name to Toby? For the men of Yashar'el is **HEBREW from the continent of Eden from the land of Yashar'el.** We are not Greek or English.

The Cepher Bible converts the name to the original Hebrew name instead of a false and misleading name to satisfy not the poor masses to make them feel safe but to hide not the truth that HE who gave authority is **THE HEBREW GOD YAHUAH. And also, it added back The Apocrypha as in the 1611 KJV.**

This information is either true or false, you be the judge to see if I am telling the truth or giving out false or misleading information, or if the glaze and the slumber of sleep are falling from eyes or heart. Or like the song "I can see clearly NOW." Amein.

And this is to my HEBREW Sisters quit trying to be like the non-melanin woman and show your hair as it is, as YAH has given to you. You don't have to go and get some hair that is not of your nature or color, but **keep it real** and let the world be aware of your greatness and power. Your hair is your beauty that surpasses them completely. You don't have to have lipstick to show your lips because YAH gave you lips to show and it is all-natural. UNDERSTAND who you are. BE YOURSELF and please don't try to be like the non-melanin because without makeup what would they (non-melanin) women look like? Come on Sisters BE YOURSELF, **Hebrew Women of YAH** because the non-melanin is trying to imitate you. Because your skin tone (the color), hair, lips, and hips make them jealous and you are trying to emulate them, WHY? Be glad of **WHO YOU ARE! WHY BECAUSE THE CREATOR MADE YOU AS YOU ARE. YOU ARE SPECIAL!**

You will see this name written in this book as Ad-am. The reason I did this is that I believe the pronunciation as it has been said is incorrect. The GOD of The Bible is known as THE GREAT I AM and HE made another person in HIS Image and HE called him ad-am and in other words another Add (AM). One in HIS IMAGE.

These are My Words, do as I did and study to show thyself approved by GOD and see If I was led by THE RUACH or led by a man. Amein. Do you think this is true? This earth does NOT belong to man, but to HIM that created the earth.

Israel Shabbaths

Holy Days

1) The Seventh Day	Leviticus 23:3
2) The Passover (First Month, Fourteenth Day	Leviticus 23:6
3) The Feast of Unleavened Bread (First Month Fifteen Day	Leviticus 23:6
4) The End of The Feast of Unleavened Bread	Leviticus 23:8
5) The Feast of The First Fruit	Leviticus 23:9-14
6) The Festival of The Pentecost	Leviticus 23:15
7) The Feast of Trumpets(Seventh Month, First Day)	Leviticus 23:24
8) The Day of Atonement (Seventh Month, Tenth Day)	Leviticus 23:27
9) The Feast of Tabernacles(Seventh Month, Fifteenth Day)	Leviticus 23:34
10) The End of Feast of Tabernacles	Leviticus 25:8
11) The Jubilee Year	Leviticus 25:3-4
12) The Seventh Year Sabbath	Leviticus 25:3-4

CHAPTER 1

—— ❧ ——

Elohiym

In the beginning, ELOHIYM created heaven and then the earth. Everyone believes something. You believe something He exists or you believe He doesn't. So, you believe HE is or HE isn't. It is important to believe in what is right. Pilate asked YAHUSHA a question: "WHAT IS TRUTH?" YAHUSHA states in **John 17:17**, *"Thy WORD is Truth."* *Most people believe* in a supreme being or some type of god. The figure in the newspaper states that about 90 percent of people believe (in a supreme being). We have been told all our lives about The GOD of The HOLY BIBLE. I believe in The GOD of The Hebrews of The HOLY BIBLE. This is The GOD of (Abraham) Avraham, (Issac) Yitschaq, (Jacob) Ya`aqov (Israel) Yashar'el, and (Moses) Mosheh. Some people believe in the very existence of a GOD and some believe NOT in the very existence of GOD. In addition, I feel sorry for you because without HIM nothing would exist that does exist.

HE is all power and all knowledge and HE is everywhere. HIS power is too unimaginable for me to even try to describe, but I would say it is like thousands of tornadoes and man is like a sheet of tissue paper. This is the reason alone that every knee will bow. HIS power is enormous. It feels like a great enormous magnet that cannot be dethroned. You may ask how I know this. I will discuss this in a later chapter. All I know is that ELOHIYM does exist. ELOHIYM is more than just the head's belief, but the heart's belief. Your head's belief, you will not die for, but heart's belief you will for. Will you die for THE LIVING ELOHIYM? The HOLY BIBLE states that it is a terrible thing to fall into the hands of the Living GOD.

We have heard about many other gods and the only true and LIVING GOD is YAH THE FATHER, THE SON YAHUSHA, THE HOLY SPIRIT RUACH HA'QODESH. I am not here to prove the existence and HE will not interfere with your choice or HE may give you an option. In fact, HE may just help you with your choice of not wanting to know HIM.

What is life without ELOHIYM? LIFE without ELOHIYM is impossible. All the money in the world cannot possibly be enough without ELOHIYM in our lives. I was given a vision of hell. What is hell like? There is gloomy darkness. There seem to be miles and miles and miles of depth. There is hunger and pain. There seem to be compartments. If you step outside your compartment, you experience greater pain. It seems as though men are climbing on the jagged rocks, trying to escape, but they are experiencing complete and utter failure. Their attempts are altogether futile. There are children and families huddled in groups, waiting. The air appears cold and dreary. The jagged rocks are very pointed and sharp and the men are struggling, but going nowhere and this is a part of their eternity. After this vision, tears came to my eyes. Why? Because you requested to be without ELOHIYM. Once in hell, there is NO WAY TO ESCAPE period. Once in hell, you are there until the lake of fire and there you will be forever. What is forever? The Cepher Bible in the book of Sirach [**Ecclesiasticus**] **18:10** *"As a drop of water unto the sea, and a gravelstone in comparison of sand; so are a thousand years to the days of eternity."* In other words, it is endless. To not believe in ELOHIYM is not foolishness. You either believe or do not believe that ELOHIYM exists. Can your disbelief stop my belief? Can guns, stones, destruction, bombs, or money destroy my belief? All I know is that I believe in The GOD of the Bible and everything HE said or says, I believe everything HE said, I believe and there is nothing that will deter me from that thought process and knowledge. THE GOD I believe in is the same The GOD of Avraham, Yitschaq, Yashar'el, and Mosheh. I am not trying to prove the existence of ELOHIYM or that HE exists. All I know is that HE does exist. It goes further than you or I can ever imagine. This GOD created heaven and earth in seven days. HE is GOD. If you choose to exist without ELOHIYM, HE will grant your request. ELOHIYM has given us free choice.

GOD is the name commonly given to the ultimate source and power of the universe and subject of religious devotion. "But THE FATHER'S true name is YAH" (**Psalm 68:4**). We all have our ideas of who we think the true GOD is. This project wasn't to determine if GOD exists but to clarify a few things. We all have been taught about the death of YAHUSHA and HIS resurrection. We can get all types of ideas, suggestions, discourse, hypotheses, and rhetoric about GOD and how HE intervenes and does not intervene in man's affairs in this life. Every individual is like a cake. You ask me what I mean. What information we acquire in this life determines how we will turn out or at least it should. If we were taught how to cook a cake by our mother, but someone gives us additional information about that cake it changes our previous way of doing things. The only thing I want to point to would be what The Bible (THE WORD OF YAH) states and what man has already stated for years. ELOHIYM is not a man and ELOHIYM is not a dumb animal. Why did the Israelites try to make ELOHIYM into a golden calf? Even if you look at nature, a calf cannot talk. In the beginning, ELOHIYM created man in HIS image. Since ELOHIYM created man in HIS image, why make ELOHIYM into a tired, dumb ole calf that has to be guided? Animals have to eat and drink water. Animals can't do what ELOHIYM can. So, why a dumb animal in the image of my ELOHIYM?

In addition, HE is known as the living and true GOD. THE GOD of the Bible loves to be worshiped and praised. Praise ELOHIYM and HE will show up in your life. It's been said Lucifer took the singers out of heaven and the singers are now mankind replacing those singers. Indigenous people have the totem pole, which is the placement of their gods.

Deism is a naturalistic belief in the existence of a supreme being. The word *deism* is derived from Latin *deus,* meaning "god". While the terms were used interchangeably, in recent usage, they have different implications. Deism and theism concur in acknowledging the existence of GOD as the first cause of the universe. Thus, they are differentiated both from pantheism which identifies GOD with the universe and from atheism, which denies GOD existence. Theism accepts Man, for the most part, has always had thoughts of a higher power or deity in his mind. In Roman mythology, there were many gods. The supreme Roman leader among the gods was Jupiter. In Greek mythology, Zeus was the supreme leader. Do you see the similarity between Zeus and the name Jesus? Did the Greek use a similar name as Zeus for our Son of GOD name who was born not only in the tribe of Judah but Hebrew by His great grandparent Avraham. You see, the New Testament was translated from a Greek translation. The goddess whom we see with the blindfold is dike (justice). Nike is the goddess of victory. We in the Hebrew community serve The GOD of Avraham, Yitschaq, Ya`aqov(Yashar'el), and Mosheh. He is called "I AM." The reference to this is in **Exodus 3:14** "And GOD said unto Mosheh, "I AM THAT I AM," and HE said," Thus shalt thou say unto the children of Israel," "I AM hath sent me unto you." This is the first time GOD identifies HIMSELF to a man by a name. Man has always, for the most part, placed someone with more power above or over himself to GOD 's immanence and providence in the universe. ELOHIYM presumably created a well-ordered universe endowed with immutable laws, which has thereafter operated without further divine intervention. This tenet of the impossibility of divine intervention conflicts with the traditional Hebrewism belief in divine providence and revelation.

Now it has been declared throughout the ages that most people have declared a belief in some type of deity. Let me declare that I believe The GOD of Avraham, Yitscahaq, Ya`aqov Yashar'el, and Mosheh created everything that we see today in this present universe. Go out at night, look into the sky, and look at the enormous wonders of the big, blue, beautiful, and majestic sky and space. Just look and wonder how it was made so marvelously. You will be amazed at the thought pattern it took for this to be. ELOHIYM has so much power that it is hard for our little finite minds to comprehend something of that magnitude. Your idea of GOD does not matter because ELOHIYM is self-sufficient. HE can create honey from a rock

(**Psalm 81:16**). HE can create whatever HE wants to create, and HE does not have to have your opinion. GOD is GOD, and there is no other ELOHIYM like the one I serve. In addition, I will die for this belief and knowledge and fact. All ELOHIYM wants is for us to join HIM, and we will have eternal life with HIM. ELOHIYM is all power, and HIS presence is everywhere. There is no place where you can escape from HIS presence. Once we make it to heaven, we will have our Ph.D. (PRAISE HIM DAILY). Moreover, where would we be without HIM? ELOHIYM is the potter, as the book of **Jeremiah (Chapter 18th)** states and we are the clay.

One day ELOHIYM is going to set HIS tabernacle and live with man on the new earth and man and ELOHIYM will dwell forever together Revelation 21:3. And it will only be your belief that will hold you back from this promise of YAHUAH. Please accept this invitation because the only alternative is **CONDEMNATION DISASTER FOREVER AND FOREVER and complete regrets forever and forever.**

What may we say about ELOHIYM? ELOHIYM is loving, righteous, pure, merciful, graceful, kind, generous, faithful, and just. ELOHIYM is awesome, merciful, and righteous. We will not know the full story of why right now, but just be faithful. **Exodus 24:10** says" *And they saw the GOD of Israel, and there was under HIS feet as it were paved work of sapphire stone and as it were the body of heaven in HIS clearness.*"The children of Israel saw ELOHIYM and were left wondering about the sight of ELOHIYM that they saw.

If ELOHIYM does not exist, then what man can justify what or who can determine what is right and what is wrong? Who or what can determine right or wrong? The standard of right and wrong is a part of our makeup or the DNA code. In every line of DNA, it says "**GOD IS ETERNAL.**" Psalm 105:7b states *"His judgments are in all the earth."* The GOD of Avraham, Yitschaq, Ya`aqov, Mosheh has established the pattern of good and wrong in man. In other words, you have two men on an island alone; which man has the ability to tell the other man what standard to live by? There has to be someone with much greater intelligence and magnitude to make those choices. **Psalm 105:7b** states" His *judgments are in all the earth."* Police officers do not give one another speeding ticket, generally. Is this fair? In addition, we pay their salaries and they do this to the general public. If ELOHIYM does not exist, then how did we get here? By the great boom? Where did this boom come from by magic? I know it makes you wonder, but don't wonder because we will NOT have this answer now. NASA (National Aeronautical Space Administration) states it was a big bang. NASA is now trying to determine what is behind the big bang at this present time.

The evolutionary theory states that we came from apes or gorillas. May I ask a question? Why did not all the apes change? Why do we still have apes not changing? If a man came from the sea, why did not all the amoeba change from the sea? ONLY A SELECTED FEW, isn't this weird, but you may say your information is weird also, but I have an Intelligent Being creating ALL you and I see, but what you have are just theories and questions. Maybe evolution is just a big hype of deception or theory to get you to not believe that ELOHIYM is a Person (Entity) with so much superiority we know so little about. ELOHIYM IS FATHER SON HOLY SPIRIT. HIS mind is so much more expandable than our finite mind. HIS will is HIS will, and there is nothing we can do about HIS will and HE sees and knows everything is going on right now and we give an account one day because of what HE will be done.

The GOD in the BIBLE is the everlasting GOD. **Hebrews 11:6b** states, *"For he that cometh to GOD must believe that HE is."* We must believe that ELOHIYM exists to be blessed. Go back and think about how things came into existence: this world, the galaxies, the sun, the moon, and the stars by chance or an INTELLIGENT BEING? Do you think all the sensitive nerves in your body were by chance? ELOHIYM knows the number of hairs on your head. ELOHIYM is NOT a figment of our imagination. If you had all the parts to a watch and placed it in a box, can you shake the box and the watch comes together? What do you think? ELOHIYM is real and deserves to be praised and glorified. When we glorify

ELOHIYM, HE, in turn, glorifies us. ELOHIYM'S power is so great that words are not in place to describe that power that HE has. Pa'al states it is unlawful to even try to describe Heaven. You can compare HIM to a great and powerful magnetic field that bends things at its whims or will. ELOHIYM is the only GOD worthy to be praised. ELOHIYM is the covenant, GOD. He stated that before one title of HIS word fails, heaven and earth will pass away. Amein, ELOHIYM has established HIS WORD by a covenant or testament-the old and the new. Read HIS Words to establish the truth. Psalm 105:8 states *"HE hath remembered HIS Covenant forever, the word that HE commanded to a thousand generations."*. Who is ELOHIYM? GOD is THE FATHER THE SON THE HOLY SPIRIT. This is the GOD I serve. ELOHIYM is one in Unity, idea, and concept, but three distinct persons of identity. It is strange, but this is the GOD of The Bible, and it is the GOD I serve. ELOHIYM is HOLY and right. <u>ELOHIYM IS GOD THE CREATOR of all we see.</u>

I was talking to a woman the other day, telling her about this book. I stated to her that GOD is a position. GOD corrected me on that. HE stated, "I AM the full position of everything. I AM THE SUPREME OF ALL. There would be no you without ME. I AM mankind's great source of relief. Many do not know ME but serve other elohiym, elohiym of the wrong origin. I AM THAT I AM, as I told Mosheh on my Mountain of Glory. I declared to Mosheh my minister, of who I AM. There are no other gods. I AM THAT I AM. I AM your relief. I am your source of consciousness. I see all, and there is nothing out of my power except to lie and fail. I can't fail. Failure is not an option. When you seem to have gone as far as you can go, I will send help. I am a great help. Where you can't see I see. When you are about to give up, I will send help. So, when all seems lost, don't give up, for I see it all and I will be there to support you. Go on and see the end. GOD is. GOD is self-existence. You see, many translators of my Holy Words have messed up my sacred text, and they will be punished, led by their father, satan. satan has deceived those who are my people. Israel has not been forsaken, as it is written in the eleventh chapter of Romans and **Isaiah 42** and **43**. As my servant and Apostle Pa'al are NOT wrong, I AM still The GOD of Israel and not those so-called Israelites. For MY people are the same ones My Son sought out and died for. For My, Son became a new man, and now I have received My People Israel back by the resurrection of My Son, YAHUSHA. Yes, His name is YAHUSHA and not Jesus, the Greek/English name. You see I am responsible for all things, good or bad. I take the blame, but I have also been given an escape plan. I sent My Son to retrieve Israel only, but the plan also included the other nations in the plan of salvation. My Son's name in Hebrew means "THE FATHER'S SALVATION", and all who believe can now be accepted in MY calling to the world's salvation. Salvation was for Israel only. The church is made of gentiles or other nations, but the church did not, did not, did not replace My son (Yashar'el). Believe that. I AM The GOD of all, but I love Yashar'el and hate Esau. Remember many years ago, I told Pharoah to let my people go, and now I will retrieve Yashar'el out of their disbelief, for this earth is coming to an end. Be ready because the horn of My Son will soon cry, and once again, I will have Israel with Me again and this time forever. Never no, not ever will I leave Yashar'el alone again to suffer at the hands of Esau. Esau's hand is about to end, and the most terrible condition he will have. The earth will shake, rock, and roll for what they have done to Yashar'el. Esau will regret, but that regret will be too late, for the other nations have done to Yashar'el and I will return and all that Esau/gentiles have done to My people. Esau has hanged, stripped, boiled in water, boiled in sugar, boiled in oil, and stripped Yashar'el of his name, dignity, family, daughters, sons, and manhood, hanged Yashar'el by a pole and burned at the stake, having a picnic, laughing and you Esau, will pay for all this. I have not forgotten. For you have done all this and so much more. Whatever your small and corrupted mind has devised, you did, and so much, much more you will endure Esau for I hate Esau and love Ya`aqov. A love that has endured through the ages. I remember and I will push my fury and anger for what you have done to Yashar'el. I will repay what you have done. Just remember the rich man and Lazarus, the beggar. And now the table is reversed or turned, for now, I will avenge Yashar'el. I AM the GOD that repays. Remember! Remember! Remember! I will repay with my fury. You are laughing now, but that laugh will be reversed. Do not ask why because you know. You failed to show mercy and grace, but as you showed no mercy, neither will I. For those who are still living and you are mistreating, My people you will also be repaid. My name is YAH. **HALLELUJAH!**

Psalm 68:4 says *"Sing unto ELOHIYM. Sing praises to HIS name. Extol HIM that rides upon the heavens by HIS name, YAH, and rejoice before HIM."*

Every Sunday we say HIS name, but we see it differently. You said, "we spell it wrong ." We have the word spelled "HALLELUJAH". The j is pronounced with a y. Why? There is no j in the Hebrew language: "Ha-luh-loo-yuh". In the 1611 KJV, there were no words or names that started with the letter j because the j was not formed until 1633. In the 1611 KJV, it was Iah. The letter i in the English language is sometimes pronounced with a y so thereby we have YAH. The letter j didn't exist till 1633. So, we have THE FATHER's name. When we say GOD, it is singular, but in Hebrew, we have ELOHIYM meaning GODS. Our GOD is one person with one mindset, but three distinctive personalities:

THE FATHER   YAHUAH
THE SON   YAHUSHA
THE HOLY SPIRIT   RUACH HA'QODESH

Do you think ELOHIYM existed?

CHAPTER 2

—❦—

The Passover Lamb of GOD

YAHUSHA was the Passover lamb for the entire world. The BIBLE states in **John 3:16**, *"For GOD so loved the world that HE gave HIS only begotten SON, that whosoever believeth in HIM should not perish, but have everlasting life."* This was done so that we may live in eternity with Him. **John 1:29** states `` The *next day John (Yahuchanon) seeth YAHUSHA coming unto him and saith, Behold the LAMB of ELOHIYM, which taketh away the sin of the world."* This was done so that we may live in eternity with HIM (ELOHIYM). Adam's sin (disobedience, missing the mark) caused a great separation between man and ELOHIYM. It would take a lamb (male firstborn) without blemish to bring (reconciled) and ELOHIYM back together again. You may ask why. The answer is love. ELOHIYM, so loved that HE offered HIS only begotten (unique) SON that he offered HIS life just as Yitschaq offered his life as a living sacrifice. So, we may once again become one again and not separated from HIM. In ELOHIYM'S SOUL, it took this. ELOHIYM thinking is so very much superior to our small finite mind. We must believe in this to receive salvation (eternal life). YAHUSHA offered HIS life so that we may live forever with HIM. ELOHIYM so loved that HE created <u>events</u> so that we may live forever with HIM. If there is no bloodshed, there would be no remission of sin (**Hebrew 9:22**). ELOHIYM orchestrated everything in this universe for HIS pleasure. **Revelation 4:11** reads *"Thou art worthy, O YAHUAH ELOHAYNU to receive glory and honor and power, for thou hast created all things, and for thy pleasure, they are and were created."*

I gave my granddaughter a cookie for my pleasure, (but I asked her mother first) and her hands were attached to my pant leg and she, of course, placed her hand on my pant leg, *which* created a spot on the pants leg from the cookie juice mess on her face. I had the pleasure of giving her the cookie and I had the pleasure of cleaning the spot off my pant leg because she could not do it herself even if she wanted to because she was too young. Why? She did not know-how. It was my pleasure to give her the cookie, but it was also my pleasure to get the spot off my pants. I said that to state this. GOD gave man this world, and Ad-am disobeyed ELOHIYM, but ELOHIYM took pleasure in getting the stain of sin from HIS son, Ad-am, and it was by the begotten (unique) SON YAHUSHA HA'MASHIACH, who took on a body of human flesh, left heaven and came to earth to save man from a burning hell. Adam could NOT do anything to or work for his salvation because our righteousness is as a filthy rag in the eyesight of THE HOLY GOD (**Isaiah 64:6**).

There is something about ELOHIYM in His nature, make-up, attributes, and being that takes blood to redeem man's soul. It takes blood to redeem man to ELOHIYM. Ad-am was the first man, and he saw GOD slay the first animal's life to redeem his soul and to place that skin of that animal on him and Eve (Chuah). Blood essentially has the power to redeem man. REDEMPTION POWER. Of all things to use in the universe, ELOHIYM required blood to be shed for the redemption of sin. **Hebrews 9:22**b states, *"And without the shedding of blood is no remission"* (to release). You see how precious blood is, but the man continues to take life on a very whim (like it is nothing) with no regard for the individual's family members who will miss that loved one. Why would a man take another man's life? Because of all the covetousness and the hate in this present world. Remission means dismissal or release, such as of debt MESSIAH'S blood gave man his freedom from the penalty of spiritual death. Eternal death is spirit eternally separated from ELOHIYM. Do you want to be eternally separated from ELOHIYM?

YAHUSHA (GOD) let man slay HIM on the CROSS, but some people do NOT believe this happens. YAHUSHA (GOD) let a man beat HIM with a whip, which had at the end, rocks, metal, and bones that tore into the flesh of YAHUSHA (GOD) and HE bled. YAHUSHA (GOD) let man place those thorns around HIS head, which penetrated the layers of skin and flesh in HIS forehead and HE bled. YAHUSHA (GOD) let man spit in HIS face and pluck HIS beard. YAHUSHA (GOD) let man mock HIM and when HE could have come down from the cross and right this wrong, HE stayed so that we could come up with HIM on resurrection day because without the death on the cross there could NOT be a resurrection from the grave. So those who wear that idol of the cross why are you not also wearing the tomb? I know why because you don't realize TRUTH. For without the cross, there is no resurrection and without the cross, there would NOT be a resurrection because they go hand in hand. YAHUSHA (GOD) allowed man to hit HIM upside the head with a reed. YAHUSHA (GOD) allowed man to whip HIM up the hill. YAHUSHA (GOD) allowed man to drive those spikes into His wrists and His feet, nailing HIM to the cross and HE bled and forever, these will be permanent marks in HIS wrists and feet. YAHUSHA (GOD) allowed man to drive a spearhead into HIS side. YAHUSHA (GOD) did all this for you and me because of man 's sin. Guess who was at the cross? The Hebrews nation and the other nations in which the KJV would say gentiles' nation. Why do you think HE did all of this? So, that we may live with HIM in all of eternity. If YAHUSHA had not died on the cross and rose again, where would you be at this very moment? For man was <u>REQUIRED</u> to bring a perfect sacrifice for his sin to the altar. AT the altar were men both Israelites and the other nation. For man's ELOHIYM required man to (redeem) bring a perfect lamb to be sacrificed for his sin. **YAHUSHA WAS THE SACRIFICE FOR MAN SIN THAT ELOHIYM REQUIRED. ELOHIYM TOOK ELOHIYM AND OFFERED ELOHIYM UPON THE CROSS AND ELOHIYM WOULD RAISE UP ELOHIYM AFTER THREE DAYS AND THREE NIGHTS! THIS SACRIFICE END MAN DEATH (SEPARATION) SENTENCE ETERNALLY SEPARATE FROM ELOHIYM PERIOD only if you believe. And YAHUSHA rose from the tomb along with others Matthew 27:52-53. HALLELUJAH!**

Death is not just physical, but also spiritual and eternal. Listen! Spiritual death is separation from ELOHIYM forever unless you become redeemed. What is death? Spiritual death is the state of being eternally separated from ELOHIYM? Can you imagine being without the things in this present world? "What things?" you say. ELOHIYM is light. Before there was a sun, there was light. **Genesis 1:3** states' *"And GOD made two great lights, and there was."* The sun did not come into existence until **Genesis 1:6** "And *GOD made two great lights, the greater light to rule the day and the lesser light to rule the night "* Water is something that is needed in this life also. Food is something else that is needed in this life. When physical and spiritual death occurs and you are eternally separated from HIM, these things you will not exist in forever; The LAKE OF FIRE will be your home forever. You may say "Well, my friend will be in hell, so I will party all the time." That is a great deception. You have been thoroughly deceived to believe that lie because you will be in so much misery and more misery in hell forever not stopping as if a bird would fly for one grain of sand and fly back to pick up another grain of sand. You will not be able to find your friend in hell because **Isaiah 5:14** says *"Hell has enlarged itself."* Death does not mean passing on from this life and getting placed in a grave and that's it. We are like pecans. What you and I see is a <u>hull</u> or <u>shell</u> and the person inside is completely different. We are a triune being body, soul, and spirit. The body dies, but the soul and spirit will live somewhere in heaven or hell. We will one day pass on and we better be ready because no man knows the day when we will reach the end of our lives. Physical death, I call it the door to eternity. And the only way to enter through the door safely is to have ELOHIYM'S plan of salvation. Those basketball players leaving after a victory and going back to campus had never thought or imagined that their lives would end that very night. Life on this earth is not eternal, but ELOHIYM has made life or death eternal in HIS plan. You will have eternal life with HIM or eternal life separated from HIM. And this life where you go will be eternal and these two shall not ever meet again.

YAHUSHA came to earth so that we would not have to die and spend eternity away from HIM. YAHUSHA died so that we may see eternity with HIM. When we accept YAHUSHA as ADONAI and SAVIOR, YAHUSHA passes death from us forever. This is the reason HE is the Passover's lamb for the world. **John 1:29** says *"Behold the Lamb of YAHUAH, which takes away the sin of the world."* All lambs are born in the springtime. MESSIAH was The Lamb for YAHUAH. In the first chapter of Luke, the angel Gabriel came to Miryam in the sixth month of Israel's calendar, and Miryam conception took placed in Israel's sixth month which is Elul, which is like august/September to us and we go back three months and THE MESSIAH was born in the month of Sivan, which is like May/June our time and not wintertime. This holiday that we celebrate, designated as Christmas is actual paganism and has nothing to do with THE MESSIAH's birthday.

I remembered December 26 2015 because that was the day of the tornadoes that came through DFW in the evening time. People lost their lives and properties that day.

The Israel calendar is on the moon cycle.

The MESSIAH died for 1) political and economic reason **John 11:48** says *If we let HIM thus alone, all men will believe on HIM: and the Romans shall come and take both our place and our nation.* 2) He died to become a new man also **Deuteronomy 24:1-4** YAH divorced Israel as in **Jeremiah 3:8** He had to get HIS wife back so HE became a new man. 3) He died for the sin of the world so the man and GOD can be reconciled again. **John 3:16-17 Hosea 13:14 2 Baruk 54:16-19 Micah 7:8**

Do you think The MESSIAH was The Lamb of GOD? Do you think HE was born on December 25th?

Do you think HE is the first GOD and was born to a Hebrew mother and her name is Miryam?

CHAPTER 3

Salvation

The Bible (ELOHIYM'S WORD) of ELOHIYM (THE FATHER) and YAHUSHA (THE SON) RUACH HA'QODESH (THE HOLY SPIRIT) world. **John 5:22** YAHUSHA is going to ask you "Why did you not believe?" What reason can you give HIM that will satisfy that question? You then see those nail-scarred hands and feet before your very eyes. Now what. You are in this world, You are in this world and You are in this world and the only way, the only way, and the only way to escape spiritual and eternal (separated forever) are to be born again by your spirit, recognizing that you are a walking dead person (zombie) who needs a SAVIOR. Except as the BIBLE says, you cannot see THE KINGDOM to be a part to dwelt in THE KINGDOM except states in **John 3:3** *"Except a man be born again, he cannot see THE KINGDOM OF ELOHIYM." There is no way around this statement.* **Hebrew 6:18** *states, "By two immutable [unchanging] things, in which ELOHIYM couldn't lie, we might have a strong consolation, who have fled for refuge to lay hold upon set before you, which hope we have as an anchor of the soul, both sure and steadfast"* Psalm 138:2c reads, *"For thou hast magnified <u>thy word</u> above all thy Names"* It is impossible for ELOHIYM to lie. Luke 16:17 says *"And it is easier for heaven and earth to pass, than one title of the law to fail"*

In other words, what GOD said will be true. There is no other way out of the situation of sin you are in. Accept ELOHIYM'S truth or accept ELOHIYM'S consequences of not accepting HIM as savior you must be born again. *Except for* means "exclusively" "only for" or to make an exception. Therefore, to see the KINGDOM OF ELOHIYM we must be born again. This is the only escape clause to the covenant (contract) by blood ELOHIYM has made with man. The KINGDOM is ELOHIYM'S place. ELOHIYM is a king and HE has a standard. And well we are in this flesh it cannot ever please ELOHIYM, but once we are born again all things become anew. You must meet HIS standard. What is HIS standard? HIS standard is HOLINESS! How can we become HOLY? Only through believing what HE did upon the cross and being raised from the tomb. To be justified (make right), you must accept YAHUSHA HA'MASHIACH as ADONAI and SAVIOR.

You may have seen *The Oprah Winfrey Show* when she gave out all those gifts at no cost and you may have noticed how fantastic the gifts are. Guess what? Oprah does not have anything that will even significantly compare, even slightly to what ELOHIYM has in store for us all who are trusting in HIM. **Psalm 2:12** states *"Blessed are all …. that place their trust in HIM."* What is the opposite of blessed? The opposite of blessed is cursed. **Psalm 1:5b-6** says, *"Therefore, the ungodly shall not stand in the judgment, nor sinners in the congregation of the righteous...but the way of the ungodly shall perish."* In HIS KINGDOM, there is total rest from the grudgingness we go through trying to make it from day today. No one will rule over you unjustly as today judges, police officers, mayors, bosses, presidents', governors, etc. ELOHIYM is JUST.

Salvation is ELOHIYM'S plan and HIS alone. Man was separated from ELOHIYM by Adam's disobedience of eating the wrong fruit. And so thereby we were all guilty of Adam's disobedience. Have you ever lied, stole something, lust upon another man's woman, lust after another woman's man, have you, or cheated someone or even a business? All of this is because Adam ate from the wrong fruit tree. There were two trees in the midst of the garden of **Eden,** not Africa. The trees were 1) The tree of knowledge of good and evil and 2) The tree of life, but **Ad-am** followed his woman. Ad-am followed the voice of his woman instead of HIS FATHER. And men are still following the voice of their woman instead of GOD. The BIBLE mentions hoary heads and men cover it up. Since salvation was designed and implemented by ELOHIYM'S and no one else. So then who can take it away from you? Salvation is life (living) with ELOHIYM. Why do we need salvation? We need salvation because **Romans 3:23** says *"For ALL has sinned and come short of the glory of GOD"* and ELOHIYM has established the standard for HIS KINGDOM. It would be like I come inside your home and you have rules which I MUST follow if I want to continue to abide in your home. No smoking of any type, no running, no drinking alcohol, no eating off the floor, no pets, etc. HIS standard is HOLINESS and we become holy by believing what HE has done on the cross and the resurrection and this through HIS SON YAHUSHA HA'MASHIACH.

What the KING says is what matters the most. King Ahasuerus in the book of Esther made a law for all wives to honor their husbands after Queen Vashti had refused to come to him at his request, but she refused and lost the queenship because she got the big head and didn't do as the king had requested and got put out of the kingdom. Your parents made rules in their house and you had to follow those rules or there were severe consequences for your behavior or at least I hope so. Can you refuse ELOHIYM? Go ahead if you dare. Go right and receive the consequences for your disobedience to ELOHIYM. ELOHIYM is the king, with ALL power and grace. He is ELOHIYM and no one can dethrone ELOHIYM. I have one question. How did everything get started? And it is here because YAHUAH allowed it.

Is your salvation **BASED on work** or **GRACE?** Do you want to earn your salvation from your work? Is salvation based on what you do or what or who you believe in, what ELOHIYM has done? Are you assured of your salvation? What does the WORD OF ELOHIYM say? Since ELOHIYM has transferred our souls from death to life, when sin, again does HE transfer our souls back to death? How much salvation do we need or to be free from sin(death)? When we are born again, does HE take salvation away from us if we sin? How much work do we have to do to maintain our salvation?

Remember **Hebrew 9:22** There is no remission of sin without a blood sacrifice. So, with each lie told, you have to bring a blood sacrifice, but YAHUSHA HA'MASHIACH is our blood sacrifice forever. When HE died over two thousand years ago, that blood sacrifice ended ALL sins then now and forever. We are forever forgiven for all of our sins, by YAHUSHA HA'MASHIACH death on the cross. Just accept what HE did and QUIT all the guilt of your sin because you are forgiven and thank YAHUSHA HA'MASHIACH for the one blood sacrifice when HE gave HIS life for our sins. For how long? **FOREVER, but don't just sin because you are forgiven because this is when rewards come into play. This could cause physical damage to your life.** Get caught in adultery and you could die or be on the street looking pitiful. Go rob a bank and die. Can a drowning person save himself? You are drowning in sin and YAHUSHA is your only life jacket.

ELOHIYM's salvation is free (no shipping and handling fee) and it is offered to the entire world. All you have to do is accept HIS word and believe with your whole heart in YAHUSHA HA'MASHIACH as ADONAI and SAVIOR. We **MUST**(to be obliged or bound to by an imperative requirement) believe in the YAHUSHA'S death, burial and resurrection to receive salvation(eternal life). What is salvation? Salvation is THE WAY ELOHIYM (THE GREAT

I AM) of Avraham, Yitschaq, Ya`aqov, and Mosheh has established (Do you remember in the book of Exodus YAH created a way for Yashar'el to escape Egypt?) the way that man may be joined to HIM again. The question may be "How do I gain eternal life?" That is simple. Believe In what ELOHIYM has done for you and me. YAHUSHA HA'MASHIACH (ELOHIYM THE SON) suffered and died so that we may live with HIM. (Many believe that a quarter is silver in your pocket or purse, but it is not. This is how belief works. It only has power because you believe it to be so and because it is used as a medium of exchange. Try to give someone a fake quarter, you believe it is a quarter, but they do NOT. This will cause trouble.) In addition, I am thanking YAHUSHA every day for what HE has done for me eternally. Salvation denotes deliverance, preservation and eternity secured. Salvation is personal assurance that we WILL forever live with YAHUSHA HA'MASHIACH forever and eternally. We have made a personal statement (decision) in faith (we believe GOD is and that GOD THE CREATOR exists) and believe that YAHUSHA died because we are sinners and we accept the fact that YAHUSHA died on a cross and rose again three days and three nights later from the tomb.

So, you believe that you CAN work for salvation? You cannot work for salvation; **Isaiah 64:6** states *"We are all as an unclean thing…. our righteousness is as filthy rags."* What are filthy rags? A filthy rag would be a menstrual bloody rag or a rag we wipe our butt with after sitting on a commode and that which cometh out. An auto mechanic finishes working on a car and wipe his hands on a rag. Filthy rags period. Do you think about a filthy rag? Would you use it again or simply trash it?

No matter how much you work, you cannot ever be pleasing to the HOLY GOD. ELOHIYM is HOLY and the only way to please ELOHIYM is to be HOLY. Our righteousness is as a filthy rag in HIS Eyes. What is a filthy rag? That would be the rag we use to wipe the manure <u>from</u> rear ends or it could be the rag a woman uses for her monthly cycle. This is what our righteousness is compared to The HOLY GOD. Therefore, I ask you, ARE YOU TRYING TO WORK YOUR WAY TO HEAVEN? We work for rewards not for the show because it is RIGHT to please a HOLY GOD. So, quit working and accept ELOHIYM and HIS WORD because heaven and earth would pass away if HE lied.

I will never forget the time when I was wondering if I was saved? There was an evangelist who stated," Just accept you are saved." When I heard that, I accepted from then on that I was saved because it was ELOHIYM who saved us and not you yourself. ELOHIYM sent that evangelist in the midst of our congregation to speak those words to me because it has made a profound effect on my life and thinking. I receive ELOHIYM'S Word. And this I know that I am SAVED from condemnation and the coming destruction of planet earth! HALLELUJAH (All praises to THE FATHER). The word Halle means All praises In the KJV we see the name JAH **Psalm 68:4.** This is The FATHER's name, but it is pronounced with a y so we have YAH.

Therefore, to receive salvation, all one has to do is confess to ELOHIYM, "I need you to be my Savior. I am a sinner and I am in agreement with you, ELOHIYM." You want to be in accordance with what HE said that your SON died for my sin and rose from the tomb. Salvation is BASED on belief and confession, belief and confession, belief and confession and not works. Salvation is based on what YAHUSHA HA'MASHIACH (THE ANOINTED ONE) did and did alone. Everything else that we go through is an ordinance to follow after confession is made. Some people think that you have to get baptized, speak in tongues (baptized in The HOLY SPIRIT), be dealt with fire, get your feet washed, etc to be saved. These are just ordinances(causing confusion in the body of HA'MASHIACH the called out ones)to be followed because you are SAVED(not condemned for destruction). None of these things will be used to determine ELOHIYM'S salvation. There were two thieves on the cross along each side of YAHUSHA. One thief said come down and save us and the other thief said don't you see this man is innocent, but we are guilty and this thief believed and YAHUSHA said to him "Today thou shalt be with me in Paradise." The one thief was accepted because he BELIEVED. He was NOT baptized, there was no fire over his head didn't speak in tongues and he sure didn't get his feet washed. Did you see anything like this in the scenario? So, do not let anyone confuse or confute you about salvation. Ordinances are followed because you are saved, but have NOTHING to do with the salvation period. Once you are saved, you are saved forever because it is based on what YAH has done and not what you have done. ELOHIYM sets the standard for salvation. It takes a GOD to satisfy GOD. HA'MASHIACH was the only lamb of ELOHIYM, so that we may have eternal life, peace, and joy with ELOHIYM (THE FATHER) forever and forever. Therefore, ELOHIYM (THE FATHER) sent YAHUSHA HA'MASHIACH (THE SON) to die _for man_ to reconcile with HIM to justify us and make us have the right relation between ELOHIYM and man. THE CROSS bridged the gap between ELOHIYM and man. You may ask "How was that done?" YAHUSHA HA'MASHIACH was born to be the Passover Lamb for the world. YAHUSHA was born of a woman, reared up like all of us, HE slept, ate, and used the facility after HE ate, suffered by getting beat, slapped, spitted on, the crown of thorns shoved on his head (these thorns penetrated the skin on HIS skull, carried the cross, was nailed hands and feet to that cross, was mocked while on the cross and finally saying to HIS FATHER, **"IT IS FINISHED."**

I have a question? Can a drowning man save himself? Can a drowning man continue to keep himself saved? Now the answer to those two questions, since you did not save yourself, there is nothing you can do to continue to keep yourself saved. No matter how saved you are (which is a misnomer), there will always be areas for improvement until YAHUSHA HA'MASHIACH judges you. The reason I stated that this is a misnomer is because the standard to be saved cannot be measured because it is based on YAHUSHA HA'MASHIACH'S death, burial, and resurrection and not on anything I do, but I accept and believe and confess that HE IS ELOHIYM and that I need HIM every day.

If salvation is based on works, how much work must you do to be saved? How many sins must I not commit to be saved? How do I please THE HOLY GOD? What can I do to work on HIS plan? Salvation is based on what HA'MASHIACH did and did alone. Salvation is not based on deeds. Rewards are based on deeds, not our salvation. Don't openly display your deeds because you have already been given your rewards. Once again, ELOHIYM saved you, right? It is ELOHIYM who will continue to save you by your beliefs and that is ELOHIYM. YOU are right and I am completely wrong. Someone can outwork me because of money, power, and position, but YAH saves all.

And this is the record, that GOD hath given to us eternal life and this life is in HIS SON; he that hath the SON hath life and he that hath not the SON of GOD hath not life. **(1 John 5:11-12)**

For GOD so loved the world that HE gave HIS only begotten SON, that whosoever believeth in HIM should not perish, but have everlasting life. For GOD sent not HIS SON into the world to condemn the world, but that the world through HIM might be saved. He that believeth on HIM is not condemned, but he that believeth not on HIM is condemned already because he hath not believed in the name of the only begotten SON of GOD. **(John 3:16-17)**

Verily, verily, I say unto you, He that heareth my WORD and believeth on HIM that sent ME hath everlasting and shall not come into condemnation, but is passed from death unto life. **(John 5:24)**

*If thou shalt confess with thy mouth the ADONAI YAHUSHA and shalt believe in heart that GOD hath raised HIM from the dead, thou shalt be saved (**Romans 10:9**)*

*For by grace are you saved through faith and that of yourselves; it is the gift of GOD, not of works, lest man can boast. (**Ephesians 2:8-9***

*Not by work of righteousness which we have done, but according to HIS mercy, HE saved us by the washing of regeneration to HIS mercy, HE saved us by the washing of regeneration and renewing of THE HOLY GHOST, which HE shed on us abundantly through YAHUSHA HA'MASHIACH our SAVIOR, that being justified by HIS grace, we should be made heirs according to the hope of eternal life. sin separated us from ELOHIYM. (**Titus 3:5-7**)*

*But our iniquities have separated … you and your GOD and your sins have hid HIS FACE from you, that HE will not hear. (**Isaiah 59:2**)*

ELOHIYM came and took the yoke and the burden of sin off us and placed it upon HIS Shoulders. Many are concerned about lost salvation when in reality, salvation is based on what ELOHIYM did and ELOHIYM did alone on Mount Calvary. I thank GOD for giving HIS SON, YAHUSHA HA'MASHIACH, who took sin and conquered death forever to those who simply believe in what HE did and did alone. ELOHIYM makes us RIGHT in HIS Eyes. ELOHIYM died for us so that we may, in return, live with HIM both now and forever. The only wise GOD is our SAVIOR, both now and FOREVER. Please accept YAHUSHA HA'MASHIACH as SAVIOR before it becomes too late for your soul. The eunuch in the book of Acts of the Apostles (chapter 8) accepted YAHUSHA HA'MASHIACH as ADONAI and SAVIOR and was baptized. What he was reading came from the Old Testament. And guess what, he went home and had an understanding and he explained to those in from whence he came. Just because YAHUSHA has died for your sins doesn't mean we continue in those offenses because you are forgiven because lying, stealing, killing, gossiping, defrauding, using foul languages, doing drugs, etc are an offense to THE RUACH HA'QODESH (THE HOLY SPIRIT) who is now living in you. You are grieving THE HOLY SPIRIT. And if you continue in these offenses, you will make your life here on earth grievous on earth, but there will always be forgiveness by YAHUAH because of HIS SON DEATH and resurrection, but **GRIEVE NOT THE SPIRIT or your brother or sister.**

What is a testament? A testament is a will, covenant, contract, or instrument in writing by which a person declares his intent as to the disposal of his estate and effects after his death. You have the word testator. A testator is a person who leaves a will or one who testifies or is a witness. ELOHIYM has given man HIS covenant in writing and oral communication. We have no excuse, but we make excuses. "I did not want to obey", "I did not seek because I did not take the time", "I did not know", "I did not care", "I felt ok", "I had too many responsibilities", "I knew, but I…", "It is always I". Do not make the excuse of "I" because ELOHIYM'S GRACE will not be able to redeem you at the time of judgment because at that time it is too late.

What is grace? Grace is ELOHIYM'S unmerited favor toward man. GRACE IS NOT MERITED OR EARNED. GRACE is given. ELOHIYM'S grace caused salvation. ELOHIYM'S grace saw Ad-am in his disobedience and ELOHIYM'S grace caused the first animal to die and its blood to be shed and Ad-am skin to be covered by his act of disobedience. Grace could be an acronym:" GOD REDEMPTION AT CHRIST EXPENSE." Without grace, there would be no salvation. We could not earn salvation because ELOHIYM in HIS wisdom, established GRACE. Grace is not what you and I could ever earn. We would be the most miserable men and women without grace headed to hell and then to the lake of fire that burns until eternity. Grace is given. If we could earn GRACE, then a man would have something to say, but GRACE has allowed everyone to simply accept what ELOHIYM has done and nothing else. We would all be lost if ELOHIYM'S GRACE had not stepped up. GRACE, what more can we say, but yes? "Yes ADONAI, YOU are great, and nothing can surpass your GRACE, so that I may see your face in peace. GRACE to wrap my sin so you will only see YAHUSHA HA'MASHIACH your SON. Amein, amein, amein!

ELOHIYM saw the need before the foundation of the world and GRACE was a part of HIS being more than sin. Sin (missing the mark) broke the relationship between ELOHIYM and man. It took blood. The blood from the lamb, without blemish to bridge, to reconcile, to restore ELOHIYM and man, so that man and ELOHIYM can now have fellowship together again. satan tried to break the relationship between GOD and man. It's like a woman who is jealous of another woman so she TRIED to circumvent the relationship between the woman she was jealous of but YAH already knew. There will be a new heaven and new earth and ELOHIYM wants you to be a part of this new heaven and new earth. This earth CANNOT be saved. This earth is CONDEMNED. You can think what man says will save this earth or you believe what ELOHIYM says what will happen to earth. You may feel this can't happen, but I am **TELLING** and **WARNING** you this is going to **HAPPEN.** Please believe **THIS** because in the book of revelation Yah is going to create a new heaven and a new earth.

Everything will be renewed and GOD will live upon this earth and GOD and man will dwell together.

1) ELOHIYM is ALL Powerful and 2) HE cannot Lie

HE states in this blood covenant that heaven and earth would pass away if HE lied. If heaven and earth would pass away, there would be nothing at all. HE would become nothing and be non-existence. It would be like a person with Alzheimer's. Nothing would exist.

For behold, I create new heavens and a new earth, and the former shall not be remembered nor come into mind. **(Isaiah 65:17)**

And I saw a new heaven and a new earth, for the first heaven and the first earth were passed away, and there was no more sea **(Revelation 21:1)**

But the day of YAHUAH will come as a thief in the night; in the which, the heavens shall pass away with a great noise, and the elements shall melt with fervent heat, the earth also and the works that are therein shall be burned up. **(2 Peter 3:10)**

In the mouth of two or three witnesses shall every word be established. **(2 Corinthians 13b)**

The former heaven shall depart and pass away; a renewed heaven shall

Appear, and all celestial powers shine sevenfold splendor forever. **(Enoch 93:1)**

And the hour comes which abides forever and the new world comes which does not turn to corruption those who depart to its blessedness and has no mercy on those who depart to torment and leads not to perdition those who live in it. **(2 Baruk 44:12)**

For unto them shall be given the world to come, but the dwelling of the rest who are many shall be in the fire. **(2 Baruk 44:15)**

ELOHIYM and not the devil or the devil ways to cheat, kill or destroy. We are alive to ELOHIYM and dead to this world's system and fashions. We become citizens of another KINGDOM (THE KINGDOM OF ELOHIYM). As Pa'al said, we are NOW ambassadors of MASHIACH, another dimension of ELOHIYM'S WORD is true. HE has established witnesses and you can believe or not believe, but this world we live in today will be **DESTROYED,** and a new heaven and a new earth will be created. "How will this be done, you ask?" Because I serve ELOHIYM, who has all power. You can place this in the bank vault, the most secure place here on earth. *Repent* (change your mindset) means to change, to abandon sin, and to turn from sin out of penitence for past wrongdoings. You come into agreement with ELOHIYM. You realize ELOHIYM is CORRECT and how you are wrong. You change your way of thinking and align yourself with ELOHIYM. It then becomes a love affair. You will believe with your heart and not with your head. Your head's belief is completely different from the heart's belief, which is a faith that you are willing to die for. There are people who will give their lives for their system of beliefs. Their belief is their belief but it is RIGHT in their eyes. This is exactly what causes a man to die for a cause. Heart belief and not head belief. Are you willing to die for the belief that YAHUSHA HA'MASHIACH IS ADONAI AND SAVIOR AND THAT HE ROSE FROM THE DEAD AFTER <u>THE THIRD DAY?</u>

When salvation occurs, ELOHIYM transfers our soul and spirit from death (separation from HIM) to life. ELOHIYM does it when we have our hearts' belief. ELOHIYM transferred our soul to HIS kingdom of ELOHIYM. HA'MASHIACH has prepared a place for us. We become alive in the kingdom of ELOHIYM and are no longer walking dead. ELOHIYM becomes alive in our soul and we want to follow HIM that we can't see. ELOHIYM becomes more important than life here on this earth because we see the end of this earth because everything will be gone. We do not commit suicide to be with ELOHIYM, but we set out to do HIS Will and to bring others to HIS kingdom, even if it causes us to lose our lives here on this earth, but we are led by THE RUACH HA'QODESH in ALL things. What ELOHIYM wants you to become more important to HIM than things that are on this earth. For what HE wants it may not be what you want to have because everything has its <u>timing.</u> Because of HIS Plan. Avraham and Sarah wanted a child. **(LISTEN, PLEASE PAY PARTICULAR ATTENTION TO THIS.)** <u>**YAH has a plan**</u>. <u>**YAH has a Will**</u>. The MESSIAH had a <u>**specific time to be born and die**</u> (you see this is **YAH'S PLAN** and it ain't our). <u>**A specific and a particular TIME**</u>. Why do we ask? If (it is timing) Yitschaq had been born too soon that would have thrown everything off schedule. Yitschaq had to be born then Ya`aqov, Mosheh, David, Daniyel, and so on. Each person has a particular time to be born, but we don't see it because YAH KNOWS WHEN. Nat Turner was to be born at his time. Martin L. King and Malcolm X were born at a particular time because YAH said so. Each person has a particular job to do and I **was to be born at this particular time FOR NOW**. Why? I know now, but YAH knows the full term of my life. And I have to apply this to my life because sometimes I get upset, but I am in HIS Hands. So, I chill and be quiet and I pray (talk to YAH) because **HE is** fully aware of ALL in my life. You see in the first chapter of the Bible YAH brought life and in the seventh chapter, HE brought to rest for HIMSELF. What day did YAH rest from HIS work? I know some of you may not be able to believe this, but look at your life and maybe you will be able to relate to this information. In the movie "It's a Wonderful Life", George Bailey wished that he had not been born and the angel showed him what would have happened if he had not been born. If David had not been born when he was born he would not have been killed, Goliath, someone maybe, but David was born at that time to kill Goliath. And this leads back to who his parents are and to their parents and so on. Like Shalomah (The king of peace after David, his father which was the result of his brother's death) said "There is a time for all things."

ELOHIYM knows our future. Therefore, the events that occur in our lives are for a reason and it is HIS Will, not ours but HIS Will and they are for HIM and HIM alone. And HE determined the way we should go. ELOHIYM wanted Yonah to go to Nineveh; but Yonah said I'm going to Tarshish. Yonah tried to redirect ELOHIYM by trying to escape to Tarshish, but ELOHIYM redirected him. Yonah went to Nineveh through the whale's belly for three days and three nights. And this is the reason we have **Matthew 12:40**. ELOHIYM told Avraham that his seed will be afflicted in spiritual Egypt for four hundred years and that "It has been fulfilled!" ELOHIYM is ELOHIYM and HE Knows our future. Amein, amein, amein or so be it.

This world of the satanic systems is feeding us lies. We are trying to live as long as we can in this polluted, forsaken world of ours. This world is cursed. You see on TV to take this pill for this, get on this diet, get this operation, take this formula, exercise for $20,000 (lol) an hour to lose weight, and on and on so that we can live or save our lives. Take the vaccination so you won't harm others. I am not against pills, diets (you do know diet is what you eat) so eat healthy, diet, exercise, or have your operations, but none of these things will save your life, because you will eventually physically die. Your body is going to give up and you will be spiritually alive or spiritual dead (separated from GOD). This is a fact, Jack. You will physically die and then what? Are you ready (spiritually alive right now) to meet ELOHIYM? Listen up. This world system will not give you the entire truth. After drinking so much, your body will throw up, or you will die or you will have a hangover. Go on a date and you may be raped or contract HIV, get impregnated only to be satisfied for just that particular moment. Now what? Get all those credit cards and you cannot pay them all back or make minimum payments. Please get the entire picture. We take partial pictures and say "That will never happen to me." We opened a door, but we never got the entire picture. A lot of adults said the same thing, "It won't happen to me." And guess what? Right now, teenagers are missing, on drugs, living life, never making it back home, just on the streets. Listen up, YAHUSHA is coming back very real soon.

There is a problem in America right now of not going to the church house. Why do I say this is a problem? Because our children will not go to the church's house because the adults are rearing our children. We have a generation of children who are waiting for hell to grab them. When one generation changes, future generations change. Look at the nation Yashar'el they built a golden calf to worship in Mosheh's generation and that calf was destroyed, but during the king of Yashar'el Jeroboam built two golden calves. WHY? No one told him and sure did not read it anywhere, but he took counsel. Did no one know this history? What does this have to do with salvation? The answer is that what you do in the house affects your children in various ways. Where did you learn you need YAHUSHA HA'MASHIACH for salvation? In the street, maybe? At school? No, at the church's house. Give your children the same opportunities you had before it's too late. Pastors tell the truth. One problem is that some pastors are seeking fame and fortune and not rightly dividing the word of truth. Parents, we should set the example at home. I have had my shortcomings, but I have tried to instill the words in their direction whether they appreciated it. What I can't say, but I did what I could to acknowledge GOD when I talk to them as adults. The bible says train up a child in the direction they should go. If THE MESSIAH didn't come to earth and lived and then DIED and ROSE AGAIN then as Pa'al said we are still sinners headed to a disastrous end. What do you think? Do you not think there is A or THE CREATOR of man or do you think it was a big boom, of course, there is because THE CREATOR's voice is The Great Boom. Just think of what you are saying and how intelligent this system is and how great your body works? You plant seeds in the dirt and it grows into something else that it wasn't and yet the seed remains in them to grow again into something it AIN'T.

Do you believe in YESHUAH?

CHAPTER 4

— ❧ —

LOVE

YAHUSHA stated before He left in **John 13:35** "*The world shall know you are my disciples*".... You ask what is it? He states to have a love for one another. Many of us say we love one another, but look at what is going on in each family. We are brothers and sisters and we can't get along. We come from the same loin. All of the humankind came from these three brothers: Shem Cham and Yapheth. Unbelievable, huh? Many of us who come from our father Ya`aqov b.k.a. Jacob, a Hebrew, who is the father of the twelve tribes of Yashar'el aka Israel and we are calling each other n_ _ _ _ r or n_ _ _ a. We, whose foreparents were shipped on those filthy nasty slave ships are using a word taught to us by our slave master to describe our brother and sister, it should NOT be, but we who do this are still caught up in the slave master mentality. You should regret this because when you see THE SON OF GOD are **YOU** going to say H N_ _ _ _ r? Just think before you say anything to your brother or sister because our children are repeating what they hear that is coming from your heart. This word IS NOT a sign of love, but ANGER and WRATH and it is not a love word, but a very negative word that is a curse and not a blessing. So be it amein. So, when you are judged, what are you going to say to justify the words that are coming out of your mouth? What is your escape?

Love seems so hard to demonstrate and act upon. We may say the wrong thing and people take it the wrong way and we just pop off. We will give our brother and sister a piece of our mind. "I give you a little piece of my mind." The next thing you know, we are fighting, cursing, or dying. Why do we stir up anger in our brothers and sisters? Like Marvin said, "There are too many of us dying." Why is it that we cannot all just get along? Why do we continue to hurt one another when there are plenty of resources for us all to require the things needed to participate in this day-to-day environment? Why can't we use the fruit of The SPIRIT, not the fruits, but the fruit of THE SPIRIT there are no fruits on that tree, but it is one fruit. You see this is one fruit not a variety of fruits. Do you see apples, oranges, plums, bananas, cherries, pecans, and peaches on the same tree? Do you not know that YAH is looking at us right NOW. YAH knows what we need at all times. Did HE not count the hairs on your head? HE knows! We need to express loving-kindness and quit trying to defraud one another. Help when you can. Be positive when you can. Man loves your woman and woman loves your man. Come together and seek the betterment of each other and FORGIVE one another as I have forgiven you. **Galatians 5:22** says *"But the fruit of THE SPIRIT is love, joy, peace, longsuffering, gentleness, goodness, belief, meekness, temperance: against such,* **there is no law put in place."** **Let peace be most of ALL who call themselves a Believer in the church (The called-out ones). You are a believer and you and the woman can't get along. She alone and you alone in the same house. DIVORCE, but not on paper just waiting for death? WHY? Husband grabs that woman's hand and woman PLEASE don't reject this offer, but be kind and not mean, but consider YOURSELF, but accept this lovingkindness. Man, dance with your woman. Turn on some music, whatever you want to hear. Man, have some fun. Lighting up, take it easy, don't be so grumpy. Man, take your woman and hold her close to you, cook her a meal or take her out, be considerate and just don't take each other for granted anymore, but be loving and gentle and go for a walk and most of all be patient with each other. Give each other a break. Breaks are good. Because once the other has departed from this earth you will forever regret how you treated one another for where we are just here for a moment and then we are gone FOREVER to be in our place of eternity. So, be understanding and say baby let's talk and be most of all understanding one to another and let there be peace and love between you two because The Called One (The Church) starts at home for if there is no peace at home then how can the body of HA'MASHIACH be at peace? Those who are not divorced (you are married, but yet you act like an unmarried person, but YOU ARE NOT OBEYING THE COMMANDMENT of coming together as one. Kiss and hug each other every day. And say "I love you Babe or Baby.") remember it is up to you to amend and forgive one another as I have forgiven you. What are you going to do to be grumpy for thirty years living in the same house for a person you can't stand. Be loving not hateful. Because, whether we know it or not, it is a part of the law of marriage to come together and we are** *refusing that commandment. So, WHATEVER YOU ARE HOLDING IN YOUR HEART YOU ARE KILLING YOURSELF PHYSICAL AND EMOTIONS, and guess what you are making your relationship most very difficult on you and your partner, by holding onto this (YOUR) ANIMOSITY or whatever you are holding in your heart LET IT GO. BE AT PEACE WITH ONE ANOTHER. REMEMBER WHAT I SAID "BY THIS SHALL THEY KNOW THAT YOU ARE MY DISCIPLES.* And you are in someone else's kool aid. Stay in your lane. We need to love one another and care for our sisters and brothers. We won't do it. We want to do it our way. *"My way is the only way."* Seek peace and compromise and let us seek ways of thinking because unless your breath leaves your body, you can make it. We steal. We lie. We covet. We destroy. WHY? If we were to love one another like very close friends, then would we have these problems we have now? Nevertheless, I confess that I believe every sin is because of covetousness. A man will often say, "I love you baby", when, instead, it should be, "I lust for you." What sounds best: "I love you" or "I lust after you." **Love** and **lust** are both four-letter words, but their meanings are millions of miles apart.

What is love? Some of us think love is an emotion. My emotions change every day or moment. What moment I am in determines how I feel. Therefore, love has to be more than an emotion. Love is often confused with what we say when we are in the heat of things. We say it so often and, on a whim, we do not mean it. We say we love, but let a mistake be made. Is love expressed then, or is it an emotion? The Bible states that ELOHIYM is love. ELOHIYM'S love is perfect love. Love is seeking for the betterment or the best out of others for the highest good.

Let us look at how we treat that LOVE in today's environment. We turn our backs and do whatever may come into our small and infinite minds. Parents kill their children. Husbands kill their wives. Wives kill their husbands. Children kill their parents. We rape women. Men rape other men. What makes a man want to rape a man or a woman? We spread our diseases around, knowing they will kill others. Husbands cheat on their wives. Wives cheat on their husbands. Boy's state" I will kill you if I catch you cheating and you have NOT put a ring on that finger." We defraud one another by various means such as money, taking things back that we have worn just for a day by leaving the tag on (this is our mindset before we went into the store). We lie, steal, commit murder, incest, drunkenness, fornication, child abuse, mental abuse, racial hatred, child molestation, human sacrifice, homosexuality, transgenderism, questioning our gender, lesbianism, pornography, and drugs of all types and all sort of other evils. These greedy industries corporations and internal revenue services (a corporation) create stressful situations for individuals. We create frivolous lawsuits so that we may get some money. We do every damnable act our conscience comes up with. Let us refrain from these devices and turn to ELOHIYM. As the song says "What the world needs now is Love sweet love". What greater love can one do for another than to give HIS LIFE for you? Did THE MESSIAH say to the woman tell My disciples and Kepha bka Peter?

YAH loves earth so much 1] HE stated in the Revelation 21:3 That **HIS** Tabernacle is with men and **HE shall dwell with us** and we shall be HIS people. 2] If you look at the word **earth** and put the h in the front, you will **heart**. YAH placed HIS Heart into the earth and we shall forever be with YAHUAH. Look at what HE has done for man. 3] HE gave HIS only begotten (**unique**) SON that man would not be condemned to The Lake of Fire forever, but many don't or won't accept this concept and would rather believe HE IS **not** because you think YAH is a liar. As The SON if you believe in GOD believe also in ME because no man can get to THE FATHER except, HE believes I AM.

Does ELOHIYM show us HIS Love?

CHAPTER 5

—— ✺ ——

Passover

The question now maybe "What is Passover?" Passover is the celebration of the Israelites, which is done on the fourteenth day of the month of Nisan or Abib (between march/April) when our foreparents escape from bondage and freedom from the Egyptian's Pharaoh. It is the day that death passes over all of Yashar`e'liy who had the blood on the doorpost. The Hebrew Passover or "Pecach" in Judaism holiday commemorates The Hebrews' liberation from slavery from The Egyptians and the "passing over" of the forces of destruction or death or the sparing of the firstborn Israelites when YAHUAH smote the land of Egypt on the eve of the Exodus. The festival thus marks the first and most momentous event in our Hebrew/Israelites history.

Passover begins on the fourteenth and ends with the twenty-first (or outside of Israel and among Reform (so-called) Jews, the twenty-second day) of the month of Nisan. On these seven (or eight) days, all leaven, whether in bread or other mixtures, is prohibited, and only unleavened bread called *matzo* or *matzah or matstsah, may be eaten. The matstsah* symbolizes both the Hebrews' suffering while in bondage and the haste with which our foreparents left Egypt in the course of the Exodus. Passover is also sometimes called The Holy Day of Unleavened Bread. Passover Is often celebrated with great pomp and ceremony, especially on the first night, when a special family meal called the *seder* is held. At the *seder*, foods of symbolic significance commemorating the Hebrews' liberation are eaten. In addition, prayers and traditional recitations are performed. Though The Holy Day of Passover is meant to be greatly rejoicing, strict dietary laws must be observed and special prohibitions to restrict work at the beginning and of the end of the celebration.

This gives you something to think about of YAH, allowing the triumphalist escaping of The Hebrews from bondage by the hands of the Egyptian pharaoh. The Hebrew's Passover or Pesach or Pecach in Judaism (Yahudah) Holy Day commemorates our Hebrews' liberation from Egyptian bondage or slavery and the passing over of the force of destruction or death or the sparing of the Israelites' firstborn to those who the blood was on the lintel of the door in the shape of a cross. And YAHUAH smote the Egyptians in their land on the eve of the Exodus out of Egypt. This Holy Day thus marks the first and MOST DAY in the momentous event of our foreparents history.

It is too bad the high priests objected to certain things this week and were glad to do some other damnable things at other times. What do I mean by that? The chief priests **urged** the people to say, "CRUCIFY YAHUSHA [ELOHIYM]" (Mark 15:11) and they were willing to plot HIS death and be really secretive about their desires (Matthew 26:3). Yet they would not enter the hall of judgment because they would have become defiled and could not eat during the Passover. I guess they had not heard the laws of "Do not covet" and "Bear not false witness" and "Thou shalt not kill." Those laws don't matter, but I can't enter the judgment hall because **<u>I will be defiled</u>**, but your THOUGHTS YOUR ACTIONS are all defiled in the eyesight of GOD. In actuality, your actions speak louder than your words. This is why it states in the book of **Psalm 138:2b** says, *"for you have magnified your word above all your name."* Remember the two sons: the first son said no, but went and did and the second son said yes and did not, who got the greater reward, the one that yes and did not, or the one that said no and did? You be the judge. *And YAHUAH spoke unto Mosheh and Aharon in the land of Egypt, saying "This month shall be unto you the beginning of months. It shall be the first month of the year to you. Speak ye unto all the congregation of Israel, saying in the tenth day of the month, they shall take to them every man a Lamb, according to the house of their fathers, a lamb for a house. And if the household is too little for the lamb, let him and his neighbor next unto his house take it, according to his eating, shall make your count for the lamb. Your lamb shall be without blemish, a male of the first year. Ye shall take it out from the sheep or goats. And ye shall keep it up until the fourteenth day of the same month, and the whole assembly of the congregation of Israel shall kill it at evening. And they shall take of the blood and strike it on the two side posts and the upper doorpost of the houses, wherein they shall eat it. And they shall eat the flesh in that night roast with fire and unleavened bread, and with bitter herbs, they shall eat it. Eat not of it raw nor soden at all with water but roast with fire, his head with his legs, and purtenance thereof.*

And ye shall let nothing of it remain until the morning, ye shall burn with fire. And thus shall ye eat it, with your loins girded, your feet, and your staff in your hand, and ye shall eat in haste. It is YAHUAH'S Pecach "(Exodus 12:1-11)

The day of Passover was always (supposed to be) celebrated in the first month on the fourteenth day in the evening, which is actually the closest to the fifteenth day to the Yashar`e'liy. An example of this would be, when do we celebrate the fourth of July? The answer is, of course, the 4th of July. Does the fourth of July fall on a Friday every year? Does Juneteenth (June 19th) fall on the same day every year? The answer is an infallible no. It does not matter to us what day it falls on, sunday, through saturday. We are going to barbecue food, drink our drinks, sing our songs, play our music and dance our dances. The Yashar`e'liy was to **ALWAYS** celebrate The Passover or Pecach on the 14th day in the first month which was called Nisan. This day **COULD** have fallen on any day of the week: the first, second, third, fourth, fifth, sixth, or Shabbath (the day of rest,) the only name of any day of the week designated by YAH as the day of rest, the Israelites were so structured, that they would not even fight wars on that day they rested and this how constricted they were about the seventh day, why, read Numbers 15:32-41. The lamb's blood was shed and the lamb was roasted and eaten and the bones were not broken. HA'MASHIACH is the Lamb the lamb of ELOHIYM for the world. He went into Jerusalem on the tenth day and was asked a number of questions and no fault was found in HIM as Pilate said. And HE was nailed to the cross on the fourteenth day of Nisan and HE died on the cross in the evening. YAHUSHA was placed in the tomb on the 14th/15th on the Hebrew calendar and spices were placed on HIS body and HE was wrapped in linen, and He rose again after three nights and three days. In Hebrew, culture night was before the day as laid out by YAH. He went into the TEMPLE The HOUSE OF GOD and was examined by the Pharisees and Sadducees asking different questions and YAHUSHA answered those questions and like the Passover's lamb was **FOUND without any blemishes.** The Hebrews/Yashar'el brought their next day in the evening time. When 6:01 pm started this began the next day. In the book of Genesis, states the evening and the morning….. Oftentimes we have overlooked these min-ute details about YAH'S Word. This is so very important, but pastors/teachers are just sleeping and dozing through the words. WAKEUP people. So, the fourteenth day starts on what we referred to as the thirteenth day in the evening. YAHUSHA is the Passover Lamb for the entire world. YAHUSHA was prepared to die for you and me. ELOHIYM is an ELOHIYM of order. John

1:29 reads "*The next day, John [Yahuchanon] seeth YAHUSHA coming unto him and saith, Behold **THE LAMB OF ELOHIYM**, which taketh away the sin of the world!*

You see the calendar has been screwed up by man because the first month of the year **IS NOT** January 1st, but the first month starts on the new cycle of the new moon in the spring and NOT January 1st as we have been told, **look at how meteorologist describes the first day of spring.**

Did Passover happen?

CHAPTER 6

—— ✦ ——

Avraham and Yitschaq Symbolic of YAHUSHA'S Death

Many of us believed that the Israelites only had one Shabbath day or period and this is completely contrary to what The Bible says. We have to go to The Old Testament (Covenant) to get the best understanding of the Israelites' Shabbath periods. We will also discover the symbolism of the death of YAHUSHA in The Old Testament when Avraham took Yitschaq to offer as a burnt offering **Genesis 22:1-14**. In these verses, we have the father, the begotten (unique) son and [willing offering (this is found in the book of **Yasher 22:40-42** in which is not in today KJV but it was in the 1611 kjv], two servants, (the two thieves along the side of The Messiah), the ass (The Messiah rode into Jerusalem), and a journey of three days and three nights (the resurrection as recorded in **Matthew 12:40**). Avraham had three days and three nights of thinking about offering his only begotten son. Avraham was instructed by ELOHIYM to take his only begotten son, Yitschaq, and offer him a burnt sacrifice. Yitschaq was well into age at this time. We do not know his exact age in the book of Genesis, but in the book of Yasher (Jasher) Yitschaq was 37 years of age and Avraham would be 137 years of age. Yitschaq was old enough to know what was about to occur. In the book of Yasher, Yitschaq voluntarily offered his body because Yishamel was bragging about his circumcision and YAH heard Yitschaq making this statement. Avraham followed ELOHIYM'S instructions. ELOHIYM stated, "I will instruct you as to where to go."

Avraham took Yitschaq on a journey of **three days** and **three nights,** with two servants and an ass with the wood. HA'MASHIACH rode into Jerusalem on an ass. They arrived at the location and Avraham left the two servants. The two servants are representative of the two thieves on the cross. After **three days** and **three nights**, they arrived at the location and went up the mountain. Avraham had **three days** and **three nights** to reconsider this sacrifice while on this journey. This was **three days** and **three nights** to reconsider not sacrificing his unique son. satan tried to discourage Avraham from completing his objective. They arrived at the location and went up the mountain. HA'MASHIACH rose out of the tomb after the third day ended. HA'MASHIACH gave HIS life on a mountain. satan tried THE MESSIAH not to complete HIS task by trying to shame HIM. Yitschaq was instructed to carry the wood. HA'MASHIACH carried His cross. Yitschaq asked his father, "I see the fire and the wood, but where is the lamb?" Yitschaq was willing to give his life as YAHUSHA. He asked HIS FATHER if it was possible. Avraham tied Yitschaq to the altar. HA'MASHIACH WAS NAILED (bound) TO THE CROSS. Avraham went to sacrifice his son. YAHUSHA cried out to HIS FATHER by stating "It is finished." ELOHIYM, HIMSELF provided a ram. There was a ram in the bush. ELOHIYM stated that HE would provide HIMSELF as a sacrifice in **Genesis 22:8**. ELOHIYM completed HIS sacrificial offering for us to see HIM one day.

Avraham the father, Yitschaq the unique son (begotten), two servants, the ass, three days and three nights journey, Yitschaq carrying the wood. HA'MASHIACH rose at the end of the third day.

Did you know that the Bible does not state Avraham told Sarah what he was going to do? Some people even those closest to you may not understand the journey you are going on because we all do not have the same journey and it may not be for them to understand how YAH is working in your life, so sometimes you need to just hush and let YAH work it out in your life because it between you and YAH and not those trying to discourage you. So, just hang in there because YAH got you in His Hands.

Did you know that Avraham saw the promise that ELOHIYM had made to him? You say Yitschaq was much younger than his father, Avraham. Yitschaq could have REFUSED, but he was willing, like YAHUSHA, to give his life as a living sacrifice. What promise? **Genesis 12:2** says, "And I will make of thee a great nation, and I will bless thee and make thy name great and thou shalt be a blessing." Avraham was a hundred years old when Yitschaq was born unto him. **Genesis 25:7** states *"And these are the days of years of Avraham's life which he lived, a hundred threescore and fifteen years."* Here is the math:

100 + 3 scores (20 years = 1 score) + 15 =years of Avraham's life
100 +60+15= 175 years= Avraham's total life in years.

Genesis 25:20a states, *"And Yitschaq was forty years old when he took Rivqah to wife."* When Yitschaq took Rivqah to be his wife, his father, Avraham, was 140 years of age. Avraham is 100 years older than his son Yitschaq, so that would make Avraham (100 + 40= 140) 140 years of age. **Genesis 25:26** states "And *after that came to his brother out, and his hand took hold on Esau's heel, and his name was called Ya`aqov, and Yitschaq was threescore years old when she bore them."* Therefore, Avraham would be 160 years of age when Esau and Ya`aqov were born (100+60 = 160 years). Furthermore, Avraham saw Esau and Ya`aqov for fifteen years. What information did Avraham pass on to his grandson in those fifteen years? Avraham saw the Promise of ELOHIYM of the nation that ELOHIYM had promised to him.

This is missing in today's society. Men are not leading their boys to YAHUSHA. YAHUSHA is the X factor missing in today's society. We go everywhere, but to ELOHIYM'S word to find our answers today. We have taken corporal punishment out of society. Today we just talk to them, maybe, put them in timeout. We want to do it man's way. ELOHIYM said to instruct and not to spare the rod to correct and reprove our children's ways. Would our world turn out better if we were to seek ELOHIYM'S way and not man's way?

When I was ten years of age my dad told me I want the house cleaned and do not let anyone in the house. He got home early and the house was not clean and someone was in the doorway (not in the house) and I took off (ran away). There is an old song by the group The Temptations called "Runaway child." And one of the lines says "Getting kinda hungry you forgot to bring something to eat." Well, I wasn't thinking about hunger, but the pain was on my mind and a bed to lay in wasn't on my mind either, just the pain. We don't think we just react when we are young and dumb. I was gone for a while and he (my dad) came looking for me and when I saw him I took off and he had to hurdle a bike to catch me. He was so upset at me, he caught me, took me to the car and I asked if I could get into the back seat because I was planning to run away again and he slammed my head against the dashboard (no padding on the dashboard) in the front seat of a 1955 Bel-Air. When we got home, he went to work with an extension cord and I was crying saying I won't do it anymore, I won't do anymore, but the sting of that whopping left an impression on me and Monday morning when I got to school my friends asked me why was your Dad chasing after you. What could I say? I was ten years old in the fifth grade), but I lived through it and that was 58 years ago. The whopping has left a great impression on my mind since then, but we won't do as YAH says, but we are so smart that we won't follow GOD'S way, but we have our way. Sometimes we can go to the extreme as in my case but follow the GOD way and not a man because who knows the best THE CREATOR or you.

Some men believe man evolved from apes when apes are still walking around and we have not even remotely seen any possibility of any apes changing into a man today? I wonder what happened? Answer these evolutionists: Why do we still have male and female ape species here on earth? What caused the change at first? Why is the change still not happening? Can someone please tell me what has happened since the change suddenly stopped? I know there was never any change. It was just a lie by a man who came up with disorder, topsy-turvy and higgledy-piggledy theory.

Do you see the salvation plan in Avraham and Yitschaq going on this journey?

CHAPTER 7

— ✦ —

Israelites Day(s)

We need to first establish how the Israelites' day(s) are determined. **Genesis 1:5** *"And the evening and morning were the first days."* He called night first and then day last. And the evening and the morning and not the morning and then evening. So, the Israelite's' day begins in the evening and not when the sun rises. But our day now started at midnight, which is DARK. This is actually a night in our present time.

THE RUACH HA'QODESH gave me clarity in my mind as to why the evening is first. It is difficult for a man to determine one day from another, except we know in Texas that in the wintertime, it becomes cold and, in the summertime, it is hot, but let us say you are closer to the equator. You cannot tell one day from the other. We can determine seasons, but one day appears like the others. THE RUACH HO'QODESH gave me consciousness, clear-cut, incisive alertness about the phases of the moon. The moon is the determining factor for us to determine our days because it goes from a new moon (no light) to a waxing crescent, the first quarter, a waxing gibbous, a full moon (full of light), a waning gibbous, the last quarter, and a waning crescent in a period of almost thirty days.

The Israelites' day is broken into eight watches of three hours each: The day begins at the first watch 6 pm to 9 pm, the second watch 9 pm to 12 am, the third watch 12 am to 3 am, the fourth watch 3 am to 6 am, first watch 6 am to 9 am, the second watch 9 am to 12 pm, third watch 12 pm to 3 pm, fourth watch 3pm to 6 pm. (see **Luke 12:38** and **Matthew 14:25**).

There was no sunday, monday, tuesday, wednesday, thursday, friday, or saturday because all these days are related to some type of god that this world has ascertained to be a god. These are false witnesses to this world system (which is going to the lake of fire). A system to deny the very existence of THE CREATOR of all we see. Our system is the first day of the week, the second day of the week, the third day of the week, the fourth day of the week, the fifth day of the week, the sixth day of the week, and the seventh day of the week in which is called The Shabbath (The day of rest).

The Hebrews calendar starts with the new moon and ends with the waning crescent. The new moon starts most of the middle in the first part of the month that we are under now. The false new year starts off this present calendar is January 1st. Our new year under The Hebrews' calendar new year day was march 13, 2021 (The beginning of our new year in the month of Nisan which happened in the springtime and NOT wintertime), and the first month ended on April 11, 2021. January 1, 2021 (this is a pagan holiday) is not a day to be celebrated by Hebrews because our new year starts in the springtime and not the wintertime. It may seem as though I am destroying all your ideal of what you thought was the truth, but we have been led by false information for so long that we no can longer know or distinguish WHAT IS TRUTH, but we have been following a false god of belief and the truth have been hidden from our lives, that we can no longer see the truth because we have been living in a lie for so very long that we can't see **TRUTH** when it is standing before our eyes. YAH is trying to reach us with truth, but as **Husha 4:6 (Hosea)** said, my people are **destroyed** for a **lack** of **KNOWLEDGE** because they **REJECTED IT! Please don't reject this knowledge, but learn by reading.**

Do you see the difference in the way our times are established and Israelites days are established?

CHAPTER 8

Shabbath Days

There is more than one Shabbath day or period in The Bible, but we have been ever so taught only about one. **Exodus 31:13** says "Speak *thou unto the children of Israel, saying, Verily, my Shabbaths. Ye shall keep, for it is a sign between me and you throughout your generations that ye may know that I AM YAHUAH MEQODDISHKEM."* The question that came to me is, ``Why the '<u>s</u>' at the end of the word if there is just one Shabbath day?" The Bible says in **2 Timothy 2:15,** *"Study to show thyself approved to ELOHIYM."* **Leviticus 19:3** reads, *"Ye shall fear every man, his mother, and his father and keep my Shabbaths. I am YAHUAH ELOHAYKEM. "I* had the same question why the s is at the end of the word Shabbaths if there was only one-day Shabbath. The answer had to be in the BIBLE. It is either referring to the seventh day of Shabbath throughout the year or is totally referring to more than one day. So, I had to go back to the Old Testament and study the Israelites' Shabbath and The Passover because of the perception that is totally out of concept with the Old Testament.

The Israelites (we) had several Shabbath days or periods of rest. They were days for prayer, fasting, and reverence (worship) to YAHUAH and YAHUAH alone. These were HOLY DAYS. Do you recognize this word? If not, here it is the *holiday.* The worldly method is to party all for oneself. Israel was to acknowledge those days to ELOHIYM and ELOHIYM alone. HOLY DAY and *holidays* are completely different ideas and methodologies of giving thanks for the day and persons. A Holy Day is a man serving ELOHIYM. A holiday is a man serving flesh, man, the world system, or itself and not ELOHIYM. Like I stated earlier, the Israelites had several Shabbath days according to **Leviticus 19:3** *"Ye shall fear every man his mother, and his father, and keep my <u>shabbaths.</u> I AM YAHUAH ELOHAYKEM.* **Exodus**

31:13 *"Speak unto the children of Israel, saying, Verily my <u>shabbaths</u> ye shall keep: for it is a sign between me and you throughout your generations; that ye may know that I AM YAHUAH ELOHAYKEM that sanctify you."* And verse **14** says *YE shall guard the Shabbath therefore; for it is holy unto you: every one that defiles it shall be <u>cut off</u> from among his people"* And this whole nation eventually went into captivity because of not keeping theses Shabbath. Remember the "s" at the end of the word Shabbath. This logically means more than one day. The answer is in The WORD of YAH. The first Sabbath, according to the scriptures is the seventh day of rest, when ELOHIYM ended HIS work, which is saturday as named by a man. The problem occurs because of our concept or our way of stinking thinking. This causes disturbing stinking thinking. Our thinking has been astray from THE CREATOR and we take on the stinking thinking of a man who has no way of wanting to know ELOHIYM ways. Our thinking has been corrupted and disfigured that we can't or refuse to recognize ELOHIYM's true way because we have been led by devils. And we see the word Shabbat and we are conditioned to think inside the box. Come out of your box and refresh and renew that stale and moldy stinking thinking brain of yours.

"And on the seventh day, ELOHIYM ended HIS work, which HE had made. (**Genesis 2:2**) *"Remember the Shabbath day, to it holy. Six days shall you labor and do all your work. But the seventh day is the Shabbath of YAHUAH ELOHAYKA; in it, you shall not do any work, you nor your son nor you maidservant nor your cattle nor you strangers that are within your gates.*

For in six days YAHUAH made the heavens and the earth, the sea, and all that in them is, and rested the Shabbath, and hallowed it. (**Exodus 20:8-11**)

Six days shall work be done, but the seventh day is the Shabbath of rest, a holy convocation; you shall do no work therein. It is the Shabbath of YAHUAH in all of your dwelling. (**Leviticus 23:3**)

In addition, as you read this, you will notice that it was a period of rest for all, including the beasts and no work. **Leviticus 23:24** states, *"Speak unto the children of Israel, saying, In the seventh month <u>on the first day of the month</u> shall be a <u>Shabbath</u>, memorial of blowing of trumpets, a holy convocation."*

Did you notice the word Shabbath in the verse? Is this the seventh day, as in **Leviticus 23:3**, as you just read in **Leviticus 23:3** which states the seventh day? **Leviticus 23:24** states the first day of the seventh month. Please answer the question. Does July first the seventh month fall on the same day of the week each year? Does your birthday fall on the same day of the week each year? The answer is inexplicable no. Please keep this in mind as you read this book.

Also on the tenth day of this seventh month, there shall be a day Yom Kippuriym; it shall be a holy assembly unto you, and you shall afflict your souls and offer an offering made by fire unto YAHUAH. And you shall do no work in that same day: for it is Yom Kippuriym, to make an atonement for you before YAHUAH ELOHAYKEM. For whatsoever soul it be that shall not be afflicted in that same day, he shall be cut off from among his people. And whosoever soul it be that does any work that same day, the same soul will I destroy from among his people. You shall do no manner of work: it shall be a statue forever throughout your generations in all your dwellings. it shall be unto you a Shabbath of rest, and you shall afflict your souls: in the ninth day of the month at evening, from the evening unto evening, shall you celebrate your Shabbath. **(Leviticus 23:27-32)**

As you can see with your own eyes, the word Shabbath is expressed throughout this passage. This is the third time Shabbath is mentioned in the scriptures. As you have read in **Exodus 31:13** and **Leviticus 19:3**, the word Shabbaths actually means referring to different days of the calendar year and not just the seventh-day Shabbath. Israel's Shabbath day was Holy Days (rest, prayer, fasting, worship, reverence, thanksgiving, and praise) ELOHIYM wanted Israel to glorify HIM and not themselves. ELOHIYM wants us to be real in HIM. And these days were to remember how YAHUAH brought them through different events that occurred in their lives and actions and they are NOT to do any work on those days at all and all rested including those that were servants.

1) The Sevenths Day	Leviticus 23:32
2) The Passover (First Month, Fourteenth Day)	Leviticus 23:6
3) The Feast of Unleavened Bread (First Month Fifteenth Day)	Leviticus 23:6
4) The End of the Feast of Unleavened Bread	Leviticus 23:8
5) The Feast of the First Fruit	Leviticus 23;9-14
6) The Feast of Pentecost	Leviticus 23:15-21
7) The Feast of Shofaroth (Trumpets)	Leviticus 23:24
8) The Day of Yom Kippuriym(Atonement)	Leviticus 23:27
9) The Feast of Cukkoth (Tabernacles) (Seventh month Fifteen day)	Leviticus 23:34
10) The end of The Feast of Tabernacles	Leviticus 25:39
11) The Jubilee Year	Leviticus 25:3-4
12) The Seventh Year Shabbath	Leviticus 25:8

You see **THE** word ***Shabbath*** in each of these verses referring to different days of each month and not just the one-seventh day Shabbath. In addition, you see with your own **EYES** The Sabbaths in **Leviticus 19:3** and **Exodus 31:13**; and you cannot just assume this concern only the seventh-day shabbath which began on Friday at 6 pm until Satur6 pm. There are similarities between Israelites' Passover and YAHUSHA's Death. This is the one picture of YAHUSHA's death that was in The Old Testament. See if you see as I do.

"And YAHUAH spoke unto Mosheh and Aharon in the land of Mitsrayim, Saying This month shall be unto you the beginning of months. It shall be the first month of the year to you. Speak you unto all the congregation of Israel, saying in the tenth day of the month, they shall take to them every man a lamb, according to the house of their fathers, a lamb for a house.

And if the household is too little for the lamb, let him and his neighbor next unto his house take it, according to his eating, shall make your count for the lamb. Your lamb shall be without blemish, a male of the first year. You shall take it out from the sheep or goats. And you shall keep it up until the fourteenth day of the same month, and the whole assembly of the congregation of Israel shall kill it at evening. And they shall eat the flesh in that night roast with fire and unleavened bread, and with bitter herbs, they shall eat it. Eat not of it raw nor sodden at all with water but roast with fire, his head with his legs, and purtenance thereof. And you shall let nothing of it remain… (**Exodus 12:1-10***)*

And when HE came into the temple, the chief priests and the elders of the people came unto HIM as HE was teaching and said, "By what authority dost thou these things? And who gave thee this authority?" And YAHUSHA answered and said unto them. "I also will ask you one thing, which, if you tell me, I in likewise will tell you by what authority I do these things. The baptism of Yahuchanon (John), whence, was it? From heaven or of men?" And they reasoned with themselves, saying, "If we shall say from heaven, HE will say unto us, "Why did ye not believe him?" But if we shall say of men, we fear the people, for all hold Yahuchanon is a prophet." And they answered YAHUSHA and said, "We cannot tell.

And HE said unto them, "Neither tells I you by what authority I do these things." (**Matthew 21:23-27**)

They went to the Pharisees and took counsel on how they might <u>entangle</u> HIM in HIS talk. And they sent out unto HIM their disciplines with Herodians, saying, "Master, we know that thou are true and teaches the way of ELOHIYM; in truth, neither carest thou for any man, for thou regardest not the person of men. Tell us, therefore, what thinkest thou? Is it lawful to give *tribute unto Caesar or not? But YAHUSHA perceived their wickedness and said, "Why tempt ye me, you hypocrites? Show me the tribute money." "Whose is this image and superscription?" They say unto HIM, "Caesar's." Then saith HE unto them, "Render unto Caesar's the things which are Caesar's and unto ELOHIYM the things that are ELOHIYM'S." When they heard these words, they marveled and went their way.* **(Matthew 22:15-22)**

And no man was able to answer HIM a word; neither durst any man from that day forth ask HIM any more questions. **(Matthew 22:46)**

Exodus 12:1-3 The Israelites took a lamb into the house on the tenth month of Nisan, the first month. **Exodus 12:5** This male lamb or male kid was without blemish **Exodus 12:6** At the evening time on the fourteenth, the lamb was killed as instructed. The lamb was roasted and eaten that evening time. At 6 pm it was the next Shabbath day Feast of unleavened bread when they ate the kid or the lamb which would have been on the 15th of Nisan. The blood was placed on the sides and upper posts of the door. This is a picture of the cross. The scriptures state that they were to take the lamb or kid the first year without blemish into the house for four days and examine and to keep it safe so it would be without and stay without blemish. Remembering what Cain offered to YAH, he offered things with blemishes. YAHUSHA was the first male in HIS family.

YAHUSHA as the Bible says the first-born Son of Miryam. Notice what the Bible says: firstborn not only born. So Miryam DID NOT STAY A VIRGIN as so many of those in Catholicism have been deceived to believe. The MESSIAH had four brothers and sisters **Mark 6:3** and **Matthew 13:55**. And YAHUSHA's mother's name **WAS NOT** Mary as we have been deceived to believe. Mary was not English or non-melanin. Miryam was born to Hebrew parents and having Hebrew parents she has **melanin** in her skin tone making her a person of **color. We have been deceived by a man who wants to take credit for all things but REFUSED to tell the truth and because of this, THE LAKE OF FIRE awakens for them.**

YAHUSHA entered Jerusalem on the tenth day of the first month. This day has been referred to the world as palm Sunday, but that is so terribly wrong. Was it a Sunday? I think not because the scriptures say 3 days and 3 nights. YAHUSHA had to be examined by the household of Israel for four days because HE was The Passover's LAMB of YAHUAH as **John 1:29** says, to be without blemishes. This is where the leaders TRIED so hard to entangle HIM, but you can't entangle or entrap GOD. The leaders asked different questions and they

COULD NOT entangle HIM, but HE was The Passover's Lamb for all of mankind. When YAHUSHA entered Jerusalem it was the beginning of the Passover celebration as outlined in The book of Exodus twelfth chapter.

YAHUSHA is ELOHIYM (THE FATHER THE SON THE HOLY SPIRIT), The Passover's Lamb for the world. For ELOHIYM so loved man that HE gave HIS only begotten SON to save us from the destruction and condemnation of hell. When a building is condemned the next thing that happens is destruction, but HE saved us from destruction only if you believe. We have discussed the Shabbath days for the Israelites, which is the beginning of knowing and understanding YAHSHUA's death and resurrection. If we fail to understand The Israelites' Shabbath days, we cannot fully understand how ELOHIYM THE FATHER THE SON THE HOLY SPIRIT intended on YAHUSHA (THE SON) to die. ELOHIYM is THE ELOHIYM of order and not confusion. **John 19:31** says, "The Jews, therefore because it was the preparation, said that the bodies should not remain upon the cross on the Shabbath day, for that Shabbath day was a high day." **It says that this Shabbath was a high day** meaning it is a very important day and not a regular Shabbath day, but it was an important Shabbath day of the twelve Shabbath's period. **Do you see how we have been a mistake**

CHAPTER 9

—— ❧ ——

Passion Week/Passover Week

The list below shows what happened during Passover Week

- Tenth Day ---- The lamb was taken into the home.
- Eleventh Day ----- The lamb was examined
- Twelfth Day ------- The lamb was examined
- Thirteenth Day ----- The lamb was examined
- Fourteenth Day ---- The lamb was examined/ slain in the evening (Passover).
- Fifteenth Day - Twenty-First Days--- Unleavened bread served.

This list shows what happened during YAHUSHA'S Passion Week

- Friday (Ninth)----- YAHUSHA rode into Jerusalem. **(Mark 11:1)**
- This is referred to as Palm sunday, but it is totally hypocritical that it is not Palm sunday
- saturday (Tenth) --- YAHUSHA was examined in the temple.
- sunday (Eleventh) --- YAHUSHA was examined in the temple.
- monday (Twelfth) ---- YAHUSHA was examined in the temple.
- tuesday (Thirteenth) ---- YAHUSHA was examined in the temple.
- wednesday (Fourteenth)---- YAHUSHA suffered and was slain by 3 pm
- HE gave up the ghost and was placed in the tomb by 6 pm
- wednesday evening (Fourteenth/Fifteenth) --- YAHUSHA first night in the tomb (High Shabbath day according to **John 19:31**)

- thursday (fifteenth) YAHUSHA first day in the tomb.
- thursday evening (Fifteenth/Sixteenth) YAHUSHA second night in the tomb
- friday (Sixteenth) YAHUSHA second day in the tomb
- friday evening (Sixteenth/Seventeenth) YAHUSHA third night in the tomb.
- saturday (Seventeenth) YAHUSHA third day in the tomb
- saturday and appears in the holy city (Seventeenth) YAHUSHA was <u>resurrected</u> from the tomb. Along with others that were resurrected from She'ol **Matthew 27:52-53**

In summary, whom will you believe in, man or ELOHIYM? **AS HOSEA SAYS HAVE KNOWLEDGE, BUT YOU REJECT THAT KNOW, AND AS ISAIAH SAID THE BOOK IS OPEN BUT BECAUSE YOU ARE UNLEARN MEN WILL NOT INTERPRET THE WORD CORRECTLY BECAUSE YE ARE UNLEARNED. You have a book but refuse to learn from that book!**

WITNESSES
    Matthew 12:39-40 Matthew 16:4 Luke 11:29-30, 32, 1 Corinthians 15:4
    Matthew 27:63 Mark 8:31 John 2:19

May I ask a question, is there anything too hard for our ELOHIYM to do? If ELOHIYM can become human, what can HE not do? I thank you for reading these words. When I wrote He was examined, HE was questioned and they (HIS people Yashar'el rejected HIM) they could find **no faults** as Pilate said before His death on the cross and even one of the thieves on the cross alone both sides state we are guilty of our crime, but this man has no faults. ELOHIYM states in **Psalm 138c,** *For thou hast magnified **THY WORD** above all **THY NAME.*** ``

Do we understand this?

CHAPTER 10

❧

What We Have Been Taught

The question is "Why am I writing this, you may ask?" I am writing this to cause confusion, friction, and controversy or to put clarity where clarity needs to be <u>IN THE WORD OF GOD.</u> Let me be first apologetic, but forget that because I don't have to be apologetic because when judgment day comes we will be made sorry about different situations in our life, but I DON'T have to be apologetic for telling THE TRUTH. I pity the fool who would constantly want to be lied to, but let WORD OF GOD be true and everyone else studies to show thyself-approved to ELOHIYM and not to a man. YAHUSHA states in HIS WORDS that there would be division in the family. We have all been taught that YAHUSHA died on friday evening and rose early Sunday morning. Questions came to my mind when YAHUSHA states the following;

For as Jonah was three days and three nights in the whale's belly, so shall the SON of Man will be three days and three nights in the heart of the earth. (**Matthew 12:40**)

And they shall mock HIM and shall scourge HIM and spit upon HIM and shall kill HIM, and after three days rise again. (**Mark 10:34**)

And HE began to teach That the SON of man must suffer many things and be rejected of the elders and the chief priests and scribe and be killed and after three days rise again. (**Mark 8:31**)

And when the people were gathered thick together, HE began to say, "This evil generation, they seek a sign, and there shall no sign be given It but the sign of Jonah the prophet." (**Luke 11:29**)

Is there anything that The GOD of Avraham, Yitschaq, Ya`aqov and Mosheh (Chabar his Hebrew name given to him by his Hebrew parents, well least one of his names) cannot do? I want to know, do you have a problem with Yonah in the belly of the whale for three days and three nights? Three days is three days and Three nights is three nights. The BIBLE says

WHAT IS YOUR PERSPECTIVE OF TRUTH?

three days and three nights and not part of three days and three nights. If you do not believe Yonah was in the belly of the whale for three days and three nights, then you cannot believe when YAHUSHA states HE would rise after the third day. You cannot say, "I believe part of the Bible and the other part, "I believe not." What are you afraid of? ELOHIYM will not lie, according to **Hebrew 6:18-19** *"That by two immutable (won't do, can't do, won't change) things in which it was **impossible** for ELOHIYM to lie, we might have a strong consolation, who have fled for refuge to lay hold upon the hope set before us, which hope we have as an anchor of the soul, both sure and steadfast, and which entereth into that within the veil."*

ELOHIYM'S word is a sure anchor that is holding a boat in place. The boat is not going anywhere when the anchor is tied to it, just as ELOHIYM is so sure of HIS Word that HE states that heaven and earth would pass away before one tittle of HIS word would fail. Do you believe that the pharaoh's army drowned in the Red Sea?

*Yonah is a real person (the book of **Jonah** and **2 Kings 14:25**) and the whale was real. This was no fairy tale, but this is a real problem in today's society. We believe or have heard too many fairy tales. YAHUSHA states that this is the only sign HE would give the Pharisees. If you have a problem with Yonah, then how can you believe in the death, the burial, and the resurrection of YAHUSHA HA'MASHIACH?* The Bible states that heaven and earth would pass away if HE (ELOHIYM) lies. If we believe in ELOHIYM, we have to take into full account that what HE has stated is true. ELOHIYM is all true. There is no lie in ELOHIYM. We cannot say, "I believe this is true and this is not true." ELOHIYM does not deal in or with half-truths. It is all true and nothing but the truth. Who are we to believe? I believe ELOHIYM'S word states the truth and nothing but the truth.

You may have heard of the TV show called *"Perry Mason"* and the person is sworn in. That person would ask "Do you promise to tell the truth, so help you, GOD?" The person would say "I do." Sometimes as mortal men, we at times cannot or will not accept the fact that ELOHIYM can do what HE wants to do anytime because HE has a will and a Plan and things are in HIS Timing and not our timing because He has a Plan and HIS Plan will be done no matter how we cry out to HIm. Some men say use your faith, but that has been so misstated because the verse leaves out a single word and one word left out a sentence can change the entire thought. **Romans 1:17** says "The just shall live by faith", but that scriptures came out **Habakkuk 2:4** which says...but the righteous shall live by his belief and that he is NOT a mortal man but ELOHIYM. The reason I say this is because The MESSIAH

SAID "If your faith is the size of a mustard seed you can say to the mountain go into the sea **Matthew 21:19**. So, we can refuse to believe, but once again you reject knowledge and my people are destroyed because they reject knowledge. Can we as Hebrews, Israelites, Believers just take half-truths and live by them? Should we accept what He said as half-truths or believe that HE is all righteous, equitable, impartial, and unbiased truth? A few questions came to my mind, so I set out to answer them by studying the word of YAH.

According to **2 Timothy 2:15** "*Study to show thyself approved to GOD a workman that needeth not to be ashamed, rightly dividing the word of truth.*"

ELOHIYM'S word is true. If Micahel Jackson can turn himself into a non-melanin then what can my ELOHIYM not do? ELOHIYM is ALL power. And HE can place this earth in this part of the universe in a fixed position and have the sun and moon rotate around the earth and they rotate every twenty-four hours as HE has ordered. ELOHIYM holds everything in place and this earth will be renewed as HE has said. The moon and sun never get out of their orbit and yet the stars stay within their geographical boundaries. ELOHIYM creates spring, summer, fall, and winter. HE created this atmosphere. Now that a GOD!

I set out on my study or my quest for the right answer. We have already established the Israelite days and the time slots for each day. First, let us look at what the scriptures say and what man has said about the resurrection. Many of us believe or were taught that YAHUSHA rose on the first day of the week (sunday morning) and died at 3 pm on friday and was placed in the tomb before 6 pm and stayed all night friday night all day saturday and all night saturday and rose early sunday morning. Right, that is what we have been told all our lives, but have we come from the scripture? This book would not have been written. Is this what you believe right now? Let us see if the scriptures validate or support this thought, concept, idea, or thinking.

Saying "Sir, we remember that deceiver said, while He was yet alive, after <u>three days,</u> I will rise again." Command therefore that the sepulcher be made sure until the third day, lest HIS disciples come by night and steal Him away and say unto the people, "He rises from the dead, so the last error shall be worse than the first (**Matthew 27:63-64**)

And He began to teach that the SON of man must suffer many things and be rejected of the elders and high priests and scribes and be killed and after three days rise again. (**Mark 8:31** "*For as Yonah was three days and three nights in the whale's belly, so shall the SON of man be three days and three nights in the heart of the earth.* (**Matthew 12:40**)

Either these scriptures are wrong or incorrect or our teaching is wrong? Which do you believe? What do you believe, these scriptures or what you have been taught? Let every WORD OF ELOHIYM be true and let the word of a man be not true. If you look at these scriptures, there is no way YAHUSHA died on a friday and rose early sunday morning. **Can GOD count?** You are making GOD a liar and GOD CANOT LIE. Is HE(GOD) a bumbling fool? He said three days and three nights NOT part of a day and certainty 2 nights, but 3 days and 3 nights. Let us count friday at 3 pm, friday night (**first night**), saturday (**one day**), saturday night (**second night**), and early sunday morning he rose. Where are the other night and the other days? If you are a Bible student settling for something incorrect that it will not cut it. Why have we been so content with false teaching? These pastors/teachers lie about HIS death and birth. These pastors/teachers have inherently rendered the flock of ELOHIYM with ignorance, mismanagement of thoughts, stupidity, sleepless and slumbering eyes. The reason is that we are sheep and someone has to tell you the truth. Please don't just follow a man's word and not listen to THE HOLY SPIRIT THE RUACH HA'QODESH THE WORD OF THE REDEEMER.

And when HE came into the temple, the chief priests and the elders of the people came unto HIM as HE was teaching and said," By what authority dost thou these things? And who gave thee this authority? And YAHUSHA answered and said unto them, "I will ask you one thing, which, if ye tell me, I in likewise will tell you by what authority I do these things. The baptism of John (Yahuchanon), whence was it? From heaven or of men?" "And they reasoned with themselves, saying, "If we shall say from heaven, HE will say unto us, "Why did ye not believe him?" But if we shall say of me, we fear the people, for all hold John as a prophet." And they answered YAHUSHA and said, "We cannot tell." And HE said unto them, "Neither tells I you by what authority I do these things." (**Matthew 21:23-27**)

They went to the Pharisees and took counsel on how they might entangle HIM in HIS talk. And they sent out unto HIM their disciple with Herodians, saying, "Master, we know that thou are true and teachest the way of ELOHIYM in truth, neither carest thou for any man, for thou regardest not the person of men. Tell us, therefore, What thinkest thou? Is it lawful to give tribute unto Caesar or not?" But YAHUSHA perceived their wickedness and said, "Why tempt ye me, ye hypocrites? Shew me the tribute money." And they gave HIM a penny. And HE saith unto them, "Whose is this image and superscription?" They say unto HIM, "Caesar's" Then saith HE unto them, "Render therefore unto Caesar's the things which are Caesar's and unto the things that are ELOHIYM'S. When they heard these words, they marveled, left HIM, and went their way. (**Matthew 22:15-22**)

And no man was able to answer HIM a word; neither durst any man from that day forth ask HIM any more questions. (**Matthew 22:46**)

They were not able to embarrass HIM, they were trying to find fault in HIM or find a blemish in HIM. Our SAVIOR withstood any questions. HE was faithful and without blemish. We today are like the Israelites of yesteryear because we refuse to accept ELOHIYM'S WORD as facts and truth forevermore. ELOHIYM states in **Psalm 138c** *"For thou hast magnified THY WORD above THY NAME."* And ELOHIYM counted **you** more than HIS UNIQUE SON's own physical life because HE knew the eternal depth of death and consequences of our decision if HIS SON did not give HIS life for us. Remember the scourging he went through because he was beaten with that whip that contained metal, bones, and glass and this **_RIPPED_** through HIS flesh. Any person going through this would have driven them insane, but HE endured to bring us to salvation, but we don't have to go through this all we have to do is to say yes to what HE has done for us. Amein And we so carelessly deny we sin because sin is in our nature. **So, PLEASE DON'T DENY WHAT THE MESSIAH DID EVEN BEFORE THE CROSS. HE ENDURES THIS FOR YOU. AND MANY DENY HIS WORK WANTING TO ESTABLISH THEIR RIGHTEOUSNESS TO GOD, PLEASE YOU FOOL.** The fool has said In his heart **"There is no GOD."** (**Psalm 14:1**) Now all I can say is "I pity the fool" because the fool has NO idea where the fool is headed, but it is a place of regret, of darkness, a place of no mercy, but a place of suffering and a place of eternal hopelessness and only the echo of silence, and screaming hoping for an end, but no end(an hour after hour after hour) is in their sight, but the total insanity of mind going on FOREVER with no end because they REFUSED to believe I exist. **Do you see the deception?**

CHAPTER 11

———— ✤ ————

When Did YAHUSHA DIE

YAHUSHA states HE would be in the tomb for three days and three nights. Let us look at how we have been taught all our lives about the death, burial, and resurrection of YAHUSHA. All night friday, all day saturday, and early sunday morning, HE got up; that is the basis of what we have been taught. If we look at this, this is certainly not three days and three nights. When YAHUSHA died that day, hundreds of lambs or kids lost their lives that day also. This was according to YAHUAH'S Plan. This started before the foundation of the world was even created. All this was according to timing because Miryam had to be born and Yoseph had to be born and Avraham had to be born and Yitschaq had to be born Ya`aqov had to be at a particular time. Please think about that. All of this is according to a percipe arrangement of timing. You could probably hear those thousands of sacrifices crying out all over Israel as they were slain for Passover celebration all over the countryside and the hustling and bustling came to a complete rest to observe YAHUAH'S victory over the Egyptians when the death occurred to all the firstborn in the land of Egypt without the blood on the doorpost.

*And <u>when the Shabbath</u> [What Shabbath day?] <u>was passed</u>, Mary, Magdalene and Miryam the mother of Ya`aqov and Shalom **had bought** sweet spices, that they might come to anoint HIM*

> *[YAHUSHA]. And very early in the morning on the first day of the week, they came unto the sepulcher at the rising of the sun.* (Mark 16:1-2)

> *And that day was the preparation, and the Shabbath drew on. And the women also, which came with HIM from Galilee, followed after and beheld the sepulcher and how HIS body was laid. And they returned and prepared spices and ointments and rested on the Shabbath day, according to the commandment.* (Luke 23:55-56)

The question that comes into my mind is when did those women buy the spices? These women BOUGHT(past tense of buy) these spices specifically for the body of YAHUSHA and for HIS burial only, as the scriptures state. The Bible does not state they had these spices on hand, and even if they did have the spices on hand, would they have used older spices to anoint YAHUSHA'S body? To prepare spices for a body, it would be hard to imagine them having that much spices on hand in the first place to anoint THE ADONAI YAHUSHA HAMASHIACH'S body properly. If YAHUSHA had died on a friday evening, the next day would have been the seventh day, The Shabbath. The marketplace <u>was not open</u> on the Shabbath, but was entirely closed. Would someone break THE LAW to assist these women to buy spices? Read, **Numbers 15:32**, all this man was doing was picking up sticks. So, I ask when did the women buy those spices? Tell me, bible scholars, tell me and tell me please what day, what day what day? There must be some discrepancy in THE WORD OF ELOHIYM, bible scholars, tell me what day, Please! When did these women buy these species? The Bible states that the Shabbath was past, so when did they buy those spices for the YAHUSHA'S body. The Bible states this was a real event of buying spices for YAHUSHA Body. What are we going to do? The BIBLE MUST BE WRONG? THE BIBLE (THE SCRIPTURES, THE WORD OF ELOHIYM) is wrong or our teaching is incorrect? Are we going to believe in some of the events in the BIBLE or we going to believe in all events in the BIBLE? We have been taught that there is only one Shabbath day in our culture. The women were headed to the tomb early the first day of the week before the sun rose (our calendar sunday morning), but this was the Shabbath of unleavened bread day also Shabbath day also and the women were on their way to the tomb (breaking the law) to anoint YAHUSHA'S body. We have been taught that The Yashar'el had only one Shabbath day, but The BIBLE points to 12 Shabbath periods. We have been taught Israelites' Shabbath starts at 6pm on friday and ends 6pm saturday evening. This has been traditionally taught by the ones that write history. So, if The Shabbath had passed, I ask again when did these women buy these spices? If the next day was sunday, the markets were NOT open in the evening, and they were on their way before the sun rose on the first day of the week. There is NO way they purchased <u>those spices</u> on their way to the tomb and prepared them early sunday morning. There is no way they purchased the spices between 6:01 pm saturday and before the sun rose early sunday morning because <u>the markets were not open.</u> The scriptures state that they rested after the Shabbath Day according to ELOHIYM'S WORD. The scriptures state that that the Shabbath had passed when they bought these spices. What type of quantity would it have taken to cover HIS body? Since the scripture states this was a **high Shabbath day** when YAHUSHA died (**Yahuchanon 19:31**) because this day was NOT ever to be forgotten because YAHUAH brought our foreparents out of slavery from The Egyptians bondage, The Passover **Exodus 12:1-14**. So, there had to be a day or days in between HIS Death and HIS resurrection? Are we going to sweep this information under the rug?

Mark 16:2 "And in the morning on the first day of the week, they came to the sepulcher at the rising of the sun." So, if they purchased those spices after the Shabbath, you have to take into account another day before they went to the tomb. If YAHUSHA died at 3:00 pm on friday, He was placed in the tomb between 3:00pm and 6:00 pm (because they had to get Pilate clearance because Pilate was unaware that YAHUSHA had died already and the guard pierce HIM in the side and Pilate gave the okay and Yoceph wrapped Him in linen and lain HIM a new tomb) on a friday. The Israelites' seventh day Shabbath begin at 6pm on friday and the Shabbath ends at 6:00pm on saturday evening, when did these women purchase these spices? **John 19:13** says, *"The Jews therefore, because it was the preparation, said that the bodies should not remain upon the cross on the Shabbath day (for that Shabbath day was a high day) and besought Pilate that their legs might be broken and that they might be taken away."* Why is there a distinction between those Shabbath days. There is obviously a difference, so there has to be more than one Israelites' Shabbath day. If it is not so, why declare a high day? So, by distinguishing the day, it shows a difference. This proves that there is more than one Shabbath day to the Israelities. We are often convinced that the seventh day (saturday) is our only Shabbath day, but ELOHIYM'S WORD is completely telling us something different from what man says from his lips. It doesn't matter what you think, but THE WORD OF YAH is true and the words of men are fables or just pure lies and untruth.

I did say we because the Isarelites **ARE THE MY PEOPLE IN THE BIBLE.** The nation of Israel or Yashar'el ARE people with dark skin tone or people of color not black, not Negro, Not African American and sure not Ni---r. Mosheh if he was non-melanin could he become more non-melanin and Yoceph standing before his brothers and he recognized them, but all of his brothers saw were just Egyptians. We are your neighbors, friends, coworkers, husbands and wives, ballplayers, and because the white evangelical Christian group has hidden this TRUTH. For they know and **WON'T** tell their congregation. We are the people who were in bondage in the spiritual Egypt the Americas and we were in bondage from 1619 to 2019 and

NOW we are awaiting the Exodus away from this planet to heaven and then we are coming back to a new earth and we will forever live with YAH as **Revelation 21:3** says.

The Israelites considered The Passover as the highest day of the Shabbath(s). This day was to be a memorial to us forever. A memorial for us leaving Egypt. The death of the Egyptians' first born or whosoever did not have [the lamb's blood or goat's blood without blemish] the blood on the lintel of doorpost for death to passover their household. We have been led by the traditions of men for so long and we fail to see what The WORD OF ELOHIYM says. We have become complicit, compliant,or acquiescent and go along without questioning anything or anyone. If something doesn't make sense ASK A QUESTION. We should question anyone and anything when The BIBLE says something completely different from what the leaders, teachers, and pastors say. We have become afraid or have placed man on the pulpit to be worshiped. ELOHIYM is only to worship and Reverend. We have The WORD OF ELOHIYM, and we should follow The WORD OF ELOHIYM and not man. The blind can't teach the blind. We have become afraid to ask questions to the ecclesiastical order. We have become afraid to step on toes, but ask questions because no man is above THE WORD OF ELOHIYM. If you want to understand something, then ask a question. Some people will not accept what they see right now, but **2 Timothy 2:15** states, *"Study to show thyself approved to GOD, a workman that needeth not be ashamed rightly dividing the **WORD OF TRUTH.**"* When I am before YAHUSHA in judgment, I will not declare that I didn't know or was afraid to tell the preacher the truth. ELOHIYM wants us to have HIS TRUTH. If you want the truth then ask ELOHIYM. If we fail to ask for the truth or seek for the truth, then we are failing ourselves and we get what we have. ELOHIYM THE FATHER purposely intended for YAHUSHA HAMASHIACH (THE SON) to die for our sins. ELOHIYM is ELOHIYM of order and not confusion.

You see My brothers in the ministry has abandoned me for what I believe to be TRUTH and I know that they think I am crazy, but that is ok for you see ELOHIYM has not and never will abandon me because many are under the tutelage of old teaching, failing to understand that we are the MY people in the bible and not Christian for we are Believers of WHAT THE MESSIAH THE SON YAH did on the cross to redeem us from the curse of sin (eternal death, separated from YAH forever) and HE THE SON OF YAH arose from the tomb after three nights and three days in the tomb and when He rose He brought back with HIM those that were righteous so HE declared because of father Avraham. **(Matthew 27:52)**

The Israelites' day always started in the evening. YAHUSHA was out of the tomb on the first day of the week, which is sunday to us. You have to remember that HE very well could have come out of the tomb at 6:01 pm saturday evening because the 7th day had ended and the Israelites' next day starts in the evening time. **Genesis 1:5, 8,13,19,23,** and **31** says evening first and then morning. YAHUSHA was already out of the tomb when the women arrived to anoint HIS body early on the first day of the week. YAHUSHA was resurrected way before the sun rose. It is very easy to see that YAHUSHA came out of the sepulcher after the sunset saturday evening for us or by the Israelites' time this was the next day or first day of the week to them because the word sunday is NOT in the WORD of YAH. Remember how HE folded the napkin that was about HIS head. YAHUSHA rose early sunday morning between 6:01 pm on (saturday evening or night to us) and before the women arrived early Sunday morning. YAHUSHA rose on saturday evening (night to us); that is not three days and three nights. Let us count friday night as one night and saturday as one day. YAHUSHA was out of the tomb early sunday morning before the sunrise in a new face and body except He still had the marking of the nails in HIS body. Where are the other days and nights? We have one day and one night and not three days and three nights. What are we to believe, The Bible or a man moving and lying lips? Sounds like someone is speaking with a forked tongue. If we close our eyes to the truth of this matter, it will not be revealed, unless our eyes are opened. Since YAHUSHA rose on the first day of the week, when did women buy those spices? If YAHUSHA died on Friday and the next day was the seventh day of rest (Shabbath Day/Saturday), when did HE die? As you can see, the preaching that YAHUSHA died on Friday and rose on Sunday morning is inherently incorrect, misrepresent the truth, misleading, wrong, and a darn lie. If it is not true then it is a lie and we tend to appreciate lies more than the truth. If, SINCE YAHUSHA had to die earlier in the week to get three days and three nights. Or some say He didn't die on the cross and if He didn't die on the cross, we are still sinners headed to condemnation, but **HE DID DIE on the cross** because NOW there is NO condemnation because He also arose from the tomb freeing us FROM CONDEMNATION of our sin. Whom are you going to believe either The BIBLE is wrong or man is wrong? Who will you believe? Anyone who teaches anything else but THE WORD of YAH is headed down to the road of destruction. PLEASE DON'T BELIEVE THAT ENTITY! Many say Pa'al the Apostle was wrong. So, if Pa'al is wrong then The New Testament of The Messiah is written in vain and The Apostles die in vain because according to those led by devils

THE MESSIAH was not THE LAMB OF GOD. You lying devils because the man had to be redeemed or be eternity lost separate from ELOHIYM and it was only by ELOHIYM offering HIMSELF as a PERFECT SACRIFICE just as The Old Testament states because it took ELOHIYM to satisfy ELOHIYM. Because ELOHIYM became senseless to **THE** blood of lamb, goat, and oxen.

YAHUSHA was placed in the tomb before the Shabbath began which was wednesday before 6pm so this was on the 14th day of Nisan. Yoseph wrapped Him In linen and closed the tomb and Passover is celebrated and the evening which is **the 15th of Nisan <u>The First Night</u>** HA'MASHIACH is in the tomb. The next day is Thursday the day of unleavened bread, Shabbath day also. This is **the 15th day. The <u>First Day</u>** HA'MASHIACH is in the tomb and the women rest. The markets are closed. This was **the 16th of Nisan the <u>Second Night</u>** (because The Israelites' days started in the evening time around 6pm so in our time it would be the next day for them) HA'MASHIACH is in the tomb. The next day is Friday **the 16th Day of Nisan. <u>The Second Day</u> HA'MASHIACH is in the tomb.** The women bought the spices on the 17th before the Seven day Shabbath begins and prepared them. **17th Day of Nisan is the <u>Third Night</u>, HA'MASHIACH is in the tomb.** The next day is saturday, the 18th day of Nisan. The <u>**Third Day**</u> **HA'MASHIACH is in the tomb**. This is three days and three nights. Emphasis is placed on words we see in the Bible. At the end of **THE THIRD DAY, THE RESURRECTION of HA'MASHIACH from She'ol was 6:01 pm The beginning of the next day for Hebrews/Israelites/Yashar`e'liy and when He arose others arose with HIM.**

We have the word day before night even though the three nights were complete before the three days and that is because the day is greater than night.

So, did YAHUSHA go into Jerusalem on Palm Sunday? This day was labeled as Palm Sunday. This is what we call this day palm sunday right? Well, this is so very wrong also because He had to be examined for four days. YAHUSHA was crucified on the fourteenth day of the month of Nisan (Abib), in the evening. This started The Hebrews day of unleavened bread Shabbath day, the fifteenth of Nisan (Abib). <u>YAHUSHA is The PASSOVER LAMB of GOD for humanity.</u> YAHUSHA rode into Jerusalem on the ninth, went into the temple each day and he was examined by the scribes and Pharisees by them asking HIM questions and they could find no faults and finally, **Matthew 22:46** says *"And no man was able to answer HIM a word; neither durst any man from that day forth ask HIM anymore."* HE was slain on the fourteenth that was a Wednesday evening and gave up the ghost to HIS FATHER. As you can see, ELOHIYM has kept things in order as HE did in the beginning, evening-morning (this is referring to the beginning of day and night) as the death of YAHUSHA entails.

HA'MASHIACH is the WORLD'S PASSOVER LAMB some will believe and some will not, but by accepting YAHUSHA as ADONAI and SAVIOR, eternal death or separation eternity passes over you and you are no longer under condemnation. You will not come to complete ruin. HA'MASHIACH has built the bridge for man to ELOHIYM forever. Accept YAHUSHA as Savior. YAHUSHA is ELOHIYM'S GRACE.

GOD REDEMPTION AT CHRIST EXPENSE

Events That Happened During YAHUSHA'S Passion Week:

Mark 11:1-11: YAHUSHA rode into Jerusalem (Eventide/Friday).

12-14: YAHUSHA cursed the fig tree (Saturday).

15-19: YAHUSHA cleansed the temple (eventide).

20-26: YAHUSHA gave a morning lesson from the fig tree(Monday).

27-33 YAHUSHA authority was questioned.

Mark 12:1-12: YAHUSHA shared the parable of the wicked husbandmen.

13-17: The Pharisees asked a question about the tribute of Caesar.

18-27: The Sadducees asked a question about the resurrection.

28-34: The scribes asked about The Great Commandment

35-37: The question of David's SON was asked

38-40: YAHUSHA denounced the scribes.

41-44 : The widow's offering was given.

Mark 13: 1-23: YAHUSHA shared about the signs of the end.

24-37: YAHUSHA taught about The Coming of the Son of Man.

Mark 14: 1-2: The chief priests plotted against YAHUSHA

3-9 : YAHUSHA was anointed at Bethany in Judas' father (Simon the Pharisee)

10-11: The conspiracy of Judas began (Tuesday)

YAHUSHA celebrated Passover with His disciples

Peter's denial foretold.

YAHUSHA prayed at Gethsemane.

YAHUSHA was betrayed at Gethsemane.

YAHUSHA was betrayed and arrested.

Mark 14:53-65: YAHUSHA was presented before the high priest.

14:66-72:   Peter denied YAHUSHA three times

15:1-5:   YAHUSHA was presented before Pilate.

15:6-9:   YAHUSHA was sentenced to die

15:20-47:   The crucifixion ensued (9:00 am -3:00pm Wednesday).

So, unless YOU read, what is OUT THERE you WILL NOT GET A FULL UNDERSTANDING of TRUTH LED BY THE SPIRIT OF TRUTH. You will be going by someone else's information, which may not have full and factual disclosure of truth because, if you don't read, you could be led by those giving out false information to you that could very WELL be in the state of darkness themselves and even blindness from what they are giving out. You see there was a slave bible which left OUT information that would have identified us as "The MY PEOPLE In The KJV." Remember Apollos in **Acts 18:24-28.**

So, what day did YAHUSHA die? Did HE die on good Friday and was raised early Sunday morning?

CHAPTER 12

— ❧ —

Listen Up

We have ideals, ideals and ideals about salvation, Shabbath days, tongue talking, church doctrines, YAHUSHA's death and resurrection and so on. Are our ideals based on what the BIBLE (YAH WORD) says or are they based on a preacher's mouth? We cannot base salvation on our beliefs. When it is based on our belief, then people are led astray. An example would be two blind persons trying to guide each other through a forest, tree, hills, dales and ditches and we all fall off a cliff, in which neither can see the way. ELOHIYM has **ALREADY** dealt with salvation issues and even Pa'al stated, "I have fed you with milk and by this time, I have expected you to move on to other issues." Just like the men in the book of Acts of the Apostles, we continue trying to **add** to GOD's salvation plan. The men in the book of ACTS of the Apostles wanted the Gentiles to be circumcised to [have ALL of salvation (a misnomer).] Just another step that was not necessary, just like people have done today, like feet washing, water baptism and speaking in an unknown tongue. Salvation is **BASED** on what **THE MESSIAH DID ON THE CROSS and AROSE FROM THE TOMB. IF YOU BELIEVE THIS YOU ARE SAVED AND SEALED FROM ETERNAL SEPARATION PERIOD. THERE ARE NO OTHER STEPS FOR SALVATION. HALLELUJAH! YAH DID IT ALL.** Who came up with this plan? So, tell me WHY you are trying to add to HIS plan. It would be like I have a house plan and you are butting your nose into the design of my house. STAY IN YOUR LANE! Did I ask you for your input? Well, this is GOD'S PLAN and He has all authority over HIS plan so quit adding to HIS Plan. I am excited, joyous, exhilarated, thrilled, enthusiastic, exuberant and intoxicated with this THE GOOD NEWS.

YAHUSHA HA'MASHIACH did it all with no help from me and you. If circumcision had to be added to salvation, that would have left women out of GOD'S Salvation plan altogether. Can you imagine a man in his 60's,70's, 80's or 90's getting circumcised to receive salvation? We still try to add to ELOHIYM'S perfect plan. YAHUSHA stated, "Believe and confess and thou shalt be with me in Paradise."

Man has continued to always put his idea of what salvation is instead of studying The BIBLE and let the BIBLE determine what salvation is. Man does not have a place he can offer me more than what heaven can offer. We burden the people down with different situations to make them think they have to obtain salvation this way and that way. The BIBLE simply states to admit you are a sinner and believe what THE SON did on the cross and rose again from the tomb confess and thou shall be SAVED and no more that is all. Let ELOHIYM'S Word be true and every man a lie unless it agrees with YAH. There are those who believe YAH does not exist and these writings are from someone who is DEAD, but we believe in writing from people who are dead and people (instructions) who we have not seen, but I have to see GOD to believe HIM? Do YOU see nature? A man plants different seeds in the ground (the RIGHT type of dirt and not sand) and it grows into a fruit and in that fruit, seeds and it rains and the sun shines, isn't that amazing? But you want to see GOD. Our body CANNOT STAND TO BE IN THE EYESIGHT OF A HOLY GOD! Man will say feast days, unknown tongues, circumcision shabbath days, washing of feet, water baptism and Holy Days must be followed for salvation to be completed. HOGWASH! Your filthy thinking. Who has bewitched you? The BIBLE should be the only source that determines how one becomes saved and not saved. ELOHIYM of heaven WILL be the final authority on salvation. ELOHIYM does not lie or will not lie. ELOHIYM that I am referring to is The ELOHIYM of Avraham, Yitschaq, Ya`aqov and Mosheh. ELOHIYM'S WORD should be the only source we can rely on and instead of some man words. When David tried to bring THE ARK into the city Uzza died because David did not follow the instructions of carrying THE ARK, but when he followed the instructions of carrying THE ARK he was successful. Did the children of Yashar'el deliver themselves from Pharaoh's army? YAH provided for their **YESHUAH**. When man places his two cents into ELOHIYM'S WORD, he can screw up ELOHIYM 'S HOLY WORD. So, listen most of all to THE HOLY SPIRIT to see if that man's word agrees with what is written. THE RUACH HA'QODESH will never leave us astray. We have been indoctrinated by man's word, but is it GOD'S WORD or a derivative of the truth? And this is when confusion comes in. Because we are listening to a man that we have placed our trust in, but our trust should **ALWAYS** be in YAH and never a man. There is a saying "I want to get more saved." **CAN WE GET MORE SAVED?** REALLY! WOW! **No, you can't!** What happens is that we can become more AWARE of who we are in THE CREATOR'S Heart. We are sons and daughters of THE LIVING GOD. Can we become more sons and daughters of THE LIVING GOD? Example, once you are born into a family you will always be your parents' child no matter how old you become. You may deny them, but your parents will always (I hope even in times they are upset with you) be for you even in the death of you. We will cry. You will forever be their child. My youngest daughter became angry with me and she said "I ain't going to be your friend anymore," and my response was "You will always be my daughter."

Listen up because with our small and silly mind, we will screw up ELOHIYM'S WORD with our demon in nation (denominations) thinking. This is the reason Pa'al wrote in **1 Corinthians 1:12-13,** *"Now this I say, that everyone of you saith, I am Pa'al: and I am Apollos: and I of Kepha: and I of MASHIACH. Is MASHIACH divided? Was Pa'al crucified for you? Or were you immersed in the name of Pa'al?"*

On the radio, I heard this question: "Can I lose my salvation if I continue to sin?" I was so distraught when I heard this. It ate at me like a moth on a pair of new wool pants. Different listeners came on the radio airwave, expressing their views about salvation. Their opinions ARE NOT BASED ON THE WORDS OF ELOHIYM. The question is, Can I lose my salvation? Is it your to lose, or it is ELOHIYM'S Salvation plan for man? Oftentimes we want to possess everything. If salvation is your plan, yes, you can lose it because you are stating it as your (ownership). Man can lose anything that he places his hand on. Since ELOHIYM has established salvation. It is ELOHIYM and ELOHIYM has offered salvation to you to not ever lose HIS PLAN. Salvation is ELOHIYM and ELOHIYM alone. YAHUSHA states to one of the thieves on the cross *"Verily I say unto thee, Today thou shalt be with ME in paradise."* **(Luke 23:43)** One thief admitted that they deserve their punishment, but this Man hath done nothing amiss. Now YAHUSHA did not come down from the cross to baptize the man in water or issue an edict thou must be baptize with water or be filled with THE HOLY GHOST (speaking in tongues) and yet YAHUSHA states," Today thou shalt be with ME in paradise." Salvation is NOT based on how much sin you accumulate, but it is based upon a belief because as long as you are in this body you are going to sin, but THE MESSIAH, THE LAMB of GOD covers that sin period. So how can you lose what GOD DID and Did alone?

There are those who don't follow the teaching of Pa'al. They feel like he was wrong and that is your right, but listen 1) Did Pa'al see YAHUSHA on the way to Damascus 2) Was Pa'al a Hebrew 3) Was Pa'al a Pharisee 4) Was Pa'al converted and if you answer yes to all of these questions then believe Pa'al because we all will be in the front of YAHUSHA HA'MASHIACH to give an account and what will be your defend again what he wrote by THE RUACH?

I was going to a club one night (I was way off course or direction in my life, with going with the crowd, I was depressed and did not realize it) had my suit on looking good and I was smoking a marijuana cigarette, while driving (this was in the year of 1981 this so very illegal) and I believed that THE MESSIAH died and rose from the tomb and I was filled with The SPIRIT, but I was in a depression mode) And THE SPIRIT asked me if I wanted my children doing this and my answer was "NO." Was I saved? Yes! Now this is not a license to sin because there are consequences for sinning. But to some of the people on the radio they would have stated no, he is not saved, but according to THE SPIRIT I was, but I grieved THE SPIRIT and needless to say that was the last time I did that. So many times I have grieved THE SPIRIT, but HE has never no not ever abandoned me because of HIS GREAT LOVE for us for He has stated I will not, no, not ever forsake you. Even though it seems I have been forsaken, THE SPIRIT will never no not ever abandon us because as the song says HE LOVES ME. Because HE knows why we do what we do and HE will always love us because we are in The family of GOD.

ELOHIYM is HOLY and JUST and what rules apply for one, then the same rules apply for all. What we do (our actions) affects our rewards at judgment. Once we believe and confess with our tongue that HE, YAHUSHA is HA'MASHIACH, salvation has been made in our life as long as it is heart believe and not head believe. Will you die physically with this confession or will you deny that THE MESSIAH even existed and don't accept what HE did upon the cross and arose again? If someone put a gun to your head, will you not admit that HE died and arose from the tomb? It is what we believe and confess. Are you going to admit you do not believe? Can you unconfessed that THE SON OF YAH IS NOT ELOHIYM? You see, my salvation is based on what GOD has done for me and nothing else. So, I won't be afraid of what man can do to this physical body. I am so very tired of denominations (demon in nations) that each preacher preys on people's minds for their money (to build a great temple, but the homeless are on the street and go into a such large debt to build such a building) and this is not ELOHIYM'S way. Denominations should be accursed and all the body of YAHUSHA HA'MASHIACH comes together to accomplish what the BIBLE tells us to do. **1 Corinthians 1;12-13** states, *"Now this I say, that every one of you saith, I am Pa'al: and I am Apollos: I of Kepha: and I of MASHIACH. Is MASHIACH divided? Was Pa'al crucified for you? Or were ye baptized in the name of Pa'al? Did Kepha, Pa'al and Apollos die for you?* "The answer is NO. It was YAHUSHA HA'MASHIACH and by adding things to salvation, we place needless burdens on ELOHIYM'S people. I know a woman that has NOT been baptized. What do you think she is thinking that she is not saved because she has not been baptized and now fright is set up to confess this. What a psychological job is going on in her brain. **Acts 8:5** says, *"Then Phillip went down to Samaria, and preached MASHIACH unto them.``* **Acts 8:35**, *"Then Phillip opened his mouth, and began at the same scripture, and preached unto him YAHUSHA."* Listens, pastors, you do not have ownership of ELOHIYM'S people. Pastor, you are just stewards (leaders) over ELOHIYM'S people. Preachers who want to be worshiped are no better than satan himself wanting to be god. ELOHYIM is ELOHIYM. ELOHIYM is not a man. Therefore, people stop referring to ELOHIYM as a man. ELOHIYM is not a man, but ELOHIYM is three persons THE FATHER, THE SON (GOD/MAN), THE HOLY SPIRIT HE is ALL power. ELOHIYM has so much power that we cannot fathom HIS mighty power with our finite mind. Nature obeys HIS command. Can any of you move a mountain? YAHUSHA states that the faith the size of a mustard seed can move a mountain into the sea. Have any of you moved a mountain? Our faith is in ELOHIYM alone. We cannot move mountains, but my faith in ELOHIYM and ELOHIYM can move that mountain. Listen up, people, do not be deceived. YAHUSHA is coming again and will you be ready? Do not be deceived because some of the preachers are into fame and fortune, which will eventually come to light.

ELOHIYM got me to look at the life of Pa'al the gentiles' apostle and if you will review his message, what would you see? Pa'al traveled from town by sea or land. His life was in perils of robbers, waters, wilderness, viper, his Israelites brother and false teachings. Pa'al had an eyesight problem also. He at times would not ask the congregation that he visited for an offering. His life was not easy traveling around the region of Asia minor. The reason this was done was so they (the called out ones) would not get the wrong idea about THE GOSPEL (The message YAHUSHA saved).

1 Timothy 6:5 says, ``*Perverse disputing's of men of corrupt minds and destitute of the truth, <u>supposing that gain is godliness</u>: from such withdraw thyself.*" From The Cepher bible in **Mattithyahu 19:24** states "*And again I say unto you, It is easier for a rope to go through the eye of a needle, than for a rich man to enter into the Kingdom of YAHUAH.*" This makes a better translation than the kjv. What does this mean to withdraw from men preaching such information because it is the wrong road? Bad teaching misleads people. Remember Jim Jones and the Guyana tragedy. It sets up false ideas and is on the wrong road. If you are in your right mind and have the activity of all your limbs, you are blessed. Be thankful and give out a HALLELUJAH!

Not so today in many congregations. Some congregations take up as many as five offerings on a Sunday. So many preachers will rape their congregation to pay for a musician that is lover of another man flesh. That is living in a sinful lifestyle. We need to rethink the way we use the money that is collected every sunday. There are congregations where men are living the gay lifestyle or the DL (Down Low, pretending, masquerading). We need to revisit and reevaluate what ELOHIYM said to do. If needed, we can praise ELOHIYM with our voices alone. We oftentimes do not want to hurt that brother or sister, but we must confront those living in such a lifestyle that is not YAHUSHA, like manners and reevaluate our actions in YAHUSHA'S CHURCH. YAHUSHA loves all, but continuing in blatant sin when you come to the truth is what YAHUSHA told the woman caught in adultery sin "No more!" Why? Because if she continues to lie with other men (that is NOT her husband), it will continue to be a problem and physical death could come if HE is not there. YAHUSHA states that HE loves us no matter where we find ourselves and HE will forgive all sins period. YOU ARE FORGIVEN no matter what. Should we sin so that GRACE may abound? NO!

Recently a group of young people went to a music workshop and they the impression that there were so many people practicing homosexuality that they felt that need to wear a sign that says "I am not gay or lesbian." This type of behavior should not be even named among The Called Out Ones. How messed up is our leadership that puts up with such lifestyles of sin? For if we sin, we have an advocate, but sooner or later your sin will be judged here on earth and in heaven and what will you say? Because in this body we are going to have trouble and The MESSIAH knows all your faults and HE knows the sin you are dealing with.

As Pa'al states in Ephesians 4:28, *"Let him that stole steal no more: but rather let him labor, working with his hands the thing which is good, that he may have to give to him that needeth."* In other words, shall we continue to sin that grace may abound? NO! Therefore, if you are caught up in sin, do not participate in it because sin is wrong! Shall we who are a part of the body of HA'MASHIACH continue to hurt HA'MASHIACH? HA'MASHIACH took the punishment of scourging for you and me. As you are participating in your sin (no matter what it is), HA'MASHIACH flesh was open up for you and HA'MASHIACH took the beaten of the whip in which at the end of the whip was bones, metal and rocks and HIS Flesh was open up for you and me to give the right to ask for forgiven because we can get caught up (for it feel good to the flesh, but it is wrong) in our fornication, adultery, drunkenness, stealing, defrauding one another and business, abusing (physical, sexually, emotional, drug and spiritual), raping, cursing out one another, calling us by name that should not be like M.F., nigg_r and, suicides, homicide, greed etc. We feel like it is okay to do these but it AIN'T for we are grieving THE RUACH and MASHIACH paid the price for our sin by the scourging and we are just so happily shroud off as nothing at all. Oh, ole sinful man I am to just shroud off how The MASHIACH was taking that beaten so I can do my sin. Oh, sinful man I am to disregard what HE did and HE did that for me so that I may live with HIM forever in peace. I praise ELOHIYM HE cared more than I can say and I offer HIM praises with a million tongues would not be ENOUGH. YAHUSHA IS SOON TO COME. He knows our work and we will be judged by HIM (**Yahuchanon 5:22**) and HIM alone. Thank ELOHIYM for HIS SON YAHUSHA HA'MASHIACH of Nazareth. YAHUSHA was born in the town of Bethlehem, called out of Egypt, suffered in Jerusalem, died on the cross and was resurrected from the tomb by THE FATHER out of the tomb. YAHUSHA HA'MASHIACH is soon to come back.

Even movies show things that are going to happen. Everyone needs to look at the movie called "Greenland." What it shows is the hopelessness of man because this earth will be destroyed and where will you be when this earth is destroyed? Man thinks this earth can be saved. Read **Revelation 8:10-11**. This is why the super-rich have ungrounded luxurious bunkers, but GOD promised in **Isaiah 65:17** and **Revelation 21:1** a new heaven(s) and a new earth. So, believe GOD because HE has made the way we shall escape this destruction to us that believe HE IS amein. Because HE said this will happen, but many won't believe because they think HE doesn't exist, but I assure you HE does live. So, believe in what HE said amein! I do believe that HIS SON is my escape goat for eternal life with HIM amein. And there are other disaster movies and TV shows: The One Hundred, Deep Impact, San Andreas, 2012. Geostorm, or Contagion. These show the futility of man because this earth is coming to an end. You can escape by believing what YAH has said, but if not then you are headed to condemnation forever and ever.

Do you Believe what you have been told?

CHAPTER 13

—— ❧ ——

Days and Months How They Were Generated

ELOHIYM states in **Genesis 1:14**, *"And let them be for signs and for seasons, and for days and for years….."*

A calendar should be a defined system that determines a solar year and no more. A solar year is about 365 ¼ days. Man has concocted different calendars in his history to celebrate himself. Isn't it strange that our calendar starts in the month of January as the first month? Wouldn't it be served if our year actually starts in March instead? It would be March, April, May, June, July, August, September, October, November, December, January and February. This would correspond better with the seasons of spring, summer, fall, and winter. If we started our calendar as such, this would bring so much confusion because our neck or our thinking has been so indelidate with confusion all our life and we have been in this way for hundreds of years being misled going in the WRONG direction that it would take a miracle to change the mind of man because we have been led this way for so very long. It is like our neck going in the wrong direction all my life and someone would try to turn your head it would break your neck because our neck is stuck in going the wrong direction because we have gone this way ALL our lives of being misled because we feel we are in the RIGHT DIRECTION, but we are going in THE WRONG DIRECTION. ELOHIYM changed the calendar for the Israelites. They were set with the calendar they had and all of a sudden, ELOHIYM changed the first month to correspond with the season. Anyway, what I found out about the calendar and the days was amazing.

Man has in the earlier century always placed some type of superstitions, gods or holidays on days. We believe in Santa Clause, leprechauns, Valentine's Day, Cupid, Easter bunny, fairies, and the great pumpkin today. The Romans believe in mythology, the Ides of March and gnomes. Men worship these days through ignorance of the true existence of the living ELOHIYM (as Pa'al states to the unknown God) of Avraham, Yitschaq, Ya`aqov and Mosheh.

The Roman calendar was a lunar calendar consisting of ten months of about 295 days. The seventh month, eighth month, ninth month, and tenth month were logically named September, October, November, and December respectively, Latins words indicating the position of these months. A Roman leader could change the calendar anytime he got ready. The month of July is named after Julian Caesar and august is named after Augustus Caesar. According to legend, Numa Pompilius (about 1700 BC) added January and February.

Julius Caesar wanted to reform the calendar. He met with a Greek astronomer named Sosigenes as an advisor in 46 BC. The calendar was changed to January 1,45 BC. Thus we had the Julian calendar. Today, we live under the calendar called the Gegorian calendar. This name came from Pope Gregory XIII.

As the book of Daniy'el said he shall think to change times.

The Council of Nicaea (these ungodly men) in AD 325 felt the Julian calendar was twenty-four hours in error to determine the vernal equinox in 46 BC. they attributed a lag of four days and moved the date back from march 25 to march 21 and then it would be stable. The celebration of easter was then determined based on march 21. Pope Gregory XIII felt the Julian calendar was deviated. Easter, a spring holiday, eventually ended up in the middle of summer by the solar year, and Gregory cut ten days off in 1582 of October 4, Thursday and the next day was October 15, 1582, Friday.

THE MEANING OF EACH DAY

sunday = day of the sun god
monday = day of the moon god
tuesday = The Germanic god of war and sky; also Roman and Greek
wednesday = Woden's day = the chief Teutonic god = an ancient people, probably Germanic or Celtic origin

thursday = Thor's + daeg day, actually translation ode its Latin name, dies Jovis Jupiter's day. The old English form thursday was Thunresdaeg; thunres is the genitive of Thundor, the ancestor of the modern word "thunder." Thundor was also the name of a Germanic thunder god; the Norse form of thundor is Thor. Since thunder was one of Jupiter's attributes, the two gods were associated and Thor's or Thundor's name was given to Jupiter's day: Roman god of the sky Thor = Norse myth. The god of thunder

friday = Freya's day = Norse myth = the goddess of love and beauty; Germanic

saturday = Saturn day = Roman myth = the god of agr

NAMES OF THE SO-CALLED PLANETS

Earth named by THE CREATOR HIMSELF and the only one in Bibles.

Mercury = Roman myth = the god that served as a messenger to the other gods and himself; the god of travel, commerce and thievery.

Venus = Roman myth = the goddess of love and beauty

Mars = Roman myth = the god of war

Jupiter = Roman myth = the supreme god of the pantheon, husband and brother of juno and patron of Roman state

Saturn = Roman myth = the god of agriculture

Uranus = Greek myth = earliest supreme god, a personification of the sky, son and consort of Gaea and father of Cyclops and Titans

Neptune = Greek myth = the god of the sea

Pluto = Roman myth = the god of the dead and ruler of the underworld

NAMES OF THE MONTHS

January = Janus = Roman myth god of the gates and doorways, depicted with two faces looking in opposite directions

February = festival of purification, of Sabine origin

March = Mars= Roman god of wars

April = Latin *aprilis*: Aphro, short for Aphrodite, Greek goddess of love, perth. orig. a goddess of love

May = Mai= an Italic goddess = Greek myth the eldest of the Pleiades (2) Roman goddess association with Vulcan (3) Vulcan was the god of fire and metalworking

June = Latin Junius Juno = Roman myth, the principal goddess of the pantheon, wife and sister of Jupiter and patroness of marriage and well-being of women

July = Latin Julius after Julius Caesar

August = Latin Augustus after Augustus Caesar

Sempter = Latin meaning seventh month

October = Latin meaning the eighth month

November = Latin meaning the ninth month

December = Latin meaning the tenth month

The question is maybe, why did I present all of this information? The reason is simple: man has always believed in a higher being. We just did not know who HE IS. If all of the children of Noach (Shem, Cham and Yapheth) had just believed in ELOHIYM, this world would NOT be in the state that it is in right now. This world is lost. Seeking water in dry ground. We are like the tv show lost in space. We lost our place long ago and ELOHIYM has always been trying to get our attention. He has used different ways, methods and means to reach man such as storms, disasters, famines, books, prophets, preachers, apostles, teachers, dreams and nature. ELOHIYM is JUST. He will come back and will we be ready? Man has been given each day a name of a god, but ELOHIYM did not request this, but man instituted these days' names, planets' names and the months. Man has Flipped the entire process. ELOHIYM gave each day a number, but not a name and HE sure did not give the day a name of a god that does not exist. He stated in Genesis the first day, second day, third day, fourth day, fifth day, sixth day and Shabbath. It was a man who came up with these different names that do NOT relate to ELOHIYM. In closing, ELOHIYM will be served and praised by us that recognize HIM as ELOHIYM of this universe solely owned by HIM? The reason I said so-called planets is because the sun is NOT the center of this universe. The earth does not rotate around the sun. For if it did, why do we see that circular ball in the sky and the same size as the moon? You say, "Carl, you aren't a scientist." and I will say, "I sure am not a scientist, but I see what I see and I have the common sense to believe YAH and His written word." So, you can believe these fools and yes, I did say fool because THE BIBLE says **The fool** has said there is no GOD so thereby these fools have gotten the word enthroned, encapsulated, encamped and bewitched to disregard what is before your very eyes and to disregard what is written and you would rather believe a lying man than to believe what GOD says is true. Come on man look into the sky and you see the sun, don't you? If the sun was 93,000,000 million miles away from earth, then HOW BIG WOULD THE sun BE to see that circular thing in the sky? How big would it be if it was 93,000,000 miles away from earth? What is the truth? Does this make any sense to you? You and I see the sun almost everyday. We see it in the sky, that ball! Does it appear 93,000,000 million miles away from earth? So, as you see **the sun IS NOT** the center of the universe, but **earth**. I am just asking. If mercury is the closest so-called planet to the sun would we **NOT SEE IT**? Can you see the sun in the firmament (the edge of the sky) every morning? But if I planted photographs and published books for over a hundred of years and kept this facade going and on. What would you believe? You see we are taking information from people who do not think there is A CREATOR. Can you believe them? YAH placed the moon and the sun in the firmament of the sky and the firmament is the arch of the sky. One time I asked google "When are lambs born?" and "It said in springtime." I asked that question again some months later and this time it said, "In spring and winter." **So, someone knew I was questioning** and got into the system and ADDED information to go with their agenda. So, this world system will give out wrong information, publish it and pay people to keep this facade going and going like the energizer rabbit, so it will make me look foolish and this world system right. We have been told that mercury is the closest planet to the sun and then venus and so on and earth is the third planet from the sun right. And since the sun rotates around the earth as YAH instructed it to, thereby what man has as established to be true then his (man) hypothesis is incorrect because the sun rotates around the earth as YAH has said and it will continue to do as YAH instructed the sun to do so. So the sun can't be as a man has said, but as YAH has said. So, since **the sun is not the center** of the universe, then everything else is a charade, deception, fraud, embellish lies, subterfuge, and concealment of the truth to hide, what YAH said is THE TRUTH and to have you to believe NOT that HE IS, does exist. So since the sun is not the center of this universe by 1) is not 93,000,000 million miles away from earth. 2) if it is, how big is it?

And the moon is not 250,000 miles from earth. So then there is no venus, mercury, mars and so on as we have been taught. You and I can see that circular thing in the sky called the sun by YAH, but we can't see mercury and yet we have sunrise and sunset everyday. The sun rises in the east and sets in the west. Why, because YAH said so and it does. You see I can paint and publish information and it will be so acceptable for hundreds of years and to deter from that information it would be very difficult for you to see through the maze of disinformation because it has been acceptable and the truth seems like a lie because you have believed the lie to be true. I would have to break or snatch your neck to get you to turn your head. If only you could see and acknowledge what I see and know, then we can turn to the truth. Amein. These preachers saying amen and women are so very wrong and misleading because the word was translated or transcribed wrong or changed incorrectly (so incident like this was planned because this confusion was in the plan or allows to happen as so), but these men will regret what they have done to get this fame for at the end they will be condemned with no possibility of parole but an eternity away from THE LIVING GOD. It is **AMEIN** and not **amen**. I said in my heart this world has been confused by the god of this earth which is the house of satan and men are following the house of satan. When you don't have all the information you will just follow the information you have and this will lead to CONFUSION and unrighteous thinking, but as Husha said my people are destroyed for a lack of knowledge because they have **REJECTED THE KNOWLEDGE**. There are a bunch of fools walking around this earth because they are the living dead, zombies. Any thought zombies are not real, but we have people preying on people's body, soul and mind (the way they function and react to those things around them). **YOU SEE I KNOW THE TRUTH!** Many will deny this because they will believe their father, the devil, the adversary of **YAHUAH**!

ROMAN HISTORY

The Roman calendar year originally began in March and ended in December. They only had ten months. The names of the other months were derived from Latin numbers. July's name was derived from Julian Caesar but it was the fifth month which would have been Quintilis meaning the *"fifth month" in Latin* and August name was derived from Augustus Caesar which was the sixth month and in Latin would be named Sextillis meaning the *"sixth month"*. September, *the seventh month, is from septem* "seven". October was consequently the eighth month as its name suggests : October is derived from Latin *octo,* eight. November the ninth month, is from *novem,* "nine" : December, the tenth month, is from *decem* "tenth.

THE THREE PRINCIPLE CALENDARS

GREGORIAN		HEBREW		MOSLEM	
Name	Days	Name	Days	Name	Days
January	31	Nisan*(Mar-Apr)	30	Muharram	30
February	28 (29)**	Iyar (Apr-May	29	Safar	29
March	31	Sivan (May-Jun)	30	Rabi al	30
April	30	Tammuz (Jun-Jul)	29	Rabi II	29
May	31	Ab (July-Aug)	30	Jumada I	30
June	30	Elul (Aug-Sep)	29	Jumada II	29
July	31	Tishri (Sep-Oct)	30	Rajab	30
August	31	Heshvan (Oct-Nov)		Sha'ban	29
		In some years	29 (30)		
September	30	Kislev (Nov-Dec)		Ramadan	30
		In some years	29(30)		
October	31	Tebeth (Dec-Jan)	29	Shawwal	30
November	30	Shebat (Jan-Feb)	30	Dhu'l-Qa'dah	29(30)
December	31	Adar* (Feb-Mar) leap year	29(30)	Du al-Hijjah	29(30)

*Hebrew months were alternately 30 and 29 days long. Our forefathers' year was shorter than the Gregorian calendar year. It was a total of 354 days. Therefore, about every 3 years an extra 29 days the month of Vedar was added between Adar and Nisan. Nisan was anciently called Abib, the first month of post-exilic calendar, sometimes called the first month of the ecclesiastical year.[8]

** (Leap Year)

The Gregorian calendar is all screwed up. The first month is in the winter, whereas our (The Hebrew) calendar month starts in the springtime, which is correct. The Hebrew Calendar starts at the new moon and that is the first day of each moon for Hebrew. And the next month starts on the next new moon. Why the Gregorian calendar starts in the winter is so strange, but it has gone on for years and we have been formatted to believe this is correct, but it is wrong. It is a man trying to change times. That made me want to say "Huh!" JUST THINK ABOUT THAT AND SAY TO YOURSELF, "WHY IS IT LIKE THAT? And many will celebrate January 1 as the new year, but it is totally not in alignment with YAH's Word. Just like the people in the movie "The Matrix" not realizing they weren't in the real world, but attached to a machine and the machine was allowing them to believe they live outside that machine, but the machine was feeding off of them. We don't have an accurate year because one group did this and one group ousted days. YAH IS the only ENTITY that truly knows the calendar year. We are in the last days.

The Hebrew calendar month starts with the new moon in march and the next month starts on the next new moon. It runs on a lunar calendar instead of a solar calendar because one day looks like the next. The Hebrew new year starts in mid-march of the Gregorian calendar. And the next month starts on the next new moon. In other words, it is the cycle of the moon. The Hebrew calendar runs from spring, summer, fall and winter. The Gregorian calendar runs from winter, spring, summer, fall and winter again. Which calendar **makes** logical sense? I am just asking, but because this is the world that we live in. **THIS SHOULD NOT MAKE SENSE to a Believer in THE WORD OF YAH.** Men wanting to become women and women wanting to become men. These are topsy turvy. Right has become wrong and wrong has become right. We are headed to a deadly end of this society because YAH will correct all this wrongness and it WILL be too late for some because they have damn themselves away from YAH.

How can man explain this?

CHAPTER 14

My Experience

We can discount many things in this life. We can discount clothing, furniture or our future. There are some things we'll never be able to explain in this life. We just have to accept things because YAH has control over ALL things in this universe of HIS and life goes on. ELOHIYM may give us the answer, but HE doesn't have too. HE is not <u>obligated,</u> just ask Iyov(Job), but Yoceph got his answer. Why things happen in this life, we may find out or we may not find out, but when we find out, what do we do with the information? Why things happen in this life is another question. Sin separated us from ELOHIYM and ELOHIYM holds the answer to all questions. What a person experiences may be discounted, but to that person, what they experience, they experience, so to that person, that experience cannot be discounted to them. Mosheh met ELOHIYM in different way from Ya'aqov and Ezekiel met ELOHIYM in different way from Isaiah and Jeremiah met Elohiym different from Daniyel and Daniyel went into the den of lions and Hanniah Mischael and Azariah had difference experiences. In some things in this life, we just have to lean and rely on The FATHER of this universe to answer when we see HIM. All I know is that HE in HIS wisdom knows what is best for all of us. HE and HE alone can only give us the correct and the best answers to all questions Romans 8:28 *"And we know that **<u>ALL THINGS</u>** work together for **<u>good</u>** to them that love GOD, to them who are **THE CALLED** according to **<u>HIS purpose.</u>** You see it AIN'T your purpose, but **HIS PURPOSE.**

I stated in my foreword that I know ELOHIYM is real. The reason that I know this is through a personal experience I had in the year of 1990. I have danced in the Spirit. I speak in unknown tongues, THE RUACH moves through me all of the time. The first time I spoke in unknown tongues I was on my knees at home, I was 17 years of age at that time when this occurred. I have been given revelations. Did I ask for this, no, but I have experience this (not boasting, but at times I would it never would had happen, but if it never would had happen then I would not be writing this book, just to live a normal day life) I have seen a person possess with a demon

(I knew this person). This person came into the church house, hopped (because he had lost a leg and was on crutches) into the pulpit and started ranting. One of the reasons this person may have become possessed is because of the bitterness in his soul for the lost leg, because I knew him. THE HOLY SPIRIT chased that demon from our midst. One demon got into our musician and I have never seen someone run that fast out of the church house with such great speed and velocity. I know this woman. She stated she saw this person levitate in the church house. Can I doubt her, yes, but I won't because she saw it. Why would she lie about that? What does she have to gain, but she saw that. Someone stated experience is the best teacher, but I would say ELOHIYM is the best teacher because HE gives men wisdom to follow.

The apostle Pa'al had a great experience. **2 Corinthians 12:1-4** states*"It is not expedient for me doubtless to glory. I come to visions and revelations of YAHUAH. I knew a man in MASHIACH above fourteen years ago, (whether in the body, I cannot tell: or whether out of the body, I cannot tell: YAHUAH knows) such a one caught up to the third heaven. And I knew such a man, (whether in the body, or out of the body, I cannot tell: YAHUAH knows;) How that he was caught up into paradise, and heard unspeakable words, which it is not lawful for a man to utter."*

I have heard that ELOHIYM wants to give us revelations and we should be quiet about them because people may get the wrong idea. I am just a man used by ELOHIYM. I am a very weak man who has fallen a great bit to sin, but ELOHIYM got me up. I have suffered with bouts of depression, but like a boxer who was hit with an uppercut or haymaker and staggered back to the corner, ELOHIYM helped me and revived my soul (my inner emotions) so that I will meet my destiny. Yoceph, Isaiah, Daniy'el, Jeremiah, Ya`aqov, Pa'al and Miryam the mother of YAHUSHA (Mary) all have gone through, but it is all due to YAH. ELOHIYM's grace and mercy covers me and sometimes I stagger, but ELOHIYM revives me and lets me know how much HE loves me. I am not saying I am Apostle Pa'al for we are just mere men, used and guided by ELOHIYM. Pa'al is Pa'al and Carl is Carl. Pa'al shared with us his weakness. You see we are just mere mortal men used by ELOHIYM. We are both just vessels for different choices.

One night while I was sleeping on my bed next to my wife (ex-wife now) and my infant child in the middle, an angelic host lifted me and with great velocity, we were off. It was pretty quick at the place we arrived. He dropped me off and flew away. I was placed in front of two great tall doors. I was on my knees wearing a sackcloth outfit. The doors were as tall as the walls. The glory was shown over the walls. When the angelic being dropped me on my knees, I felt no pain. The door carving had such beautiful carvings, that is hard to assign words to. The first thing I actually noticed or realized was the air. It was pure and so very clean. The air we breathe is full of dust and downright dirty (nasty). Our example would be the vacuum cleaner. This is the air we breathe. Have you ever seen the dirt and dust in a vacuum cleaner, well this is what we breathe. I WAS BREATHING AIR. I was breathing air of the highest QUALITY. I was breathing. The floor I was on was gleaming like gold. My skin color was the same. What I recalled next was the opening of the doors and I entered the room. How I entered the room, I do not know. All I know is that I was in this amazing room. The room seemed extremely vast and it had a strange darkness. When entering the room, I was still on my knees. I do not know if my eyes were opened or closed; All I remembered was the darkness. I heard my name called and it was not with an audible voice as your dad would call you, but I heard my name called. I just felt my name called. The power felt like a powerful and very great magnet upon me. It felt like a large gravitational field pressing on me. The power was enormous and tremendous. When my name was called, I was sliding across the floor backward like a little leaf as a great wind was blowing. It was like the power of thousands upon thousands and millions upon millions and billions upon billions and trillions upon trillions of tornadoes. Fear fell over me and the next thing I remember was that I was gone. I don't recall this incident taking no more than five to seven minutes. This will always be a part of my life.

You see angelic beings are all around us and we just don't realize it. YAH has assigned these beings to look over us. One night I got up to use the bathroom and I saw this angelic in white and I spoke to him and he just backed out of the room. So if you get nervous about someone near you. It is just the angelic being that has been assigned to watch over you. This happened about five years ago.

The older I get, the more this experience has come alive in my life. I am soon approaching what ELOHIYM said to me back in 1988 the opportunity to meet ELOHIYM again. Some may feel that I am trying to be the big man. Who am I? I am just a man. There is nothing special about me, but this one thing I do know is that ELOHIYM exists and HE has a place for all who believe in HIM. I wonder why I was chosen. I wonder how many people have had such an experience, but are afraid to express it because of what people may think that they are crazy? THE BIBLE SAY GOD HAS NOT CHANGE. What HE did years ago HE IS STILL THE SAME GOD, we just have to believe HE IS **Hebrews 11:6c**. I told this so people will know that ELOHIYM exists and HE loves us that HE will give us all what HE knows we can handle in this life. I am now more than ever before approaching my physical death to the meeting with YAHUSHA so that HE will say good and faithful servant. You can always doubt a person's experience, but that does not make it less authenticated to that person. YAHUSHA stated to the man in hell that even if one was raised from the dead, his brother would not believe. One in hell there is no escape. Some people may believe that I am crazy, but it does not matter because ELOHIYM IS ELOHIYM and HE will be the final judge of all things. Now you can believe or not believe, but ELOHIYM does exist. You can accept this information or not; It's all up to you. When you take your last breathe in this body, you will be headed to one place eternally and you will forever regret that decision of not believing and this I promise because it is a place of eternal suffering and regret, but that dumb and stupid decision you made you can't take it back because it will be eternally REGRETS of sorrow and unbelievable pain forever and forever and condemnation. FOREVER. Heaven or Hell? It is my hope that you chose eternal life instead of eternal death (separation from life). I know people who are so steadfast in their belief that there is no Heaven or Hell that it is eternally sewn in their heart that they CANNOT escape this eternal doom. You may not think so, but what you think now is becoming a constant reality for you now. Once you are at this point there is no second chance, no point of return (IT IS IMPOSSIBLE FOR GOD to get you to open your heart and eyes and mind to HIM that HE sees the darkness in your soul and just let you go because all you see is hopelessness), no forgiveness, no mercy, just endless pain, misery and thoughts of your past of if I would have, what I should have or what I could have. This will be your end unless you receive ADONAI YAHUSHA HA'MASHIACH as your YESHUAH (SALVATION). **Do you believe there is a Heaven the Place where ELOHIYM resides?**

CHAPTER 15

Temperance

What is temperance? Temperance is self-control. Temperance is like setting the temperature dial on the air-conditioning gauge. Without temperance, you are just like a wild beast in the jungle. A male lion will kill his cubs to have sex with the lioness. You are willing to do anything to crave that hunger within your mind, to satisfy the hungriness that is running out of control in your head, mind, soul or heart. You are like two electric lines crossed. You are hell-bent to practice all types and matters of sins without temperance. You are not interested in ELOHIYM'S ways but your way and your way only. You have no self-denial. Two men will think it okay to let the spirit (Ruach) of homosexual activity control them and they will KNOW EACH OTHER like a man and woman. Two women will KNOW EACH OTHER like a man and woman. Man and woman will get to know animals as man and woman. Man and woman will know OUR CHILDREN as a man knows a woman. You have NO SELF-CONTROL. You are all in your flesh.

According to **Leviticus 18:22-23**, *"Thou shalt not lie with mankind, as with womankind: it is abomination. Neither shalt thou lie with any beast to defile thyself therewith: neither shall any woman stand before a beast to lie down thereto: it is confusion."* **Romans 1:24** states, *"Wherefore YAHUAH also gave them up to uncleanness through the lusts of their hearts, to dishonor their own bodies between themselves."* **Galatians 5:19,** *"Now the works of the flesh are manifest, which are these; adultery, fornication, uncleanness, lasciviousness."*

This behavior is completely out of control. This spirit of homosexualism is getting so predominant that a person will need to ask, "Do you have a boyfriend, girlfriend or spouse (husband/wife)? I heard this statement: "Who is so and so?" "She is my girlfriend." I did not want to ask what she meant by girlfriend because she could have meant a friend girl, but I found later she actually meant the same thing as a boy would tell his friend, "My girlfriend." But now it is wide open and a man will now say "This is my husband." and a woman will now say "This is my wife." Is ELOHIYM pleased with this behavior?

Is there anything wrong with this behavior? You know what, it doesn't matter to me, but it matters to HIM that created everything we see. I didn't make this law. I am just following HIS Rules. Can I change GOD? Man seems to think HE can change GOD mind set about what HE established as right and wrong. To man it is not wrong, but ELOHIYM called it confusion. What matters to ELOHIYM should matter to us. This worldwide view has crept into the so-called church. Church leaders are not opposing this view because it is not popular. So, they are just letting it be whatsoever it is. And this is why Pa'al used the term "lead captive silly women" because how can two men or two women condone this behavior and feel it is, okay? Church members, when you participate in such behavior, your reward will be eternally lost because GOD stated that you change the natural use of the body and dishonor your body. When you are thinking of temperance, it is not only about me and me alone, but it is also about the individual that makes up this world's environment each day. What is the best way to handle a situation? These evil spirits have consumed and captivated your mind and convinced yourself that it is okay to have at each other because I say the meaningful words "I love you," but ELOHIYM has no desire to see this activity among HIS people (let the world have its opinion). This is simply lust and not love because we should all live in harmony with one another and at the end of this life we will be in the presence of THE SON of ELOHIYM to get our rewards whether good or bad. ELOHIYM created Adam and Chuah (This is her Hebrew name, Eve was transcribed into english) and not Adam and Ernie and Eve and Marie. Never has time changed so much that a **does NOT CONDONE, but man does.** <u>Who opinion matters, GOD or man?</u> This is the spirit of confusion? What are you going to say to ELOHIYM THE ALMIGHTY? You are going to say YOU are wrong and I am right? ELOHIYM created Ish (man) and Ishah (woman). Because Chuah was the right person to plant his seeds in to populate the earth, but now we have artificial insemination so we don't necessarily have to have physical contact anymore to have a baby. Oh this is so very backward to think that a child does NOT need a dad. One man can have a hundred children and not be the father to those children and they need a father in order to grow up and develop on this planet called earth, according to THE CREATOR, but not to man.

In this world, if we operate under the gift of temperance, we would be so further in this world if the gift of temperance was operational. We need temperance even more today. Just the other day this teenager thought he had the right of way and left the gas station and shot out with great speed making a right turn and I was going straight and he claimed he had the right of way. Which by all means he did not, but ass-u-me he did. I was at a stop sign and traffic going east and west had the right of way and I could not turn. The person blew their horn from behind me and because that person thought I had time to turn east and as soon as traffic cleared, I turned, but he got inpatient that person got into the wrong lane to turn east and this was a two way road and he was simply going about eight blocks down the road, but because of his short temperance and in such a hurry to go nowhere. This person's thinking and driving ability is very poor and has no business behind the wheel because that driver is very dangerous because that person's driving ability is truly horrible. And we both tried to turn east at the same time and that person was on my rear end. What about courtesy driving? Where has it gone? It's all about me and about the other driver. There are demons or imps and these world systems are influencing us to promote actions that are detrimental to life (salvation). In my earlier life, if I had used temperance, my life would possibly be so much different now. So where I am right now is where I should be because all things are controlled by GOD because HE can be allowed or not allowed. What I would do is follow my weak mind and now I have dug holes and now I am depending on ELOHIYM for help because HE stated I will never no never forsake you. HE allowed us to do what we do and we suffer and realize how wrong we are and HE LOVES us so much and raises us up and grace and mercy allow us back in HIS grace. When we dig a hole for ourselves, it gets too deep and we need ELOHIYM to help us out. ELOHIYM is trying to get our attention, but we go ahead and create the mess and ELOHIYM in HIS wisdom has used these situations not only to get glory, but also to show me my error and to be a witness to HIS plan. There have been things I have done which could have led to jail, but it was HIS grace that did not allow it and it was time I was in jail to show me something, but HIS grace and mercy was with me because HE has a particular plan for me to do which is not finished yet.

In the book of Genesis, Yoceph used temperance when Potiphar's wife called for him to go to bed with her and he refused. If Yoceph had not used temperance and had gone to bed with Potiphar's wife, his life may have gone a different route. ELOHIYM told Yoceph in a dream about how HE was going to use him. Was the TEN COMMANDMENTS in effect when Yoceph declined the invitation of Potiphar's wife? Yoceph a young 17 or 18 years old teenager, a young and healthy teenager REFUSED the body of another man's woman. The TEN COMMANDMENTS were not established, but his home training was always in his heart. Where do you think he learned not to take advantage of the opportunity to be with Potiphar's wife? Look at this situation and think, would you have the temperance to refuse this woman and even threaten you? And also, she stated she would take care of any situation that comes up.

We need temperance to work in our lives today. Credit cards, music, wine, strong drink, cigarettes, sex, illegal drugs, prescription drugs, food, clothing, money, tattoos, make-up and so on. All these can cause us to be out of control. Temperance is what we need for teenage boys who think they are adults. I have found it difficult to discuss things with teenagers because of no temperance. It is like a train going ahead full of steam, no controls on a course and no brakes. A teenager feels like they know it all and they do not realize that satan, flesh or this world system is leading them toward the wrong and dangerous side of the road.

ELOHIYM is trustworthy. So, seek temperance to check those sexual hormones that are completely out of control. You may ask, "Why obey? I have to fulfill my needs." Your needs will bring on changes that you are not ready to experience. ELOHIYM states, "Take heed to my words and obey ME. I would rather send satan to hell all by himself instead of sending those who failed to believe that hell exists. Remember, you are to obey your parents and adults in the church because where you are going, they have been. So be faithful and remember when you are called upon ME and believe with, thou heart I will always be with you are called upon ME and believe with thou heart I will always be with you both now and forever. Amein, Amein, Amein, Amein, Amein, Amein, and Amein. Remember to repent and confess to HA'MASHIACH because that is the only way that you will see ME in peace both now and forever and ever more because I AM ELOHIYM of all flesh and you can meet ME in peace or MY furious Hell and The Lake of Fire where forever you will be."

If we had obtained temperance, many car accidents would not have occurred. We see cars go through red lights all the time, only to be stopped by the next red light and I ask why. If a young girl had obtained temperance, then she would not be lying around with that boy (this could be caused by other things also). They could have waited to get married and may not have all of this baby mama drama or baby daddy drama. You are not married and he brings another baby around you, and you get upset. Why? No temperance! You are wrong because you slept with the boy and you are not married (but you trusted and now what do you have) and he is ignorant or just plain stupid to flaunt and downright stupid because of this. Flaunting and no temperance have caused many deaths. Our society would be very different with temperance. What is it today? Do you have to go to bed to prove your love or lust? Young ladies, your life is better off if you do not commit your body to the sexual demand of a boy who will get his jolly and communicate to his buddies how he got you. Listen to The Word of YAH. **1 Corinthians 6:18** says *"Flee fornication. Every sin that a man doeth is without* (outside*) the body; but he that committeth fornication sinneth against his own body."* **1 Corinthians 7:1** states, *"Now concerning the things whereof ye wrote unto me: it is good for a man not to touch a woman. Nevertheless, to avoid fornication, let <u>every man have his own wife,</u> and let every woman have her own husband."* With temperance, all this baby mama drama may not be occurring.

King David would not have entered Bathsheba if temperance was working in his head (heart). Adultery, lying, covetousness, fornication, drunkenness, credit card abuse, stealing, killing and so on are the results of no temperance. YAHUSHA left us an example. Look at temperance, there would be all types of situations that we would not have entered in if temperance was operational. Temperance means control, the same way we control the digits of a radio station or the air-conditioning in a car or a house. Our emotions take control of our lives and we go into all sorts of violent situations against ELOHIYM'S Word not for the good, but for the satisfaction of our small mind and hungry soul.

Remember this: lying down with a person may seem like a small thing or it may seem like a real big deal. You may say, "I love you", captain of the football team, but he bragged to his friends, saying, "I bagged her last night." After you have had sex now what? Choosing to have sex is not like anything you can take back because The BIBLE states your whole state of being is conscious (spiritual awaken) and alive when you are having sexual intercourse. Once your virginity is gone, it is gone with no return. Who knows? You could have a baby on the way, HIV or STD for a little bit of pleasure, and the STD may be with you until your physical life ends.

If the drunk had temperance, then the wreck would not have occurred. If the fan that is overdrunk had temperance, the fight would not have occurred. The baseball player would not shoot himself up with steroids if temperance were in place. The basketball players would not have jumped on fans if temperance were in place. Bosses or investors would not have committed suicide jumping out of windows if temperance were in place. Husbands would be willing to ask for directions if temperance were in place. This is why we have a Savior, so we can get forgiveness in whatever state we find ourselves in. This man has two sons and one son said, "Father, give me my stuff." So, his father gave his son his stuff (This was not the son's stuff, but the father 's stuff because he was still alive) The son failed on hard times and after spending his stuff. He was in the pig pen and he was hungered and was about to eat the stuff he was feeding the pig and he remembered his father had servants fairing better oft then he. He stopped and went home and his father forgave him, without him really even asking for forgiveness. The son realized his mistake and his father is there willing to forgive. Our Savior is willing to forgive us no matter what state we are in. Just realize that HE IS ALWAYS LOOKING AT US! HALLELUJAH.

People get their ideas from their environment. The environment could be families, friends, associates, books, television media, radio, personalities, sport legends, games, songs, words, school and so on. My daughter took driver education and right now, I have instructed her to place her seat belt on. Where does she get this idea NOT to wear her seat belt? Maybe from her mother because her mother doesn't wear her seat belt until she sees a cop. I considered it dangerous not to wear your seat belt. What does all of this have to do with salvation? This answer is what you do in the house affects your children's decisions the most. People do not go to church right now. Where did you learn you need salvation? In the street maybe, at school, home or in the church house? Children are a product of the environment they are in. I have a saying that people are like cake. What ingredients go into a cake will determine how that cake will turn out. I cooked a German chocolate cake and left one ingredient and guess what? It did not turn out right. What goes in has to come out. People are of the same nature whether melanated people or non-melanated people. We have young boys who think, who think they are men by going to bed with a woman and a woman refuses and these dummies get all upset. Why? Because of the environment. She is NOT required to go to bed with you dummy because some other women allow you to go to bed with her at her ease. Man, you wicked, bent and plain crazy. The woman you are treating like that is someone's mother, sister, aunt, grandmother and so on. Many have been misled because remember what YAHUSHA said to the woman at the well **Yahuchanon 4:18** *"For thou had five husbands; and he whom thou hast is not thy husband: in that sadist thou truly."* You see ELOHIYM and man look at marriage differently. Man look at marriage like this. He pays for the license, says his vows and places a ring on her finger and kisses his bride, but ELOHIYM looks at marriage as this. When you join your body with a woman you have become one. This is the only way that YAHUSHA could have made that statement. And the majority of people will disagree, but YAH has a perspective and man has a perspective and who perspective is right man or GOD? And many thought you were just fornicating, but YAH saw the first woman or girl you join your body to as your first woman. That is why we need a SAVIOR because we are an adulterous person. Is the woman or man you are with is this the first person you laid with as man and woman? And please don't start an argument. All I am trying to do is to get you to think, how you think and from YAH perspective because we need a Savior for what we have done so that we may be at peace with HIM. And many are thinking we are just fornicating. Yes, that is true, but you are also joining your body and becoming one and you are also **investing your time** with another person that is not approved of by YAH. And you think YAH doesn't see this. Oh baby, you are so terribly wrong. HE even knows your very thoughts. Many thought they had never been married or had a husband or wife? According to YAH yes, but according to man no. Listen up child if you are not a virgin and have joined your body with another person, you have been married. So, the first person you so-called hooked up with was your first and the person you are with now is someone else's husband or wife and we do this continuous and adulterous people we are! Now you know why we need a SAVIOR. Even your thoughts are adulterous, why?

Matthew 5:27-28 says, *"Ye have heard that it was said by them of old time, Thou shalt not commit adultery: But I say unto you, That whosoever looketh on a woman to lust after her hath committed adultery with her already in his heart."* This world system, flesh and satan are ALL corrupted and headed for hell and The Lake of Fire. Therefore, in closing, acquire and maintain temperance and ELOHIYM will be very well pleased. Call on YAH because this system we are under these last days is coming to an end and there will be a new beginning for all. Some Will go to eternal life and others will go to eternal death. Some will say "I don't believe you." An atheist said when it was raining," If there is a GOD let it lightning in three seconds." He counted 1, 2, 3 and after he said 3 the lightning flash and after that he said," Very disturbing." So when he is judged what can he then say? These very words will meet him when he is before THE KING of kings. For The Mark is coming to you soon. Amein (So Be It). **Do you possess temperance?**

CHAPTER 16

— ✦ —

Forgiveness

One of the greatest gifts given to man is ADONAI YAHUSHA HA'MASHIACH, SAVIOR and THE PASSOVER LAMB of ELOHIYM for the world. ELOHIYM gave us YAHUSHA HA'MASHIACH so that we may have peace with HIM forever and ever. ELOHIYM created man in HIS image. From THE MIND of THE CREATOR man was created with all the nerves running throughout our body all things working in harmony. Just think of your body and how marvelous you are. There are so many different types of doctors, each an expert in their field of medicine wow. ELOHIYM and man were separated from fellowship by man's bad choice. So it was The blood and resurrection of YAHUSHA HA'MASHIACH that joined ELOHIYM and man back together once separated by man to choose the wrong tree. There were two trees in the midst of The Garden of Paradise, the tree of life and the tree of the knowledge of good and evil. Man chose the latter tree and it took death on the cross and the resurrection to join GOD and man together again. We are no longer separated by sin and now its belief; The blood of YAHUSHA HA'MASHIACH and the resurrection has brought man back into the good grace of The FATHER. The prince of this world is now defeated and we have the opportunity to be with ELOHIYM forever and ever by ELOHIYM'S offering forgiveness for our sins. We are to offer forgiveness to one another also. You may think that is hard, but put yourself in his place. Turn the table around. YAHUSHA came and endured such bad treatment that a dog should not have gone through that, but look at what man did to YAHUSHA. He (man) ripped into the flesh with the whip, he (man) spit in YAHUSHA'S face, he (man) hit YAHUSHA upside the head and with a reed and placed a crown of thorns around HIS Head, but we will not offer forgiveness when a brother or sister has done us wrong. Everything will never no not be 100% percent again, but forgive and fellowship, but just be aware. This is just an example. Owe you money well don't loan them anymore money, but forgive. Can we compare any wrong that has been done to us with what our ADONAI had to suffer to gain us? I say again, can you imagine being beaten and forsaken by your friends? Your dad seems to turn his back on you and you are in this situation that you did not do anything to deserve this type of treatment, but you did this for others who? Your dad is unable to bear to look at your face and your father is now stepping back because he has become so grievously sick looking at your face and losing all feeling for you. The intimate contact and relationship you had with your dad and you and your father is now stepping back. It is like a lost child in the shopping mall and you search hard, trying to find your parents and they stay aloft, avoiding your steps and your cry or calls for help.

Kepha asks YAHUSHA a question in **Matthew 18:21,** *"YAHUSHA how oft shall my brother sin against me, and I forgive him? Till seven times."* We as a man want to place a limit on our forgiveness. How can we do that? YAHUSHA did not place a limit on our forgiveness. How can we do that? YAHUSHA did not place a limit on us. YAHUSHA is king and HE bent down and gave HIS Life toward us HE WAS Commend to do so that we may be with HIM. We are to endure so at the rewards station, we can claim our reward.

It is a commandment to forgive. **Matthew 18:35** states, *"So, likewise shall my heavenly FATHER do also unto you, if ye from your hearts forgive not everyone his brother their trespasses."* **Colossians 3:13** states, *"Forbearing one another and forgiving one another if any man have a quarrel against any: even as MASHIACH forgave you, so also do you."*

This Commandment of ELOHIYM is to be followed no matter how we feel concerning something. If we do not follow THE COMMANDMENT, then we are just wrong as the person we are supposed to forgive. Oftentimes, we feel we are better than the person we are supposed to forgive, but when that person asks for forgiveness and we say nay, that puts us in a worse condition than the one who asked for forgiveness. You may ask why? Because the person who asked has given that burden over to the petitionee and the petitioner no longer carries that burden or load of not asking, but have laid all of the weight on your shoulder, the petitionee. This is the reason that is expressed throughout the BIBLE: it is better to give than to receive. There is power in our words. We need to realize that according to The WORD when we stand or kneel before HA'MASHIACH and those rewards that we could have obtained are gone and they are gone for eternity. So, the saying sticks and stones may break my bones but words will never hurt is so wrong because words hurt. All your life, you here, you are stupid.

Each and every day more than likely you will be just that because you think so, but if I tell you each and every day you are blessed and smart, you will be just that hopeful unless something in your environment throws you off course. We will then realize how powerful forgiveness is. Thanks be to ELOHIYM for HIS greatest gift to us who believe, YAHUSHA HA'MASHIACH, The ELOHIYM of this universe and all we see and do not see. You have the option to forgive and not to forgive. You can comply with ELOHIYM. It is your option, but if I was you, I would comply with the MASHIACH.

Now this is only for us that are The Call Ones. Let THE RUACH always be your guide. Should there be a matter of forgiveness in any situation or is there a place of no forgiveness with us who say we are believers? Husbands cheat on wife and wife cheat on husbands, find out the reason and go on from there. If a man or woman has given all? What do you think? Can you forgive or will you forgive? We are in a quandary, how can we go on? Do you forgive me? Neither should there be a matter of forgiveness in any situation and this applies to Believers only because if a man or woman says they are a believer and they continue in their abuse toward you, please don't stay in that abusive relationship because someone is still following the world viewpoint. In other words, should I stay in a relationship when I am being physically and emotionally abused? Move on, get away because you were NOT TOLD to be someone's punching bag. We have people who ask for forgiveness and it is given but it WAS NOT from the heart and they repeat this same cycle of asking and abusing, but their ways are the same! You got an eye missing, but he or she baby please forgive me and "Okay I will but from a distance." This forgiveness is not a get out of card jail, but a recognition of who you are.

Job's (Iyov) trouble did not cease until he prayed for his friends, **Iyov 42:10** says, *"And YAHUAH turned the captivity of Iyov, when he prayed for his friends: also YAHUAH gave Iyov twice as much as he had before."* When we forgive, this action will create a nuclear activity in our life. Unforgiveness binds, controls, and weakens us physically, spiritually and emotionally. It creates hardship, loneliness, heartbreak and all types of ailments. Never getting a good night of sleep. And this has been scientifically proven. In other words, It Will Kill You. Holding grudges ain't good because then come other things such as hate, envy, demons, depression, other illnesses such as high blood pressure because so go ahead and be unforgiving and you may feel you are justified by not forgiving, but this will bring all types of calamities in your life. YAHUSHA states in **Matthew 5:44**, *"Pray for them which despitefully use you."*

Romans 12:19-20, *"Dearly beloved, avenge not yourselves, but rather give place to wrath: for it is written, Vengeance is mine; I will repay, saith YAHUAH. Therefore, if thine enemy hunger, feed him; If he* hopely *give him drink: for in so doing, thou shalt heap coals of fire on his head."*

This is not operating this way at all. You do wrong to me and I will do wrong to you. You give me an iron bed and I give you an iron bed, but ELOHIYM says not so; instead of hate, give love and HE knows exactly what HE will do. It is not our place to seek revenge by gun, bomb, destruction or evil speaking, but to seek ELOHIYM and HIS LOVE will provide all our needs. Because no ONE needs to go to hell because it is a place that only satan and his followers should go. If we were to follow HIS Word, this place would be a much better place for our needs. In closing, if you believe in THE GOD of Avraham, Yitschaq, Ya`aqov and Mosheh follow HIS Words and everything will be alright. If after asking for forgiveness and it is not forgiven, then the burden is NOT UPON your shoulder, but to the person you asked. This is like tennis. Once you hit the ball over the net that person has to return it. Game set match.

Let me ask one more question. When YAHUSHA rose from the dead, was there anything written or discussed about Kepha's failure of denying YAHUSHA not once, but three times? The answer is NO. MASHIACH knew this would happen because it was foretold and by being GOD HE foreknew and YAHUSHA made a very special request and HE said "Tell *my disciples and Kepha…"* We have been given the ability to forgive, so forgive and you will be forgiven or the tormentors will be after you. **Have you ever asked for forgiveness?**

CHAPTER 17

— ❧ —

The Age of Moral Accountability

What is the age of Moral Accountability? No one knows but ELOHIYM. What we do know is that ELOHIYM would not destroy the town of Nineveh because of 120,000 souls, which could not discern between the left hand from the right hand. The Rapture is going to occur and we will have no idea when. When The Rapture occurs, will your child be at the age of moral accountability and not know who ELOHIYM (YAHUSHA) is and have repented? We have a generation of children right now who do not know ELOHIYM and who do not care to know ELOHIYM. This generation is lost. Since this generation is lost, they do not know the way. This is the situation before the flood. If you are lost, you are in a bad and terrible way. ELOHIYM is just. We were often led to believe the age of moral accountability is at the age of twelve years because YAHUSHA stated in the temple it was time HE was about HIS FATHER'S business. What an assumption? He was referring to HIS HEAVENLY FATHER. He was twelve when HE made this statement. HE made an open confession to those around HIM. It doesn't mean HE was not aware before then. To conclude that the age of accountability is twelve years of age is very deceptive because The BIBLE does NOT declare this information. I have seen people accept MASHIACH at the age of eight years. In America, there are churches all over and if our little one fails to believe in HA'MASHIACH, it is our loss and ELOHIYM'S loss.

I wrote a letter to my stepdaughter that she has two little ones who need to know The HA'MASHIACH'S death burial and resurrection. I wrote to her, asking how she learned of HA'MASHIACH death burial and resurrection, in the streets, school or church house? The answer is the church house. If you learned (why) of the death, burial and resurrection of YAHUSHA HA'MASHIACH through the church house, then we must take our children to the church house so they will obtain the same information as you and I received. Some people may be against this and call it indoctrination, but have you also been indoctrinated to a certain belief of not also. Yes, or no? What is ahead of your ability of not believing? I know, but you would not believe even if I told you so, buty your ending is doom. YAHUSHA is coming back. In addition, those who have reached the age of moral accountability will be left to suffer the tribulation, if they have not believed. What is the age of moral accountability, three year of age, four years of age, five years of age, or six years of age? Since we don't know; Parents, what is the age of moral accountability is, then instruct your children in your home, instead of waiting for the pastor to teach your children and take them to church and you be there with your children. I know we have messed up, but straight up and do what you can do at this time. You can only do what you know what to do. That is all we can do and move on because the sun will come up in the morning. Because in today's society, we are so concerned about me and me. Pray before a meal and give thanks because someone is worse than you. Man did not have any shoes and then he saw the man with no feet, but in all things give thanks. And maybe they will ask, "Who do you pray to, father and mother?" What is going on right now? Have you asked YAHUSHA for the answer? Then the burden is on HA'MASHIACH to resolve. YAHUSHA stated HE would never leave us or forsake us. The RUACH HA'QODESH is there to guide you in all situations. Do not let satan take advantage of you by taking your children to the church house because you know they should know HA'MASHIACH. ELOHIYM had instructed the passo to post HIS words on the doorpost. Let us gain to ELOHIYM'S Kingdom by doing what YAHUSHA did. GO to The CHURCH house!

Deuteronomy 11:18-21 states, *"Therefore shall ye lay up these my words in your heart and in your soul, bind them for s sign upon your hand, that they be a frontlets between your eyes. And ye shall teach them your children, speaking of them when thou sittest in thine house, and when walkest by the way, when thou liest down, and thou risest u. And thou shalt write them upon the doorposts of thine upon thy gates: That your days may be multiplied, and the days of your children, in the land which YAHUAH swore unto your fathers to give them, as the days of heaven upon the earth."*

It is our business as parents to make sure our children come to know YAHUSHA in HIS fullness. Would it not be a shame that YAHUSHA came and took you in The Rapture and left your child or grandchild to suffer the tribulation and then possibly The Lake of Fire?

We may feel it is a game and think we have all the time in the world, but time is running out. Let's say your child dies. Has he or she become knowledgeable of the death burial and resurrection of MASHIACH? Will they be carried to heaven by an angel or will they experience eternal death (separation from THE FATHER) and The Lake of Fire? Parents, answer the question right now. Are your children ready? Will they see YAHUSHA in peace? Parents, ELOHIYM has left us a great responsibility and we will be judged on how we carried out the requests of ELOHIYM. ELOHIYM is just and right. We can make all the excuses we want, but if you have time for gossipping (conversation on the phone), shopping, excessive eating, having entertainment, using the internet, vacationing, playing video games, movies, reading a novel, going to concerts, etc. Then we got time for our children to present the plan of salvation. If they don't listen, keep at it. The anagram A.S.K. keep asking, keep seeking and keep knocking. Always A.S.K.

Our children are our greatest asset. Our children are very important. All of my children have knowledge of HA'MASHIACH as ADONAI and Savior. How they mature in YAHUSHA has been between themselves and YAHUSHA because every tub has to sit on its own bottom. Each one will be before The SAVIOR and be rewarded. In other words, give an account of their duty. We need to talk to our children about what we have discovered about YAHUSHA. The things that are occurring in our society because it points to HIS COMING back soon. HE is coming back soon and will your children, friends and cousins be ready when HE COMES? I am now ready to see YAHUSHA. I am now ready to offer whatever, including my life. We must deny ourselves and pick up our cross daily.

Luke 9:23 states *"And HE said to them all, If any man will come after ME, let him deny himself and take up his cross daily, and follow ME."*

Do you think there is an age of accountability?

CHAPTER 18

The Rapture

What is The Rapture? This is NOT accepted by ALL Believers. Many are split three ways on this, but who are we to be split? All I know I believe what The BIBLE says and that is what I believe. The MASHIACH YAHUSHA said in Yahuchanon 10:16 *"And other sheep I have, which are not of **this fold**: them also I must bring and they shall hear **my voice**; and there shall be one-fold, and one Shepherd."* There is but one-fold only! When YAHUSHA used the word this (used to identify a specific person or thing close at hand or being indicated or experienced). This fold. There is NOT two-fold, but one-fold period. Who was YAHUSHA talking to in this verse? He was talking to HIS FOLD. Who is this fold **YAHUDAH**. YAHUSHA was born Hebrew and not Judah because the original name was Yahudah, but HE is First SON OF ELOHIYM. So thereby HE was born Hebrew in the tribe of Yahudah and not Judah. The letter j did exist until 1633 so everything has been screwed up to cause this confusion going on right now. The word Judah did not exist until the letter j was formed. Let's get this straight PLEASE theology teacher, teaching not the truth (but you ALREADY KNEW, BUT YOU DID NOT TELL GOD'S PEOPLE **SHAME ON YOU**), but pacificing the masses to get them to believe your lies from the school of the cemetery. So, first YAHUSHA is a Hebrew and He was born to Miryam and not Mary and He was born in the tribe of Yahudah not Judah and not on December 25, but we still are celebrating that lie by giving each other gifts and putting trees in our houses, which has nothing to with MASHIACH, but a pagan holiday and the beat goes on. The church

(the Called Ones) thinks it has replaced Ya`aqov, but YAHUAH loves Ya`aqov with an everlasting love and Ya`aqov cannot ever be forgotten. The other fold in this verse are The called out ones and as says **1 Thessalonians 4:16** the voice of an archangel, they shall hear my voice. This event YAHUSHA HA'MASHIACH will come back for HIS Body and we will forever be with ELOHIYM as **Revelation 21:3** says that The Tabernacle of YAHUAH is with men and YAHUAH SHALL be with them. The Bible states that MASHIACH is The Head of the called-out ones. **Ephesians 5:23** *"For the husband is the head of the wife, even as MASHIACH is head of the called-out assembly: and HE is the Savior of the body.*

Some will think they are safe because I follow The Law. What happened will you sin? Are you covered by The Law? When you break The Law, you **HAD** to have a blood sacrifice for your sin.

When The Rapture occurs, the believers (who are the saints), the body of YAHUSHA HA'MASHIACH, who are the called-out ones **Romans 1:6,** *"among whom are ye also called of YAHUSHA HA'MASHIACH:* Will be snatched out of this earth and our bodies will be changed from corruptible to incorruptible from mortal to immortality from dead to alive in HA'MASHIACH. Who wants to go through the tribulation of not being able to buy or sell or not to be able to eat unless you have The Mark. Would YAH condemn us like that? I will say NO, but those that refuse to believe will have to endure or be beheaded because 1) no Mark 2) will not worship the beast 3) name of the beast 4) number of his name. We will not be condemn as the world as

1 Corinthians 11:32 says. This YAH along with HIS Holy Angels and the saints who had previously died (coming back for their bodies) and those that are here on earth to be with MASHIACH forever. We are taken back and will eventually come back to earth and there we shall remain forever.

Acts 1:11 says *"Which also said, Ye men of Galilee why stand here gazing up to heaven? This same YAHUSHA, which is taken up from you into heaven, shall so come in like manner as ye have seen HIM go into heaven."*

YAHUSHA left on a cloud and only HIS believers saw HIM leave. The angels state HE would come back in like manner or fashion. He left on a cloud and would come back on a cloud to receive those who believe in HIM to HIS home.

YAHUSHA states in the book of John, "I go to prepare a place for you so where I am, there ye may be also. **1 Thessalonians 4:13-17** says *"But I would not have you to be ignorant, brethren, concerning them which are asleep, that ye sorrow not, even as others which have no hope. For if we believe that YAHUSHA died and rose again, even so them also which sleep in YAHUSHA will YAHUAH bring with HIM. For this we say unto you by the Word of YAHUAH,* *that we which are alive and remain unto the coming of YAHUAH shall not prevent them which are asleep. YAH Himself shall descend from heaven with shout, with the voice of an archangel, and with the shofar of YAHUAH:and the dead in MASHIACH shall rise first: Then we which are alive and remain shall be caught up together with them in the clouds, to meet YAH in the air: and so shall we ever be with YAHUAH."*

These verses state that HA'MASHIACH, with the voice of an archangel and we who are alive, would meet them (those who believed before death) in the air. The bodies of our loved ones who are dead would meet us in the air. When these verses were written, there was false information spreading and Pa'al was instructed to write down the correct information, so that we may have this information today. People were led to believe there is no resurrection of the dead, but if there is no resurrection of the dead, then how was HA'MASHIACH raised from the dead as well as the other resurrected from the graves also as it is stated in **Matthew 27:52**? We would be most miserable if HA'MASHIACH was not resurrected from the dead. Some people will explain everything away if it does not fit what they have been taught. Why not just believe what you read? If something is red, why would I tell you it is blue?

1 Corinthians 15;51-54 says, *"Behold I show you a mystery; We shall not all sleep, but we shall be changed, In a moment, in twinkling of an eye, at the last trump: for the trumpet shall sound, the dead shall raised incorruptible shall put on incorruption, and this mortal shall put on immortality, then shall be brought to pass the saying that is written, Death is swallowed in victory.*

These verses state we will change at that moment in a blink of an eye. As quick as you can blink, you will be changed. The moment The Rapture occurs, that person who was standing close to you will be swooped up (slambammthankyoumaam) and gone as well as the person you are about to pay for your morning breakfast, coffee, soda, filling up the gas tank, your bride missing from the wedding, your groom missing from the wedding, the argument you were having, drivers from cars missing freeway back up because drivers are gone, hitting the golf ball, swimmers in the swimming pool gone pilots gone and so on. CHAOS on a large scale. Some people will feel this is a joke, but it is real. What will you do? My question is, what will you be doing at the time of the Rapture? Think about this for a moment? What were you doing last night? Will you not have not forgiven someone? Will you be using profane language when YAHUSHA makes the call? Will you be engaged in some sort of adulterous relationship? Will you be fornicating with another man or a woman with another woman or will you be with another woman that is not your woman or will a woman be with another man that's not her man? **WHAT WILL WE BE DOING AT THE TIME OF THE RAPTURE?** How much chaos will be going on in this present world when the Rapture occurs. Ha'MASHIACH has called His Body to HIM. Therefore, the people who are left are those who had an idea of HA'MASHIACH but never confessed and those who do not believe in the ELOHIYM of Avraham, Yitschaq, Ya`aqov and Mosheh in this world because there two people in this world Believers and Unbelievers. Can you imagine what this world will be like when everyone that believes is GONE at the same time? How are you going to explain? Right now in the movies they are saying aliens and people will believe this, but the chaos is left and martial law will go into effect and then The Beast system will have total control and now if want to eat without the mark you won't be able and where will you live because to live somewhere you will have to take the mark and just how long will you be able to endure such things?

Let's say The Rapture occurs at rush hour traffic in the morning or in the evening. What type of traffic jam will there be? There will be empty cars all over the roads in the USA. People will be looking for drivers. Airplanes will be unable to land because there is no one to help land the planes, air traffic controllers or planes falling from the sky or planes crashing into buildings. Accidents will be all over. Telephone lines will be tied up for hours. Cellular Towers will be tied up or down, unable to call home to check on children, parents, friends or neighbors. Children coming home and parents gone. Your doctor is performing surgery on you and all of sudden he (the doctor) is gone. A doctor performs surgery on a patient and he comes out to tell you, "Your spouse is gone." And you say, "What do you mean, gone where?" What type of turmoil would this event trigger for such a worldwide event? Tragedy? When this happens, what do you think the world would do? The USA would be in a colossal mess because of all the things we have created to operate on. We are so dependent on automobiles that it will take a grand effort to clear the roads. Let me say this: it will certainly be a mess. Children will be crying, parents crying, husband crying, wife crying and why? All you had to do was believe and confess that YAHUSHA HA'MASHIACH died and rose again because GOD states you are a sinner and you need HIM to live. It will be a total chaos, train running off the track, shoppers missing, children missing, police officers missing, firefighters missing, ballplayers missing (can you imagine being at a ball game and all of sudden you see clothes laying around and wondering where are the bodies) doctors missing, telephone repair person missing, nurses missing, taxi drivers missing, teachers missing and so on. This will be total chaos. Your world has changed all of a sudden. Food supply will be limited and eventually man will turn to cannibalism. How long can you go without eating? Guess who will be on the menu? No house and no bathroom, no toilet paper. How long can you live like this? Why suffer this? And all you had to do is believe. You believe that a quarter in your pocket is made of silver? Just believe. That quarter in your pocket is not silver, look at the edge of it, but yet man places ridges around a fake quarter to get you to believe it is.

The man of sin will institute his ways and you will not be able to buy or sell without the mark. The mark of the beast is 666 and his kingdom is being set-up. What is the mark? The system is completely computerized. Right now, coins are being threatened to be taken out of this system we are living under and next paper cash. Some societies in Europe are already headed that way. 5G is available now. This is to make the system faster, but also more dangerous because we don't see that it is affecting the quality of the air. The Food and Drug Administration (FDA) has approved for a biological chip that will be implanted into the human body and with satellite, and this is how it may happen or maybe you will be scanned or tattooed because The Bible states you will **<u>NOT</u>** be able to buy or sell. It was approved a few years ago. In addition, if you accept the mark of the beast you will NOT see ELOHIYM in peace. You will be judged and be found guilty because you have pledged allegiance to the beast and sentenced eternally from ELOHIYM and there, you will be placed away from ELOHIYM forever and never again to see the light, just utter darkness and weeping and gnashing of teeth. This what the covid vaccine is about is a precursor to the mark. It is not the mark, but a precursor to it. The federal government is trying to mandate something that is NOT LAW because laws are not instituted in The USA by one man, but by The House and The Senate and then The President signs into law. If one man can pass a law then we are no longer free.

The biological chip which can be placed anywhere in the body. It has already been implemented and approved by the FDA.

1 Corinthians 1:7b states, *"waiting for the coming of our ADONAI YAHUSHA HA'MASHIACH."* **Colossians 3:4** states," *When MASHIACH, who is our life, shall appear, then shall ye also appear with HIM in glory."* **Philippians 3:21** says," *Who shall change our vile body, that it may be fashioned like unto HIS glorious body, according to the working whereby HE is able even to subdue all things unto HIMSELF."*

We will be changed. The Rapture, you may feel it will not occur. Can ELOHIYM lie? Some people don't believe the teaching of Pa'al, but Kepha (Peter) had trouble understanding Pa'al also so I understand as **2 Kepha 3:15-16** says. He gave Pa'al insight on this and we will be gloriously changed when we join our SAVIOR. YAHUSHA is our ARK of Safety. As in days of Noach, so shall it be of the coming of the SON of MAN. They were eating and drinking, marrying and giving in marrying. You may say," How can a loving ELOHIYM do such a thing? You never read The Old Testament where this loving GOD destroyed several communities because of how they treated strangers. ELOHIYM is LOVE and JUST. JUSTICE demands that HIS WORD be obeyed.

The reason that we need to accept YAHUSHA HA'MASHIACH as ADONAI and SAVIOR is that this planet earth is ending as we know it. It will be recreated, anew, renewed or whatever words come into your brain. ELOHIYM states in the book or Yahuchanon (John) that a meteorite will hit planet earth and the rich know this and this is reason it says **Revelation 6:15** says," *And the kings of the earth, and the great man, and the chief captains, and the mighty men, and every bondman, and every free man, hid themselves in the dens and in the rocks of the mountains;"* The name of the meteorite is called Wormwood, and it take out one-third of the rivers. Look at the movie "Greenland" and you will see how hopeless you are without ELOHIYM.

Revelation 8:10-11 states, *"And the third angel sounded, and there fell a great star from heaven burning as it were a lamp, and it fell upon the fountains of waters; And the name of the star is called Wormwood: and the third part of the waters became wormwood; and many men died of the waters, because they were made bitter."*

Many have seen the movie Deep Impact. The actors and actresses portrayed the very emotions that we would feel if we knew that this world was coming to an end, and we were all touched with the realization that lives were about to end. Look, look, look at this verse. This is a description of an asteroid or meteor. Have you ever been hit by a piece of hailstone? It hurts! A hailstone is just a small object moving through space at such a great velocity. What do you think of something with much larger capacity at an even greater velocity hitting the earth? What type of damage that can do to this earth?

ELOHIYM wants you to accept HIM because this world will soon end. This is all you have to do is accept what ELOHIYM did on the cross. Accept you are a sinner. Believe HE died on the cross and rose from the tomb and make the confession and you are saved from condemnation because it is not based on your work, but what HE did and did alone and not based on your work and you are saved forever because you not basing your salvation on your work, but HIS works. **ACCEPT the fact that a drowning man CANNOT save himself he needs help and YAHUSHA is that help!**

So many people are following corrupt and destructive ways. Things are upside down. Man is having sex man. Women is having sex with women. Man has a wife and a man on the side. Man is having sex with beast. Woman is having sex with beast. Man is having sex with child and women is having sex with child. Anything goes. Do what you feel you can do. ELOHIYM loves you and me with a love that surpasses our understanding that HE gave up HIS SON to suffer what HE suffered so that we can get back to HIS arms. It was like two people who love one another but had not seen one another for s great time and He promised that I will never no not let you go again. ELOHIYM came down from heaven. ELOHIYM took the abuse and HE was HE ABUSED for me and you, yes, with great pain and we so careless sin, but you are forever forgiven that sin price has been paid. I think about a song by Titus Showers `` It's *gonna be alright"*. And the great word HE loves me oh how HE loves me. It brings great tears to my eyes and they are full right now. **Oh, HOW HE LOVED ME, but it's gonna be alright.** Where does this madness end? ELOHIYM took the abuse from man so that man may be saved. How else can ELOHIYM show HIS LOVE for man and we can at least say Thank you each every day because if HE had not done what HE did we would be in such a terrible state, but HE LOVES ME. Say this Oh," HE LOVES ME." The MESSIAH states in **Yahuchanon 10: 16** there shall be one-fold and that one-fold is Yashar`e'liy only and not the church for the one fold is YASHAR'EL because HE stated there shall be one fold only and that fold is YASHAR'EL. The MESSIAH was speaking to Israel. **Zechariah 2:11** says, *"And many nations shall be joined to YAHUAH in that day, and shall be MY people: and I will dwell in the midst of you…*So THE MESSIAH'S fold is Israel and the called-out assembly bka the church cannot replace Israel. All of Israel shall be saved **Romans 11** and this spiritual Israel.

2 Baruk 30:1-2 says, *"And it shall come to pass after these things, when the time of the advent of HA'MASHIACH is fulfilled, that HE shall return in glory. Then all who have fallen asleep in hope of HIM shall rise again."* **2 Baruk 51:3,** *"Also as for the glory of those who have been justified in my Torah, who have understanding in their life, and who have planted in their heart the root of wisdom, then their splendour shall be glorified in changes, and the form of their* *face shall be turned into the light of their beauty, that they may be able to acquire and receive the world which does not die, which is then promised to them.*

There is a coming destruction to this planet and where or how do you escape this destruction **Revelation 21:1**, **Yesha`Yahu (Isaiah) 51;6, 65:17, 66:22**, **Hebrews 2:5,**

2 Kepha (Peter) 3:13, Mattithyahu (Matthew) 24:35 and **Tehilliym (Psalms) 148:6** says, *"HE has also stablished them forever and ever: <u>HE has made a decree which shall not pass.</u>"*

If you don't think there will be a Rapture *then* there will be an end to this heaven and earth.

Do you believe this?

CHAPTER 19

—— ❧ ——

Physical Death (The Plea)

What is physical death? Man has and always will try to escape physical death through various means such as surgery, exercise, eating right, nutritious information, medication, and so on and so on and so on. You know what, this is futile because physical death is a reality and it is totally out of your control. People pass on for whatever reason every day and any age. We die and that is just the fact. Have you seen the commercial where the man exercises, runs every day and drinks the right water, only to be wiped out by a bus? Death is like taxes; it will occur. YOU CANNOT ESCAPE PHYSICAL DEATH! Physical death will happen. Death Is a part of physical life. You are born, you live and then you die. Is your great-great-great-grandfather living? Since most of us have never ever met our great-grandfather, physical death is assured. Why do we think we can escape physical death? Think about it. There is no doubt about physical death: it will occur and then after physical death, the judgment.

Some people may state that exercise is to improve this life. Okay, I will give you that, but physical death will occur and that is a fact, Jack. Therefore, since physical death is inescapable and realistic, we must be prepared for judgment or eternal life or eternal existence. You are here NOW and what can you do about it? For we must all be ready. Why, because physical death is guaranteed unless The Rapture occurs first.

This earth is going to burn up. Remember the movie "Knowing." Where do you think you can escape? There is but one way to escape eternal death and that is to believe in the death burial and the resurrection of YAHUSHA HA'MASHIACH. This is our escape clause from eternal death. YAHUSHA states in Yahuchanon, "I AM the Way, I AM the Truth and I AM the Life." The word "The" makes this statement so definite, defining, ending and resolute. There is no escape clause from this statement. You believe YAHUSHA or not believe YAHUSHA; This is your only option. YAHUSHA is either telling the truth or HE (THE SON OF ELOHIYM) is lying. ELOHIYM (THE FATHER THE SON THE RUACH HA'QODESH) CANNOT, CANNOT and I mean cannot lie and I mean cannot stand a liar and most of us can't stand a liar.

The BIBLE speaks of three deaths: (1) spiritual (2) eternal and (3) physical. All three deaths can occur in a person's life. We as believers sometimes do not realize what physical death actually is because if we did, we would not be doing all of this boo-hoo and boo-hoo. Physical death to most is very devastating. Should it be? Life here on earth is so very short. It likes the water that evaporates. Physical death is going to be a reality and to some not, but we have known someone that has died. There are people that have died that I missed so very much, but I know they are in great comfort. What we see is not that real person, but the image of that person. Physical death is like leaving this shell (the body) and going into eternity forever. We are going into another realm. I compare it to something like this, your body is like a pecan shell and what is inside that shell is the real you. Majority of the time what is inside the pecan is good, rotten and just not ripened. Where you go will be upon your belief of who YAHUSHA HA'MASHIACH THE SON THE CREATOR of all things is in your heart and confession. You can play around if you want to, but your decision will have eternal consequences. I pray that you make that decision with a contrite heart, while it is still beating. Don't be like Avram's brother Haran who could not make a decision. Read **Jasher 12:19**.

Can you imagine being without things in this life? Water is something that is needed in this present life. You may say my friends, my friends will be in hell, so I will party all the time. Do you remember, after ALL of that partying that hangover? Would you want that feeling for eternity? You will not be able to find your friend in Hell because it will be utter darkness and there is no telling what is running across your feet or your body. You are there in complete misery. Hell is not the only place you will abide. You will be waiting for judgment and be condemned to the Lake of Fire. Heaven and Hell are completely different. In heaven, there is light, pleasure, joy, peace,and great smell (the oxygen is so pure, not filled with dirt as this present world). In Hell, there is total darkness, pain, hunger, misery, stench like the trash we smell today or the constant foulness of the air like that that comes out of your butt. What is life without ELOHIYM? LIFE without ELOHIYM is impossible. All the money in the world cannot possibly be enough without ELOHIYM in our life. I was given a vision of hell. What is hell like? There is a gloomy darkness. There seems to be miles and miles of depth. There is hunger and pain. There seems to be compartments. If you step outside of your compartments, you experience tremendous pain. It seems as though men were climbing on the jagged rocks, trying to escape, but they were experiencing failure. There were children and families huddled in groups alone, waiting. The air appears cold and dreary. The jagged rocks were very pointed and sharp and the men were struggling, but going nowhere and this is a part of their eternity, an existence of waiting on judgment. In the book of **Ecclesiasticus 18:10** says, *"As a drop of water unto a sea, and a gravelstone in comparison of the sand; so are a thousand years to the days of eternity.*

So, if you think you are tough enough, go ahead if you dare to think you can spend eternity away from YAHUAH.

Physical death to a believer is completely different from a sinner. Physical death to a Believer is joy, rest, peace and assurance. There are no gasoline stations in heaven. You will not to pay for any more electric bill, gas bill, telephone bill, water bill, grocery bill, automobile note, mortgage, clothing note, no speeding ticket, credit card bill, wireless phone bill, home phone bill, no lawsuit, cable television bill, rent bill, football entertainment, no insurance bill, theater entertainment, no irs taxes, county taxes, city taxes and whatsoever bill you can come up with. This is one reason the nation of Israel was looking for The MESSIAH. It is living in a clean environment with no one ruling over you unjustly. There are no Federal Reserve Notes in heaven (The place where ELOHIYM resides). No unruly police officers to give you a speeding ticket and no one to continually make laws for this world to operate.

Physical death should be if you understand eternity is a part of it; that would be the most devastating part of it if you are not saved. We think of physical death as the finality of existence, but The BIBLE declares it is just the beginning to a totally different experience for everyone. Physical death from this life is a very different experience that we can never even imagine. For some people, physical death will be life and for some physical death will be eternally separated from GOD forever. This current life presents so many problems and the things we seek after will soon come to naught. The BIBLE asks, What would a man exchange for his soul? In other words How much is your soul worth? What is the value would you place on your soul? Would you take all the money in the world, all the land, all the food, or all the control and power for your precious soul? What would you give in exchange for that part of you that will live forever and eternal? Sometimes I think some people think that there is no forever eternity. You are right now trying to improve something on you. This life is full of vanities or empties because this earth will be replaced and now what. The house you are living in will be done away with so be ye ready.

Death to an unbeliever is completely opposite from a believer. Your place is terrible. You will reap the filthy air every day and you will never to be able to rest and to utter destruction, disease, corruption, darkness, weeping and constantly hearing how you could have avoided all of this trouble, by accepting these words, "I believe that YAHUSHA died and rose from the dead for me and because I am a sinner and I trust HIM to lead me to the promised land." Trust ELOHIYM what HE says about Hell. **Isaiah 5:14** says, **"Therefore hell has enlarged herself, and opened her mouth without measure: and their glory, and their multitude, and their pomp, and he rejoiceth, shall descend into it."**

Hell is a real place and by accepting the fact you are a sinner, ELOHIYM has no other choice than to send you to hell by your decision because you chose not be with HIM in heaven. Some people do not believe in the devil or satan, but as Constantine stated, HE believes in you. This will be your worst decision that you will ever make by not accepting HA'MASHIACH as ADONAI and SAVIOR because Hell will be your home not for one, two three, four, sixty, eighty, a hundred and twenty, one thousand, three thousand years, but forever and a day. How long is forever? You may say, "Well, I live just as good as some believers, "but where you place your safety is in yourself and not what ELOHIYM has said. You failed to look as the believer has recognized the fact that we needed a SAVIOR to meet ELOHIYM in the safety of HIS Arms. ELOHIYM sent YAHUSHA to save the world and not to condemn the world, but the choice is yours. We the Believer realized we were drowning (a sinner) and could not save ourselves, but we reached out and grabbed that vest (YESHUAH HIM) and now we are safe in HIS Arms. You the sinner will exist (because you failed to realize how unimportant HE is to you, in other words you say HE IS NOT IMPORTANT to you, you have more clout than HIM) forever in the nakedness of Hell, forever thinking of the time you could have avoided this misery. You are now in hell by your choice and your thinking because **you refuse to accept** that YAHUSHA being ELOHIYM came from Heaven to save a wretched sinner like you and me. The Bible, ELOHIYM HOLY WORD states, "*For ALL have sinned and come short* " **Romans 3:23**. All does not leave anyone out because the word all is inclusive.

All is an inclusive word and not an exclusive word. So, make the decision to accept YAHUSHA or accept forever the utter destruction of hell and its force. Thank ELOHIYM for HIS SON YAHUSHA HA'MASHIACH of Nazareth. To the only wise ELOHIYM, our Savior. Can you imagine being thirsty and hungry and never being able to satisfy that desire? You are in this world, and there is no escape from eternity. And you say I believe that I will just go away. Where did you get that idea from, a man? Who thinks he knows and has not experienced death? Listen to this one man experience **Luke16:24** *"And he cried and said, Father Avraham, have mercy on me, and send El`azar, that he may dip the tip of his finger in water, and cool my tongue: for I am tormented in this flame."* ELOHIYM does exist. I serve The ELOHIYM of Avraham, Yitschaq, Yashar'el, Yoceph and Mosheh. You have the option to believe or not believe. Whom you believe in will determine your eternity. You can meet YAHUSHA in peace or you can face HIS wrath. YAHUSHA will judge all. **Yahuchanon 5:22-24** *For The FATHER judges no man, but has committed all judgment unto The SON: That all men should honour The SON, even as they honours The FATHER. He that honours not The SON honours not The FATHER which has sent HIM. Amein Amein, I say unto you, he that hears my word, and believes on HIM that sent ME has everlasting life, and shall not come into condemnation; but is passed from death unto life.``*

As you have read, YAHUSHA, ELOHIYM'S SON, will judge all and not The FATHER. All means the total does not exclude but include the total and the absolute. The ELOHIYM I serve as a Believer is not Buddah, Muhammad, Mars, Jupiter, Saturn, Venus, Mercury, but THE FATHER THE SON THE RUACH HA'QODESH. As I have stated, you have the option to believe or not to believe. This choice is yours. You just have to make the correct choice. You state how I know how to believe. The Bible is the true words of ELOHIYM. HIS COMMANDMENTS are not hard or grievous. Should you lie, steal, or hurt someone? No, because it is built into your being. These things should grieve you? **Yahuchanon 17:17b**, states *"Thy word is truth."* It is simple; The land or country of Israel exists? Yes, Jacob (Ya`aqov) and He came from Issac (Yitschaq). Ya`aqov name was changed to Yashar'el. He has a son called Yoceph. Yoceph was held in Egypt for 13 years. Does The nation of Egypt exist? Yes. We believe in Pharaoh because of the pyramids and the hard evidence of their tombs. The Bible confirms Pharaoh. The Bible confirms an Apostle called Pa'al and he was thought to be an Egyptian **Acts 21:38** and he traveled around Asia and Greece and was a prisoner in Rome, Italy. Pa'al preached HA'MASHIACH. These are the very real places and individuals that did exist and exist today and in history? Were there not Roman soldiers at the cross? Was not Pontius Pilate over The trial of MASHIACH? ELOHIYM says HE wants us to believe us to believe HE IS. **Hebrews 11:6c** states HE IS. Once you believe that ELOHIYM is, you will never have to experience eternal death ever again. If you believe in the ELOHIYM of Avraham, Yitschaq, Ya`aqov is factual, then you are covered by HIS blood and eternal death passover. Just like the Israelites were covered by the blood during The Passover (The evening of The Passover, the blood of an innocent lamb was placed on the door of each Israelites family), so we are then covered by the blood of YAHUSHA HA'MASHIACH and eternal death will Passover us also. This blood was placed on the two side posts and on the upper doorpost of the house. This was in the form of a cross. YAHUSHA died on a cross for our salvation and ELOHIYM raised HIM from the dead so that we can be with HIM forever and forever.

Physical death as we call it from man's viewpoint is devastating. We cry and holla and fall out and why, because our thinking is all screwed up. I think of my loved ones that have passed and I think I must go that route also just as King David said **2 Samuel 12:23** *"But now he is dead, wherefore should I fast? Can I bring him back again? I shall go to him, but he shall not return to me."* Physical death is the door to eternity. If you have HA'MASHIACH, it is eternally with ELOHIYM. If we choose not to accept HA'MASHIACH, it is eternally separated from ELOHIYM is awful and in this present body, we can no way imagine the finality of the situation and how much trouble you are in on that decision you have made. ELOHIYM has given us HIS grace, mercy and time to make the correct choice or decision. We often think this life is hell, but this life is heaven compared to hell and to make that comparison is foolishness. We cannot even begin to compare this life to hell because to be eternally separated from ELOHIYM is total ineptness and vain existence. In this life, we have light, food, water, fruits, housing, day, night, seasons, time, mother, dad, temperature, clothing, and love. Separate yourselves from ELOHIYM and you will be in total darkness. Do you want an idea of hell? Go to jail. It is cold and you will be in total darkness. You are locked down, but still you have some options such as getting food and so on. Hell is like a place completely opposite of heaven. No one has even mentioned the smell (I was led to write this because there is no mention about the smell anywhere) that you will encounter each and every day and forever. The BIBLE mentions darkness, weeping and gnashing of teeth. Can you imagine the smell of garbage that is seven days old in the house, stale food, rotten eggs, the funk of a skunk, filthy diapers, human manure, twenty-fours a day seven days a week and never getting any relief? Can you endure those smells for the rest of your eternity, never escaping that scent, not being able to move around and rats and maggots running across your body, never getting any relief? Can you imagine being locked in a room

6X6 with all the manure in your room and never not ever escaping that for eternity? These are small examples of what hell could be. Hell is like the rich man who had his time here on this earth and he died and in hell he lifted his eyes. He asked Avraham to send Lazarus to dip the tip of his finger in water to cool his parched tongue, but Avraham was unable to fulfill the request because it is impossible to pass from death to life.

Eternal death is simply eternally separated from ELOHIYM without any benefit. Believers should not fear death (separation) because we won't be separated. What is fear? **Wisdom of Solomon 17: 12** says *"For fear is nothing else but a betraying of the helps which reason offers." Believers should not fear death (separation). The BIBLE states in* **2 Corinthians 5:8** *"Absence from the body presence with YAHUAH."* Once again, absence from the body presence with YAHUAH. When a believer dies, we go into peace and we are talking about the freshest air one can ever breathe. Lazarus in the book of Yahuchanon (John) died bodily twice, so absence from this body presence with YAHUAH. Lazarus is not among us today, but in the presence of YAHUSHA. Physical (body) death is when our soul and spirit separate from this shell. The shell has come to cessation. Spiritual death is not believing or not coming into agreement with ELOHIYM that you are a sinner and need a Savior. You refuse to agree with ELOHIYM that you needed HIM. You refused to accept YAHUSHA HA'MASHIACH as your ADONAI and SAVIOR, Eternal death is when you are totally separated from ELOHIYM with no chance of repentance. Physical death came into your being; you never confess acceptance to ELOHIYM that you need HIM. Your body is separated from your soul and spirit and you are eternally doomed to come to complete ruin and will never see ELOHIYM in peace for eternity. Your soul and spirit will forever be away from ELOHIYM with no reprieve from the governor or pardon from the parole board. Lost for eternity and suffering to no end all because of lack of belief and not confessing with thou heart that HE rose from the dead because you were a sinner.

Therefore, when you act out at a funeral, that person is NOT in that body you are seeing. That person is either with ELOHIYM or awaiting their sentence and now suffering while waiting for their final destination for eternity. The people in the movie *Final Destination* thought they could escape physical death, but it is always waiting to take us into ETERNITY heaven or hell. So, if you are not saved, agree with ELOHIYM. Accept that you are a sinner **Romans 3:23**. Believe that ELOHIYM raised HA'MASHIACH from the dead **Acts 2:32**. Confess that YAHUSHA HA'MASHIACH is ADONAI **Romans 10:9** and thou shall escape eternal death which is separate from ELOHIYM **FOREVER**.

Here is the problem. You requested to be without ELOHIYM and ELOHIYM granted your request. You stated in your heart, "I do not need ELOHIYM '' and the decision you made is eternal. Even the singer Sting in a song called "Rushing Water '', part of the lyrics mention the story of Jonah. What will be his excuse? Eternal consequences! Can you imagine the bonehead decision you are making to be without HA'MASHIACH? All you had to do was believe and HA'MASHIACH would have saved you from eternal doom, destruction, ruins and realization of hell. How can I believe it? Have you ever been a passenger on a plane? Did you check to see if the plane was equipped with enough fuel to make it to your destination? Did you check to see if the pilot had his license? Did you make sure the plane was operational? The answer is no because you believe the airline (American, Delta, AirTran or Southwest) has already checked or will check everything. All you did was simply believe. Believe they did all of these checks. The only thing you did was simply check your bag(s) and give them your ticket and walk on the plane. BELIEVE ELOHIYM! **Yesha`Yahu (Isaiah) 65:17** states, *"For, behold, I create new heavens and a new earth: and the former shall not be remembered, nor come into mind."*

The Revelation of YAHUSHA HA'MASHIACH to **Yahuchanon 21:1** says, *"And I saw a new heaven and a new earth: for the first heaven and the first earth were passed away; and there was no more sea."* **2 Peter 3:10** declares, *"But, the day of YAHUAH will come as athief in the night; in the which the heavens shall pass away with a great noise, and the elements shall melt with fervent heat, the earth also and the works that are therein shall burned up."* **2 Corinthians 13:1b** states, *"In the mouth of two or three witnesses shall every world be established."*

A thought came to me; will ELOHIYM turn His hearing off when you are in hell? The answer is HE will give HIMSELF anemia because *HE states in* **Isaiah 65:17** *that the former things* **SHALL NOT** be remembered nor come into mind which means we won't remember anything or HIMSELF about our past, it will ALL be forgotten forever. How can ELOHIYM do that? HE IS THE GREAT I AM. Your pleas for mercy will go unanswered, because you will not be heard, but forever forgotten. I feel for the people who were given a chance but are now forever forgotten to the abyss of doom, regrets and no hope at all, but are eternal lost and forgotten. All you will hear will be the chance or a chance you had and it will be echoed back to you. You had the opportunity to accept YAHUSHA HA'MASHIACH. Hearing the statements that will be echoed back to you. Mocking you for eternity. If you are a nonbeliever accept the fact you will one day die and then what will happen to you or what will you experience after physical death? As I stated before, your great-great-great-grandfather is probably not living, so what do you think will happen to you? You have a choice of the pure smell of air in heaven or the foul and corrupted air of hell. But physical death can be so horrendous for those left behind. All of the arguments and disagreements are now gone. Now what? Remember HE states I will never not ever forsake those that believe in me. For you are in My Hands. So get up and wipe the tears from your eyes and look up to ME for I AM always with My children. So hold fast to the faith to a faith that doesn't end with physical death as I was with Avraham Yitschaq and Ya`aqov

(Yashar'el The Righteous). So, I AM with you, The Yashariym. So remember I AM with MY Children forever and ever. Be not afraid, but remember as it says in the book of Iyov (Job) your days have been determined and his steps and the number of his months are already determined. So, quit sobbing because your time to your end is already determined by YAHUAH. And to those that are reading this and you don't believe WHAT YAH did for you, you will regret that decision because it was an eternal decision. And your pleas for mercy will not be heard because YAH will not remember the old earth, but we who believe HE IS will be forever at peace with no regret. **THE ONE DECISION PLEASE DON'T BE IN THE GROUP OF REGRETFUL DECISION. Amein.** Who is our protector? **Proverbs 16:33, 21:3, 29:25, 30:5b.** The Cepher Bible says **2 Corinthians 5:8** We are **confident,** I say, and willing rather to be absent from the body, and to be present with El-YAHUAH. And you are believing and thinking like the world that a mask or vaccine will protect you from physical death. You have been DECEIVED. How are we going to explain that to HIM?

Where will you be after physical death? Do you BELIEVE in what HE HAS done on the cross and was raised by YAH for eternal life and that all it takes. Do YOU BELIEVE?

CHAPTER 20

Tongue Talking

One of the greatest debates or misconceptions in the church today is being filled with The HOLY SPIRIT or The HOLY GHOST or THE RUACH HA'QODESH and the evidence of talking in an unknown language. A whole denomination was predicated or affirmed because someone has taken a misconception of The Word of YAH. Let me first say I have no problem with tongue talking in the unknown language because I believe in the entire BIBLE. I do not try to justify some things in The BIBLE, but I believe Pharaoh's army drowned in The Red Sea. Now does talking in tongue mean that I am filled with The HOLY GHOST. The answer is flatly and distinctly no. Before you put this book down, let's see what The BIBLE says about being filled with The HOLY SPIRIT. I was a member of The Church of GOD In CHRIST. Talking in the unknown language was one the main points in their doctrine of being baptized in The HOLY SPIRIT. Pastor C. H. Gerald would say, "Go in dry devil and come out as a wet devil." When you are filled (CONTROL) with The HOLY GHOST, you will have love for one another as YAHUSHA states, "By this shall all men know that ye are my disciples, if ye love one another." **Yahuchanon 13:35** says, *"Love is the greatest gift we can have one to another." The devil can speak in a tongue, but will he express love? Sometimes we can get people to focus on something to continue in our doctrines because we hold on to doctrines instead of truth. Are you filled (CONTROLLED) by The HOLY SPIRIT not speaking in an unknown tongue.* I would rather be filled with love than to speak in an unknown language.

Pastors, I guarantee that you have members who are BOUND because they do not speak in an unknown language. YAHUSHA came into this world to give us life and freedom, to take the sin burden off our shoulders and place it on HIS shoulders. Pastor, release the burden and face the truth. The BIBLE states to diligently search the scriptures. **2 Timothy 2:15** *declares, "Study to show thyself approved to GOD, a workman that needeth not to be ashamed, rightly dividing the word of truth."* The leaders of today have to realize that The BIBLE is true. What did Pa'al mean when he states, *"I thank GOD, I speak with tongues more than ye all."*

1 Corinthians 14:18 So, let's study.

The word "filled" when translated means controlled, where it says filled. When the believers spoke according to **Acts 1:8-9**, *"And how hear we man in our own tongue, wherein we were born? Parthians, and Medes, and Elamites, and dwellers in Mesopotamia and in Judea and Cappadocia, in Pontus, and Asia, Phrygia and Pamphylia, in Egypt, and in parts of Libya about Cyrene and Strangers of Rome, Jews and proselytes, crete and Arabians, we do hear them speak in our tongues the wonderful works of YAH,"* They spoke in languages of different people and not in an unknown tongue. The HOLY SPIRIT (RUACH HA'QODESH) is ELOHIYM with all Authority of THE FATHER and The SON. THE HOLY SPIRIT does not cause confusion. We will oftentimes bind and burden people with our beliefs, which are not based on the entire BIBLE, but we take one or two scriptures and go off the reservation or off the script. *We are to unburden people and not burden them. We need to unburden the people and let ELOHIYM mature us to HIM YAHUSHA HA'MASHIACH.* In the book of Acts, the second chapter, why did those men suspect Kepha and the group were drunk? Those disciplines must have been dancing around because they assumed the men were drunk because of the staggering the disciples were doing. If they were drunk, why did each man hear their language plainly? If one is drunk the police officer will hear slurred speech and you will be under arrest, but they hear their own language. Why do you think THE MESSIAH took time and made a scourge and chased those money exchangers out of the temple and overturned tables. It upset the Pharisees and Sadducees, but THE MESSIAH was upset by the deeds these men were doing in THE PLACE OF WORSHIP to HIS ABBA. The early church of Hebrews tried to place additional things of the Hebrew culture for the other nations to come into the fold like circumcision and if this was the case then this would have left females out of the fold because a woman can't be circumcised. YESHUAH is based on what The MESSIAH did on the cross and being raised again after three days and three nights and nothing else. Water baptism is not a condition to be saved, but you are baptized because it is an ordained, but NOT required as some in today called out ones have determined. You are baptized (IMMERSED in Water) because you are SAVED from the eternal Lake of Fire.

The evidence of tongues was the proof that the group of Samaritans at Cornelius' place had received THE RUACH and this was evident to Kepha (Peter) who was in attendance. **Acts 8:17** states, *"Then laid their hands on them and they received The HOLY GHOST."* Here is one reason why speaking in tongues was important when first started. Acts 10:46 says, *"For they heard them speak with tongues, and magnify YAH. Then answered Kepha,"* An unknown tongue was important when Kepha preached to the other nations. Yahud had no dealing with the other nations (gentiles). The other nations were considered dogs and no Yahud would come into contact with any other nations. ELOHIYM allowed Kepha to know how HE felt. He allowed Kepha to open his mouth and speak unto all flesh. Therefore, ELOHIYM endowed The other nations to speak in unknown tongues. This allowed the gospel to be for ALL. Praise HIM. Praise HIM for HIS goodness. If Kepha had not done what he had done, ELOHIYM would have had to open The Gospel up another way, but Kepha went as instructed and opened his mouth and ELOHIYM blessed. ELOHIYM blesses all who open their mouth to praise HIM.

Control is what The HOLY GHOST wants. He wants to lead and guide you. THE RUACH HA'QODESH will direct our path or way. HE will not lead us wrong. ELOHIYM is THE FATHER THE SON THE RUACH HA'QODESH. In addition, *ELOHIYM* works for the betterment of man and the only way to be led is by HIS SPIRIT. Therefore, to be filled is to be led. To be led means you are controlled. So follow THE RUACH HA'QODESH, and He will always lead you down the right road and that road is the straight and narrow and those who are controlled will be with ELOHIYM one day.

I spoke in tongues at home on my knees. I didn't have to say all the ritual things of thank you "Jesus" repeating that phrase as we were taught to receive The HOLY SPIRIT. What pastors fail to realize is that speaking in tongues is one of many gifts. Pa'al asked a few questions in

1 Corinthians 12:29-31 *"Are all apostles? Are all prophets? Are all teachers? are all workers of miracles? Have all the gifts of healing?* **_do all speak with tongues?_** *Do all interpret? But covet earnestly* _the best gifts_ *and yet I show unto you a more excellent way,"* If you answer each one of those questions, the answer is of course, no. But we are so hung up on a gift of tongues that means little to the body of MASHIACH unless it is interpreted. In chapter 13 of 1 Corinthians, the WORD states to have LOVE is the greater gift to desire. What good are these gifts unless love is expressed? Love is what YAHUSHA told HIS disciples the sign that will show them to be different from everyone else. Pa'al states He speaks with the tongues of men and angels and in chapter 14 of 1 Corinthians, he thanks ELOHIYM that he speaks with tongues more than all, but in turn, he states he would rather speak in a language understood rather than a language not understood. We are the body of MASHIACH. The human body has so many different body parts.

The church today do not know or will not recognize what prophecy is because we believe that it is not active, but the gift is alive and well and ELOHIYM will endow that gift more as HIS time to Rapture the church (the called out ones) and we shall hear from ELOHIYM because HE is ELOHIYM and ELOHIYM is all by HIMSELF.

The BIBLE states we are baptized in HIS body. **Galatians 3:27** declares *"For as many of you as have been baptized into MASHIACH have put on MASHIACH."* Speaking in tongues is a gift. You do have to work to receive a gift. If it was not a gift, then you would have to work to receive it. I received the gift of tongues and spoke in an unknown tongue at home on my knees on my couch and ELOHIYM simply gave me the gift, but there are other gifts beside speaking in tongues. Do you work for gifts? How much do you have to work for the gift? What about the gift of prophecy, healing, miracles, discerning, interpretation, faith, wisdom and knowledge? Let's seek the best gift to edify THE BODY OF MASHIACH.

Ephesians 5:18 says, *"be not drunk with wine, wherein is excess; but be filled with The SPIRIT."* Remember, in the place of filled, use control. THE RUACH HA'QODESH is not a thing or power, but HE is ELOHIYM with ALL Authority as ELOHIYM THE FATHER THE SON. I know this sounds strange to some, but look at the scriptures and not the preacher or doctrine. Our lives would be so much better off if we just listen to THE RUACH HA'QODESH instead of the binding doctrines of men, which does nothing but bind, burden and condemn us to their doctrines and not to THE RUACH HA'QODESH. LISTEN UP!

I have heard of a pastor stating we have a tongues-talking school. He stated we would teach you to talk in tongues. I do not know if he was kidding. Since the unknown tongues are a gift, how can you teach a gift? Can you teach someone miracles or prophecy? THE RUACH HA'QODESH gives a gift or gifts and a man cannot teach what THE RUACH HA'QODESH gives. Listen up! Man cannot teach a gift that is freely given by THE RUACH HA'QODESH for the edifying of the body of MASHIACH. If you want a gift, ask ELOHIYM for your gift. What GOD gives is for edifying the body of MASHIACH and no more and not for your pleasure. YAHUAH will give the gift that is needed for the body of MASHIACH.

What we fail to see in this life is that the satan, luficer, devil believe in you and he is seeking to take you to hell. satan realizes that he is going to suffer for eternity. ELOHIYM did not want man to go to hell, but justice says so. LISTEN UP! Please heed ELOHIYM'S warning and receive MASHIACH as ADONAI and SAVIOR. There will be a new heaven and new earth. **Isaiah 65:17** states, *"For, behold, I create new heavens and new earth: and the former shall not be remembered, nor come into mind."* Revelation of YAHUSHA HA'MASHIACH to **Yahuchanon 21:1** says *"And I saw a new heaven and a new earth: for the first heaven and the first earth were passed away; and there was no more sea."* **2 Kepha 3:10** declares, *"But, the day of the YAHUAH will come as a thief in the night; in the which the heavens shall pass away with a great noise, and the works that are therein shall be burned up."* **2 Corinthians 13b** says, *"In the mouth of two or three witnesses shall every word be established."*

Question: have your pastors explained to you what will happen to you if you are not filled with THE RUACH HA'QODESH (evidence of tongue talking) if you were to die or The Rapture occurs?

Once you accept THE MESSIAH THE MASHIACH, as ADONAI and SAVIOR The GODHEAD is there with you, THE FATHER THE RUACH HA'QODESH and THE SON are all presence with us who believe. **Is tongue-talking real?**

CHAPTER 21

— ✤ —

Trust vs. Love

Love is (a) the attraction, desire or affection felt for a person who arouses delight or admiration or elicts tenderness, sympathy, interest or benevolence; (b) a devoted affection; (c) an assurance of love; (d) a warm attachment or devotion; (e) the benevolence attributed to GOD as resembling a father's affection for his children; (e) a man's adoration of ELOHIYM in gratitude or devotion; and (f) the attraction based on sexual desire.

Trust is an assured reliance on some person or thing, a confident dependence on the character, ability, strength or truth of someone or something. Belief (a) is where confidence is placed in a person or thing, a basis of reliance, faith or hope and (d) dependence on something future or contingent, confidence, reliance, dependence and faith. Trust implies an assured attitude toward another, which may rest on blended evidence of experience and more subjective grounds as knowledge, affection, admiration, respect or reverence.

Which is greater in a relationship, love or trust? What is needed most in life for humans? You get your choice of one and one only. I choose love. I have been through a lot in my short life here on planet earth. The reason I chose love is because ELOHIYM says to love. ELOHIYM does not say anywhere in the scriptures to trust man. Some people may say, "If I can't trust you I can't love you." Love and trust are not the same thing and every one of us humans has made a mistake. **Psalm 91:2b** states, ``*In HIM will I trust.*" **Psalm 100:5b** declares, *"HIS TRUTH endureth to all generations."* Before, there was The TEN COMMANDMENTS Yoceph, Ya~aqov's (Yashar'el) son, knew not to commit adultery. Trust can be lost between each other, but love is enduring. Love is not lust. Love is not an emotion. My emotions come and go. Lust comes and goes. Lust is about a body part we hunger after and it comes, you desire it and it goes after being satisfied. Love is an enduring and lasting part of a relationship. It is not getting a climax and then leaving looking for the next climax. Without love, you may as well say quit. A preacher stated love is an acronym for my Life Offered for Victory Everlasting.

I know of two marriages that failed because even though they say until death do we part, they failed to realize the vows they stated to one another. One failed because the man's credit was terrible and the second failed because he lied about something concerning his business. Maybe in their heart they meant until your credit dies. These relationships were not based on love, but based on an ideal of this worldly system. Anytime it is based on this worldly system it is based on a missed astrayed system because all we see will burn up. Your relationship should not be based on things that will come and go. I know we need things, but YAH knows this also and HE promised to deliver all our needs. Sometimes we are not patient. We will face ELOHIYM at the end. Whatever route you decide to follow, YAHUSHA will see you at the end. If our relationship is based on love, they will last. We can follow ELOHIYM or flesh (is self spelled backward with the h left off) or this world system or satan and his imps. Some people may wonder why man lies? Does ELOHIYM forgive lying, but will you forgive? We never know what ELOHIYM has in store for us and which direction HE wants us to go. We can be like the wife in the movie *Seabiscuit* who got depressed when her only son died and missed out on the greatest part of the man's life with the horse, or we can be like the second wife, who shared in the glory and fame. Since forgiveness is attainable for all things, why not forgive instead of divorce? Love is one of the greatest gifts in a relationship. You see, forgiveness goes right alone with love. They are like two peas in a pod, love and forgiveness.

The reason THE RUACH HA'QODESH led me to write this passage is because there was a discussion that was going on. This young man stated that this one woman messed it all up for all women and that he would never trust again. This thought could have come from how he was rear-up. I will speak as ELOHIYM has made me and I will not hold back my tongue this time. I stated you could have a relationship without trust. I went to state ELOHIYM does NOT tell us to trust a person. We will never totally understand a person. What makes them tick? We place our heart there and we get hurt and so we want trust. Listen to yourself. Can you rely on yourself not to ever change, make a mistake, be on time, fail, burn something up and so on?

I stated I love my wife, but I do not trust her. I cannot put my faith, assurance, reliance on any person because we are all human. To err is human: to forgive is divine. When you place your trust in a person there will be failure, but love can overcome those errors. Look at ELOHIYM, He loved man so much that HE gave HIS only begotten SON for us to receive us back with HIM. **HE counted HIS SON DEATH AND RESURRECTION WAS OF LESS VALUE TO RECEIVE US BACK. HIS LOVE for US OUTWEIGH THE DEATH OF HIS SON.**Then (the women) asked me where I kept my money. What money has to do with trust, I do not know because if you do not have the money, you should have love. There should be at least in all marriages LOVE. As the BIBLE says For **THE LOVE OF MONEY**. Money has so messed up our life. Are you placing your trust on a piece of paper with a number in the corner? That is pitiful! They asked me what bills I paid: once again, what does trust have to do with that. I have no idea what these women are referring to. Unless you are placing your trust into money, bank account or a job. Tell em, "Who do you place your trust in?" I told them I place my trust or faith in ELOHIYM and ELOHIYM only. ELOHIYM promised to FULFILL all my needs. One person made the comment, "So ELOHIYM will comes down and places the money you need in your hands." I repeat, "ELOHIYM provides everything I need." A person who makes a statement as this does not know ELOHIYM. If your relationship is based on money, then when failures happen, then you will leave, but love will be there even in the failures because there is a GOD who sees and HE has the fixed, but you can't wait, you got to go. This person is very ignorant of ELOHIYM. For if they knew ELOHIYM, they would have **THE VERY FIRST** realization that it is ELOHIYM that wake you up this morning and everything on planet earth is HIS and HIS HANDS alone. Did HE not have the ravens to feed, to bring Eliyahu (Elijah) the prophet bread and flesh in the morning and in the evening. A raven. We are dealing with people who have no idea of THE GOD in THE BIBLE is real and people who do not care because all they see is what they see, but like the prophet said open his eyes so he will see there is more on our side then there side see **2 Kings 6:17**. They kept asking me about my money and what bank I keep it in. I had to bear the situation that I am in right now. One woman stated that trust must not have been in my wedding vows and I stated no. I really do not remember, but if trust was in the marriage vows, we must remove this word because ELOHIYM does not ask us to place our trust in one another, but man does want us to trust one another. I checked the wedding vows and trust was not there. I guess you can say that maybe our world is based on trust. Creditors trust us to make payments, for checks to go through the system and not to be as a racquetball that bounce all over the place. **Proverbs 25:11** states, *"A word fitly spoken is like apple of gold in pictures of silver.'* **Proverbs 12:25b** states *"But a good word maketh it glad."* Maybe we should reexamine the vows and remove the word trust because trust should only be placed in ELOHIYM, THE CREATOR.

Our idea of trust is whacked. Most people believe if you cannot trust your spouse, the marriage is over. The worldwide view state, I guess, you must have trust between each other. Is that true or false? Does ELOHIYM ask us to trust one another? Let me repeat, does GOD ask us to trust one another? Or does ELOHIYM ask us to love one another? Can we 100 percent trust someone? Or can we completely love someone? Repeat! Can we 100 percent trust someone? Or can we completely love one another? Answer these questions. What would happen if we were to love our spouse as The BIBLE says to do? The BIBLE says in **Yirmeyahu 17:5**, *"Thus saith YAHUAH; Cursed be the man that trusts in man, and makes flesh his arm, and whose heart departs from YAHUAH.* **Proverbs 3:5-6** *"Trust in EL-YAHUAH with* <u>all</u> *your heart; and lean not unto your own understanding. In* <u>all</u> *your ways acknowledge HIM, and HE shall direct your paths.*

I asked this question: Can you trust? What is the meaning of trust? This is the definition of trust: assured, reliance, reliance on the character, ability, strength or truth of someone or something; one in which confidence is placed; dependence on something future or contingent or hope. NOW, CAN YOU TRUST ANYONE, not just a little trust? ONLY PLACE YOUR TRUST IN ELOHIYM! To look at trust, we cannot look at it from the human viewpoint at all. We must look at it from ELOHIYM'S viewpoint. ELOHIYM'S view is what counts in this life and not what we want or think. It would be like your child forsaking your information and going by your next door neighbor's opinion. That child valued your neighbor's opinion over your information. How would you feel? I would feel awful. I would be wondering, what did I do to get this type of treatment from my child. We feel we know what is best for OUR child. We humans often look strictly from our viewpoint, which is very wrong because we do not listen to ELOHIYM. This is a completely wrong way to look from our small frame structure. If we look at it from ELOHIYM'S viewpoint, we will see what HE said in The BIBLE. The BIBLE is ELOHIYM'S WORD and this is HIS TESTAMENT for man. We look at it from our very small, finite, cripple, handicapped and selfish mind-set. Our capacity to sin is so great that we have a hard time controlling our eyes. Our eyes wander, our desire is strong and temperance places us under the control of ELOHIYM'S SPIRIT. ELOHIYM is the only keeper for our life. It is kinda like we tell our child "I have already been where you are going."

The definition of trust is reliance, confidence, assurance, faith and hope. Can you rely completely on someone to do things? The answer is no. Can you completely love? We have words like eros or ahab for love which is sexual, philagathos which is brethren love and agapao which is social love. The answer is yes. We need all these loves. LOVE overcomes any fault or frailty. Husband and wife often forget the eros, but it is needed. Husband and wife hold hands and give each other a peck on the cheek and hug one another and put satan in check because if you are a believer, why do you have all of this anonymity toward one another. Straighten yourself out because sooner or later we are going to leave this earth. **SO LOVE ONE ANOTHER and QUIT** this behavior acting like an unbeliever activity of walking around the house and saying in your mind I can't stand you. **DO YOU NOT KNOW YAHUAH IS LOOKING AT YOU**. HE said by this they (unbeliever) shall know you are my disciples. Are you a believer? Husband and wife not obeying HIS commandment. Let it not be among believers. You should know your wife as Kepha said to be understanding. I checked the concordance on the words "love" and "trust." The word "trust" had about 1,700 scriptures dealing with the word "trust". The same concordance had over 4,700 verses for the word "LOVE". The word "trust" in the concordance was in relation to ELOHIYM only. In fact if you talk the t off the first of trust you will have rust. So if you trust in anything else it breathes CORRUPTION. ELOHIYM tells us to trust HIM because HE will not fail us or leave us. We can place our total faith in HIM, our assurance, our total reliance in HIM. We can depend on HIM 100 percent. It may seem as though HE has abandoned you, but HE is right there helping you to mature in HIM. If HE stated something to you HE will see you through. Yoceph went through 22 years away from his family, but YAH did it for a number of reasons, but HE never forsaken Yoceph even though it may seem HE did. And Stephen was preaching this great sermon and the men did not want to hear him any more and they beat Stephen with stone, but he saw the SON of Ad-am sitting on the right hand of YAH and then he slept. Some may live and do and others will do and have physical death, but we who believe will forever be with YAH because HE promised to not ever forsake us HIS children. Can you depend on so and so 100 percent? If you cannot, how are you trusting? Trust is built into our DNA. I hope that the person whom you trust does not let you down. If the person fails you, then will you have love when the trust is gone? Two rappers met and had a baby and NOW he called her a side chick and she gave that man her body but her trust was in him and now he wants her gone. Where did she place her trust? Does she love him, but she did place her trust in him and now what? What type of relationship did he have when he was young? Maybe she should have gotten counsel before having the baby? This situation is a mess. How many of us have gone through this same type of situation over and over and are not on the same level not resolving those issues. You and the man are not on the same level. Write down what you want before you lay down men and women or more problems will occur than what you bargain for. Because of lust. If this rapper had loved her they WOULD NOT be having these issues, but to lust after someone is the issue. A person can say "I love you", but what are those actions behind those lips? And they think it is funny, but this could result in a physical death. So think before you lay with that person because that person could be turning to witchcraft to get revenge. This is just a warning.

So why do we trust? YAHUSHA stated, "Ye love one another, as I have loved you." We are to love one another, but to trust is not what ELOHIYM says. If we love one another, this is ELOHIYM'S COMMANDMENT. How can you say, "GOD I love You" and hate your husband and hate your wife and hate your brother? HE said to love your neighbor. ELOHIYM'S LAW, ELOHIYM'S ORDER, ELOHIYM'S TEACHING or ELOHIYM'S COMMANDMENT. ELOHIYM commands man to love his wife. The BIBLE tells a man to love his wife as MASHIACH loved the church. The BIBLE tells the wife to submit, reverence the husband as unto the ADONAI. Man is to submit to his wife also but not to obey his wife as many men do, but nowhere does it command us to trust one another. If we trust someone, that is not The ELOHIYM'S Commandment, Law, Order or Words. Man wants to trust one another. May I ask why? I can slip off and do anything, but ELOHIYM cannot fail us. HE is assured of HIS WORD. The Bible tells us about ELOHIYM'S love for man and not GOD's trust for man. So to trust man is not right, but to trust ELOHIYM is right. If you feel you have to trust, then feel free, but LOVE is ELOHIYM'S ORDER. Love exceeds trust because when I have fallen, LOVE picks me off and dust me off and put me back to the way I should do,but to trust someone is so very grievous. I had a friend that said he needed $100.00 to pay his rent and he said I will give it back (I needed it back so I could pay my rent), well that didn't happen. And so I moved on money lost because he had a drug problem that I was unaware of. So to say I trusted and lost, but that does not stop me from loving him and praying for him. You never know what condition that person is in if you trust them. But as The BIBLE He shall guide your steps. Love is the most dominating magnitude of all relations. Women and men run into problems because of a lack of love from one parent or both. Have you ever heard of women having problems in their marriage because the Dad was absent from their life and also men suffering for the lack of a mother in their life and all of this is from their childhood? If your spouse fails in some way to love you and be overcome to infidelity and that spouse covets another. All trust in the relationship is gone. Do you think that spouse is going to ever trust you again? ELOHIYM does give you an option to forgive or not to forgive. You can get a divorce, but love is the greatest key, but if you forgive, don't keep bringing it up because that is emotional abuse and you keep harping on it and harping and this could lead to physical abuse or death. Go to counseling. Did The MESSIAH keep harping to Kepha I knew you were going to deny me three times? He said "Tell my disciples and Kepha." If you are feeling so righteous remember you have committed adultery by even imaging in your heart. Examine why it occurred and be an adult and reason among each other and move on, but if the situation doesn't change then you are heading to the road of death to the marriage (divorcement). If you can't forgive then move on because anything death needs to be buried because if not the total atmosphere will be fouled. Love conquers any faults. And please don't go back to your old way and always remember how you got where you are right now. So many regrets, but regrets can be so deadly, but move on because YAH states that I will be with you always and forever. Guess what you cannot change your path, but remember HE LOVES YOU SO MUCH that He gave HIS UNIQUE SON to save you from a burning hell.

Look at the Prophet Ovadyahu's life. ELOHIYM has been through what you have been through. He divorce Israel and cast Yahudah out also, but because of HIS SON, HE claimed Yashar'el and Yahudah back. ELOHIYM has not told us to trust in one another, so if we trust in one another, that is not found in HIS Word. So should we trust one another or should we love one another? How will you answer this question one day? ELOHIYM has instructed us HIS WAY and HIS WAY is truth. Listen up. Follow ELOHIYM or follow man. IT IS YOUR CHOICE. If there is no forgiving, there is no LOVE! **Can we say I love you and not forgive you of your wrong?**

CHAPTER 22

— ❧ —

Prayer

Kepha cried, "ADONAI save me" and before then he asked, "ADONAI, if it be you, bid me come unto you on the water."

So, then what is prayer? Prayer is the effective two-way communication (talking, praising, uplifting, following, obeying, doing, requesting and listening) with and to ELOHIYM. Prayer is a two-way avenue. It is not just one way. You ask and ELOHIYM does. No Baby! You got it all wrong. Kepha cried out "Save me." And HE does what is according to HIS will and not our will. HE guides and we SHOULD listen, but sometimes we get it astray. Look at Yonah. The BIBLE states we should pray one for the other. Instead, we gossip and talk about an individual and that could have been us in that person's shoes. Have you ever been in an awful situation where there seems to be no help? So pray for one another instead of tearing each other down. Why, it could have been you in the shoes of whom you are running down. Why, because you are human, who YAH has placed on this earth. So sow good seeds and not evil seeds. Remember in HIS word that HE said, you will sow what you reap and you will sow more than what you reap. Why? In an apple tree, it will grow apples on those branches and in those apples are SEEDS. We should pray because we don't know what ELOHIYM has planned for our life and what HE has planned for someone else's life. What we don't know is how ELOHIYM is directing someone else's life? We just don't know and we talk about that person. Please admit that and say I'm so sorry because you just don't know. So pray that what that person is going through you won't have to go through what that person has or is going through. You see we are under **HIS Will** and plan and not our plan. Some are chosen to give their life for **HIS plan** but it is ALL in HIS Will and not our will. So be prayerful. You see someone on the street be prayerful and if they ask be led by THE RUACH to help if you are led to do so because you will never know.

ELOHIYM is like a painter. A painter paints a picture and when he finishes painting the picture, he quits working on it and frames the picture. HE is the painter, and HE may have to go and touch it up before he finishes it, but once it is framed, he is finished. ELOHIYM has a plan for all HIS people (some to bring a baby into this world and your job is done and some to ask a question to get a person he encounters to do a job that HE wants done etc. You see it is ALL about HIS timing for things) and when HE is finished painting our portrait and when HE has worked it all out in our life, HE brings us to HIM. ELOHIYM is finishing up the work in our life, HE will bring adversities in our life to complete us. Your adversity is completely different from mine. HE will provide a way to give you shelter. HE may want you to be homeless, but HE will provide a way to give you shelter. I would say that the majority of us would not want to be homeless and living in the street. ELOHIYM states HE would never no not ever leave us nor forsake us, but sometimes it seems as though HE is not there. Look at Yoceph's life. Twenty-two years he was separated from his family, but YAH protected him. Accused of raping a woman and he had no rights because he was a stranger in the land of Mitsrayim. Daniy'el lowered into the hungry lion's den. Hanniah, Mishael and Azariah were placed into the fiery furnace. Yonah's lot was drawn and thrown overboard and spent three nights and three days in the fish belly because YAH had prepared that fish especially for Yonah. If Yonah had not done what he did then Mattithyahu 12:40 would not have been written. HE is there looking for HIS children. **Proverbs 16:33** says, *"The lot is cast into the lap; but the whole disposing thereof is of YAHUAH."* And we think YAH has forgotten us, but HE can't. Why because we are a part of HIS Plan. ELOHIYM is right there, building you up. So do not faint, but pray (communicate) then listen to HIS Word but have to also read HIS Word. If you are in a situation right now, relax and give HIM thanks to help you in times of need because HE sees ALL you are going through. So please do not faint. In other words, don't **give up.**

When we pray, we should be making a specific request (not being greedy and requesting something outlandish, but be led by THE RUACH) and when we make a request, it is a burden and that burden leaves us and it goes to the person we make request of. Did you know that we make requests to people all the time? We make a request to people and since ELOHIYM has given us the abilities to fulfill that request we should do, but sometimes fear comes in. When a person asks for something and we do not fulfill that request and we are able to fulfill that request, then we are falling short on our blessing toward ELOHIYM. Remember what HE said When I was hungry, thirsty, sick, a stranger, naked, and a prisoner **Matthew 25:35-39**. When we pray we just don't do all the talking but we also listen. Give praise. You have a pair of lips, one tongue, two ears and one heart. So listen and obey. You see YAH has the very best for you and sometimes we can turn HIS mind-set and sometimes we can't. Ezekiel asked YAH that he would not defile himself and Avraham requested to YAH that the cities and area around Cedom and Amorah not to be destroyed if ten's righteous souls could be found and Shalomah prayed to YAH not for wealth, but for wisdom and his father David prayed constantly to YAH. He asked if I should go here and even wrote songs of praise and thanksgiving. This is the same principle when YAHUSHA told the disciples on how to pray. **Matthew 6:12** declares, *"And forgive us our debts, as we forgive our debtors."* Don't be like the one man who owes a great debt and he was forgiven his great debt, but he could not forgive a man that owes him a much much much lesser debt. Oh how foolish we can be. How can we ask something from THE FATHER and not forgive those who we are to forgive? Pray for one another. I pray for you and you pray for me. When a person asks for something, they have actually laid their burden on you and either you can fulfill the request and be blessed or you will not fulfill the request and not be blessed.

Prayer can be summed up to ACTS.

A = Acknowledge or Adoration - You tell ELOHIYM all about HIMSELF. You let HIM know who HE is. You magnify HIM. Make HIM large. You tell HIM how much ELOHIYM is to you. Tell HIM how wonderful HE is.

C = Confession - Tell HIM all about yourself. Tell HIM that you agree with HIM and HIS WORD. Confess to HIM about your ways and how disturbed you are to yourself. Confess your sin.

T = Thanksgiving - Give HIM thanks for all things. Give HIM thanks for HIS words. JUST give HIM thanks and you will find out how graceful HE is because there is so much to be thankful for. Look at your life and you have so many working parts.

S = Supplication or requests - After, giving thanks, make your requests to ELOHIYM and your requests to ELOHIYM and your request will line up to HIS Will. You can go boldly before HIS throne.

My prayer is that we who believe to believe with our whole heart. YAHUSHA is coming back and to those who do not believe as of yet, I want you to believe that YAHUSHA died and rose again. Make this confession openly. **Romans 10:9** says, *"That if you shall confess with your mouth ADONAI YAHUSHA, and believe in your heart that YAH has raised him from the dead you shall be saved."* If you are not saved and when the Rapture occurs, satan (man) will offer the mark of the beast, which you will have to accept if you are going to be able to sell and buy. If **you** receive the mark, you will be doomed to the eternal Lake of Fire. I have given you knowledge, but you reject knowledge as **Husha 4:6** says.

Man has already come up with a biological chip. This chip was approved early last year by The FDA (Food and Drugs Administration). This chip will be programmed and handled by the satellites in the sky. You have heard of "OnStar System" and ``LoJack System". The OnStar system is installed in the newer GM models. This system allows your automobiles to be tracked from whatever points on the earth. It is the newest tracking device like GPS (Global Positional System). This same system will be in place after The Rapture to keep you from buying and selling. It is a way of control. The reason this is implemented is because The BIBLE states in **Revelation 13:16-18**, says *"And he causeth all, both small and great, rich and poor, free and bond, to receive a mark in their right hand, or in their foreheads; And that no man might buy or sell, save he that had the mark; or the name of the beast, or the number of his name. Here is wisdom. Let him that hath understanding count the number of the beast: for it is the number of a man: and his number is six hundred threescore and six."* Man desires to control one another. Please do not accept the mark.

YAHUSHA is coming back in HIS full glory one day with HIS angels and those who have died in MASHIACH and to receive us, who have believed to live with HIM for a thousand years. We, who are the saints, hold fast to our belief in ELOHIYM. We will ALL HAVE TO FACE YAHUSHA. **Yahuchanon 5:22** declares' *"For The FATHER judgeth no man, but hath committed all judgment unto The SON."* Will you face HIM in peace or justice? If someone asks for forgiveness, give it. We who have offended someone, ask for forgiveness. Forgiveness is all a part of love. ELOHIYM so loved man that HE saw the need and offered HIMSELF for an offering. ELOHIYM so loved man that HE gave HIMSELF in the place for us. ELOHIYM, thank you. It is up to each one of us to offer the gift of salvation to those who do not believe. When we see the Lake of Fire and our loved one or enemies going into The Lake, then we will come to the full realization of HOW GREAT OUR SALVATION IS.

ELOHIYM has so much power until we cannot grab the concept of HIS power. ELOHIYM is pure power. We men have very little control over anything in our life. We do not wake ourselves up. ELOHIYM does. We control what we place in our mouth and the body takes over. We go from place to place because we are directed by this bodily desire. We go to work to place clothing on your back, housing over your head and food in your belly. We do not even control our desire because the body does not like hunger and nakedness. Most people do not like their body, so we try to improve it.

ELOHIYM is total power and control. It is my prayer that each believer comes to the realization it is all about ELOHIYM and not us. We want it to be about us, but it is all about ELOHIYM alone. Man became alive because ELOHIYM breathed the breath into man and man awakened. ELOHIYM will be glorified. ELOHIYM is able to get honey out of a rock if need be **Psalm 81:16** says, *"HE should have fed them also with the finest of the wheat: and with honey out of the rock should I have satisfied you.* ELOHIYM cannot lie and HE will not fail HIS promises. YAHUSHA is coming again. HE is ELOHIYM and ELOHIYM is ELOHIYM alone. We should be subject one to another. In other words, if you hurt, I hurt. I thank ELOHIYM for HIS great and enduring love. ELOHIYM cannot deny HIMSELF. Let us go out and tell people to praise HIM and HIM alone. No man deserves to be worshiped. It is my prayer that we worship ELOHIYM totally. It is like a man and a woman knowing each other. Totally with no clothes on, but completely naked before each other and not hiding anything. Let's get intimate with HIM, For HE is love. The greatest gift ELOHIYM could have offered us was HIMSELF. I praise ELOHIYM for whom all blessings flow. Praise HIM creatures below. I thank HIM because HE is ELOHIYM. This is my prayer that all believers come to love one another. It is my prayer that my family will be safe and it is my prayer that the church, the called out ones will come together and praise HIS HOLY NAME under one roof. ELOHIYM is love. I thank HIM because it is all about HIM and HIM alone. Find a place to worship and realize there is no way out, but ELOHIYM, ELOHIYM, ELOHIYM and ELOHIYM. Thank ELOHIYM, thank ELOHIYM and thank ELOHIYM. And your adversaries were placed in your life by YAHUAH'S Will also to help you grow and mature to who you are. Just think about that. Amein. **Should we pray?**

CHAPTER 23

———— ✦ ————

I Will Extol Thee

What is it that men's eyes are **SO** blind to the truth OF ELOHIYM? ELOHIYM is! ELOHIYM is all ability and control and ever present. HE is OMNISCIENT, OMNIPRESENT, OMNIPOTENT and OMNIFICENT. ELOHIYM is SOVEREIGN. The song states HE got the whole world in HIS Hands. To ELOHIYM, to ELOHIYM, to ELOHIYM who gets all the glory? Who is man that we should glorify, or who am I that I should be glorified? The question that comes to my mind right now is, "If what I am going through was it ordered by GOD?" satan has his agenda, which is directly opposed to ELOHIYM. Does ELOHIYM tempt man? The answer is definitely and unequitable **NO**. ELOHIYM tests man. ELOHIYM has HIS Will, satan has his plan. Man and Woman were placed in The Garden and YAH <u>allowed</u> the serpent to do what the serpent did, but YAH already knew this and some people may ask, "Why" and all I can say is, "HIS Will to be so." ELOHIYM has set HIS Will in place and satan tried to destroy GOD'S Will. However, what ELOHIYM has will, will go through. Therefore, what I go through was ordered by ELOHIYM, so HIS will, will go through. To us who are **the called out ones** everything we go through, ELOHIYM has a purpose for it. We may not know at this time why we are going through, but ELOHIYM knows and please don't faint because HE SEES US. We do not know at this time why we are going through, but ELOHIYM knows.

You see I am speaking to myself. Because this way seems to be grinding and burdening me, but I know my end, but what I don't know is when my end will be. You see I want this, but ELOHIYM has my path set out the way that I should go, but it seems I want to fight against that just as Jeremiah (Yirmeyahu). Yirmeyahu wanted at times to just give up, but The Word of YAH was like a fire dwelling inside of his soul that he proclaimed YAH'S Word.

HE has pointed out to me that I have it better off than a bunch of people so, "I thank you FATHER for all things because you know what is best for me and others because of your plan and the timing of your plan." Oh how I would love to have a permanent place and be settled. Then HE told me to look at The Apostle Pa'al's life. Pa'al would travel from place to place and he would preach in the synagogues or on the streets and where would he go after that. Where did he sleep at night and what did he eat; (this is why he said give thanks for the food you have and for all things. Pa'al was a Binyamiyn of Yashar'el of Hebrew and he had dietary concerns he probably ate some pork which was against Yashar'el's diet), and did he have a place with air conditioning and running water and what type of bathroom facilities did he have? So, what do I have to complain about? All we hear is mainly about the epistles he wrote. He did express in the epistles about the dangers and travel he did. So be thankful for whatever condition you find yourself in and preachers are saying become a millionaires and this WAS NOT a part of the gospel, but we must be like the **Proverbial** saying **30:8** Remove far from me vanity and lies: give me neither poverty nor riches; feed me with food convenient for me: Because at the end of this life you will be required to be a millionaires, but what did you do with what you have. Did you help?

Yoceph had no idea why ELOHIYM let him go to be a slave and prisoner in Egypt, but ELOHIYM had foreseen what was ahead and HE allowed Yoceph to go through what he went through. ELOHIYM had a purpose. ELOHIYM told Yoceph in a dream that his dad and brothers would bow down to him. Yoceph was seventeen years of age when the dream was coming into fruition. Yoceph had no idea that he would have to go through what he went through, but he endured the treatment of his brothers and Yoceph was young and sometime when YAH give us something it hard to keep it to yourself, but it was meant to be because YAH could have let it happen without giving Yoceph the dream, but YAH has a purpose for those that are chosen. Yoceph was chosen among all his brothers. YAHUSHA was chosen to die and to bring HIS people back to HIM and the world. Yoceph did not know how it was going to occur, but ELOHIYM knew and had seen, and ELOHIYM was with Yoceph even on his way into Egypt. You have to read the book of Yasher. Yoceph had no idea that he would be brought into Egypt by the son of Avraham's Ishamelites and that there would be an argument between the other sons of Avraham the Midianites. What ELOHIYM did was give Yoceph a dream with virtually little or no details on how it was going to occur, but HE showed him the result of the dreams. What ELOHIYM gives are commandments. And the events that occurred after the dream, there was no way, I suppose, that Yoceph had any idea it was going to happen that way. You see, it is all about ELOHIYM and it is HIS Plans for our life. We can request, but it is HE in which everything comes into fruition. The only thing we can do is plant and water, but HE gives the increase. GOD has HIS Hand on the thermostat and HE knows how to control the temperature. He could have let Hanniah, Mishael and Azariah be burned up in the furnace as Avram's brother Haran was burned up in the fire or let Daniy'el get eaten by the lion, but it was not meant to be. Let me stand on ELOHIYM'S Word. ELOHIYM cannot lie. ELOHIYM cannot lie. So what we are going through right now, is it ordered by ELOHIYM? The book of Psalm tells us to Praise ELOHIYM. **Psalm 145:1-2** states, *"I will extol you, my ELOHIYM, O King; and I will bless your name forever and ever. Every day will I bless you; and I will praise your name forever and ever."*

I like the KJV version because some versions have left out the word "extol," which to me changes the concept, the meaning of this Psalm. Will you extol ELOHIYM every day? Extol means to highly praise. I had some pain in my gum and the pain in my legs and instead of complaining, I praised ELOHIYM for the pain. Why," you say" because of the pain, ELOHIYM wanted me to learn something. The pain let me know I have gum and teeth. The pain could be far worse. I could have lost my eyesight. ELOHIYM is there when we are in pain. Why pain? Pain is a result from Ad-am eating the wrong fruit. satan tried to get Iyov to deny ELOHIYM because of the pain. The BIBLE says Iyov had sore boils (ra ratah these boils were very painful) from the crown of his head to the bottom of his feet. Ivov stood and took the abuse from his wife (she could not stand to look at him) because he looked nothing like his former self. Can you imagine what he looked like? ELOHIYM blessed Iyov for what he went through.

What we go through is called light afflictions. Once we make it to heaven, all the pain will be miles away. We are saved. Death of a loved one, loss of job, loss of a house, loss of income, ELOHIYM knows all about your pain. I know these are real losses, but take it to heart, ELOHIYM will not and I repeat ELOHIYM will not put no more than what we can bear. THIS IS A PROMISE. ELOHIYM has you in HIS HAND and HE will deliver you from whatever situation you are in. It may not be the way we expect, but ELOHIYM knows what is best for you and me. ELOHIYM can be trusted. And besides, is there any way you can prevent yourself from going through something?

I had a rear wheel come off my automobile during morning rush hour traffic on my way home. The wheel could have come off on my way to work at night. It could have been the front wheel. When the wheel came off, I was on the far left side of the four-lane 635 freeway and it was 6:30 am in the morning and I was headed west and I had four lanes to cross to get to the service road on the right side of the freeway. ELOHIYM allowed the automobile to make it to the service road and I have no idea where the wheel went. It was like it was raptured. There were no traffic accidents. It occurred that way because ELOHIYM had seen it fit so that I would not have to deal with no insurance claim or traffic death or automobile damage would occur at that time. All I can do is say HalleluJAH! HalleluJAH! HalleluJAH! ELOHIYM is in complete control. What are you going through? Lift your head and remember the ELOHIYM that your grandmother prayed to. We serve the ELOHIYM of Avraham, Yitschaq, Yashar'el and Mosheh. ELOHIYM has a plan for you. ELOHIYM is our heavenly FATHER and when HE is finished with you on Earth, HE will bring you home. It is not about what you want; it is about what ELOHIYM wants. Our plan should be related to what ELOHIYM wants and sometimes we simply do not realize it. My wife wants me to do so and so and she does not realize or ask me, "Is this what ELOHIYM wants for you?" Sometimes we need to stop and ask ELOHIYM, "What do you want me to do for your plans?", Quit living so much for this present world. Are we trying to make this Earth our home? This world has been cursed. The world will soon end. Eventually, you will leave this world. What will you have stored up in heaven when you meet The MASTER?

The BIBLE states that ELOHIYM will wipe every tear from our eyes. If we extol ELOHIYM, this praise will bring us up to HIM and ELOHIYM will hear our praise. All we have to do is praise our ELOHIYM because HE is in control. I cannot stand a whining child. Therefore since we are made in HIS image, do you think that ELOHIYM cares for whining children?

Yesha'yahu 54:15-17 says, *"Behold, they shall surely gather together, but not by me: whosoever shall gather together against you shall fall for your sake. Behold, I have created the smith that blows the coals in the fire, and that brings forth an instrument for his work; and I have created the waster to destroy. No weapon that is formed against you shall prosper; and every tongue that shall rise against you in judgment you shall condemn. This is the heritage of the servants of YAHUAH, and their righteousness is of me, says YAHUAH."*

Whatever is out there, The CREATOR created it or it came from what HE Created and YAHUAH has control over all that HE has created. MY ELOHIYM is Sovereign, meaning it is All HIS and HE can say no or yes to any situation you are going through. ELOHIYM has full autonomy, but HE is also Wise. If HE does not have full autonomy then HE is not GOD? HE is GOD or HE is not GOD. ELOHIYM has HIS control of what satan does and satan can't do more than what ELOHIYM allows him to do. ELOHIYM can call for an end of these times, send The Rapture and bring an end to all this misery. You may ask why HE won't bring it to an end right now? Because ELOHIYM'S Word is true and because it's all about timing for HIS Plan. ELOHIYM has a plan and HE will complete HIS Plan. **Psalm 138:2** declares, *"I will worship toward your holy Temple, and praise your name for your lovingkindness and for your Truth: for you have magnified your word above all your name."* ELOHIYM'S Word is HIS bond and because HIS word is ours, HE has to complete HIS Plan.

The Hebrew men Hananiah (Chanananyahu), Mishael (Miysha'el) and Azariah (Azaryahu) were delivered going into the fiery furnace. ELOHIYM states in HIS words not to bow to idols (imagines that a man makes to worship) and they told the king we will not bow down to an inanimate object (this is why many who will take the mark are pledging allegiance to another god that is NOT **THE CREATOR**) because HE will deliver us from the fire or from your presence and into HIS presence we will be. Many don't believe there is a GOD because of the focus of this world. Broad is the way that leadeth from THE CREATOR. ELOHIYM covered them as they went into the fire. They believe that it was going to be death here or life with HIM. These are our only two options. Death or life, you choose today? Pa'al and Ciyla were beaten with a rod that brought stripes on their back and they were thrown into the inner prison and feet in stocks. Can you imagine the stinks of this prison? Their feet were in stocks or retained and they could not go too far. Where did they use the restroom? ELOHIYM is in control because at midnight, they prayed and sang songs unto ELOHIYM and ELOHIYM **DELIVERED**. **Why would men suffer such conditions, if they did not believe in THE SON OF YAHUAH? You mean to tell me that these men would go through this, what they went through for that which is not real? Tell me would you go through these conditions for something that is not real? They were NOT preaching to become rich or for wealth or for houses or for lands or for fame? ARE YOU READY TO GIVE YOUR LIFE FOR THIS CAUSE?** If they were complaining about their circumstances or the conditions or whining about their condition, do you think ELOHIYM would have come to their rescue or deliverance? Maybe? **However,** instead of complaining, they prayed and sang praises to THE GREAT ELOHIYM of this universe. They could have complained, but complaining could have made their condition worse with their backs that had just been beaten with rods. Look, you are tied up, just imagine that you can't use your hands and you are not able to move around freely in stock. **You would be saying, "Poor little me." Pa'al and Ciyla could have said we ain't doing this no more, but they prayed and sang.** We preach and get thrown in jail and beaten. Man, we quit, but they prayed and sang. Their condition could have been worse; they could have had their legs or fingers cut off, but ELOHIYM is extremely good, so let us praise HIM for all things, when we think things are worse or things are good. It could be extremely worse than what you are going through right now. Are we going to let things control our emotions on how we are going to praise our GOD, All-Magnificent, All Sufficient, All-Generous, Most Righteous, Most Holy, All Superb and The Great ELOHIYM of creation?

I complain and whine about my circumstances. I am in a hotel writing this book. I have a bed, food, clean water, automobile, phone, air conditioning and most of all running water with a toilet. Why do I moan? I should be thankful and give YAHUAH thanks everyday. **WHY**, because **HE sees** and **knows**. **AND NOW I SAY I EXTOL YOU YAHUAH** for what you are doing for me. I appreciate **YOU** because **YOU** know and when the time is right **YOU** Will.

ELOHIYM will use sin to get HIS plan through. ELOHIYM will use sin and satan to promote HIS Name. ELOHIYM will be glorified in all things. ELOHIYM will allow us to be developed so that we may come into agreement with HIM even when this (sin) is not right. **Psalm 37:23** says," The *steps of a good man are ordered by YAHUAH: and he delights in HIS way.* David praised GOD in the death of his child." Are you a good man? Then your steps are ordered by YAHUAH. The word 'good' in this text was supplied to the original language meaning well, favour, kind, pleasant or prosperity. YAHUAH orders the steps of a man when his delight is in ELOHIYM'S Words. The only way to become a good (righteous) man in ELOHIYM is by reading, studying and obeying HIS Word. **Psalm 119:105** declares, *"Thy word is a lamp unto my feet: and a light unto my path."* **Does ELOHIYM have the ability to turn the sun off and stop the sun from rotating around the earth**? The sun is not the center of the universe. The earth does **NOT** rotate around the sun. The sun rotates around the earth. YAH placed the sun and the moon in the expanse or firmament (the edge of the sky). The sun and the moon are the same dimensions. This is the reason we can have lunar and solar eclipses. **Enoch 72:47 78:3 and 69: 28.** The earth is in a fixed position, it does not move **1 Chronicles 16:30, Psalm 93:1, 96:10 104:5 Isaiah 45:18** So, since the earth does not move and the sun rotates around the earth and we have sunset and sunrise. Will you believe YAH or man. So thereby the planets do not exist as man says. We can publish pictures and write information that does not mean it is true. Many of you are reading this and saying this can't be true from what has been told to me all these years. One of the many lies man has told us. Read the tenth chapter of Joshua (Yahusha). **Psalm 135:6** declares, *"Whatsoever YAHUAH pleased, that did HE in heaven, and in earth, in the seas, and all deep places."* **1 Corinthians 10:13** declares, *"There hath no temptation taken you but such as is common to man: but YAHUAH is faithful, who will not suffer you you to be tempted above that ye are able; but will with the temptation also make a way to escape, that ye may be able to bear it."*

ELOHIYM has ordered our steps and we are only good through what HE has done for us. ELOHIYM has placed our steps and HE has provided an escape for every temptation. There is nothing our ELOHIYM has not done for us. HE will place an escape route for us and satan cannot prevent our escape from temptation. satan cannot throw any temptation our way and ELOHIYM will make a path to escape. satan has to have permission. So, what that means YAH placed the test before you and HE have the way for you to escape. ELOHIYM is in control and not satan. ELOHIYM has HIS little finger on the control of our wheel of life.

Iyov was not aware that satan was given the opportunity to turn his heart from ELOHIYM, but we know today that satan will try to destroy you. Iyov used those obstacles or that mountain to give thanks to ELOHIYM. Even if satan were to knock you down, ELOHIYM will use that opportunity to lift you back and place your feet on solid ground because what HE will go through and there is nothing that will prevent HIS will from going through. The reason we can **EXTOL** ELOHIYM is that HIS WORD is true and HE will not lie. We are HIS children. Like your Dad or mother your child will always be your child NO MATTER what that child does. And since HE has taken the time to count each hair on your head, **HE CARES. ELOHIYM** gives HIS children commandments and NOT SUGGESTIONS. Commandments are to be followed. Would you give the same duties to two years old as thirteen years old, would you? ELOHIYM is faithful. You must believe ELOHIYM is. Since ELOHIYM is, believe what HE said because heaven and earth would pass away before HIS word would fail. Who is ELOHIYM that I should praise HIM? Has

HE been excellent in the way HE has treated me? Has HE been there in my time of need? Has HE been there when I was in jail? Has he been there in my time of trouble? Has HE been there in my homeless need? Has HE been there in my time of want? Has HE been there and I will testify YES and a HALLELUJAH! Even will it seem as if I was starving HE provided and guess what HE called it a fast. What do I have to be thankful for? Let me count the ways 1] YAHUSHA HA'MASHIACH, my ex-wives, children, grandchildren, aunts, father, mother, transportation, work, food, clean water, eyesight, walking, legs, taste buds, knowledge, wisdom, bumps, bruises, not getting shot, not getting run-over, clothing, shelter, friends, lying down, sleeping, depression, music, happiness, joy, sunshine, winter, fall, spring, summer, security, dangers unseen, money, credit cards, little pain, feelings, sound mind, groceries stores, clothing stores, my wheel not coming off on the way to work and so on. It happens; HE is always there. ELOHIYM is a great ELOHIYM and HIS excellent mercy shadows all the time and I mean ALL the time. HIS excellent mercy shows all the time. HE is responsible for my ALL in ALL.

What ELOHIYM requires is a servant. ELOHIYM requires just a servant who is willing to be molded and shaped by HIM as needed. This servant is willing to give what he has. This servant is under ELOHIYM'S hand for use. These servants who are used by ELOHIYM really do not have a choice. ELOHIYM wants someone who will give their life to HIM to be used by The MASTER of the universe. ELOHIYM has given much to us. What not let HIM shape our life? Life is so short. ELOHIYM'S will will be done. ELOHIYM can do anything but fail and lie. ELOHIYM states that HE loved man so much that HE gave HIS SON to die, so that we may live with HIM. ELOHIYM is not a man that HE will lie. It Is ELOHIYM'S plan and HE is. HALLELUJAH! Praise MASHIACH. Man, we think it is us, but it is ELOHIYM and ELOHIYM alone. HE is ELOHIYM! HalleluJAH! ELOHIYM has a plan and we are to trust HIS plan because HE HAS it all worked out. **Romans 8:28-29** declares, *"And we know all things work together for good to them that love YAHUAH, to them who are the called according to his purpose. For whom HE did foreknow, HE also did predetermine to be conformed to the image of HIS SON, that HE might be the firstborn among many brethren."*

Whatever satan plans are, ELOHIYM knows them. Whatever we plan, ELOHIYM knows them. So why do we worry? We fear, do we not know we have YAH surrounding us. **Wisdom of Shalomah 17:12** declares, *"For fear is nothing else but betraying of the helps which reason offers."*

It has become what we want and not what ELOHIYM wants? We can just believe, trust and rely on ELOHIYM that what ELOHIYM says is true. ELOHIYM is to be trusted because HIS promise is that whatsoever it is according to ELOHIYM'S Plan and not our plan. We often make the mistake thinking that this earth will be our home when ELOHIYM has declared, **Isaiah 65:17**, *"For, behold I create new heavens and a new earth: and the former shall not be remembered nor come into mind."* **Hebrews 2:5** declares, *"For unto the angels hath HE not put in subjection the world to come, whereof we speak"* **2 Kepha 3:12-13** declares, *"Looking for and hasting unto the coming of the day of YAHUAH, wherein the heavens being on fire shall be dissolved, and the elements shall melt with fervent heat? Nevertheless we, according to HIS promise, look for renewed heavens and a renewed earth, wherein dwells righteousness."* Revelation 21:1 declares, *"And I saw a renewed heaven and a renewed earth: for the first heaven and the first earth were passed away; and there were no more sea. And I Yahuchanon saw the holy city, Renewed Yerushalayim, coming down from YAHUAH out of heaven, prepared as a bride adorned for her man.*

What things are we storing up here on this earth? Our value should be placed on the coming earth. When we see THE JUDGE what are we going to declare to HIM? Because everything on this earth is corrupted. Where have you placed your value? Did you help when you could? Did you feed someone or visit someone or pray for someone or did you talk down to someone? Did you look at your brother or sister and call them the 'n' word? You see we all came from two people and after the flood 3 sons Shem Cham and Yapheth. You can believe this or not. YAHUAH is so amazing. ELOHIYM feeds the birds and they do not sow, but they are sustained. He clothes the birds. ELOHIYM knows what to do and when to do according to HIS Plan. And if you fail or fall, ELOHIYM will lift you up and dust you off and place you back on the road (if you are listening) because satan doesn't like you to stand up for YAHUAH, but YAHUAH loves us. We are in YAHUAH'S Hands and when we fail, ELOHIYM will be like a mother to nurture you and like a father to discipline you and encourage you in our daily walk, all you have to listen and remember **ALL SINS ARE FORGIVEN**. So don't dwell on that sin, but remember you are always forgiven. We can't see them, but there are angels around you. Don't be afraid to fail because ELOHIYM **SO loved us** that HE gave HIS only begotten SON for our sin. ELOHIYM has seen your failures and has already forgiven because of HIS great love. YAHUAH knows your weakness and HE is NOT surprised, but HE HAS FORGIVEN, but please do not continue because your steps are numbered. Remember the parables of the two sons? One son left, learned a lesson and returned home, and the father was there, waiting for his son to return. Who knows the father may have had people to watch over his son. The younger son did not have to even ask for forgiveness because the father was concerned for his younger son's welfare. ELOHIYM will always love us and HE states in the book of Hebrews that HE will NEVER ever never, no, not ever leave us alone and **Deuteronomy 31:6, Genesis 28:15** and

2 Baruk 78:7 declares, "*For if ye so do these things, HE will continually remember you, HE who always promised on our behalf to those who were more excellent than we, that HE will never forget or forsake us, but with much mercy will gather together again those who were dispersed.*" AMEIN and HALLELUJAH! For THE GREAT ELOHIYM to NOW and FOREVER, AMEIN!

I AM the ELOHIYM THAT LOVES
EVEN THE TIPS OF YOUR NAILS
AND THE ELOHIYM THAT CARES
FOR ALL OF HUMANKIND
AMEIN AMEIN AMEIN
PRAISE ELOHIYM FOR ALL THE BLESSINGS BELOW
PRAISE ELOHIYM'S CREATURES BELOW
PRAISE ELOHIYM FATHER, SON, AND HOLY GHOST
PRAISE ELOHIYM FROM WHOM ALL BLESSING FLOW
PRAISE ELOHIYM HEAVENLY HOST
PRAISE ELOHIYM, PRAISE ELOHIYM
AND
PRAISE ELOHIYM
FOR HE IS GREAT
HE IS GREAT
HE IS GREAT
FOREVER, FOREVER
AMEIN, AMEIN, AMEIN
HALLELUJAH TO OUR GREATER ELOHIYM
WHO IS ABLE TO MOVE MOUNTAINS

WHO IS ABLE TO MOVE RIVERS

WHO IS ABLE TO MAKE A DESERT INTO A GREAT

ARID PLACE

PRAISE ELOHIYM WHO IS ABLE TO BRING

FOOD TO THE POOR

AND WATER TO THE WATERLESS

PRAISE ELOHIYM

FATHER, SON, AND HOLY GHOST

PRAISE HIM FOREVER

AND A DAY

AND AMEIN FOREVER

A DAY TO THE

GREAT ELOHIYM TIME FOREVER

AMEIN

THANKS

It is my prayer that this book has been helpful. I pray that you love ELOHIYM and most of all, host fast to HIS WORDS. YAHUSHA HA'MASHIACH is SOON TO COME for all the saints, will go back with HIM and forever we will always be with HIM. Amein, Amein, Amein.

Do you have anything that you can EXTOL ELOHIYM for? Why? Because things could be worse.

CHAPTER 24

———— ❧ ————

Color in The Bible
We The My People in The Bible

There has been a lot of deception by those that printed or published materials and also television and movies. I am here trying to rectify or clarify those errors or misinformation by liars of the printed and published and television and movies industries or should I say corporations. Did you know that it is corporations that run this country? Everyone has heard of FICO, but did you know this is a corporation and it stands for Fair Isaac Corporation. A corporation is responsible for credit score. Anyway, we have been misled by preachers spreading false and misleading information. The majority of the people in the bible were not non-melanin but were people with color in their skin tone. You see non-melanin people want to take credit for all things. They pretend like they are the only people on this earth. Look at the paintings, statues in the Vatican. Let me first say that I said non-melanin and not white because they are not white, (let this sink in your thoughts) and you are not black, but this is a result of a lack of melanin in their system or dna. And people of color have more melanin in our DNA thereby we are very unique. Melanin determines your skin color, eyes color and hair. So quit accepting that bogus designation as black or African-American because it is wrong. **YOU ARE HEBREW!**

We the people of color that has been labeled black, African-American, Negro and Ni_ _ _ _. And everyone of these labeled are so terrible wrong because first YAH called it THE LAND OF **EDEN** and not Africa **Genesis 2:8**, second we are not black because my skin is brown and my grandson skin is much lighter than mine, third the word negro is spanish meaning black and fourth the 'n' word is so much very wrong because when you see The

172

MESSIAH on The Throne judging you, will you then say I am so sorry? You see, the majority of us in americas are Hebrews whose skin tone is melanated. You see we are NOT black! Look at a crayola box and look at the color black and place that against someone you call black and pull out the brown and look, what do you see? But we have brothers and sisters whose skin tone is so much lighter than those colors, but we are called black in the united states. In the united states we all must be color-blinded? We have been blinded by lies, lies and more lies. And we accept this wrongful designation, but it is oh so wrong! The truth which people are afraid of is the truth that we are The Hebrews ``The My People of the Bible '' of whom THE MESSIAH was born into this HEBREW NATIONALITY of this world in the spring time and not on december 25th. Avram **Genesis 14:13a** *And there came one that had escaped, and told Avram the Hebrew*; The MESSIAH was born into a Hebrew family of Yahudah. Miryam and not Mary is Hebrew and Yoceph not Joseph is Hebrew. I used is instead of was because Miryam and Yoceph are in heaven. So, YAHUSHA was born with the nationality of **HEBREW.** Pa'al is a Hebrew **Philippians 3:5.**Yoceph and not Joseph **Genesis 42:6-7** Yoseph was standing before his brothers and all his brothers saw were just Egyptians, but Yoceph knew his brothers. Mosheh **Exodus:4:6-8** of the tribe of Levi of Yashar'el. A man that is non-melanin CANNOT GET WHITER. Miryam the **12th Chapter of Numbers** turning white as leprosy. Can a person who is called white get whiter?

We are basically the color of a penny the majority of us and a penny is not black and our hue is a result of the amount of melanin in our skin tone, in which THE CREATOR did this. Did I determine how much melanin I would receive? For you see **we had no choice** and Ad-am was created from the dust of the earth and Chuah came from the rib of that first man that YAHUAH created from the dust. What color is the dust of the earth? Is a hershey chocolate bar black? We have been taught ALL of our lives that we are black and we AIN'T black. How is someone much lighter color than me called BLACK? And the people from India are darker than me. Are they called black? Because they are from India and that designation was placed us wrongfully because the ones in charge wanted to keep The Hebrews blind. Because if you come to realize how much you are loved by The FATHER who gave HIS SON to reconcile you back to HIM. And maybe just maybe you would stop this hatred of one another. The killing, robbing and defrauding one another. So, since they (The people from India) are not called black therefore there is no black race period. We need to comprehend this! We have been blinded by the composed lies of history, because the men led by satan KNEW THIS and they will and are suffering for why they **REFUSED** to tell the truth, but perpetrated those continually lies that have been around for centuries, but no one stood with courage for **TRUTH**. And we have acclimated to those lies and James Brown sang a song *"Say It Loud I am Black and I am Proud."* **I AM NOT BLACK, I AM A HEBREW (melanin in my skin tone) MAN, THAT BELIEVE THE MESSIAH DIED ON WEDNESDAY AND WAS IN THE TOMB THREE NIGHTS AND THREE DAYS (Matthew 12:40) and WAS RESURRECTED BY THE FATHER and whosoever believe this shall be saved forever, because YESHUAH (salvation) is based on WHAT THE FATHER DID and not on my works period.**

We have been told that we who have darker skin have been cursed and this curse was placed on an entire group of people of Cham not Ham as we have been told. Cham had Cush, Mizraim, Phut and Kena`an,and to say that curses were placed on this entire group is oh so wrong. This cursed was only placed on the Kena`an which was Noach's grandson who looked at him and his grandmother (and you thought Noach was in the tent by himself, no baby) who were both naked in the tent and because in the book of Jubilees the earth was divided among the brothers and Kena'aniym went into Shem's territory and Kena`an brothers tried to warn him, but as he was when he was young would not listen. If we fail to get the rightful information and the full information, we will get the wrong idea about everything we have learned, which leads to a corrupt society taking their bad idea on wrong information. Do you not realize that everyone on this earth is related to one another because we all came from just one seed, but there are those who are expressing a false narrative. Just like preachers preaching riches is not to be for all because THE MESSIAH said the poor will always be with you. And whosoever HE blessed HE will because it is HIS will and not our will because HE is in control of all and so preachers STOP this false narrative. This ideological or narrative is so very far from the truth. It is a down right deception. Israel is not on the Middle East continent. There is no such thing as the Middle East continent. It doesn't exist. This was all made up. Israel is on the Eden or Alkebulan continent. You see this is not taught in schools. This curse was placed on Kena`an only and not Cham. Cham had three more sons and one of the sons still stands today and his name is Mitsrayim. It was a curse for the color to leave your body in The Old Testament. That was a curse and you had to leave camp. Look at Miryam and Mosheh skin turning and Naaman. You lost your skin color and all around you looked like a penny in color, oh no, you had to go. The **"my people"** in the bible are people with various hues in their skin tone. We are from very light to very dark skin. The word 'My' means ownership. We are the true Israelites of the Bible born to the Shem line. YAH is our GOD and we are HIS people. **Exodus 3:18** says "YAHUAH ELOHAI of The Hebrews" And The Bible says **YAH is THE VERY SAME TODAY and FOREVER. HE DOES NOT CHANGE. HE IS CHANGELESS or UNCHANGEABLE of HIS NATURE for HE cannot lie. So thereby HE is still The HEBREW'S GOD.** Many will struggle but HE states in **Yahuchanon 10** There shall be one fold and one Shepherd. Many will say, "This can't be, oh no, what and so on" because what you will read has never been explained to most of the general public because we have been misguided by lies. And this is the point of this book is to awaken your eyes to what you have been informed from this worldly deception and many will see **the truth**, but most won't accept this as truth.

It has always been the agenda of man to place emphasis over one man and should not be because of color because we don't have a choice of how we come out of the womb and who our parents are? We are ALL brothers and sisters. The non-colored people are in pictures, in all of the movies, placing themselves in the role of chieftain and these roles emphasize the non-colored, but it should be a person of color. When this is done this brings the wrong image of the truth. A picture can be worth a thousand words. I am attempting to set the record correct. Some people may say color doesn't matter or say "I don't see color." So would you eat a black orange or a black apple? So if the answer is yes, please tell the truth. ELOHIYM created man in HIS Image and after HIS likeness and no more and no less. In some translations

Jeremiah 8:21 declares, *"I am black;"* in some versions this has been changed. What happened, someone read this and changed it in their versions and some people will just simply explain this away, but in my version it says just that. ELOHIYM created man, just a man, not a man non-colored or man colored, but simply a man. In the United States emphasis is placed on the adjective and in the Spanish language more emphasis is placed on the noun. So in the United States we would say green tree and in Spanish it is tree green. We men of color have the same desire and that will be in a poem at the end of this chapter. The Cepher Bible declares

Psalm 8:4 declares, *"What is man, that YOU are mindful of him? And the son of Adam, that YOU visit him. For YOU have made him a little lower than ELOHIYM, and have crowned him with glory and honour.* ELOHIYM loves ALL and the color does not matter and HE is not a respecter of any of those who does not follow HIS Word. ELOHIYM deals with each man in HIS way. ELOHIYM'S way is the truth. We (men) have placed so much emphasis on color that is a disgrace to this world. You see, we will ALL be judged by HIS SON and what are we going to say? Because ALL need HIS Mercy and Grace. When you see THE SON when judgment time comes and you see GOD YAHUSHA and HIS skin tone is dark like mine what are you going to say? You see HIS mother was Miryam, a Hebrew of the tribe of Yahudah of the nation of Yashar'el and you thought these people looked like they are in the nation Israel today? This has been a deception led by the house of satan.

It has already been proven that in this present world every woman in the world has the DNA of the original woman who was found in Eden, a person of <u>color</u>. So if the first woman was colored, the first man had to be colored also because **THE FIRST WOMAN** came from **THE FIRST MAN'S RIB**. So why can't we accept the fact that we are ALL sisters and brothers because this is the way YAH has formed it. DO YOU BELIEVE YAH? It is YAH that has created because we were not formed from an amoeba or we evolved from apes because apes are still walking around today. Shem Cham and Yapheth, the sons of Noach, have produced what we see today. Can a husband and wife of the same hue produce children of different hue? I will let you answer that question. And this is the problem with the non-melanated man producing anything except his own hue? And this is a problem when his sister or his non-melanated women crosses over his non-melanated appearance he would be wiped out. ELOHIYM is the ELOHIYM of all flesh. **Jeremiah 32:27** states, *"Behold, I am YAHUAH, the ELOHAI of all flesh: is there anything too hard for me?"* HE is not just the ELOHIYM of the man melanated and man non-melanated. HE is the GOD of all men.

So when Hollywood makes movies and the movies display people not of the correct hue, it distorts the true picture entirely in the minds of people. Therefore, Hollywood, when you do that what are the psychological damage done. It destroys hope and trust of what you present. Can a man of color play Charles Manson? Hollywood you cannot constantly take actors that are non-melanated or actresses that are non-melanated and place them in the roles of people that are melanated. You got a group of people thinking WRONGLY but your effort to disguise truth has failed. Hollywood placed Charleston Heston in the movie as Mosheh and Mosheh has melanin in skin tone. So people think Mosheh is non-melanated. Every movie I have seen about YAHUSHA, HE is non-colored and has straight hair and probably blue eyes. In the movie, *The Ten Commandments,* the major actors were non-colored. We know now Mosheh was a man of color. What type of effect would have a people to know the truth? All children grow up with very bad idealism (believing a lie) thinking the people in that area were non-color. This DESTROYS a person's attitude. What type of physiological damage has **THIS** done to our people's behavior? If all you saw in your life were people living in their castle and you are living in your tent but you are the one that is supposed to live in the castle, what would that do to your thinking? All your life these images are suppressed into your brain, the very consciousness each and every day. How would you be? What would your state of mind be? I forgot you are not trying to educate? There is a saying "What you see you become." This information is implanted in the mind to people you have engaged for many hours. Pictures to brainwash a population into stinky and false thinking and we are engraved with this stinky thinking. Tarzan, the non-colored man in the jungle, was able to control the elephants, gorillas and chimps. On the television show *Dallas*, how many people of color did you see? Your industry reap at a very high level. It is like I was told the other day that the veins in your body move and I am 68 years of age and just found that out and it is all because I did not have the training and was not taught, but guess what NOW I know and you know because someone has told you.

All of this fantasy has created an emotional depression on an entire nationality of people that are blind to know their true identity, but ELOHIYM is NOW awakening HIS People. You see we are the MY people in the bible. The people with melanin in our skin tone are The Hebrews The Israelites who are here in the Americas, Australia, The Islands and the British Isles. YAHUAH awakens HIS people to true. We have been misled by satan's house for so long. Many thought The Holocast happened to the so-called jews who were not the true jews. The Holocast happened when our foreparents were trapped on those filthy nasty slave ships. Just imagine those conditions and you are going to tell me that it was not a holocast? **Please! Chained up together and unable to go to the bathroom and it was stinky (feces were everywhere and lying next to a dead body and they were in these conditions for up to four months).** satan has placed this world under his guise. Well, the mask is finally off. Even in the movie *The Bible,* every leading character was non-color, when the people of that land are of totally different hue. Can Morgan Freeman play the role of President John Fitzgerald Kennedy in his life story? This is what you have done, Hollywood. In today's America, we have a group of people that we do not know our true identity. We have been disguised in untruthfulness and preachers today have failed to properly correct this information and this society just shrugs it off and keeps moving in the wrong direction.

Can we get people to acknowledge the lie that has been covered up all these years that we the people whose foreparents were chained and shipped to the americas are The MY people in The Bible. Oh as The Bible says *let justice roll down as waters, and righteousness as a mighty stream.* You see we have been groped into darkness, but YAH is opening our eyes to HIS truth and righteousness. We take on the identity (names) of those around us and not realize who we are in this present world. I did mention names because why did the slave master almost kill Kunta Kinte because he did not want to take the slave name Toby? This is a tragedy ELOHIYM told our forefathers, that HE would scatter us through the world for disobeying HIS Word and now we do not realize who we are, a lost nation in the americas. Our sons grow up not knowing that as the truth is hidden and we are killing our brothers and raping our sisters because the truth has been hidden from our heart. Men and women on the street do not know that YAH has a special love for you, but you turn back on YAH and let the devastation of the street rob your brain and you die not knowing The Love of YAH for you. You are the very natural children of our father Avraham. We are kept further from the truth. ELOHIYM states in **Psalm 78**, *Who will teach our children when the truth is hidden from their eyes?* And as long as the truth is hidden, we will be further from the truth like the clouds when gathering for a great storm.

Let me ask a question. Can a non-melanated man become more non-melanated? Let me ask again. Can a non-melanated man become more non-melanated? The answer to the question is no. So I ask the question, how did Pharaoh's daughter present Mosheeh as her son to Pharaoh? And this we know that the Egyptians are dark-skinned. This is one reason Napoleon had the noses of the Egyptian's statues shot off. **Exodus 4:6-7** declares. *"And YAHUAH said furthermore unto him, Put now your hand into your bosom. And he put his hand into his bosom and when he took it out, behold, his hand was lepreous as snow. And he said, Put your hand into your bosom again; and plucked it out of his bosom, and, behold, it was turned again as his other flesh.*

What happened? Mosheh 's hand was turned non-melanated as snow. Can the non-melanated man become more non-melanated? Then he placed his hand back into his bosom and it became the color of his other flesh. Would Pharaoh have questioned his daughter if she brought in a baby that was non-color into his house? Come on now. Let's get really real. Would you not wonder that your daughter is a person of color and your husband is a person of color and the baby is non-melanated?

The Garden of Eden, where is it? The answer is Eden or Alkebulan. This was no small garden. The Bible declares that a river went out of Eden to water the garden and from there, it was parted and became into four heads. In the KJV, the names are in English. So why did KJV transposed the names into English instead of leaving the names in Hebrews? So I ask a question. **<u>Why was the truth hidden from our eyes and lies has been perpetrated as the truth?</u>** You see these people that we talk about the most in the bible are Hebrews, people of color. The twelve sons of Ya`aqov Hebrews and not English. John the baptizer's name is Yahuchanon. Yahuchanon is Hebrew. Jesus who died on the cross is not Grecians. His mother's name is Miryam and not Mary, a Hebrew. All the Apostles including Pa'al, Hebrews. The Son of YAH was born to a Hebrew's mother which makes HIS nationality **Hebrew.** When you **REJECT, you will continue to believe the lies that He was non-melanated. You can still deny the truth and believe the lie you have been told all these years, but do not disavow THE TRUTH.** Why are you so afraid of THE TRUTH? I know the Bible says man loves darkness more than light, but come into the light because there is warmth in the light and peace. You see we ALL came from one man. There are many reasons for conditional thinking: pride, ignorance, dominance, prejudice, lust, wars, hunger, divisiveness and just plain ole sin. No race is dominant because we all want the same thing. All of this fantasy of today. You see there were no words that start with letter j until after 1600. The letter j was formed in 1524. So any word starting with the letter j is a little over 498 years old. The so-called Jew of today came from where? The word 'Jews' comes from the word 'Judah', this is the fourth son of Israel a Hebrew. We have a tendency to abbreviate names: thereby we would say Ju and the enunciation of all words and create another word. Since **Mosheh** is a person of color, a Hebrew, that means his <u>father</u> **Amram** a Hebrew (person of color); his <u>grandfather</u> **Kohath** a Hebrew (person of color); his <u>great-grandfather</u> **Levi** a Hebrew (person of color); his great-great-grandfather **Yashar'el (Ya`aqov)** a Hebrew (person of color); his great-great-great-grandfather **Yitschaq** a Hebrew (person of color); his great-great-great-great grandfather **Avraham** a Hebrew (person of color); **Genesis 14:13.** We must admit that this entire land of Eden is full of people of different hues and not just non-melanated.

Art teachers have stated that white is the absence of color, but black is also the absence of color. Why do non-colored people tan? That process started many years ago and now I hear of skin cancer. Have you ever asked your parents that question? Why do we tan? But as a Hebrew man the sun is good for our being. We soak in the hormones of the sun and it helps our very well being. Watch "https://fb.watch/9EPz2RuQeL/ and you may be surprised by this **TRUTH.** You see, YAH has made us different from all other people. HE specifically gave us this hue or melanin, in which it created our hue and for a reason before the creation of the universe and people see us as dangerous, but it is YAH that has made us and we **DIDN'T** make ourselves. My skin tone and my brownness is first the result of what THE CREATOR wanted and my parents coming together as one. Why is the non-melanated man so afraid of a person of my skin tone? All I want is what the non-melanated want, peace. And whatever provides you peace, seek, but do not harm your brother because YAH created man in HIS Image.

Where did the non-melanated nation come from? Who knows but ELOHIYM? There are many assumptions in which I will not go into that because that is not my field of information. Gehazi, a servant of Eliysha, received gifts from Na`aman (who had leprosy) after the leprosy was gone from Na`aman and Eliysha asked Gehazi where he had been? Gehazi was greedy and covetous and because of this, he and his seed were **CURSED** with having non-melanated skin forever. Leprosy is not a fright for the non-melanin man because his skin is already non-melanated. It is a fright for people of colored skin and not non-colored skin. **2 Kings 5:27** declares, *"The leprosy therefore of Na'aman shall cleave unto you, and unto your seed forever. And he went out from his presence a leper as white as snow."*

When ELOHIYM says forever, HE means forever.

Genesis 3:14 says, *"And YAHUAH ELOHIYM said unto the serpent, because you have done this, you are cursed above all cattle, and above every beast of the field; upon your belly shall you go, and dust shall you eat all the days of your life:*

Yesha`yahu 65:17 declares, *"For, behold, I created renewed heavens and a renewed earth: and the former shall not be remembered, nor come into mind.*

And this is continually of that same passage where the dust shall be the serpent meat forever.

Yesha`yahu 65:25 states, *"The wolf and the lamb shall feed together, and the lion shall eat straw like the bullock: and dust shall the serpent's meat."*

Non-colored people should not be afraid of becoming non-melanated. As you can read; What did leprosy do to the skin? Their skin becomes non-melanated. Their skin becomes non-melanated. Miryam, Mosheh's sister, talked against Moseh because of his woman, and because of this, her skin became leprosy, white as snow. **Numbers 12:10** states, *"And the* *cloud departed from off the Tabernacle; and, **behold**, Miryam became leprous, white as snow: and Aharon looked upon Miryam, and, **behold, she was leprous.***

If her skin became white as snow, then she HAD TO BE of a dark skin and not as she is pictured in the movie "The Ten Commandments"? What are you going to believe, what is true, **THE WORD OF YAH** or the lies of pictures done by a deceptive and crookedness of man?

Pa'al was called an Egyptian in **Acts 21:38**. Pa'al called himself in **Philippians 3:5**

1) Yashar'el 2) Binyamiyn 3) Hebrew of Hebrews (Pa'al never declared in the scriptures that he was a christian). This is the truth. This is The Word of ELOHIYM. Ad-am was formed from the dust of the earth **Genesis 2:7** says, *"And YAHUAH ELOHIYM formed the man of the dust of the ground, and breathed into his nostrils the breath of life; and the man became a living soul."* Now man was formed from the dust of the earth, the answer is yes. What color is the dust of the earth? What color is the dust of the earth? I will let you stew on that question and let you think what color is the dust of the earth. The ELOHIYM I serve is the ELOHIYM of all flesh. He has no respect for people but loves each one of us, but ELOHIYM loves Yashar'el; HE loves Israel so much HE died to regain Yashar'el again! Hallelu**JAH**. Read, **Deuteronomy 24:1-4** made it impossible for ELOHIYM to marry Yashar'el again. If He did that it would violate the law HE wrote and if He violated His law then heaven and earth would disappear. So ELOHIYM died and became a new man so HE could marry Yashar'el His bride again. I told this to a friend of mine and he just simply shrugged it off and this is as Hosea said MY People **REJECTED KNOWLEDGE.** People please don't reject knowledge as the song said I am on my knees. Acquaintance said to me "People pay for ignorance." Man, have we paid for ignorance. Man can't get along, why? This is oh so true because if you could remodel things, you save money, but because of lack of knowledge, you pay for someone else to do it right. Ignorance is simply not nothing, but stupidity is on a different level. You see your low level gasoline light on and you go and run out of gas and then what is the price? Now that is stupid.

As far as the Cham's curse; it was on Kena`an and not his father. **Genesis 9:25** declares, *"And he said, Cursed be Kena`an; a servant of servants shall he be unto his brethren."* You see Kena`an stole this land and called it the land of Kena`an. **Genesis 9:24** declares, *"And Noach awoke from his wine, and knew what his younger son had done unto him."* There is some descriptive of who Noach's younger son is, **Genesis 6:10** Shem, Cham and Yapheth, but

Yasher 5:18 states Cham to be the youngest, but this verse is referring to his grandson Kena`an. Noach grandson Kena`an and not Cham. Do I have your attention misinformation and those providing false and misleading collaborators of truth? This is the reason Kena`an was **CURSED**. Kena`an saw his grandfather's nakedness. What is man nakedness? It is his woman. Where is that found? In The Book of Leviticus chapter 18. **Leviticus 18:7** declares, *"The nakedness of your father, or the nakedness of your mother shall you NOT uncover: she is your mother; you shall not uncover her nakedness."* Now do we have complete information or full disclosure. Noach and Na`amah his woman **(Yasher 5:15)** were in the tent. And you thought Noach was in the tent by himself. Did you forget Noach had a woman (I am using woman instead of wife because husband and wife are legal terms belonging to man's law and man's law does not overturn GOD's Law and many will say why aren't you following the law of the land because no where is the law of this land you have to buy a license to be one and for this is the reason The Messiah told the woman you have had five husbands. There were no marriage licenses back then and when a man and women joined their body together they became one. Man's view and YAH's view are completely opposite to one another. Men look at marriage, when we get the piece of paper, then we are married, but YAH looks at it when you join each other as one. Not man and man and not woman and woman, but man and woman. The other is simply wrong. So many of us thought we have never been married just once, but when you joined your body to that first woman that was your first woman or man and this will be debated, but YAH has the final say. Oh how we have been deceived. Na`amah was sleeping next to her man and after consuming all that wine they both passed out and after waking up Noach knew what Kena`an had done and Noach cursed his grandson. Kena`an showed no respect, but looked and laughed and disrespected his grandparents lying naked together and this was the cause of the curse on Kena`an. Cham had three other sons Cush, Mizraim and Phut. Out of all his descendants, there is one great nation that we know of today, The nation of Egypt (Mitsrayim). All of these years it has been stated the curse of Cham, but that is so very wrong, but the curse of Kena`an. Egypt still stands today. So if it was the curse of Cham, why is Egypt still here today? Because of The ELOHIYM'S Sovereign reign. HIS Will, will be done. Amein.

What is the nakedness of man? It is his wife and not himself as defined by The Bible. **Leviticus 18:8** states, *"The nakedness of thy father's wife thou shall not uncover: it is <u>thy father's nakedness.</u>"* So, what Kena`an saw was his grandmother nakedness, his grandmother nakedness, his grandmother nakedness and one more time his grandmother nakedness. If you have any further questions ask ELOHIYM. **Deuteronomy 28:68** declares, *"And YAHUAH shall bring you into Mitsrayim again with ships, by the way whereof I spoke unto you, you shall see it no more again: and there ye shall be sold unto your enemies for bondmen and bondwomen, and no man shall buy you."* Who did this happen to? This was the spiritual meaning of this not the actual Egypt but the americas instead and the word buy means to redeem and this verse along with **Genesis 15:13-14** happened to our foreparents who were shipped or kidnapped from The Land of Eden on those filthy nasty ships and the journey could take from 4 weeks to 4 months. Who did this happen to? We were in bondage starting in 1611 the first group of Hebrews shipped and it ended in 2019. 2019-1619 =400 years and now we are awaiting the Exodus from the americas in which I believe is The Rapture, but some don't believe, but look at our world today because man is mandating vaccines which is leading to the man of sin taking over operations and many fail to see the sign, but are encouraging to pledge their allegiance to the beast by taking the injection and implanting chips so that they may buy and sell. Men and women chained together not for a day but maybe up to 4 months and nowhere to potty, except on themselves. The voyage of the great Atlantic Ocean to the new Egypt (The USA) as YAH had promised in HIS Word. **<u>DO I need to say more?</u>**

<u>Here is a poem.</u>

Blackman Why

I ask this question and maybe you can tell me!

Why canst I be considered a man?

Why as a man black am I hated so badly?

Is it because of the skin I have or the hair on top of my head?

Is it because of the ability to jump, run, and dunk?

Why am I chased around and hated even among my very own?

Why am I looked upon as the "N" in some blue eyes in this world?

Why as a man black must I be the disgust in the eyes of some,

Where they will just simply spit on, curse, hang, drag, and burn for the pleasure of a few?

Why as a man black must I seek ways to prove I am a man?

Why as man black must I be labeled as hate?

In addition, when I lose the color of my skin, am I a man, even without the pigmentation of this skin and hair on my head?

Don't I look like your brother on the other side of our world?

As a man black, you see I desire the same as you.

"What's that you say?"

PEACE, HAPPINESS, SECURITY, and PROSPERITY.

This is all man that a man should seek!

The Jews who called themselves Jews today are not. First their foreparents were not in Egypt. Their skin tone is already white and can't become whiter. Just check the record. The word Jew is only about 498 years old because the letter j was not formed until 1524. The word Jew comes from the word Judah. When you shorten the saying you would say Ju. All Jews must prove what tribe of Israel they are from according to **Ezra 2:62** *"These sought their register among those that were reckoned by genealogy, but they were not found: therefore were they, as polluted, put from the priesthood."* There is no way the Jews of today can prove their inheritance to tell what tribes of Israel they are from. Jews today are still people of color. You may say I can't prove it also, no I can't but I can say that I am Hebrew/Yashar'el. Hebrews are people of **COLOR**. Why is Pa'al thought to be an Egyptian **Acts 21:38** and **Philippians 3:5** he states 'I am Hebrew of Hebrews', but the movies showed him to have no color in his skin tone. The record have been covered up, but on youtube someone had the names of the people that were shipped on those slave ships. Remember what YAH said in **Deuteronomy 28:64,68**. Our foreparents were shipped on those filthy nasty slave ships the greatest holocaust that happen to our people **The HEBREWS. And the news media DON'T even talk about this.** In school they (the ones in charge) want to cover these tracks by not teaching or telling the truth by insisting that it did not happen by not teaching about "The Critical Race Theory ". This is so much of a cop-out. Just tell the truth and it will set you free from bondage.

Acts 6:9 declares, *"Then there arose certain of the synagogue of the Libertines, and Cyyrenians."* (Northern Eden)

Luke 23:26 states, *"And as they led HIM away, they laid hold upon Shim`on, a Cyrenian."* (Northern Eden)

Acts 13:1 says, *"Now there were in the church that was at Antioch certain prophets and teachers; as Bar-Naviy, and Shim`on that was called Niger, and Lucius of Cyrene.* (Northern Eden)

ELOHIYM'S covenants are forever. Are we still under the law covenants as some think? If we are still under the law covenant it would require us to bring a sheep or goat or oxen to sacrifice for our sins and when THE SON died that covenant is over, but the promises of YAH are forever. If you are trying to live under the law then you would have to take off an entire year and not work because **THE LAW** required THAT **Leviticus 25:3-4, 8**. So If you call yourself following THE LAW and any that break THE LAW REQUIRES you to provide a penalty for breaking THE LAW. Look at the man in **Number 15:32** all he was doing was picking up sticks on The Shabbath and for doing that, that man lost his life for picking up sticks on The Shabbath. There was **NO EXCEPTION PROVIDED**. The Law, you either follow it whole or you are guilty of death and you are going to present yourself as having fully followed The Law, you will be found GUILTY, but my freedom is not following The Law but by what YAHUSHA did was take away the penalty and death. My YESHUAH is based on what HE did by dying on THE CROSS and coming alive again after THREE NIGHTS and THREE DAYS in the tomb and this is the LAW I FOLLOW because HE did that for man to be received of ELOHIYM. What He has stated will not be voided or phased away (**Yesha`yahu 55:11**). We will see ADONAI YAHUSHA HA'MASHIACH and know that it is YAHUSHA because HE will forever wear the nail-pierced, scarred hand and feet and side. We who are the true Israelites will forever be under the covenant of ELOHIYM has stated. We want to separate ELOHIYM'S Word, but ELOHIYM'S Word is the truth. Since ELOHIYM'S covenant doesn't fail but continues, we are to follow HIS WORD until it is fulfilled. **Deuteronomy 32:47** declares, *"For it is not a vain thing for you; because it is your life: and through this thing ye shall prolong your days in the land, whither ye go over Yardan to possess it."* ELOHIYM'S promises are as HE has stated and it will not be destroyed. Maybe this is the reason the seeds of Avram should stay away from pork because pork meat was forbidden for the Israelites to eat according to ELOHIYM's Law, but Pa`al stated by THE RUACH HA'QODESH to pray over all things because in it the book of Acts YAH has blessed all food. Too much of anything is not good.

In conclusion, non-melanated man, why do you exclude the true seeds of Yashar'el **The MY People** from all pictures of Israel out of ELOHIYM'S HOLY WORD and Hollywood images and give the entire truth of your evil and satanic agenda? Do you not know and realize that to curse Avraham seeds is a curse will be upon thou head also? And that curse shall be worse because on an apple tree there are apples and in those apples there are seeds. I have two questions: Why do non-color people tan and where does this idea of tanning your skin to become darker come from? Huh! Pa'al was asked if he was that Egyptian who caused all that trouble. Why was Pa'al asked a question like that if he was not of dark skin tone? Maybe Pa'al skin tone was that of a penny. Guess what a penny is not black. The majority of you would say copper. And copper is shiny brown, but we in The United States of America that are darker hue (not white) are labeled as black or African-American and are not black and why are the people from India not labeled black also. Black is not a race, it is color. And some that called themselves white want to be color blind. You are so sad because if I placed a black orange or green orange in your face, you would not eat it! And you say I don't see color. If you don't see color that means you are surely color blind. We who foreparents were shipped on those slave ships are the direct descendant of Avraham our great forefather of faith. Charlie Theron is an African-American because she was born in the continent so-called South Africa. **Acts 21:37-39** says, *"And as Pa'al was to be led into the castle, he said unto the chief captain, May I speak unto thee? Who said, Canst thou speak Greek? Art thou that Egyptian, which before these days madest an uproar, and leddest out into the wilderness four thousand men that were murderers? But Pa'al said, I am a man which am a Yahudiy of Tarsus."*

If we were to go back and look at your parents, grandparents, great-grandparents, great-great-grandparents and so on you would see your skin tone down in that line. If Cham and Shem are dark-toned what would be Noach skin tone or his parents skin tone? What would be Noach's father, grandfather, great grandfather, great-great-grandfather and great-great-great grandfather? You can answer that question.

This world system has been deceived by satan and his imps and he has placed a scale over the eyes of men that we cannot see what is true. The truth will set you free. Let's go out and marvel over the wondrous work of ELOHIYM and what HE has made for us the earth and the fullness thereof. There is enough of the earth for all of us to enjoy. The world is in a state of confusion because we key on such little things, not wanting to share what we have.

Muhammad Ali states that "If I you called Mr Chin and when he comes you will see he is Orientral and if you say Mr Rodriguez you will see he is Hispanic, but if you say Mr Brown you will have to wait and see if that person is melanated or non-melanated."

My six year old grandson stated, "I am not black!" Nevertheless, I was surprised, stunned, shocked and amazed at his wisdom. I said, "Wow!" He had the courage to say "I am not black." I was thinking about this before he spoke. You see his skin tone is very light and we who are calling each other black need to pay attention because to this and as India Arie said in a song brown skin and Eric Benet chocolate legs. You see we are NOT black, but we have been claiming this for years. WAKE-UP. There is no such thing as a black nation. We are HEBREW NATION. So on those applications put down HEBREW. For we are not black. We are not African-American. We not negro. We are not the nigg _ _ _. We are **THE MY PEOPLE IN THE BIBLE**. The ones that YAH led across the Red Sea, David the king of Yashar'el, Mosheh who led us to the promise land, the ones that Yahusha took over Mosheh, Shalomah who took over from David his father, Shimshon, who committed suicide, but taking down more Philistines in his death, and people who were shipped to the americas whom YAH divorced and remarried because HIS SON died and arose from the tomb after three nights and three days in the tomb and now the 400 years are ended, we are now awaiting for **The EXODUS** from the americas. This society (the non-colored) has treated us less than their household dog. THIS IS A TRAGEDY FOR THIS NON-MELANATED SOCIETY. For we are not black, but various hues from light to dark brown. We are The My People in The Bible. There are some people awakening to this truth, but the vast majority are asleep at the wheel heading into a danger zone. The non-melanated generation has stolen our identity to make themselves the Jesus, Mosheh, Jeremiah etc in the movies, pictures, television shows, books and coloring books. YAH is awakening HIS People for we who are copper tone the color of a penny and any other various hue are HIS People. You will see that we are of various shades. Why, because the non-melanated man has raped our females and place his seeds inside of our female womb and have produce children that are lighter skin and lighter coloreyes. The people in Israel are not the nation that left there. The people that left there are people of color and as the Bible says in Revelation fake Jews. We the people of color are the one in the Bible who are the true Yashar'el. The Bible prophesied about our foreparents coming to the americas. Look at this nation being punished. Covid 19 is shutting down every major event in the USA. The USA will lose billions of dollars because of covid 19. If you look at a penny it is not black, but brown. Why have you (non-melanated man) labeled me as black when in REALITY I am brown. The same color as a penny. So, please don't list me as black, African-America, negro, color or ni_ _ _ r for I now and always will be labeled as Hebrew. And the word Africa comes from a Roman general named Scipio Africanus. And my skin tone is brown and not black. Black has no status under the law. Who labeled us as black anyway and we just accepted that as right. Well it is wrong! If you look at my skin tone, it is not black and our own brother and sister will downgrade one another by calling each other nigg_ _. **STOP THAT! THIS IS PITIFUL. Did you not learn this at home? It is degrading. It has no value and we are brothers and sisters. You see, not all brown skin people came from one father who is Ya`aqov. There are many of us WHO come from one father Ya`aqov better known as Jacob. Ya`aqov who is the father of the twelve tribes of Yashar'el (12 sons and one daughter and four different mothers) are calling each other the word N _ _ _ _ _ or Nig_ a. You should regret this but it is happening. So what are you going to do when you see THE SON OF YAH and HIS complexion look like you? Are you going today hi N _ _ _ _ _? Just think before you say that word to your sister and brother because our CHILDREN are repeating what you are saying because that word is a curse and not a blessing and now I drop the mic, so it be or Amein! Because many of our brothers and sisters are still under the slave mentality! If you don't like this just beware that you will be judged for whatever comes out of your heart (mouth) Yahuchanon 5:22. What are you going to say? What is your escape because you will be there before HIM that has the same skin tone as you?** If you look at my skin tone it is not black. My skin tone and for most of us who have been labeled black, is actually copper or another hue much lighter. It is the same color of a penny. Is a penny black? Look at the color of a penny and place it on your skin or on my skin and you will see you are not black but brown. Most of the people you see that are called black are brown. Most are called black by who? Let's think this through. We have been deceived by who? Guess? Everything we have been told is through deception and deceit. Who told you what? We have been in deception since we have been in the USA over four hundred years. Our names are not the names given us. Our language and history has been construed. Our history was stolen by those slave ships over four hundred years ago and we had lived in deception by people who are not telling us THE TRUTH. We have been led by a man who knows WHO WE ARE. Our preachers have been told a lie and they teach us that lie to us. We ARE the people of Israel, Hebrews in a strange land and unknown language, from the land of Eden. The non-color **REFUSED** to inform us who we are. They have kept this DECEPTION from us, but YAH is awakening HIS PEOPLE. This is YAH METHODOLOGY. YAH is all about timing. Sarah had Yitschaq at a particular time because David had to be born at just the right (you see David had to face Goliath and so on, do you see what I mean) time and it is all in HIS TIMING and not man's timing. I had to be born to do this **BOOK** at this **TIME.** It is **ALL ABOUT THE CREATOR TIME.** Ya`aqov, Shalomah, Pa`al, Yahusha, etc had to be born at a specific time for things to be done at YAH's time. The SON had to be born and die at a specific time and date. He had to die on a specific date because HE had to spend 3 nights and 3 days in the tomb and rise again because HE was **THE PASSOVER'S Lamb. Read what happened to the lamb during passover. The lamb had to be without spot or blemish and it started on the tenth day of nisan.** As the Bible states, Israel has stumbled so the other nations could come into Israel, but the other nations' reign is coming to an end and we, THE ISRAELITES will be set free. HA'MASHIACH is. We are The MY PEOPLE of The Bible. The Apostles are Hebrews men.

Open your eyes and see. Don't be like the preachers who are preaching THE WORD but refuse to believe what they are preaching. Preaching YAH'S WORD but refusing to believe The WORD that is coming out of their mouth. We are "The MY People in The Bible. Some still won't get this truth, but are stuck in their mind-set of what they have been taught and refusing to see THE TRUTH of YAH'S WORD, THE SON OF ELOHIYM is coming for Yashar`el and the gentiles or other nations who have been grafted into Yashar`el. Take this to heart and believe that THE WORD OF YAH IS TRUE. We were the one who fulfilled the curses in Deuteronomy. We are the one whom YAH will fulfill **Genesis 15:13-14**. The non-color people who refused to see the destruction that is coming to the United States of America will be fulfilled by THE CREATOR of this universe, THE ELOHIYM (FATHER,SON, RUACH HA'QODESH THE GOD OF THE HEBREWS **(Exodus 3:18)**.

Being enslaved for four hundred years, how would that change a group of people? Language, culture, dress, lifestyle, name, food, GOD (religion). HOW DO YOU SEE YOURSELF! All of this has happened because **WE ARE THE MY PEOPLE OF THE BIBLE!** Our ancestors were called by the name of **YAH**, Mattith**YAH**u, **YAH**uchanon, **YAH**USHA, Yesha**YAH**u, Yirme**YAH**u, Zakar**YAH**u and Nechem**YAH**u. Our forefathers refused to follow THE LAW, so ELOHIYM devised another way. HE saw this before the foundation of earth began. So love YAH first and then your neighbors (brothers and sisters from another mother) for we the people who have been raped, wasted, defrauded, conned, fornicated, defeated, trounced, lese majesty, pissed on, rejected, misguided, uneducated, missed educated, misinformed, dealt harshly, treated very unfairly, treated like orphan stepchildren, degraded, criticized, mocked, spitted on, hanged, criminalized, tormented, despised, dehumanized, lied to, mistreated, looked down on, degraded, misrepresented, immortalized, justice not given equally, treated like a mongrel dog, brutalized, terrorized, unsatisfied, dragged through the garbage, oppressed, taken away, undignified, just dogged out and any other unimaginable thing that comes to their mind for our lack of knowledge of our GOD. HE IS THE GREAT I AM. THINGS COME TRUE WHEN HE SAYS SO. No one can do this. ELOHIYM ALONE HAS THAT POWER AND AUTHORITY. All this degrading because of the color of my skin of which I did not create the color of my skin, but THE ADONAI GOD CREATOR did. HE, who has made this wonderful skin of who I am. GOD chose this beautiful brown skin tone that you non-color so desire in your heart. And you think THE ADONAI GOD WILL NOT AVENGE THE PEOPLE HE LOVES for the ways you have treated us! PLEASE DON'T FOOL YOURSELF, FOR I WILL AVENGE THEM THAT LOVES ME ADONAI ELOHIYM! Amein

People have tried to restrain MY PEOPLE from their knowledge, but THE GREAT I AM (EHAYAH ASHER EHAYAH) alone is awakening our hearts, eyes and minds to HIM. MY People have been destroyed, wasted, deformed for a lack of knowledge of HIM because they have **REJECTED that knowledge.** For ELOHIYM has always been **THE GOD OF THE HEBREW** people **(Exodus 3:18, 5:3)**. Esau I hate, but Israel I Love so, say ELOHIYM's Word. Awake, O Israel, to the knowledge of who you are. Amein! Amein! Awake, O sleeping Israel, to this, for you have been raped, wasting and wandering in the wilderness of sin. ELOHIYM will awaken your eyes and your hearts and see I AM your ELOHIYM, THE GOD of The People I love and always will love says, YAH always. Don't listen to those bastards, for I will spew them out of my mouth and they shall be away from you ETERNITY to ETERNITY. Men with men, men with boys, women with women, women with girls this should not be among ELOHIYM's People, but it is. These are not YAH ways. YAH did not authorize this behavior. **Men**, teach your children to be men and women of GOD. Seek ELOHIYM WAYS and not the ways of other nations. Seek ELOHIYM and find YESHUAH (SALVATION) and peace. Amein.

ALL I WANT IS THE TRUTH

The CREATOR IS NOT CAPABLE OF OR SUSCEPTIBLE TO CHANGE (**Hebrews 6:17-18**). **KJV** says in **Genesis 15:13-14** states, *"And HE said unto Avram, Know of **surety** that thy seed shall be a stranger in a land that is not theirs, and shall serve them and they shall **afflict** them **four hundred years**; And also that nation, whom they shall serve, **will I judge** and afterward shall they come out with great substance.*

Septuagint says in **Genesis 15:13-14** declares, *"And it was said to Abram, Thou shalt **surely** know that thy seed shall be a sojourner in a land not their own, And they shall enslave them, and **afflict** them, and humble them **four hundred years**. And the nation whomsoever they shall serve **I will judge**; And after this, they shall come forth hither with much property.*

Cepher says in **Genesis 15:13-14** declares, *"And HE said unto Avram, know of a **surety** that your seed shall be a stranger in a land that is not theirs, and shall serve them; and they shall **afflict** them **four hundred years**; and also that nation, whom they serve, **will I judge**: and afterward shall they come out with great substance.*

You will notice a repeat of the same words from three different bibles surely or surety, afflict, four hundred years and I will judge, but we have been instructed wrong. These Hebrews in Egypt were not in affliction for four hundred years and it is, we who are in United States has right NOW has been in affliction for four hundred years and all this confusion come from one verse in the KJV in which teachers, preachers, bishop etc has dominant this word for so long. Let the prophet speak. Let him express the word of YAH. There were **WORD LEFT OUT OF THE KJV** in which I the prophet of YAH have come across and I am now publishing it in this book RIGHT NOW. THE TRUTH OF YAH'S WORD IS COMING TO LIGHT. You see the world teachers have misguided us THE TRUE "**MY PEOPLE IN THE BIBLE.**"

KJV Exodus 12:40 declares

Now the sojouring of the children of Israel, who dwelt in Egypt, was four hundred and thirty years.

Septuagint Exodus 12:40 declares

And the sojourning of Israel, while they sojourned in the land of Egypt and the land of Chanaan, was four hundred and thirty years.

Cepher Exodus 12:40 declares

Now the sojourning of the children of Yashar,el, who dwelt in the land of Mitsrayim, and in the land of Kena`an, they and their fathers, was four hundred and thirty years.

Now do you see what I mean? Now does the word afflict and sojourning mean the same? Yes or no. Afflict to distress so severely as to cause persistent suffering or anguish, trouble or injury Sojourn to stay as a temporary resident. As you see Genesis says 400 years and Exodus says 430 years. We have before you, three different scriptures from three different bibles to which it should cause you to think about what the KJV says. The KJV even says not to take the word of one witness, but two or three. I have given you three witnesses and are you going to take the word of one witness that has not given you full disclosure to make the right decision? When words are taken out of a sentence or paragraph it changes the content or the thought or the meaning of that sentence or paragraph or book because people WILL get the wrong idea or the wrong information and will go on the wrong road teaching the WRONG information because of words being left out. This is the one point of the SAT (Scholastic Aptitude Test) exam. When you see the truth it can screw with our present stinking thinking. So the Israelites in Egypt were not in slavery or afflict for four hundred years as YAH had say to Avram. That group was only in affliction for less than 200 years and not as HE told Avram in **Genesis 15:13-14.**

Genesis 15:13-14 was fulfilled in august of 2019. 1619 to 2019 is 400 years, baby.

The Chart in Kena`an and Mitsrayim

Genesis 12:4 Avram was 75 years old when he left home.	0 year
Genesis 21:5 Avram is 100 years old when Yitschaq is born.	25 years
Genesis 25:26 Yitschaq is 60 years old when Ya`aqov is born	60 years
Genesis 47:9 Ya`aqov (Yashar'el) enters Egypt he is 130 years of age	130 years

25+60+ 130= 215 years in Kean`an land before entering Egypt.

Yoceph is 39 years old when his father enter Egypt. Yashar'el is 91years older than Yoceph his son

Genesis 47:28 Yashar"el dies in Egypt 147 years of age	17 years
Genesis 50:22 Yoceph 54 years later dies in Egypt	54 years
Exodus 1:11 The Hebrews/Isarelites or Yashareliym are taken into slavery	64 years
Exodus 2:2 Mosheh is born	
Exodus 2:15 Mosheh escapes from Egypt	40 years
Exodus 3:1 Moshes returns to Egypt	40 years
Exodus 12:1-31 The Passover	
Exodus 13:17 The Exodus	

17+54+64+40+40= 215 years in Egypt.

215+215= 430 years of sojourning in Kean`an and Egypt.

One question **CAN YOU COUNT? CAN YAH COUNT?** So as you can read our foreparents were not afflicted in Egypt for four hundred years and everyone who says it doesn't matter is calling YAH a liar! When YAH says something HE means exactly what HE says period and HE SAID 400 YEARS and not 430 years. Our forefathers were afflicted for less than 200 years in Egypt. It was our foreparents that were shipped in 1619 and the affliction ended in 2019, but as in the time of Mosheh we are still in the struggle and NOW we are awaiting for **The Exodus and THIS EXODUS WILL HAPPEN!** You see YAH has made these promises to HIS People. As you can see police officers USED to get away with killing THE MY PEOPLE of The Bible, but HE is beginning to punish this nation as HE told Avram. You see, after this book comes out my life will end because men love darkness and this book is light because it will open people's eyes who have been shut and as the movie "Eyes Wide Shut." Many will accept this, but many won't wake-up because as many in the matrix will want their easy life and maintain their same existence or way of life as it is NOW. And many will be damned to keep their easy life!

The Bible **declares** that **GOD CANNOT LIE or FAIL. Titus 1:2, Hebrews 6:18** and **Luke 16:17** these three witnesses state that THE FATHER CAN'T LIE. The words of YAH must be fulfilled. Period. NOTHING ELSE MATTERS. The first slaves came to the United States on august 19, 1619, and if we add 400 years later, we will have august 19, 2019. The words of THE FATHER MUST BE FULFILLED. HALLELUJAH, HALLELUJAH AND HALLELUJAH! Many of you are dumbfounded and so was I when I found this out, but I accepted THE TRUTH and realize now what HE said to me in the year of 1988 and one of the reasons I was given the opportunity to meet with HIM. When a prophecy is <u>stated</u>, you have to identify the right person that the prophecy is referring to. If not, then that leads to <u>DECEPTION</u>. In which it has already. If you agree, then say AMEIN. If not, let your world go on in a state of blindness. Does THE CREATOR MEAN WHAT HE SAYS? Esau could not have Ya`aqov blessing because Esau was not Ya`aqov and it was for Ya`aqov only. Ya`aqov's blessing was Ya`aqov's blessing and not Esau's blessing.

We are waiting for THE EXODUS from planet earth. Amein. We are the people (the so called colored people, n _ _ _ _ _, negro, african-americans are the people in the bible. We are direct and true descendants of our father Avraham. Please accept this for we have been oh so wrong labeled as black when our skin tone is brown or lighter. You see black is a color and it is not a nation. No where in the bible does it mention race, but the word NATION. Say it loud I AM A HEBREW. Say it again I AM A HEBREW. One time I AM A HEBREW. Great. Let this word soak in your soul and maybe just maybe we can treat each other like brothers and sisters and quit defrauding one another trying to rape your sister or brother for you see we have one brother and his name is Ya`aqov as YAHUAH told Avram and I will make as your seeds as the stars in the sky. You are HEBREW my brother and you are not as the non-melanated has called you all of his life but you are THE MY PEOPLE IN THE BIBLE. And those white (non-melanated) evangelical christians leaders will be punished for not telling the truth. We are HIS People and no man has the right to us for we are ALL natural born people. Since we are direct descendants of our father Avraham those curses and blessings have been transferred to us who are The True people of YAH. Ask this question: how many preachers do you know that are the first born males? YAHUAH states all first born males in the Hebrew/ Yashar'el are HIS. **Numbers 8:17, Exodus 3:13, 13:2, 12, 13,**and **15**. We can argue with YAH Words, but your argument is useless. Why, can the pot argue with the maker? Many of you think Israel is across the sea, but because of the wrong information and teaching and unwilling church leaders giving out this deceptive and deceiving us to accept this wrong information and are we are led astray by false and misleading, misinterpreted information and causing climatic confusion in MASHIACH'S body. And part of **Genesis 15:13-14** has been fulfilled and now we are awaiting for the Exodus and **Genesis 15:13-14** will then be fulfilled. Israel is scattered on the four corners of this earth. Guess what other nations? You have looked at us everyday with eyes of no pity but disgrace in the United States, Canada, Mexico, South America and the islands of Bermuda, Jamaica, Cuba and Puerto Rico. The world is in crisis. The USA is in $24,000,000,000,000 trillion dollars at the time of this writing, but the true digital figure could be like $60,000,000,000,000 trillion dollars in debt. United 6 letters, States 6 letters and Dollar 6 letters and we have 666. In the word corona there are 6 letters in this word and you add each number in each letter alphabet and you will have a total of 66. And you will remember this micro (you can't see it) virus that shut the world down.

C=3 O=15 R=18 O=15 N=14 A=1; 3+15+18+15+14+1=66. And we have 666 the beast system id number.

The Israel country flag has the so-called (it is nowhere in the Word, so where did it come from?) star of David. There are two triangles merging together. This is like a man emerging into a woman. The star of David is satanic also and The USA is worshiping this devil because they are not the true Israelites of The Bible. You can't be non-melanated and say you are a child of Avraham. 1) There are six points on the star. 2) There are six triangles within the two stars when merged together. 3) There are inside these triangles six conjunction points in these stars and we have 666. And the USA worships that nation as well as its dollar. 666 represents the beast system. The United States has declared sanctions on China for human rights atrocities. You **HYPOCRITE**, look how we **THE TRUE HEBREWS NATION** have been **TREATED** in The United States of America by your so called officers of public trust. **YOU HYPOCRITE!** You have the **audacity** to make a claim like that when we **THE TRUE HEBREW** has been scourged by the non-melanated population. When we are trying to enter a building where we live and some non-melanated person feels we **DON'T** belong there and you have the audacity to claim an action against another country. Before you point your finger at someone else, look into your own house.

To say that the seeds of Avraham are not people of color is a total disgrace. Recognize the truth when you read. YAHUAH made man from the dust of the earth, from the dust of the earth. It has been the truth whitewashed and many who have perpetuated this information have lost rewards or in hell. Many believe the one you call Jesus (His true name YAHUSHA) is non-melanated (white), but HE is not; HE is in fact a person of color and all our forefathers are people of color. Many may say color doesn't matter. So since color does not matter, then why have you not told the truth? It was a poll that the majority of non-melanated people would not serve YAHUSHA if HE was melanated. You see those that say this are LIARS because whether you realize it or not color matters because it is YAHUAH who has placed us in a world full of beautiful colors. If this world was just one color, oh how boring would it be? When the sky is dark, it is night or you know there is a storm coming. When the grass is green, you know it is healthy or you can determine seasons. When the leaves on trees are brown and falling, you know it is fall. So color matters! Would you eat a black orange, but you say color doesn't matter?

But YAH'S love goes to all because we are all formed by HIM and HE knew what HE was doing. A little boy died and went to heaven and YAH has awakened that little boy's eyes I hope and he came back and he asked his dad "Why were so many n_ _ _ _ _ _ in heaven?" He has been told so erroneously by his dad. You see, all who accept what YAHUSHA ADONAI HAMASHIACH done on the cross and arose again will be accepted in heaven because it is not our work but HIS works. HE is in charge. So tell the truth because color matters. The blood running through your veins is a certain color. Let that color change. Are apples purple? Apples are red, green, gold or yellow. Would you eat a watermelon if it was green inside? Are oranges yellow? No, that is a lemon. If your bowels come out black, then what would that say? Would you say that is okay? Anyway, that may be a little graphic, but I am trying to make a point that color matters in this life. I don't want to hear that color doesn't matter because it does. So, I will turn my head to those who say color doesn't matter because you are a liar. So tell the truth, Jesus (YAHUSHA), (FIRST HE IS GOD) the SON OF YAH is a person of color and HIS FATHER YAHUAH, but HIS mother a Hebrew! Amein. The word Jew is a misnomer because this word is only about 498 years old and The True name is Yahudah and not Judah. Anyway the word Jew came from Judah. Yahudah was the fourth son of Ya`aqov, a Hebrew. If we shorten Judah we will have "Ju" and thereby Jew as of nowadays. It is all according to what we hear. Like we pronounced the word christmas as chrismus. The t is silence and we say mus instead of mass. Christ-Mass.

The American English pronunciation is so jack-up.

Great-great-great-great grandfather Avraham, Hebrew **Genesis 14:13**

Great-great-great-grandfather Yitschaq, Hebrew

Great-great-grandfather Ya`aqov/Yashar'el, Hebrew

Great grandfather Levi, Hebrew

Grandfather Kohath, Hebrew

Father Amram, Hebrew

Son Mosheh, Hebrew

Mosheh is his Egyptian name and His Hebrew name is not in the KJV, but found in the book of Yasher. His Hebrew name is Chabar, but Mosheh was given 6 other names also. I have always wondered what his Hebrew name is and YAH gave me the ability to buy The Cepher Bible and it has answered some of the questions I have. The book of Jasher has been mentioned twice in the KJV **Joshua 10:13** and **2 Samuel 1:18**. The Bible states not to take the word of one witness, but two or three witnesses. These are my two witnesses.

Mosheh is a man of color. **Exodus 4:6-7** states GOD told Mosheh to place his hand in his bosom and once he removed it turned white like leprosy and GOD told him to place his hand back into his bosom and it was changed to his other flesh.

Why did you not display this on the movie Called The Ten Commandment producers**, because you were not displaying full disclosure?** You wanted the information to be hidden and not disclose who the true people in The Bible are! Wow!

And many women of color see and copy what they see everyday on television. Trying to become like the non-melanin women by buying a wig that is no way close to your original hair and we use perms on it because you are not satisfied how <u>YAH made you</u>. Just like Chuah in the garden. Since, YAH has given you your hair, (which is way different from other) why are you trying to change what GOD gave you? Many are out there saying these **STUPID PHRASE** '<u>Good Hair</u>'. Please. We ought to be ashamed for saying that because there is no such thing as good hair. There are different types of hair, but good hair there is no such thang baby! **WHO SET THE STANDARD FOR GOOD HAIR.** Boy, we can be so stupid. And this I mean. Grow up and be yourself and **QUIT** trying to emulate someone you see everyday on the television.So, are you saying you know more than your CREATOR? You see very few non-melanin women going out and getting an afro wig and if they did you would have a hissy fit. I say this because your man would not say this because he doesn't want to hurt your feelings. AWAKEN MELANATED WOMAN and be you and be MELANATED because YAHUAH made you different for a specific reason. Like Katt Williams says it is called SELF-esteem. Be yourself who YAH has made.

Which of these two statements would have a more positive effective effect on that child?

If I tell a child everyday, **"You can do it"** or **"You can't do it."**

Galatians 3:16-17 STATES, *"Now to Avraham and his seed were the promises made. He saith not, And to seeds, as of many; but as one, And to seeds, as of many; but as of one, And to thy seed, which is MASHIACH. And this I say, that the covenant, that was confirmed before of YAHUAH in MASHIACH, the Torah, which was four hundred and thirty years after, cannot disannul, that it should make the promise of no effect.*

Listen to Dr. Edward W. Robinson on youtube who has good information to correct our thinking.

There is also a report that is called "Global Patterns of Linkage Disequilibrium at the CD4 Locus and Modern Human Origins" by The American Society for The advancement of Science

In this report we have **9 DNA patterns** whereas the non-colored society has just **7 DNA patterns.**

You see we have been brainwashed by this non-colored society.

Who do you believe we (The Melanated People in the Americas) are referring to as THE MY PEOPLE of The Bible? Who chose all of this?

CHAPTER 25

—— ✦ ——

Thou Must Be Saved

This is the most defining chapter in this book. **YOU MUST BE SAVED**. No matter what you believe, <u>**we must be saved.**</u> It is imperative to all else, riches, fame, glory and recognition. The MESSIAH asked one question, **"What would a man or woman or child give for their precious soul?"** Why <u>must</u> you be saved? Because The Bible says so. The key word in this statement is 'must." There is no way around it. Must is not maybe or perhaps it is must. Must means to be obliged or bound to by an **<u>imperative requirement</u>**, to be under necessity to, need to, to be required or compelled to as by use or threat of force, ought to, is bound to, to compelled to, to fulfill some need, or to achieve an aim. There is no way around it. You are obligated to be saved or face hell forever and forever. I don't care what men say because ELOHIYM'S Word is true. It would be like if you came into my house wanting to do what you do in your house and it goes against my rule and it is NOTHING you say that can convince me any other way. ELOHIYM'S Word is greater than any name HE has. What ELOHIYM has said will come true. ELOHIYM said thou must be saved. Since ELOHIYM has stated man must be saved, then it is true and factual. YOU MUST BE SAVED and living by The Law it won't save you but damn you because you cannot fulfill The Law. Remember the parable about who is thou neighbor. You have the priest and Levite who passed by the man on the road because The Law required them to be clean and so you can't do so and so, but the greater part of The Law is love.

ELOHIYM was talking to Nicodemus The Pharisee, a man on The Sanhedrin Council: *"Ye <u>must</u> be born again"* (**Yahuchanon 3:7b**). This is all ELOHIYM wants from us first. You must be saved, you are headed to hell when you die. If you knew that there was a cliff ahead and that below this cliff was jagged rock, awaiting for those who went that direction, would you not tell everyone who passes that direction to turn and go in a different direction? The answer hopefully would be yes. ELOHIYM has forewarned. Please say yes. ELOHIYM is calling out for people to be saved before The Rapture. There are many who believe that we are in the tribulation, but this is a precursor to that time. Read **Revelation 13:16-17** this is commerce not being able to buy and sell. We are ever so close but we are not required to have the vaccine to buy and sell. We are just required to have it only to work at companies with more than a 100 or more employees. He stated there would be pestilences (malaria, HIV, AID, West Nile, bird flu, viruses (corona, delta, omicron etc). In **Luke 21**, HE states the sea will be roaring (tsunami), and these are the beginning of sorrow. YAHUSHA, HE is soon to come. Just like HE wanted HIS people to follow THE Covenant, to follow HIS direction, and if not, they would have to suffer the consequences for their disobedience and we, the nation of ELOHIYM'S People, have suffered for not following HIS Word.

What nation does **Deuteronomy 28:68** seem it has followed, "*And YAHUAH **shall** bring thee into Egypt again with ships, by the way whereof I spake unto thee, Thou shalt see it no more again: and there ye shall be sold unto your enemies for bondmen and bondwomen, and no man shall buy you.*" What group of people have suffered more than the tragedy of being shipped on a boat tied foot to head two by two on those slave ships coming to the nation of Americas? Just imagine these ships carrying people not able to get rid of their waste products from their body and living in that mess for up to almost four months. ELOHIYM means what HE said and says what HE means. When something comes out of HIS Mouth don't just shrug it off and please pay attention. We can become so lackadaisical about HIS Word that we fall asleep reading. **WAKE-UP**! Because in the book of Luke 1:36 the word sixth is looked over. We have to dig deep. Study to show thyself approved to YAH. ELOHIYM is crying out, trying to get our attention before it is too late because time is getting full, complete, ending or winding down and if you are **TUNED IN** to **YAH'S** frequency, you should know this. This should not be new. He promised safety for us who believe in HIM. HE is soon to come, so be ye ready for HIS coming in The Rapture. There is not another way out of this earth in peace.

There are two places to go after physical death: <u>heaven or hell for eternity and forever.</u> Everything in life has its opposites north-south, east-west, hot-cold, black-white, warm-mild, friend-enemy, left-right, up-down, employed-unemployed, girl-boy, bat-ball, man-woman, male-female, or right-wrong. If you are saved, you are saved from a burning and eternal hell, Hell is a place that ELOHIYM speaks of weeping and gnashing of teeth and darkness forever. I have heard the howling and people moaning and it is forever. There is no stop. Just the constant howling of people regretting their decision. The rich man is still desiring a drop of water. Hell is a place that ELOHIYM speaks of weeping and gnashing of teeth and darkness forever and it is no telling what is running across your feet. Can you imagine that? Have you been to a place where you could not see your hands in front of your face? That is some darkness. Have you gone into a small town and traveled down a road with no lights? Well, this is what you experience. ELOHIYM informed me of the smell that will occur, that it will be foul odor continuing each and everyday. Would you like to smell the sour odor of a raw, uncooked chicken after it has been in your garbage bin in your warm house of ninety degrees for a period of two days? I think not. Would you like to smell a baby diaper in the same period? I THINK NOT. Let's think about it. Hell is dark, hot, stinky, pain and misery forever and never ending. Please think about this. I beg of you please THINK!

To miss all of this misery and discomfort and all you had to do is confess that you are a sinner, believe in your heart that YAHUSHA paid the price for your sins and you are saved. **Romans 10:9-10 says,** "*That if you shall confess with your mouth ADONAI YAHUSHA, and shall believe in your heart YAH has raised HIM from the dead, you shall be saved. For with the heart man believes unto righteousness; and with the mouth confession is made unto yeshu`ah.*" This is all it takes to become saved from hell eternity. When you rode on a plane, did you check the pilot for his credentials? Did you check to see if the plane was filled with gas? No, you did not! You just believe in your heart that the company had done what the workers were supposed to do. Just believe ELOHIYM raised YAHUSHA from the dead and you shall be saved (past tense). **Yahuchanon 3:16-17** "*For YAH so loved the world, that HE gave HIS ONLY LOVE, BEGOTTEN, UNIQUE SON, that whosoever believes in HIM should not perish, but HAVE everlasting LIFE. For YAH sent not HIS UNIQUE SON into the world to condemn the world; but that the world through him might be saved.*

2 Baruk 54:16-17 "*For assuredly he who believes will receive reward. But now, as for you, ye wicked that now are, turn ye to destruction, because ye shall speedily be visited, in that formerly ye rejected the understanding of EL ELYON.*

Yahuchanon 3:36 "*He that believeth on The SON hath everlasting life: and he believeth not The SON shall not see life; but the wrath of YAHUAH abides on him.*"

Yahuchanon 5:24 *"Amein, Amein, I say unto you, He that hears my word, and believes on HIM that sent ME, has everlasting life, and shall not come into condemnation; but is* **passed** *from death unto life."*

Yahuchanon 6:40 *"And this is the will of HIM that sent ME, that everyone which sees the Son, and believes on HIM, may have everlasting life: and I will raise him up at the last day."*

1 Yahuchanon 5:12 *"He that The SON has life; and he that has not the SON of ELOHIYM has not life."*

If you have no life, then you are dead. Death's real meaning is simply being separated from the true and living ELOHIYM forever and forever. Can you imagine that? Believe ELOHIYM (THE SON) and thou will be saved! What I found out that the English or Greek name Jesus means just deliverer. In Hebrew, it is not Jesus but YAHUSHA. The shorter version of The FATHER name is JAH *Psalm 68:4 is* where it can be found. We say it all the time. Really. See if you recognize the word "HalleluJAH". See the last three letters JAH, The "J" is pronounced with an "Y" instead of "J". So we have Hal La Lu YAH. Oh how our FATHER loves to hear HalleluYAH. And this is soooooo very strange that we say YAH when it is written JAH. What about you? So THE FATHER full first name is YAHUAH and some may say YAHWEH. YAHUAH is what is in The Cepher Bible and it says YAHWEH, YAHVEH, YAHVOH, YAHVAH, but YAHUAH is more accurate. So thereby I will use YAHUAH. Anyway the person we have been calling Jesus is a Greek name which is closest associated with their supreme god zeus. The SON of ELOHIYM was born into The Hebrew's family, mother Miryam and not Mary (english name). So HE would have had a Hebrew name which is YAHUSHA. Our leaders know this and this charade or facade is finally up and because of their failures there rewards will be taken away also. We have mistakenly called HIM by the wrong name for over 388 years. You see the letter j did not come into existence till 1633 because in the 1611 kjv there were no names that begin with the letter j but the letter i instead. It would be like if Kunta Kinte would go home, would they call him Toby? They have ALL led us with the wrong information by giving us wrong information and we are all led by the blind. Some of our leaders know this and refuse to tell the truth. Some people will definitely REJECT and deny this information and insist on using the English spelling because most will say it doesn't matter, but to me truth matters. In the 1611 KJV or KIV it was Iesus and not Jesus. Iames, Ioseph,Iacob Ieremiah, Ioel, Ioshua etc. How do you feel about what has happened? Do you see what publishers can do and this applies to paintings and so on? Oh the deception.

HIS Hebrew name means "The Father's Salvation." YESHUAH means salvation in Hebrew. HIS Hebrew name is HIS CORRECT and TRUE NAME of The SON of GOD is YAHUSHA HA'MASHIACH [THE FATHER'S SALVATION THE ANOINTED ONE] and HE IS THE SON and HIS skin tone look like **The Hebrew**.

YAHUSHA died for several reasons

1) HE was The Passover Lamb for the world	**Yahuchanon 1:36**
2) For political and economic and religion and envy	**Yahuchanon 11:48**
3) He needed to become a new man	**Deuteronomy 24:1-4**

Yahuchanon The Immerser called "Behold The Lamb of GOD '' YAHUSHA was The Lamb of GOD to take away the sin of the world. **Yahuchanon 11:48** states if we do nothing <u>all men</u> will believe and the Romans will or shall come and take away both our place and nation. In other words this would have taken away their houses, synagogues, business, government, position, lands, sheep etc. And Jealousy. When a person is jealous or envious of someone that person will do almost anything to create destruction for that person. YAH had to follow HIS Law. He issued Israel a bill of divorcement in **Yirmeyahu 3:8** and HE wanted Israel back again and according to HIS Law HE could not marry Israel again so HE had to come back as a new man or HE would have defiled the land. And now to get Israel back HE became a new man on THE RESURRECTION Day. Do you not remember they could not recognize HIM even though they had been with HIM for 3 ½ years? YAHUSHA died and on resurrection day HE became a new man and can once again get HIS first bride back. ELOHIYM [THEFATHERTHESONTHEHOLYSPIRIT]. The way it is typeset here is to show the UNITY OF THE GODHEAD and now HE can now reclaim HIS Bride without breaking HIS LAW..

Can you justify (make yourself righteous) yourself? Can you make yourself right? Can a drowning man save himself? Baby, you are drowning?

CHAPTER 26

— ✦ —

How to Touch

This chapter is dedicated to all our brothers and sisters who have been emotionally and psychological damaged due to family issues. A lot of our problems can stem from our childhood. The majority of us have come from broken families and it creates problems in adulthood. I am not a psychologist, but I am an observer of people. Men can have Mother issues and women can have Daddy issues. Some may feel this is incorrect, but unless both parents were in your household talking and counseling you, you will have issues. But as basic socially says both parents are needed. With both parents a child will have a better chance, but with GOD nothing is possible.

In today's society, there is a game between men and women. The game that is played in all our lives cuts deep into a person. The games that have messed up so many lives because we defraud our sisters and brothers with lies and promises. Men and women are paying child support and men and women are left alone to train our children. Children should be trained and not raised. Children need instructions. The games we play between the sexes are not to be, but they are so. We play the game that has messed up so many lives. satan has twisted and warped our minds that we live in a world that is confused. Why do we play these games, only to find out in the end its vanity? We seek and prey. We destroy and do not care. We see and feel no pain. We live and keep on. We show up with an empty vessel. We laugh with laughter and no glee. We sense and do not care. It is all about I, me, my, mine, and myself. We move only to not forbear. We say and do not give our hearts.

Nowadays, we have people named Slyde with no heart for his or her victims because Slyde is a narrow-minded individual, fulfilling his or her physical needs only with the touch of a person. You see this game is played by men and women and it was something that

204

happened to them years ago. You see boys and girls are sexual abused by adults and those adults were maybe sexual abused by some adults also. These problems are embedded in their souls and it is never emotionally let go and that child has the feeling of sadness all of their lives and they are never able to let this feeling go and they are beaten down and one day something triggers that emotion that has been embedded in their soul for so long. Slyde is a very well-dressed person and has a very loud mouth. Speaking loudly with no concern with what comes out of his or her mouth. Slyde is a handsome and beautiful person who comes out looking outstanding. Slyde is not satisfied with just one person, but he must seek after every beautiful and handsome body they see. Slyde could be on the DL (down low). Slyde is only after one thing and it is not the heart or emotions, but the flesh only. She just after the flesh and she moves on to another man. Never letting her guard down and she doesn't let another man get to her heart. He is not interested in exploring your emotions but your vagina. Slyde wants that conquest that head on his mantle against his wall in his mansion and the notch on his penis. All she wants is for you to satisfy her so she can get her organism and go on to the next man. Slyde wants the glory between your legs, never knowing you as his Queen Dahomey and she never wants you as her King Kane. Woman, I am sure you have met Slyde because you are left to rear little Slyde and Slydette on your own, while Slyde is prowling to see the next glory he can enter. And man of sure you have met Slydette who is prowling around to get what she after. This is the game!

The Bible states, father, let not the land become whoredom. **Leviticus 19:29**, *"Do not prostitute thy daughter, to cause her to be a whore; lest the land fall to whoredom, and the land beome full of wickedness."*

This verse says father and not mother. And a woman **CAN'T BE A FATHER!** The reason I say this is because men and women THINK differently. It is a fact because YAH made it that way. And it takes two parents to train up children and not kids. Kid is a young goat so QUIT referring to your children as kids. We NEED the perspective from both parents, but fathers are most important because it takes a man to be aware of the function of a man and sometimes the woman is often repeating things loudly and it is just like an echo. A woman generally has to sit down to use the potty, but a man can stand up to use the potty. Who made it that way? So I am not saying a woman is not needed because she is. A man will never be able to pull his breast out to feed a child and this is important. Man should be able to direct his children and protect his children because things aren't as they seem all the time.

Did you see the movie "King Richard"? He protected his daughters. A father should protect their children and know your children and direct your children and aid your children and be there for your children, but it is lacking in today's society and this is why many children are in the situation we are in. And women don't hold grudges with men because something happens but be wise in all cases because sometimes things don't go as we expected. You may say he cheated on me, ok, yes, he cheated but don't hurt your child because <u>a child needs her father.</u> What is the reason so many of our men are in prisons? And you may say I don't need a man, but LOOK at your life and examine yourself?

Today our land is full of whoredom because of us men [and institutional attitude of racism and slavery, poverty, bad thinking and not following the law of YAH(your child emulate what they see) and you think it is ok to do] The strip clubs, call girls, gentlemen's clubs, dates, prostitues, marriages, baby daddy drama, pregnancies outside of marriage and professional athlete followers (trying to get a hook-up) and celebrities (idolizing peope who sit on the commode just like you). It is all about the MONEY or the ideal of MONEY or the worship of anyone, but YAH. The Bible states that the **love of money** is the root of all evil. We are worshiping anyone else but YAH and this is a travesty for mankind. Making other people as gods. This land has become a whoredom because of the man mindset for lust and they call it LOVE! This game Slyde and Slydette are playing it well because we seek some type of relationship and we are trying to fulfill things that are not spiritual. We are open to opportunities that do not have a good spirit. Slyde and Slydette have a large ego feeling there is no man or woman they cannot conquer. They have conquered and now the thrill of the 35 second climaxx is gone and they move on to their next King or Queen, never knowing what emotional distraught mess they have brought. When you are having sex together you are bring more than your body but your spirit are becoming entwined with emotional bondage. These men and women will be who they are until they reach that point of clearness in their mind and their eyes are opened to the psychological damage they have done. Do you think a man or woman who has joined their body to a child realize what they have done to that child? We think they should by being adults but this behavior has been embedded in them since it is more than possible it happens to them. And now is the point that there has to be a rescue from this peril. These individuals have to look big in their friends eyes, but someone needs to step in and tell Slyde and Slydette this is not right and do away with this type of behavior because it is killing our community. In the Old Testament if your son did not want to work, the option was to take him out of the community and stone him and I am not saying that, but we need teachers in the family from a man in that family to lead your family. These individuals are after one thing only and it is not your mind and just to leave a mark on his belt, but they could leave you with a baby, hiv, std, and emotional distraughtness and NOW WHAT. They were not trying to obtain your mind, just time to get-off and move on and it should not be. Why are STDs spread like they are? Slyde and Slydette don't care about your spirit but your body only. Look at the social media and how this nation addresses themselves. It is all about I, me and myself. And this is the whole problem; me, myself, and I and I do not care about someone else but me, myself and I. Me, myself and I get along really well with me, myself and I, but when others come into the picture and I have to share, me, myself and I and I say no emphatically. This will not change because each generation commits this same atrocity every year. Slyde and Slydette come out of the women that a man has planted a seed inside the woman and they try to hurt those individuals of whom they were created from. Slyde and Slydette can only accomplish this repeated behavior because their peers are encouraging them to do so. These unseen forces pressuring them to show off. Father, Mother, listen and teach your children about this behavior. It rests with you to stop this lackadaisical attitude. Their attitude and ways are destructive. All they want is to pimp that whore or whoremonger and get all they can from their victim and on to the next trick. This society's evils are coming to an end.

In the book of Genesis, it states when Ad-am woke up out of his sleep, he saw and said, "woman" or like the comedian said "Wooooow man." You see YAH said it is not good that this man should be alone so HE made him someone like him. Ad-am was so amazing and incredibly happy to see what YAH made from a rib bone of his. You see when Ad-am woke up he had a rib bone missing. This was his mate that YAH gave him. In other words she was by his side. YAH walked her up to Ad-am and he was excited. If I was Ad-am, I would have looked around, grabbed her hand and touched her and would have said what he said Woooooo-man. The joy he felt and the blood rushing through his body. He had someone to share the view with no longer alone. Someone to look at beside the animals and nature to look at, someone to walk along the rivers, he saw his woman and she saw her man. Can you imagine the enthusiasm he had? Can you feel the love? Look through his eyes. Look through her eyes. What, they saw into one another? What amazement! Wow! A Hebrew translation of the word "woman" means a better man. A WOMAN. This woman was someone he could relate to. No longer would he have to communicate with Mr. Gorilla, Ms. Baboon, Ms. Sea Lion or Mr. Giraffe. YAH made him a special companion, WOMAN. Ad-am said a better man. He looked at her face, hair, eyes, hands, toes, and touched her body and looked at her face to face and looked into her eyes. He could put his hands through her hair. Ad-am looked at her and said WOMAN. As someone once said "Wooooooo-Man!" This woman was very special to him. Her Hebrew is Chuah. Chuah was the last of YAH'S marvelous creation. She came from the man's rib to be by her man's side. She didn't come from his foot bone, hipbone or head bone from his rib bone side. The bone that encases and is close to his heart. Man is not to stomp his woman or his woman is NOT to rule her man, but she is his rib bone to be by his side to help because she is right for him. You see Ad-am gave up a rib bone.

Ad-am also gave Chuah the title "the mother of all living." I wish I had a definition, but that is something you can take as it is. "The mother of all living," what a great title to be given. She came last, but was given credit for all there is going to be. She came last but is given credit for all there is. Sit back and contemplate the amazement of these words. Look at the grandeur Ad-am gave to his woman, Chuah. This shows the thankfulness, thoughtfulness, gratefulness, awareness and the carefulness Adam considered his mate. Ad-am was very lonely and something was missing and YAH knew this. The first "not good" in The Bible is when YAH said so "it is not good that the man should be alone." When he saw Chuah, can you imagine the enthusiastic feeling he felt and the thought that rushed through his mind when he opened his eyes and saw this majestic and beautiful person known as his woman? Ad-am placed Chuah on a pedestal in his heart and admired her beauty. In closing, man we should remember the admiration when we first came together with our woman. Adore your woman and never ever neglect her, but treat her like you treat your mother, sister, aunt, grandmother because your woman is someone's daughter. YAH created Ad-am and Chuah and not Ad-am and Steve or Marie and Eve, **BUT** AD-AM and CHUAH to be by each other's side. Man would you want your daughter treated as you treat your woman?

How can two believers fall out of LOVE? When YAHUSHA's commandment is to love one another!

When as YAHUSHA said, your desires overtake your heart (mind)! When our hearts are no longer looking through The SON'S Eyes. We are looking through the eyes of this sinful flesh. And we are eyeing things in this world. And we feel we can do things ourselves. And we look around and GOD is not there. And we fail in our desire because we forget our desires are in GOD and GOD alone. For it is HE who can bring us together again. I have come to realize that we disrespect one another which CREATES ALL of our problems. Men disrespect women and women not realizing or knowing their worth and this comes from me meeting people. You say something nice to a woman and her thoughts are all screwed up because she would say or think something like this *"Uhmm most men say all this to* gain *attention and after sex they are gone."* Thinking like this should not be, but this is the most probable thought of today's society. We DON'T respect each other. We just defraud one another and this is the norm to this society. Men and Women not realizing what is happening to us. We are so blind today. I know of this one woman who has not had the pleasure of being someone's traditional Valentine, but she has given up her body which means this is out of the norm. She is being used which is not appropriate because this is someone's sister, daughter, aunt, mother, grandmother etc. She has never been treated as a woman should be treated. Where is the father of this daughter?

Who formed the union of man and woman?

CHAPTER 27

—— ❧ ——

Dear Khali

What was the original plan for man? Answer to commune with ELOHIYM (FATHER SON HOLY SPIRIT). How do you get forgiveness of sin because everyone is born into sin? Babies don't have to lie, but it is in their spirit to be just angry. Look at a baby and all of this whining. Baby is not happy. There is no forgiveness of sin without the shedding of blood. Remember in The Garden, ELOHIYM shed the blood of innocent animals and gave Ad-am and Chuah coverings for their naked bodies. ELOHIYM is HOLY and ELOHIYM nature does not change. HE has a standard. ELOHIYM wants man to do the right things by HIM and one another, but no matter how hard we try, we fail in some way to do things completely right and that's why we need a savior. ELOHIYM needed a perfect sacrifice to remit man's sin forever and YAHUSHA HA'MASHIACH, ELOHIYM'S SON, was the perfect sacrifice. ELOHIYM told Avraham in (**Genesis 22:8,** *"ELOHIYM will provide himself a lamb for a burn offering?"*) that HE would provide HIMSELF. ELOHIYM stated HE was going to redeem man HIMSELF. I heard a Muslim states all he had to do was ask and ELOHIYM forgive and that is truth because HIS SON died on the cross and arose again, but they simply believe that The SON was just a man. HE is not just a man but HE is first GOD and then HE CAME through the body of a Hebrew woman and became man also and this is the only reason you can ask for forgiveness, but you don't believe HE is GOD. Well HE IS GOD PERIOD and your belief makes you not saved because it took a GOD TO SATISFY GOD PERIOD. For there is no other way we can be saved from our sins. Man could not satisfy GOD because HE became unsatisfied with the continual burnt offerings. It is like you ate a burger in the morning and ate a burger at lunch and you ate a burger at dinner and I am pretty sure you don't want a burger the next day are all. It does not matter if we eat right, dress right, sing right, dance right, love right and so on. All this is in vain without a savior. These things are called self-righteousness. The Pharisees thought they were righteous by what they did but they were clean on the outside but inward they were bastards of The Words of YAH. We can not stand before a HOLY GOD and say I am as good as you. Your righteousness is like filthy rags and HE can't stand to look at you. You see you have established your own right path or way (when your way or pass you are lost trying to find the path) to ELOHIYM instead of letting ELOHIYM establish HIS way for you. It is like you getting ahead of the guide instead of letting the guide guide you. ELOHIYM has provided the path and all you have to do is accept HIS path, but you don't want HIS path, you want your own path.

When ELOHIYM has already established the way to righteousness, all you have to do is accept what ELOHIYM has already done. Question: Can you save yourself if you are drowning? The Pharisees were on the same line as The Muslims (followers of Allah). YAHUSHA is ELOHIYM and The Prophet and The SON that The FATHER sent to redeem man to HIS KINGDOM. Amein.

If all of our righteousness is as filthy rags (women's menstrual cycle rags or the rags you clean your waste material that come out of your buttocks), what can we do to be clean and HOLY in the eyes of ELOHIYM? There is nothing, but one thing and that is to accept what ELOHIYM done on the cross.

Look at the following scriptures:

1. **1 John 2:2** *"And HE is the propitiation for our sins: and not for ours only, but also for the sins of the whole world. And hereby we do know HIM, and keepeth not HIS Commandments, is a liar, and the truth is not in him."*
2. **John 14:6** *"YAHUSHA saith unto him, I AM The WAY, The Truth, and The Life: no man cometh to The FATHER, but by ME."*
   How are you going to get to The FATHER my brother? Was this verse WRONG? Was THE SON OF YAH lying here my brother?
3. **John 17:17b** "Your Word is Truth". So is this true?
4. **Psalm 14:3** *"They are all gone aside, they are all together become filthy: there is none that doeth good, no, not one."*
5. **Psalm 130:4** "But there is forgiveness with THEE, that THOU mayest be feared."

6. **Psalm 103:12** *"As far as the east is from the west, so far hath HE removed our transgressions from us."*

7. **Proverbs 29:26** *"Many seek the ruler's favour, but every man's judgment cometh from YAHUAH.*

8. **Ezekiel 33:13** *"When I shall say to the righteous, that he shall surely live; if he trust to his own righteous, and commit iniquity, <u>all his righteous shall not be remembered</u>; but for his iniquity that he hath committed, he shall die for it."*

9. **Luke 20:42** *"And David himself said in the book of Psalms, YAHUAH said unto my ADONAI, Sit on my right hand,"*

10. **Galatians 2:16** *"Knowing that a man is not justified by works of the law, but by faith of YAHUSHA HA'MASHIACH, as we have believed in YAHUSHA HA'MASHIACH, and not by the works of The Law shall no flesh be justified."*

11. **Philippians 2:9-11** *"Wherefore YAHUAH also has highly exalted HIM, and given HIM a name which is above every name: That at name of YAHUSHA every knee should bow, of things in heaven, and things in earth, and things under earth; And that every tongue should confess that YAHUAH is YAHUSHA HA'MASHIACH, to the glory of YAH The FATHER."*

12. **Yahuchanon 17:5** *"And now, O FATHER, glorify ME with Your OWN SELF with the glory which I had with YOU before the world was."*

13. **Colossians 1:21-22** *"And you, that were sometime alienated and enemies in your mind by wicked works, yet now hath HE reconciled in <u>the body of HIS flesh</u> through death, to present you holy and unblameable and unreproveable in HIS sight."*

14. **Colossians 2:9** *"For in HIM dwelleth all the fullness of the Godhead bodily."*

15. **Acts 7:55** *"But he, being full of THE HOLY GHOST, looked up steadfastly into heaven, and saw the glory of YAH, and YAHUSHA standing on the right hand of YAHUAH."*

16. **2 Corinthians 4:4** *"In whom the god of this world has blinded the minds of them which believe not, lest the light of the glorious gospel of MASHIACH, who is the image of YAHUAH, should shine unto them."*

17. **Hebrews 3:19** *"So we see that they could not enter in because of unbelief."*

18. **1 Yahuchanon 3:16** *"Hereby perceive we the love of YAHUAH, because HE laid down HIS life for us: and we ought to lay down our lives for the brethren."*

19. **Yahuchanon 14:23** *"YAHUSHA answered and said unto him, If a man love ME, he will keep MY WORDS; and MY FATHER will love him, and WE will come unto him, and make OUR abode with him."*

20. **Hebrews 9:22, 26** *"And almost all things are by the law purged with blood; and without the shedding of blood is no remission. For then must HE often have suffered since the foundation of the world; but now once in the end of the world has HE appeared to put away sin by sacrifice of HIMSELF."*

1. ***Old Testament Psalm 22:1*** *"My ELIY, My ELIY, Why have YOU forsake ME?"*
   See **New Testament** *Matthew 27:46*

2. ***Old Testament Psalm 22:16c*** *"They pierced My Hands and My Feet"*
   See **New Testament Yahuchanon 20:25**

3. ***Old Testament* Psalm 22:18** *"They parted MY garments among them, and cast lots upon my Vesture."*
   See **New Testament Matthew 27:35**

4. **Old Testament Psalm 31:5** *"Into YOUR Hand I commit MY Spirit: You have redeemed ME, O YAHUAH EL of Truth.*"

   See **New Testament Luke 23:46**

5. **Old Testament Psalm 31:13** **"***For I have heard the slander of many: fear was on every side:*

   While they took counsel together against ME, they devised to take away MY life."

   See **New Testament Yahuchanon 11:47-48**

6. **Old Testament Psalm 69:21** *"They gave ME gall for MY meat; and in MY thirst they gave ME vinegar to drink."*

   See **New Testament Matthew 27:34**

7. **Old Testament Psalm 69:26** *"For they prosecute HIM whom you smitten; and they talk to the grief of those whom you have wounded."*

   See **New Testament Matthew 27:26-31, Mark 15:19, 20.**

Can these verses be accidental or coincidental? Or were these verses planned by THE CREATOR?

ELOHIYM brought me to heaven for a brief moment. Why, I don't know, maybe just to let you know heaven exists for those who do not believe. Khalil you stated The Holy Bible and The Koran or Quran were like sisters and both have truths. The BIBLE is YAHUSHA'S story. Questions Can you have two truths? Can two objects occupy the same space? Is 1 + 1= 2 or 1+1=5? Can the sun come up in the east one day and come up in the west the next day? Does the sun rise in the north and set in the south? Which one is true? To say they are sisters would be false because they sprout different beliefs. ELOHIYM'S Word is true and this is HIS Word and not Muhammad. Two truths. Can the earth be flat and a circle? The first truth, the earth is flat and the latter truth, the earth is a circle. **Isaiah 40:22** *"It is HE that sitteth upon the circle of the earth.* One last statement, This earth will soon end. **Isaiah 65:17** *"For behold, I create new heavens and a new earth: and the former shall not be remembered, nor come into mind."*

Revelation 21:1 *"And I saw a new heaven and a new earth: for the first heaven and the first earth were passed away; and there was no more sea."*

To My Muslim Brother

You see my brothers, we came from the same father Ya`aqov. Our foreparents were shipped on those slaves ships as it says in **Deuteronomy 28:68.** Ya`aqov's father is Yitschaq and his father is Avraham. As YAH told Avram that his seeds would be in a strange land **Genesis 15:13-14. 2 Baruk 78:4** *"And truly I know that behold all we the twelve tribes are bound by one bond, inasmuch as we are born from one father."* Mosheh's skin was turned white in **Exodus 4:6. Acts 21:38** Pa'al was identified by a Roman guard to an Egyptian. ELOHIYM made a man. Not a black man and not a white man and not a red man, but man in HIS Image. Man was formed from the dust of the earth and so thereby his skin had to be dark and YAH just made man and breath breathe into his body and he became a living soul. And his intention was just a man. Just because you have dark skin doesn't mean you get any special privileges from YAHUAH because you are filthy rags in HIS Eyesight. Man is unholy because of what Ad-am did. It is man who has placed emphasis on skin tone and we all die the same. Just because HE is melanated doesn't give us any more privilege. The non-melanated man is just as unholy as the melanated man. Isaiah established that ELOHIYM does not send out empty words or vain words.

I have a few questions. Are the promises of ELOHIYM defunct to the nation of Yahudah? Are HIS promises (blessings and cursing) everlasting or short term? In other words are ELOHIYM'S promises ended to HIS people? I will let you think about that. **Romans 11:29** *"For the gifts and calling of YAH are without repentance."* In the Strong concordance the word repentance means irrevocable. In the Merriam Webster's Collegiate Dictionary, "not possible to revoke and unalterable." It is ironclad there is no way around or no way through. It is set and finished. It is completed. It can't be changed. It is set in marble. It is set in granite.

I have learned that the word "Muslim" means followers of YAH or ALLAH. In the preface of The Holy Koran, it is said that the believers in the HA'MASHIACH and Judaism have the same book, but have totally different beliefs. Judaism believes just you Muslism that YAHUSHA was a prophet, a good man, but believers believe HE is ELOHIYM, The SON of ELOHIYM. Why is it that some Muslims have one book but believe differently also among each faction and I guess you say that Christianity is the same way. You see I am not a Christian, but I am a believer, a follower not of the name Jesus, but YAHUSHA HA'MASHIACH who has melanin in HIS skin tone. And HE is first The SON of ELOHIYM born to a Hebrew's mother and thereby HE is thereby a Hebrew by man nature. Why is it that some Muslims have one book but believe differently among different factions? Some believe it is okay to commit suicidal bombings and killing one another? I guess it is like any other religious sect. We take certain passages and establish an ideal and follow that teaching instead of evaluating the truth of that word and we are led down the wrong road of the wrong belief. There is something that has been triggered in our heart and soul by what we have heard, experienced and learned toward that direction from past experiences and relationships that we want to continue.

We have lost a generation of people who do not realize we are the original people of this earth, from Eden and not Africa **Genesis 2:8.** We are a lost people because we do not follow the words of ELOHIYM to treat one with truth, equal weight, righteousness, not defrauding one another and most of all love. We are a divided people like Yoceph and his brothers. We will not follow ELOHIYM'S Law Commandments, Directions or Teachings LOVE GOD and LOVE our neighbor. Why are we lost? Our foreparents were dragged over to the Americas stacked like sardines in a can to lie in their filth and waste (urine and feces and menstrual blood) across the long voyage, the new Egypt (**Deuteronomy 28:68**). This voyage took from four weeks to four months to complete this holocaust. Yes, HOLOCAUST! Is ELOHIYM'S

Word true? Does HIS promises end toward HIS people? The true identity of the Yahudah is hidden and we are a lost nation because we do not realize our true identity and not race because race is not in The Bible and you refer to yourself as Black but you are not. So there are people that are melanated and non-melanated. In the movie *"She Hates Me"*, you have people of copper tone (the color of a penny who are not black) in their skin trying to be gangsters or Mafia. Find your true ID and quit trying to be non-colored. We are a lost nation that does not know our true identity. ELOHIYM stated HE would scatter HIS people and we in the Americas The people of color do not realize our true ID. We have been blinded by satan through the non-colored man devices in America and England and we try to emulate him and we take on his name as if he still owes us. Just like Hananiah (Shadrach), Mishael (Meshach) and Azariah (Abednego) under King Nebuchadnezzar changed their name in the book of **Daniel,** but they were taught the word of ELOHIYM and did not bow to the statue. But we today are bowing to the no knowledge of ELOHIYM (FATHER SON HOLY SPIRIT) which is the beginning of knowledge.

Hosea 4:6	*"My people are destroyed for a lack of knowledge: because you have rejected the knowledge."*
Proverbs 1:7	*"The fear of YAHUAH is the beginning of knowledge."*
Proverbs 9:10	*"The fear of YAHUAH is the beginning of wisdom: and the knowledge of The HOLY is understanding."*
Psalm 111:10a	*"The fear of YAHUAH is the beginning of wisdom."*
Job 28:28	*"And unto man HE said, Behold the fear of ADONAI, that is wisdom; and to depart from evil is understanding."*

As long as we bow down to not learning about ELOHIYM and his ways, disregarding HIS Words, learning the devil ways, disrespecting and defrauding one another, not loving one another, stealing, lying, disrespecting our mothers, disrespecting our women, disrespecting our fathers, disrespecting our brothers, disrespecting ourselves, not following or heeding ELOHIYM'S Words, not loving, not caring, killing one another, raping our (women) sisters, drugging (herion, marijuana, alcohol, cigarettes and pain pills) one another to satisfy self, spreading our diseases, not teaching our children YAHUAH ways (a young woman had a young child in her car playing music with all type of profanity music playing and had the reap smell of marijuana all in the car. What is this child learning and she had no business with that child in that car. Question: **At what age do we expose our children to our way of sin's living life thinking it is right?**) fornicating, and misusing one another, take heed and listen because the promises of ELOHIYM **still exist** whether you believe it. We can't get rid of HIS promises because HIS promises are forever and ever. ELOHIYM abides forever and HE has maintained this earth because of HIS words (**Psalm 138:2**) No matter what you do, ELOHIYM is ELOHIYM and we must obey HIM. So, I shout to you brother. ELOHIYM is not dead; HE is alive. It is awful to fall into the hand of a living ELOHIYM and HIS WORDS endure forever and forever. There is no escape from HIS WORDS and you will agree ELOHIYM is true and right no matter what you and I think because once you feel HIS power, power so strong, you will forever regret what you have done and while you are in hell a thousands of years, wondering when the flames, the smell, the darkness will never stop and these words are echoing out of your mind of the peace you could have had, if you had only believe that ELOHIYM is true and you could have had the opportunity to say thank you ELOHIYM for saving me and you refuse to heed HIS WORDS as true. You refused HIS plan of salvation and decided to follow your way of salvation. Listen up, you can play around and be fooled by a man stating his words instead of asking ELOHIYM for HIS truth. Turn to ELOHIYM before it is too late, for ELOHIYM **cannot go back on HIS Words** because **Isaiah 55:11** and **Psalm 138:2b** because ELOHIYM'S WORDS are HIS established truth as the sun comes up in the east every day, so does ELOHIYM WORDS shine brightly each and every day. This is your chance to believe or not believe that ELOHIYM (FATHER SON HOLY SPIRIT) has established HIS WORDS and HE died and rose from the dead and became alive from the dead and is sitting on the right hand of The Father. ELOHIYM, died (paid the price) for our sins so you won't have to pay the price for sin for yourself. What can you offer ELOHIYM to satisfy the payment for your sin debt. It is like the parable one man owed a billion dollars to the king and the king forsake the debt. There was no possible way the debtor could have paid the debt. The debt was way too much. YAHUSHA paid the price for your sin, please accept HIS payment and be free from the debt of eternal separation. What do you have to lose? When we are judged for rewards not sin if you are a believer. **Yahuchanon 5:22** YAHUSHA will be like a friend if you accept HIM. There is nothing like a friend in your corner when trouble is abound.

I went over to my daughter's house to see my new granddaughter. I asked if I could give her a cookie. My daughter said yes. I gave my granddaughter the cookie and of course she stayed close to me. Guess what? The cookie created cookie juice and the saliva got on my pants that I had just got out of the cleaner. She placed that cookie juice on my pants leg. So, I got the stain out. This is the same way ELOHIYM did for us. ELOHIYM removed the stain and PENALTY. We could not pay that price.

Hebrews 9:22 *"And almost all things are by the law purged with blood; and without Shedding of blood there is no remission."* *[extinguishing or release of a debt]*

Without a blood sacrifice there is no release from the sin debt. Muslim where is your remission because a good man as you call YAHUSHA would still be a man, but I believe and KNOW HE IS THE VERY PRESENCE OF YAHUAH. Every time in the Old Covenant you needed a blood sacrifice, but since YAHUSHA died and rose this is our blood sacrifice forever. Never needing to ever produce a blood sacrifice for the lies I have told, for the gossip I have done and for every sin I have done or will do. YAHUSHA died and rose that will forever cover all of my sins. I am saved by ADONAI HA'MASHIACH'S DEATH AND RESURRECTION FOREVER.

Like a husband and wife are one so is ELOHIYM. ELOHIYM is ELOHIYM is ELOHIYM. All you have to do is believe. He has made the way and ELOHIYM exist forever. HIS Word does not change. ELOHIYM is ELOHIYM and HE must be believed that ELOHIYM is ELOHIYM or forever comes to ruin. Don't be separated from ELOHIYM forever. Amein forever and Hallelu**JAH.**

And Miryam took the timbrel and <u>the nation</u> of Israel crossed The Red Sea and Pharaoh's army drowned in The Red Sea. ELOHIYM is the ELOHIYM that will stand up for you and spare you from eternal damnation, darkness, hunger, thirst, fearfulness and devastating consequences of ruin. Amein for so it be and Amein to ADONAI YAHUSHA HAMASHIACH, SAVIOR. THE PASSOVER LAMB FOR THE WORLD

Amein

Brother

And Amein

Do you think brother you can be righteous yourself without a Savior?

CHAPTER 28

The New World Order

We are not there yet, but we are very close to the new world order. This plan is being allowed by **THE CREATOR**. <u>Have you not read what the scriptures say?</u> **Yesha`Yahu 51:6, 65:17, 66:22, Revelation 21:1, Enoch 92:3h, 93:17-18, Zephaniah 3:8f, 2 Kepha 3:13, Hebrews 2:5, Mattithyahu 24:35 and Psalm 148:6.** This plan is being allowed by YAHUAH to bring The New Heavens and The New Earth so that HE will live with us **Revelation 21:3.** Many have been deceived thinking that Heaven will be our eternal home, not so. It is THE CREATOR'S Plan before the foundation of earth was ever established. Many are praying against HIS Plan so stop it and agree with YAHUAH. Think what you are praying against corona? Oh I remember though face book prayer against this, but **DO YOU THINK YOU CAN STOP YAH'S PLAN? DO YOU?** Remember HE has complete control of what is happening to you right now. Even to bring your physical body to the ground. And many are deceived into thinking a mask or vaccine will save you. Please, fool who do you THINK you are. YAH is able to save Avram from burning up in the furnace, Daniy'el in the den of hungry lions, Chananyahu, Miysha'el, and Azaryahu in the fiery furnace, David facing Goliath and the bear and the lion, Yashar'el conquered the wall of Yeriycho, Ad-am for disobedience, Yitschaq was not sacrifice, but a ram in the bush, Pa'al was bitten, Pa'al was stoned and did not died, Stephen saw The Glory of YAH being stoned and died, Shimshon did not die in the battle of slaining the 1,000 philistines with the jawbone of an ass, Yashar'el crossing the Red Sea, but the egyptians drowning in the Red Sea, Yechizqiyahu was sieged, but Yahudah escaped destruction from the Assyrians and YAHUAH raised up YAHUSHA from the tomb after three nights and three days. So can you pray this away? Heaven is not our home because earth is our home period. YAH has a plan that will not be stopped.

What is the new world order? It is satan's plan (allowed by YAH) devised for this world to be under his complete control. He wants complete control of all this world's finance, economy, cash, food (food has been modified, seedless grapes, watermelon, gmo foods and modified corn starch), medical system (my card on my insurance ends in 666), communication system and people. He wants you to bow to him and make him god. Nothing will be out of his hands to control and we are ever so close. And I hear silence. He will have complete control of all databases of this present world. What databases? All databases! This is the captive state! Look at the movie called "Captive State." **ARE YOU TAKING KNOWLEDGE or ADVICE or COUNSEL or OPINION or INFORMATION FROM PEOPLE THAT DOES NOT AGREE OR ACKNOWLEDGE THAT THERE IS A CREATOR OF WHAT IS? Simply ask them, "Do you believe there is A CREATOR that created everything we see?"** Can you imagine one person having a complete dossier on you? All of your credit information, department of public safety, court, medical, banking, food you eat, places you go, movies you have watched, things you have purchased. They are all contained on one database at one person's control. And guess what this is happening before our eyes. Google know exactly where I go when I uses their maps and the bank has information when I swipe that card and this is the reason the cashless society will be in trouble because when cash is gone, it is simply when will **THE NEW WORLD ORDER be in place, because it is impossible to track the flow of cash, but I forgot the camera are still up as in the movie "Enemy of The State".** What did they do to him? The so called government authority **SHUT DOWN ALL OF HIS CARDS**! And I had a man tell me they can't do that and I told him they have the power to do this corruptible act. President Franklin Delano Roosevelt by executive order 6102, april 5, 1933, all citizens had to turn in their gold. And so we have it that by executive orders **THE NEW ORDER** will be. You have heard presidents of the USA mention this in their speeches. Look at these mandates issued by President Biden. All of this will be on one database for one person to control. Have you seen the movie The Matrix? Do you remember they brought Neo into the room and the agents pulled him into the room and they started to read his dossier? **THE NEW WORLD ORDER! THIS was allowed by YAHUAH because HE is going to recreate, renew or redo HIS WORLD.** And we men dispute about this and that and YAHUAH is going to do a renewal! HE shall get rid of old earth and create a new heaven and new earth. Many will follow the adversary and they will be forever forgotten and never ever given another single thought. There will be no regret from YAHUAH because there will be no remembering of the past but all things shall be new. So you can go on with your silly way but MY FATHER'S GRACE AND MERCY was offered but YOU REFUSED to bow to HIM, but bow down to HIS adversary the devil and you will always have the thought haunting you for the rest of eternity of never ending wanting rest from this torment, but your time of torment won't end. Right now on your smartphones, you are tracked. You are listened to and looked at on all your smart mobile devices, video game consoles, laptops, televisions, traffic cams, automobiles etc. And this person has complete control over all of this information on you. Just imagine this. This is THE NEW WORLD ORDER in disguise and we are in the pot and the water is beginning to boil, but YAH has an escape plan and HIS name is **YAHUSHA HA'MASHIACH** and HE is your only option. **BELIEVE PLEASE! I AM PLEADING WITH YOU WITH TEARS IN MY EYES!** THE BIBLE has informed us of this many years ago, but people refused to believe this. Do you see this? I hope so! The BIBLE said this would occur many years ago and guess what, it is happening before our eyes. People believe a person is so spiritual and we are not aware of the venom coming out of their mouth, but we follow these so-called spiritual individuals. This new world order is happening before our very eyes. ELOHIYM WROTE THE FUTURE YEARS AGO and now it is before our very eyes. All of this information is being collected and stored on a supercomputer at this very moment and we are like sheep that are saying it is okay. Have you seen the movie *"The Net"* with Sandra Bullock, where someone stole her identity? You can say that can never happen to me. Really. Well, I say it can. Have you seen the movie ``The *Manchurian Candidate"* with Denzel Washington, where they wiped him out of the picture and replaced him with someone else and gave the new media a bogus tape? This happens daily. Have you seen the television show *"Person of Interest."* Let's think this has happened in our lifetime in reality. The media is owned by corporations (or a family) and these corporations control what information gets out. Look at the 911 events. This plan coordinated events that brought in The agency of Homeland Security. Why? Billions of dollars for another agency please. When people in rural counties in Alabama can't get sewer treatment plants. Please. Newscasters are given a script from which they read every single day (they have to read or get fired from their highest paid job of which they work to get only then to be deceived) and we are following people and idolizing people who **DON'T** believe there is **A CREATOR. Ask** these people "Do you believe there is A CREATOR?" If they hesitate, watch out. Because the answer will be yes or no. Newscasters are given a script from which they read from. The antichrist is living at this present moment and his henchmen are setting up his kingdom on this earth right now. All the databases are coming together. What database, banking, medical, employment, government, criminal, biometrics (such as found on facebook of you aging and you have given over to the beast and you thought it was a game and this ancestry program of finding your relatives. Yes it is interesting, but this company has all this information on you and who in reality owes this company or corporation and you don't know but you willingly gave up this information on you and family members. Just be careful what you do.), driving records, insurance, and so on? I found out recently that anytime you file a homeowner claim, there is **A** single database that **ALL** insurance companies can go to see if there have been **ANY** claims in the history of that **ADDRESS**. They will ask and then the representative will check the insurance database to see if the information you gave is accurate. We can't escape the man of sin because where are you going to? The **PLANNED-DEMIC** is just a precursor of what is coming. **You see this WAS PLANNED!** Am I trying to scare you heaven yes!

AT&T(American Telephone and Telegraph), which was broken up and is back together again, is a large communication and entertainment corporation. Wal-Mart Inc, is one the the world' s largest retailer and other corporations are joining together to make larger retailers. Sears and Kmart have set up joint ventures and thereby one less place to obtain things. How many bookstores are there? These gigantic retailers are making it very easy for the antichrist to control the retail industry system. Retailers like Amazon where there are no cashiers. Even Wal-Mart is going to this type of set-up of no cashiers or no machine which only takes cards with a chip. I went to a restaurant in Austin Texas and they had a sign that said "card only no cash." All you have to do is have your card ready, but now you do need a card because you can use your card image on your smartphone. There are people already chipped and you can just wave your hand. In my last book I stated it will be just having your chip implanted in your hand or forehead. This is **HERE RIGHT NOW** and the person that has done this does not see a problem with this because it is convenient and you don't have to worry about thieves. This system is being formatted under the very disguise of convenience. You have been tattooed with a barcode or chip and you walk in and leave the sensor, take the payment from your account just like toll authority scan the barcode and take payment from the account you set up with them. Man, we feel the ease. Can you feel the ease, but it is all in disguise that a cashless society is coming NOW and all he(satan) has to do is implement a rule change and change the dynamic of this entire industry and issue his **executive orders or mandates.** These mandates or executive orders are not constitutional because you won't find the word executive orders in The United States Constitution of America, **anywhere.**

Revelation 13:16-18 *"And he causeth <u>all</u> both small and great, rich and poor, free and bond, to receive a mark in their right hands, or in their foreheads: And that <u>no man</u> might buy or sell, <u>save he that had the mark,</u> or the name of the beast, or the number of his name. Here is wisdom. Let him that hath understanding count the number of a man: and his number is Six hundred threescore and six.*

If you read this there are three conditions 1) the mark is a chip or tattoo 2) you know his name 3) or his number and if you do any of these things you have pledged allegiance and loyalty to the beast. This is a commerce condition of buying and selling. And you do you are damn forever from YAHUAH because your allegiance is to the beast system and not to THE CREATOR. You know about the chip on debit and credit cards. It can be tracked almost anywhere you go. Without the Mark you will not be able to buy food, water, clothing, housing, gasoline, pay utilities (water, gas, telephone, electricity), medical aids, prescriptions, coats, shoes, toilet paper, go to the movies and so on. People are being chipped with no regard that they are committing a great tragedy and eternal end possibly. Maybe the chipped can be removed? I have asked this question to YAHUAH with no response. If after having the chipped inserted into your body you may want it removed because you made a mistake, but you have gotten accustomed to it being in your body. How many of us have smartphones? I have a flip phone also and I hate to text from it. Do you think you can leave your mobile device at home now? This is just like a chip. It goes with you everywhere you go. It goes to the bathroom with you. It goes with you to the store. It is right there by your side. This is similar to having the chipped in your body. You have gotten accustomed to the implant and its conveniences. You won't leave your device at home right now. It is in the church house. Some people now don't have a paper copy of The WORD of YAH because they depend on a preacher to teach them the word of YAH instead of what The Bible says 2 Timothy 2:15 *"Study to show yourself approved unto YAH, a workman that needs not to be ashamed, rightly dividing the Word of Truth."* Now this is the bible true because we will all be before HIM when we leave this physical body and we will be at eternal peace or be at eternal condemnation and unrest forever. People may say they won't be able to track you. But is that true? Something electronic can be hacked. Sometimes electronics can go wrong and have to be reset. Have you ever lived in a house without electricity? How easy will you accept The Mark and not have all these conveniences of today? I will say it will be very difficult for you to last forty-eight hours without food. Have you ever gone without food for twenty-four? It gets hot in the summer and cold during the winter. Besides that you will be on the street because you will not have a job unless you take The Mark. All debts will be called in. Where are you now? No car, no money, no gasoline, or electricity for your vehicle, no house, no food and no way to communicate. You are in a world that doesn't care for you because you are not worshiping the beast or have taken The Mark. This is like Colin Kaperernick who kneels and refuses to stand before the American flag because of police and social injustice of a certain nation who are the true Israelites. You will get the same type of treatment because you refused The Mark. Will you give in after 48 hours, 72 hours, 140 hours, one month, two months? No food, no clothes, no water and no shelter. How long will you last before you give in? This is what coming and you will have regrets, but once you take The Mark your trouble will be over for now, but you have made the most horrendous and the most grievous error because now you will be worshiping and pledging allegiance to and for the beast and you are on your way to the lake of fire for how long FOREVER. What is forever? It is like a bird taking a gravel of sand from one end of earth and going to get another gravel. In other words there is no end. **Ecclesiasticus 18:10** *"As a drop of water unto the sea, and a gravelstone in comparison of the sand; so are a thousand years to days of eternity.* Oh how precious is your soul.

There is a book by Tex Marrs entitled *"Project L.U.C.I.D"*. He goes into great and many details on how this will occur and will continue to occur, but ELOHIYM said that no one will be able to buy or sell many years ago.

The book of Revelation of YAHUSHA HA'MASHIACH was written in the year AD 95-96. This book was well written over 1900 years. If ELOHIYM says so because HIS Words will not be void. It is assured like money in the bank. It has to be true. Man has his idea of this and that. Some feel it has already happened and so on, but what they are saying is it true? Be watchful and pray and THE RUACH will lead you into all truths. L.U.C.I.D. stands for <u>L</u>ucifer <u>U</u>niversal

(<u>C</u>riminal, <u>C</u>omprehensive, <u>C</u>onspiracy, <u>C</u>ontrolling, <u>C</u>entral, <u>C</u>omputerized) <u>I</u>dentity <u>D</u>atabase. The people who have placed this system together are simply relying on it for our <u>sense of security.</u> Safety. You cannot trust man. He will heighten your insecurity to place more control on you and in your life. In the television show like *"The Travelers"* the reason for the bomb was to bring a sense of insecurity in society to further enhance the control to The Homeland Security Department. The government is made of men who are fallible and liars. Why place these files into one man's hand to control? He wants you to believe he is ELOHIYM and he is not ELOHIYM, but the very adversary of ELOHIYM; satan is the adversary (antichrist) of THE ALMIGHTY ELOHIYM. We who are believers will not have to worry about taking the mark because we shall be gone. ELOHIYM promises safety to HIS Children **Proverbs 21:31** *"The horse is prepared against the day of battle: but safety is of YAHUAH.* Can you trust YAHUAH at HIS Word? HE states in the book of **Psalm 138:2d** that HIS word is greater than HIS Name. We will be Raptured before this goes into effect. Some don't believe this and some do, but I know I won't be here! Those who are left here on earth will have to take the mark or endure such treatment that I would not like any of my enemies to go through. You could very well be stripped of all your rights and be naked and fed to the animals etc. The man of sin will be in charge and whatever his mind directs him that he will do. Without the mark your life will be threatened with beheading and you are facing a guillotine, will you change your mind or will you take the mark? These will be your options 1) life with antichrist and then damnation forever 2) to be beheaded and be with The MESSIAH? Which way will you choose? You can choose one or you can choose two. Without the mark you will not be able to function in this world, activities like shopping or opening a business to sell stuff. What business person will close down their business for such a little injection of the flesh? You say *"It is anything. I got to feed my family."* You may not want to take the mark, but how long will you last without a bite to eat and everyone around you is eating and the food looks so delicious and the smell so wholesome? You will fail and take the mark to fill your belly for the moment and when you do, the lake of fire will be your home forever and ever. And all you had to do was accept YAHUSHA as ADONAI and SAVIOR TO ESCAPE THIS DOOM. This is the new world order. It is what is going today with the vaccine mandate and mask wearing. You feel that these vaccines and masks are your protector, but The Bible declares that YAHUAH is your shield **Proverbs 30:5b.** What is a shield for? You see this period is only seven years, but this is the beginning of plagues that will hit the late great earth during this seven years period.

ELOHIYM made a promise that I will never leave you or forsake you and this is the reason that we as believers will not be around for the mark because many people will not last without food. ELOHIYM states in HIS Words, <u>I will provide </u>for all your needs and My <u>ELOHIYM cannot lie. </u>You say I have rights. What rights? The Constitution of The United States of America has been trodden upon for years. We are just not aware that your rights are long gone. We are not just under the rule of law, but also under the rule of money. Whosoever controls the money controls you. For example, article 1 section 8 part 5 says, *"To coin money, regulate the value, and of foreign coin and fix the standard of weights and measures."* Congress does not regulate the value but The Federal Reserve System. The Federal Reserve System is a private bank that has shareholders. The constitution does not recognize paper money. The chairperson of The Federal Reserve Board determines the value of money. The coin money today is counterfeit. Counterfeit definition made in imitation of something else with intent to deceive, to make fraudulent replicas of, forgery. There is no need to put ridges on dime or quarter because these are not silver coins anymore. The only reason to put ridges on those coins is to keep them from being chipped off. Since they are not silver anymore, there is no need to continue to place ridges unless you are **deceiving the public.** Guess what, WE HAVE BEEN DECEIVED. Deceived by who? You guess?

The world is going more and more into the system of the antichrist. The reason I say this is because people are tattooing themselves. If you are used to tattooing, what differences will an implantable chip make to you? The city and state are placing cameras everywhere to make us feel safe, but it will only work if your biometrics (DNA, fingerprints, facial, iris, etc) are on file somewhere. Isn't it frightening that someone has complete control over all your information? The Constitution of The United States guarantees us the right against unreasonable searches and seizures **SHALL NOT BE VIOLATED** without probable cause. When you give up your biometrics, this **AMENDMENT** has been **TAKEN AWAY and TRASHED.** Why, all in the means of safety from robbers and terrorists. <u>I would rather be in HEAVEN,</u> where there is safety and peace with ELOHIYM peace.

Police departments are no longer departments, but are agencies. Police agencies are not near City Hall in a lot of towns. Police department referred to each department as an agency and not a department. Who works for an agency are agents. An agency is *"contracts by which one person acts for or represents another by the latter's authority."* A definition of an agent is *"one entrusted with another's business and given the authority to act for him."* A definition of a department is *"division of public administration."* This is the new world order. Police agents will be working not for our interest, but for this new world order. They are no longer working for the public, but outside the public government.

There is a movie called "*Gattaca*" that came out several years ago, where they had all of this information on this person and someone took his place and he went through all these procedures to replace this person. He broke his legs to add additional height to his body and each and everyday, he would vacuum his computer keyboard to wipe up any DNA cells from his keyboard. He did this to survive. This world is coming when the man of sin will take control and if you do not take the mark, you will be denied all your rights and be sent somewhere. It will not be nice.

I have a friend who was trying to reset his password on his computer at work. He contacted the person who reset passwords and the person asked him some questions. She asked him if he had a brother named so and so and he stated *"Yes"*, and she asked him if he had another brother named so and so and he lived at so and so. His antenna went up then and he asked her

"Why are you asking this information about my brothers to reset my password and where did you get this information from?" The person stated, *"I am not allowed to give out that information, Where I got **YOUR** information from."* She has your information and she is verifying information she has on you and your family members. Doesn't this sound strange? Welcome to **THE NEW WORLD ORDER. We are not there yet, but it is surely on its way.**

Do you think The New World Order is coming?

CHAPTER 29

Money

In The Bible, **KJV** says, **1 Timothy 6:10** says "that the love of money is the root of all evil," **NIV** says all kinds of evil, **ESV** "all kinds of evils," **NKJV** "all kinds of evil, **NASV** all sorts of evil," **Amplified Bible** "For the love of money [that is, the greedy desire for it and the willingness to gain it unethically] is a root of all sorts of evil, and some by longing for it have wandered away from the faith and pierced themselves [through and through] with many sorrows."

Money is not the root of all evil, but love of. The Ojays have a song entitled *"For the Love of Money"*. People would kill for money, steal for money to eat, cheat their insurance companies, heist art painting for money, fraud a business partner(s) or investor, kill their spouse, assassinate, steal cars, prostituted their body, offered their body for test like food and OTC, pharmaceutical and illegal (get that fix) drugs and the list go on. Oh what we do as PEOPLE do for MONEY (that small printed green stuff with a number on it). **Proverbs 22:7,** says *"The rich ruleth over the poor and the borrower is servant to the lender."* The USA has $24,000,000,000,00 or $25,000,000,000,000 trillion dollars of debt to The Federal Reserve System. But since I wrote this years ago it has ballooned to $28,000,000,000,000 trillion dollars, but someone says it may be around $66,000,000,000,000 trillion dollars. The USA brings in around $3,500,000,000,000 a year from tax revenue. The Federal Reserve System or bank is a private bank in which the Federal Reserve System prints Notes. You see we are in debt to **The Federal Reserve Bank. The FRB is a private bank which has private members and they print this paper money in which it is not authorized by the Constitution of The USA and Congress set up the legislature and borrow money from this unconstitutional entity and we are in debt. This is basically the gist of the matter.**

We have a Federal Reserve Note, before that we had Silver Certificates. What Silver Certificates meant, we could turn them in and get silver, but no more. Now, we have the Federal Reserve Note. I know this does not matter to people, but to know will make you enlightened. What is the word note? Note is a legal term meaning debt. We say it every month. "I am going to pay my house *note*. Or I am going to pay my car *note*. Look at this we say mortgage NOTE. So in legal terms, when you see or hear *"note"* it is also referred to as DEBT. So we have FEDERAL RESERVE DEBT and not note per se as THEY (THE UNSEEN HAND) want you to think NOTE and not the real word "debt" and want you to believe in this satanic system. The unseen hands of men are in charge of this totally corrupt system, wanting you to believe it is safe, but we are on the verge of destruction and total collapse of debt in this financial system and we have not been made aware about this. This is just a warning. Just think about this. And don't let money rule you, but let THE RUACH HA'QODESH lead and guide your daily walk.

This system is like your household. You have so much money coming in and so much money going out. You will go bankrupt when you have more money that is going out than what is coming in. The USA is very close to financial collapse as in 2008. There are a couple of movies called "Margin Call" and "Too Big to Fail." The people in control of this system have covered up The TRUTH of this luciferin system, but YAH is awakening HIS PEOPLE. We are totally in the hands of this system. And you knowing this won't change the system. You will be self-aware, so when it happens you will know you were told. So be ye ready for the collapse. This is like the movie *"The Matrix"*. We live and think in one scheme, but there is the real reality in which we are not aware of unless we take the red pill. TAKE THIS RED PILL and AWAKE, AWAKE, AWAKE yourself out of your slumber and open your mind and heart and realize the truth of this failing system. BECAUSE THE END IS NEARER THAN YOU THINK. YAH IS AWAKENING HIS PEOPLE. THIS LAND IS DEFILED, AND YAH IS GOING THROUGH THIS LAND EVERY DAY, SEARCHING FOR THOSE WHO ARE READY FOR this coming life. SO BE YE READY. Once upon a time, there were silver certificates and those have been replaced and kept out of circulation. And, we bank with these federal financial institutions every single day of OUR LIFE. This debt must be PAID. PERIOD! One farmer was paid not to grow crops and his dirt was taken and shipped to China. Do you think the cartel is going to release that debt? I don't think SO. Yes I said cartel because the FRB is a cartel

The constitution of The USA gave Congress the ability to borrow money. This is strange because of the different monetary systems around the world, but gold is gold and silver is silver. **Article 1 section 8** says 'to borrow money on the credit of the United States." What type of money is the USA borrowing? No two countries have the same currency. The USA borrows so-called money from the Federal Reserve Bank. The reserve bank is a private bank just like Chase and Wells Fargo. THEY ARE A CARTEL with POWER. They control the printed notes (money) supply. This is the same paper that is so-called DEMONinations. We have the Federal Reserve paper with various numbers representing different values, but the same paper with different numbers. The Federal Reserve Bank has stockholders just like Chase and Well Fargo. The name or the word "federal" is deception also to fool you into thinking it is federal, BUT it is not federal. These notes are federal indebtedness. They are valuable in our mind only as well as invaluable in reality. The coins we have in this system are also deception because silver coins are no longer silver but counterfeit. Since it is no longer silver and copper coins, but made to look like coins before 1964. Why do the so-called silver coins (quarters and dimes) still have ridges around these coins? It is ALL a delusion. Dimes and quarters today have no real value. Look at the edge of the dimes and quarter; there is NO silver but some other type of metal. It only has value because it is in our mind only. Period. Which means this is deceit, fraudulent and crookedness to the American people. We have been betrayed to the highest level of treason. Since it does not contain real silver and real copper coins, why does silver coins still have ridges? Ridges are there to continue the deception. Let's get real. These coins today are **counterfeit**, passing off as real. And this is to defraud us the American public and this is a crime to defraud by deception. The intent is to defraud us and this is a crime by definition. Who is committing or perpetrating this crime with intent to defraud? Those people who are allowing THE MAKING of those coins. What we have is monopoly money.

What is the definition of counterfeit according to *Webster? "MADE IN EXACT IMITATION OF SOMETHING VALUABLE OF IMPORTANT WORTH THE INTENTION TO DECEIVE OR DEFRAUD."* **NOW YOU BE THE JUDGE, FOR I AM THROUGH.** My life (I am not concern because as Psalmist wrote HE IS MY SHIELD AND PROTECTOR and when my job is over HE shall close my book and I will then be move on to heaven and in HIS arms I will be forever) WON'T BE worth anything after this book comes out and hits the street because the system has been exposed by greedy and corrupt men in the highest offices in this land of The UNITED STATES OF AMERICA INCORPORATION THEY HAVE ALLOWED AND COMMITTED FRAUD TO THE HIGHEST LEVEL OF THE CONSTITUTION OF THE UNITED STATES OF AMERICA, AND THE BEAT GOES ON LALALADEEDA LALADOSE AND THE BEAT GOES ON AND THE BEAT GOES ON AND ON and now look at the debt of the USA Inc. We are in a mess and there is only one hope and that is off planet earth. The situation seems hopeless. The only hope we have is our SAVIOR YAHUSHA. Because the debt WILL NEVER EVER END TILL WE SEE THE END AND GUESS WHAT, THE END IS COMING SOON. Just wait. Keep on living because some will see SALVATION and to escape this planet, for there will be a NEW HEAVEN AND A NEW EARTH. This debt will never end. What about the interest on that type of debt? The constitution also says in **Article 1 section 8** *"that Congress must provide for punishment of counterfeiting the securities and current coin of the United States.* So who is going to protect us from Congress? Congress is not following The Constitution of the United States. Our congresspeople are omitting, neglecting or co signing their duties to another entity which is NOT CONSTITUTIONAL. Their actions or lack of actions are at the highest level of treason of the constitution of The USA.

These laws were instituted to protect us from the whims of man's basic nature of GREED. Basically, this is monopoly money. Our congressperson promised, when sworn in, to defend the constitution from enemy within and enemy without. This is in The US Constitution. None of these congresspersons has fulfilled their portion of that statement and should be held accountable for not defending the constitution of the USA. The constitution says ALL debt <u>MUST</u> be paid by coins and not by printed money. **Article 1 section 10 states,** *"No State shall enter into any Treaty, Alliance, or Confederation; grant Letters of Marque and Reprisal; coin Money; emit Bill of Credit; make any Thing but gold and silver Coin a Tender in Payment of Debts;* "Anything else would not be legal according to The Constitution. There is no law higher than THE CONSTITUTION of The United States of America. You will have to add an Amendment to override this statement in The Constitution. A bill will not do, but an Amendment would have to be added. **Article 1 section 10 states** to coin Money and *It does not say to print Money.* This is where the UCC comes into being. Uniform Commercial Code (UCC) money order, bank drafts and checks. UCC IS NOT CONSTITUTIONAL. This is outside of the constitution of the United States of America. None of these things are constitutional in the United States of America, but in fact, the Constitution of the USA gave Congress the ability to determine the rate of our money and not the Federal Reserve Board.

Article 1 Section 8 To coin Money, *regulate the Value thereof and of foreign Coin, and fix Standard of Weights and Measures.* As you have just read, the law is not being followed. The USA government has been sold to enemies within the united states. Anytime someone else controls your money, they, in turn, control you by default. Can you go and curse out your boss and keep your job? Can you come to work when you want to, but if you work for yourself you control your money. WEAREINDEBT! WE-ARE-DEBT!

Money has destroyed our constitution because we are at the mercy of someone else. Who controls the money? Many people are NOT aware how bad or how delicate a shape our economy is in. You see it is controlled by the ones who are printing the money. Have you heard the term "Increasing The Debt Ceiling"? The debt limit is a ceiling imposed by Congress on the amount of debt that the U.S.Federal government can have outstanding. The U.S. is in so much debt that it had to raise the debt limit to borrow extra money to pay its debts. It is like you borrow money and you are having problems paying what you already owe and so you go deeper in debt and you borrow more money to pay those debts you already owe. Another example is you are in your house and water is a foot above your head and you add another 3 feet of water above that debt or when back in the 80's people were buying townhouses and the following years you were above the market and the following years your appraised value has crash and now you are $50,000 under the last year appraised value.

This has totally destroyed our constitution because we have become servants to the lenders. And if you keep borrowing money you are creating more problems. If you can't pay your bills then what? BANKRUPTCY! Some people say just print more paper, but we don't owe the paper we are borrowing the paper. We don't owe the rights to that paper; it is owed by the Federal Reserve Bank, which I have stated is a private bank. If all banks were to close up, what would you do? Remember in the movie "It's a Wonderful Life" what the bank had to do to stay in business? Someone stated to me, "They can't do that." The USA declared bankruptcy in 1933 and DEMANDED all citizens (required) to turn in their gold. So don't tell me they (ultra elites) can't declare martial law. THIS CAN BE DONE. The ultra elites have the ability to do whatsoever please them to do. Just stay prayerful because YAHUSHA is coming soon! Amein. The way to get around the constitution is for the president of the United States of America to issue an executive order and declare the USA under martial law.

Once martial law is in effect, watch out, we will have a total collapse of this society of THE UNITED STATES OF AMERICA!

Executive Order 11110 can still be implemented. Executive Order 11110 was written by John Fitzgerald Kennedy to get rid of Federal Reserves Notes and replace them with silver certificates, but before it went into effect, President Kennedy was assassinated by the power we can't see. Who is this power, the ones that actually run this country and the ones that control congress personnel that vote on things. They would place hits (assassination) on people and family members or expose their dirty secrets. This Executive Order will never go into effect because there will be another assassination will HAPPEN! PERIOD! It is called the unseen hand that is in the control of this nation's money supply. THE POWER. Do we realize what is going on or we are so out of mind that we just don't care? Just so nonchalant, uncaring, exempt, unapologetic and apathetic. Whosoever controls the money controls you!

Events occur for a particular reason, but YAHUAH is in full control of whatever situation that occurs or will occur. All things are in HIS HANDS and there is no situation that HE is not aware of because ALL THINGS occur because HE IS. And safety for HIS Saints are in HIS HANDS. Men may think they are in control of themselves, but at the end, you will report to YAHUSHA and then HE will judge the things that are done according to HIS righteousness.

So when martial order is declared and all the banks are closed and this one world goes into effect, be ye ready, for we the Saints of YAH will be gone and the world will be in total collapse when millions are missing and men are then wanting death, but death shall escape. THE END TIMES ARE UPON US, SO BE YE READY. FOR YAHUSHA IS COMING and the man of sin will be in control running this world. What will you do if you don't have access to your money? What does money control? Actually, most of us have a card with a chip. All our incomes are just numbers on a computer system. And we are tied to the number. LISTEN UP! Your bank accounts are tied to this system. Our mortgages are through this system. We have online bills paid. Our gasoline for cars is tied to that chip. Our food we buy is tied to that system. The majority of us don't have gold and silver on hand, but all the gold and silver won't do any good because we can't eat silver and gold coins. What will be better than silver or gold is food, water and the land free of any debts and also animals such as cows, sheep, goats, chicken and so on. Why, because when martial law comes into effect, this will be your way out maybe. But this can be confiscated also. The only way out is to escape planet

Earth. How do I escape the planet Earth is to know YAHUSHA, THE SON OF YAHUAH, THE FATHER. THIS IS THE YESHUAH THE SALVATION. AMEIN!

Let me ask one more question. WOULD YOU RATHER HAVE ALL THE MONEY IN THE WORLD OR ALL THE LAND (for planting trees, fruits, lumber etc.) WITH CATTLES, SHEEP, CHICKEN, FISHES AND WATER? What is your choice, A or B? Now what is the value of your money? The Bible also says not to charge usury. But we do because this usury is how banks make their money. How are bank employees paid? How do bankers and wealth management companies make that mighty dollar? Through our indebtedness. How is it that you borrow $300,000 to buy a house and you can pay it off in fifteen years if you make an additional payment a year? Sounds crazy. Sounds a little shady. One other thing the bank takes your money and invests it into other projects and the banks are not required to have a fractional reserve as in years passed. Let's be excellent students of what is going on around us and remember, THE SON OF THE LIVING GOD IS ON HIS WAY BACK WITH VENGEANCE, POWER, AND EVERY KNEE WILL BOW! BECAUSE HE IS KING OF KINGS AND THE VERY ESSENCE OF POWER. Power that you will beg for mercy for your evil Federal Reserve Notes of debt and orchestrating behind the scenes. YOU WILL KNOW THE REAL POWER. THIS ENTITY PERSON OF COLOR. The one you named JESUS! WHOSE REAL HEBREW NAME IS YAHUSHA. A HEBREW BY NATURE. WHO MOTHER IS HEBREW (A PERSON OF COLOR). AMEIN AND HALLELUJAH.

If we were to take all the richest people's money in The United States of America, it would not make a dent into the national debt of the United States of America. We are in their hands. Period! We are a nation insolvent and soon the debt will have to be paid. You ask, "How will that be done?" By closing all accounts. Your savings account, checking accounts, 401 k, money market accounts and any other accounts. You see all these accounts are digital numbers and with no actual hard on cash value. Think about this? The USA is insolvent; The ultra-elites are in charge of the USA wealth. We are in their hands. Period! You may say," They CAN'T do that", but remember in 1933, President FDR demanded all citizens to turn in their gold by an executive order. This was totally UNCONSTITUTIONAL. PERIOD.

NOW I have given you the red pill just to awaken you. To awaken you from your slumber or zombie status. That is all I am trying to do, to awaken you out of your slumber or zombie existence or experience or your ideological way of thinking, but it's man's greed and covetousness ways we are in this unrighteous and luficerian system of unholy and ungodly men aligning their pockets, praying to his god satan and his demons. When a person has an unhealthy appetite, an evil desire, a disrespectful and uncaring, an evil fragmentable heart to obtain wealth (money) by ANY means no matter WHAT, WATCH OUT because the sin of covetousness's relation is into play. Greed has consumed that thought pattern and there's nothing else, but greed has taken that person's conscience, which leads to death and separation from ELOHIYM FOREVER AND FOREVER unless one repent of his error ways AMEIN! Remember about the rich man that fared sumptuously every day. A friend once said and I am passing this information on, **"Searching for the truth is easy, But ACCEPTING THE TRUTH IS WHAT'S HARD."**

Did you find something that you were not aware of?

CHAPTER 30

—⁂—

Letters to the Churches

Dear Pastor Frederick Haynes III,

I was disappointed in your message at the end when you stated Jesus, THE SON OF ELOHIYM, died on Friday and rose early Sunday morning. THAT IS NOT WHAT THE WORD SAYS. Matthew 12:40 states as Jonah was in the belly of the whale three days and three nights, so shall THE SON of MAN be in the heart of earth three days and three nights. So If The MESSIAH died on Friday afternoon and rose early Sunday morning, THE SCRIPTURES ARE INCORRECT AND you are right, or THE SCRIPTURES ARE CORRECT and you are wrong, misrepresenting, misleading or fabricating the truth. Guess what I BELIEVE. Friday night <u>one night</u> Saturday <u>one day</u> Saturday night <u>two nights</u> and early Sunday morning. Where are the other two days and the other night? Something is WRONG! Preacher, so you and every preacher who PREACHES what you are saying is incoherent., not correct, misleading, delusion, and misinterpretation of the scriptures. You are supposedly doctors of The Word of YAH, but just like the Pharisees and the Sadducees. I think not. For ye are unlearned men of the precious word of YAH, but teaching the precepts of ungodly men. Is this what you have been taught to mislead GOD'S people? Remember, you and other pastors are just stewards.

When did the women buy those spices and the Sabbath day had passed already? **Mark 16:1**: "They were at the tomb before the rising of the sun." **Exodus 31:13**: Verily my <u>Sabbaths</u> ye shall keep. MESSIAH was <u>THE PASSOVER LAMB</u>. **John 1:29** "Passover day was a high Sabbath Day." John 19:31. Passover day was celebrated ALWAYS on the fourteenth day of Nisan each and every year. Passover day fluctuates from year to year. Passover could have been on the first day of the week, the second day of the week, the third day of the week, the fourth day of the week, the fifth day of the week, the sixth day of the week or the seven day of the week. Just like the Fourth of July fluctuates each year. The Fourth of July could be on any day of the week. The Passover lamb had to be in the house on the tenth to the fourteenth day without a blemish and The lamb were sacrificed on the evening of the fourteenth of Nisan. CHRIST was without blemish (**Mark 12:34, Matthew 22:46,Luke 20:40**). This is scripture and not Friday as you proclaimed on Sunday, April 7, 2019, at 11:00 a.m. service

THE WORD OF GOD MUST BE EXPOUNDED CORRECTLY. If it is EXPOUNDED incorrectly, then HIS PEOPLE will then be misled. As you know we have been misled for years believing non-colored people telling us JESUS was white and had blond hair and blue eyes, which is a fabricated lie that has been perpetrated for so many years, but that lie has been replaced with TRUTH! Do you agree? Yes or No.

2 Timothy 2:15: All I want to do is to give out information to informed the lost or to correct the wrong information that is said and not to argue but to confirmed what is the TRUTH OF GOD'S WORD because we are responsible to GOD only and not to the words that come out of a man's mouth. WHY, BECAUSE AT THE END OF TIME HERE ON THIS EARTH, WE WILL STAND BEFORE THE ADONAI YAHUSHA HA'MASHIACH TO BE JUDGED! If you have any questions, call me. I stand on GOD'S WORD. Why, because at the end, I will meet YAHUSHA (**John 5:22**) HE IS THE GREAT I AM!

Carl L Jones

CEPHER

Exodus 12:40

Now the sojourning of the children of YASHAR'EL, who dwelt in the land of Mitsrayim, and the LAND of Kena`an, they and their fathers, was four hundred and thirty years.

SEPTUAGINT

Exodus 12:40

And the sojourning of the Children of Israel, while they sojourned in the the Land of Egypt and the Land of Chanaan, was four hundred and thirty years

KJV

Exodus 12:40

Now the sojourning of the children of Israel, who dwelt in Egypt, was four hundred and thirty years.

We have here three different Bibles and words are left out of two of them. For a person to establish truthful information; You have to have ALL of the correct information or you will be going down the wrong road and others that you pass information to. Do you get it? It will be your fault? You see I was going down the wrong road, but NOW I have the right information and I am passing it on.

Preachers Failed

Preachers PREACH THE WORD OF GOD, but they don't believe HIS WORD. Preachers PREACH CHRIST died on Friday at three o'clock and was raised from the dead early Sunday morning. NOWHERE IN THE BIBLE DOES IT STATES CHRIST DIED ON Friday at three o'clock and rose early sunday morning. MESSIAH was the perfect sacrifice of YAH ELOHIYM THE PASSOVER LAMB as **John 1:29** states. MESSIAH died on the fourteenth of Nisan as well as thousands of lamb that day. HE was the perfect lamb of GOD. This Passover day was a high day. The Israelites had twelve Sabbath periods and this was a high day as said in **John 19:31** and **Leviticus 23:5**. YAHUSHA states HE would be in the tomb for three days and three nights (**Matthew 12:40**). Who is telling the TRUTH, man or GOD? This has nothing to do with salvation, but it has to do with TRUTH OF GOD'S WORD. **John 17:17** states HIS WORD IS TRUTH! Pilate states, "I find no fault in HIM." The Passover's lamb had to be without fault for four days before he was sacrificed on the fourteenth of Nisan. This day fluctuates each year just like The Fourth of July. This lamb had to be without blemish. The Pharisees tried to trick HIM, but could not (**Matthew 22:46, Mark 12:34, Luke 20:40)** CHRIST was the perfect lamb without blemish, but preachers PREACH Friday night one night, Saturday one day, Saturday night two night and then early Sunday morning. He arose from the dead after three days and three nights from the dead as the scriptures say. Anything else is not true, but that would be not scriptural, but a LIE! THE SCRIPTURE SAYS THREE DAYS AND THREE NIGHTS. This man's traditions of thinking are so wrong and mistaken by the scripture which are facts. Just like easter, easter eggs, easter candy, easter bunny are all paganism is mixed up CHRIST AND THE WORD and it will not mix. This is Roman Catholicism and NOT THE BIBLE. These traditions of men are misleading and false. We teach our children falsehood and lies instead of THE CREATOR'S WORD! The name Jeus was not translated but substituted. In the 1611 KJV, it was Iesus. This is really bad because some names were changed because the "i" still exists today. I have a problem with the name Jesus. This was the name I was saved under and now I find out HIS true name. Should we still be using the English name at all as savior since it is a false name? The name Jesus is false and misleading. We need the truth and nothing but the truth. Maybe it is all about the money, the reason we won't use the correct name or maybe it is just custom. We have gotten so used to using that name Jesus. Do you think this is hypocrisy? The people in the 1500 would have the same question because all they ever heard was Iesus and not Jesus. THE SON OF ELOHIYM name is misleading. This makes no LOGICAL sense at all today. How was this done without an uproar? ALL THESE LIES OF MEN. So, if you went to Spain, would your name change? I will let you ponder on that information, but I do know that OUR SAVIOR WAS NOT BORN WITH THE name JESUS, but we do use it.

CHRIST THE SON OF GOD was killed for several reasons 1] political, economic, and religious (**John 11:48**)] 2] HE was The REDEMPTION LAMB for the world **John 1:29**. Without the shedding of blood, there is no redemption of sin. All sinners were to be bring their offering before ELOHIYM, CHRIST WAS brought before ELOHIYM by Israelites and Gentiles (Roman Soldiers) NAILED HIM to the cross and HE WAS THE PERFECT OFFERING SINLESS LAMB SO man can NOW be redeemed to ELOHIYM by THE PERFECT PASSOVER LAMB. BUT ELOHIYM ALSO RAISED HIM FROM THE DEAD AFTER THREE DAYS AND THREE NIGHTS. 3] HA'MASHIACH was sacrificed to become a new man. In Jeremiah 3:8, ELOHIYM divorced Israel and according to The Law, once the first husband divorced his first wife, he could NOT ever marry his first wife again, no, not ever. And ELOHIYM wanted HIS love back. And according to The Law that HE created it was impossible without defiling the land. It would bring defilement to the land (**Deuteronomy 24:1-4**). So CHRIST DIED and became a new husband and a new man when HE arose from the dead and ELOHIYM can now get HIS FIRST WIFE back

Israel, because HE became a new man for the woman HE loves. Remember they did not recognize HIM after the resurrection.

As it states in **Romans 11:1**. Pa'al is talking about a certain people and it was not the church. HIS people are Israel. Who is Israel? Pa'al states in **Philipians 3:5** he is Hebrew of Hebrews, Israelites and Benjaminites and **Acts 21:37** (the confusion of the Roman soldier) Avraham an Hebrew **Genesis 14:13**, Mosheh an Hebrew Exodus 4:6 (what color was his skin tone), GOD OF THE HEBREWS **Exodus 3:18**, Gehazi, what was his skin tone turned to **2 Kings 5:37**, Miryam Mosheh's sister what is her skin tone turned back to in **Numbers 12:1-14.** None of this is my opinion, but a fact presented to us by GOD'S WORD. Everyone I mention is a person of color. Their pigmentation is dark and not white. Gehazi and his seed were turned white permanently and forever, but the others are like my skin tone darker or lighter. We have been deceived by leaders who knew the TRUTH, but refused to expound the truth. **Opinion**: a view, judgment, or appraisal formed in the mind about a particular matter. **FACT:** actual, the quality of being actual, a piece of information presented as having objective reality. I have presented you with facts and not my opinion. And let's see who is right man or GOD?

Genesis 15:13-14 has not been fulfilled as of yet as many people have believed that it has been fulfilled over in Egypt land (That is a LIE also), but in Genesis it is relating to spiritual Egypt which is The United States of America. You see YAHUAH has made promises and some of those promises are curses. Our foreparents were placed on those nasty, FILTHY slave ships (**Deuteronomy 28:68**) because they failed the law and became disobedient. As The Bible states, our forefather stumbled, but GOD remembered HIS WORDS over 399 years ago and the 400th year is upon us when that nation will come to destruction. Part of the nation of Israel is in The United States and look how we have been treated, but ELOHIYM **PROMISED** that HE will avenge that nation for us. People in Israel are not the true Jews. We who are here in the United States are the true Jews (Hebrews). You got people (the church in the United States) who feel they are supporting the Israelites AND THEY ARE NOT because that nation had to fulfilled and be subject to **Deuteronomy 28:68** or you will make YAHUAH a liar and YAHUAH can't lie. Look at The United States right NOW, stores closing, tornadoes everywhere, extreme weather, a nation deeply in debt to the tune of $22,000,000,000,000 trillion dollars of debt and this nation's money supply grows deeper and deeper each and every day in debt. Where does money come from? (WHAT

HAPPENS WHEN YOU CAN'T PAY YOUR DEBT?) The Egyptians gave their lives over to the government **Genesis 47:13-25**, flooding, opioid, crisis, immigrant crossing causing the court system to be further and further behind, insurance companies getting inundated with claims and possible filing for bankruptcy, killings, crisis on every border, teachers' pay, property taxes system out of line, bees dying, food getting called back, measles outbreak, and viruses such as coronavirus with no cure. Look at THE WORD AND STUDY THE WORD and not the words coming out of my mouth and pastors' mouth but GOD'S MOUTH because HE WILL FULFILL HIS WORD (**Isaiah 55:11**, **Isaiah 65-17**, **Revelation 2:1**) You don't have to believe me, but believe this GOD WILL FULFILL HIS WORDS WHEN THE TIME IS! AMEIN. Our forefathers are the people who were in Canaan Land/ Israel and Egypt. They were the ones shipped to the spiritual Egypt the United States of America and as ELOHIYM said, HE shall exodus out of that nation with great wealth. Be ye ready because THE CHRIST IS COMING FOR ISRAEL ONLY and The Church the called-out ones that has been grafted into Israel by the death, burial and RESURRECTION of ELOHIYM'S SON THE HA'MASHIACH

Letter 2

My question to YAH is, "Where are we going?" This world is dying! Trees are dying! Birds are dying! Fish are dying in masses! Bees are dying! Once the bees are dead, how will food be pollinated? Then who will become food? I DON'T WANT TO LIVE IN THAT WORLD! But GOD ANSWERED THE QUESTION: THINGS ARE IN HIS CONTROL! There is no hope for The United States of America! ELOHIYM STATED HE will judge that nation! THAT IS A PROMISE OUT THE CREATOR'S MOUTH! The United States is $22,000,000,000,000 trillion dollars in debt. This debt will be more when this book comes out. It takes a million billion to equal a trillion dollars. If we took all the assets of the richest people in The United States, it would NOT make a dent in that debt. Since GOD has made this PROMISE of judgment against that nation. Our people have been in affliction for almost four hundred years. GOD WORDS MUST BE FULFILLED. Praying will not stop the judgment of THE CREATOR.

We are comfortable in our houses, running water, air conditioning, filled bellies, nice cars, televisions in every room, freezers filled, we have our jobs, income, heat on, lights on, bathroom facilities, Wal-Mart, stores galore, filled closets, schools, hospitals and so on. All these will stop. WHEN? The question is <u>WHEN</u>. So look for the judgment of The United States in the form of debts, drug addiction, infectious disease with no cures, panic, mass hysteria, homelessness, food shortage, stores closing, bankruptcies, stock market going down, flooding, foreclosures, INSURANCE COMPANIES GOING OUT OF BUSINESS (Do you think the insurance companies can continue losses as in California wildfires?), unemployment, fires, suicide, murders, mass killings, tornadoes, drought, more sexual transmitted diseases with no cure and you will see all these are coming more and more against this nation. We pray for those who are in darkness to come into the LIGHT OF LIFE before it is too late. Why, because the judgment of GOD is COMING fast. The year 2019 is fifteen days away. YAH'S (GOD) WORDS WILL BE FULFILLED! So as in the days of Noah, people were going about life and The Flood cleansed the earth. BE YE READY, FOR THE CHRIST IS COMING BACK FOR ALL BELIEVERS IN HIM! Hebrews, Israelites and The Church, THE CALLED-OUT ONES, THE RAPTURE WILL OCCUR SOON. ONLY THE FATHER KNOWS. JUST BE READY. Ask your congregation how much they believe THE WORD OF GOD 10, 25, 50, 75 or 100 percent.

P.S. If we look at the record, The Hebrews/Israelites were in slavery/affliction less than two hundred years, so **Genesis 15:13-14** has not been fulfilled as of yet. HalleluJAH (**Psalm 68:4**)! All my life, I have been labeled WRONG. The TRUTH came to my eyes earlier last year. Now I am presenting you with the TRUTH. I have been labeled on my birth certificate Negro, called by non-colored people the word n _ _ _ _ r. I have been labeled colored, black and African American. The people in charge of this labeling will not like this. Who Was in charge of labeling people? Is a penny black? My skin tone is a little darker shade than a brand new penny. So who was even reporting me as black. Sorry, I am not black, but my skin tone is brown. All these labels HAVE BEEN INCORRECT. I am of the true seed of Avram. Thereby, I am Hebrew/Israelite. HALLELUJAH! We are the true Israelites and not the non-colored people.

IT WAS A CURSE FOR A HEBREW/ISRAELITE TO BE WHITE. Pa'al is a Hebrew/Israelite (**Philippians 3:5**). YAHUSHA is a Hebrew/ISRAELITE. Mosheh is a Hebrew/Israelite (**Exodus 4:6**) Avram is a Hebrew (**Genesis 14:13**). Miryam, Mosheh's sister a Hebrew/*sraelite* (**Numbers 12:10**). In **Exodus 4:6-8** Mosheh placed his hand in his bosom and when he took it out it was white like leporous and when he placed his hand back into his bosom and took it out, it turned again as his other flesh.

*When I first wrote these letters, I was not thinking about the power of YAH, I was just thinking about these present conditions, but YAH is more than able to produce what we need. I was so misunderstanding of HIS POWER and that there is nothing HE can't do, but we are totally in HIS Hands. HE is able to sustain us period. HE said in

Genesis 28:14 "*And your seed shall be as the dust and you shall spread abroad to the **west**, and to the **east**, and to the **north**, and to the **south**: and **in you and in your seed shall all families of the earth be blessed.***

Who are the seeds of Ya'aqov?
To the reader was YAHUAH lying in this statement? Yes or No.

Letter 3

Miryam started a dispute with her brother Mosheh and GOD (YAH) heard it and turned her skin leporous. Gehazi's skin and his seed were leprous forever. This is where the non-colored Jews came from, but they had to be separated **(2 Kings 5:27)** from the True Israelites. GOD HAS MADE A WAY FOR ALL TO COME TO HIM. This is through HIS SON'S RESURRECTION FROM THE DEAD. If we believe this, all shall be saved whether Hebrew/Israelite or The CHURCH. CHRIST DIED AND ROSE AGAIN FROM DEATH so that we will forever be with YAHUAH. AMEIN! I ask again does the TRUTH MATTER? YES or NO. If you don't believe this you will be as hopeless, LOST FOREVER ETERNITY AWAY FROM THE CREATOR.

When the prophecy goes out, it will be completed. What comes out of YAH'S mouth, it will be completed. It will not be void **(Isaiah 55:11)**. Esau could not obtain Jacob's **blessing** because YAH already know what will happen because HE has seen it. To say otherwise is disservice, disinformation, dishonest and downright disrespectful. The information that we have been taught is INCORRECT. The seeds of Avram were not in Egypt four hundred years, so **Genesis 15:13-14** HAS NOT BEEN FULFILLED as of yet. Millions upon millions of people have been misled going down the WRONG PATH by the wrong information by those who are SUPPOSED to BE IN the know! Seminary teachers, pastors, evangelists, you are teaching your flock and leading them down the wrong road. Many people are being led by the Pope, and their teachings are inherently bad. Their priests' flesh are burning, and they go after little boys, false teaching, the virgin Mary as a god, false teaching. **Mary didn't stay a virgin.** YAHUSHA is called first born **Matthew 1:25**. YAHUSHA had brothers and sisters **Matthew 13:55-56.** So to say virgin she was, but Yoceph knew his woman many times. I don't want an apology; we can CONTINUE to believe these lies that go on or we can have faith and believe THE WORD OF YAH and what HE said. THE WORD OF YAH IS TRUTH. THE WORD OF YAH MUST BE COMPLETED. This has nothing to do with salvation per se but about completion of HIS WORD. YAH states IF HIS WORDS ARE NOT COMPLETED or fulfilled, the heaven and the earth would pass away (**Matthew 5:18, Luke 16:17).** Either YAH is a liar or YAH is TRUTH? These are your options.

The letter J was not in the 1611 KJV so KJV would be KIV. So the name JESUS didn't exist. So in the 1611 KJV, it was Iesus and not Jesus. So we have not a translation, but a substitution. Every name in the KJV was not translated but substituted. Why? Peter's name in Hebrew is Kepha, Matthew Mattithyahu, Mark Marcus, Luke Luqas, John Yahuchanon, Isaiah Yesha`yahu, Nehemiah Nechemyahu, Jeremiah Yirmeyahu. **2 Chronicles 7:14** *"If my people, <u>who are called by my name</u>, shall humble themselves, and pray, and seek my face, and turn from their wicked ways; then will I heal their land."* The FATHER name is YAH **Psalm 68:4. Now do any of those people have YAH a part of their names in the KJV?** Like The Bible states, a people that would not know HIS NAME **Yesha`yahu 52:6.** We have been blinded not knowing HIS name but we are *"The My People in The Bible."* What is the opposite of knowing? And that would be **not knowing.** Because the TRUTH has been stolen from our eyes (mind) and heart. The blessings and the curses in **Deuteronomy 28** have applied to one group of people only. **Deuteronomy 28:68** Our foreparents were placed on those FILTHY and nasty slave ships and shipped to every corner of this earth. Our foreparents were placed in yokes of iron. **THIS IS ANOTHER THE HOLOCAUST** in which no one want to discuss. And we are still suffering from this bondage and affliction today in the United States of America where we are in the book as three fifths of a man. How can a so-called police or peace officer shoot an unarmed so-called African American (Hebrew) and get away with a sanction hit and be found free? How can a peace officer arrest a twelve year-old for selling his own CD, but this CURSE of **Genesis 15:13-14** will be ended by THE CREATOR and this nation will be punished for what it has sown. The sower according to the law gets more back than what he has sown. What this means is that you sow an apple tree and you get a lot of apples off that tree and there are a lot of seeds in one apple from that tree with a lot of apples.

Now I have checked several records and none of them have shown the Hebrews/Israelites in bondage (affliction) for 400 years. The original Exodus out of Egypt was not after 400 years. It did not occur as it states in **Genesis 15:13-14**. Do you think YAHUAH is slow? The Hebrews were not in Egypt for 400 years. The Hebrews did not go into slavery until after Yoceph's death. There is not 400 years between Yoceph's death and Moseh's birth. The first slaves arrived in the america in August 1619 and it will end soon. Check the record. This is what I found. The first group of Hebrews went into bondage after Pharaoh who did not know of Joseph's (Yoceph) death (**Exodus 1:6-12**). In other words, after his death, the Hebrews went into slavery and were still in slavery at Mosheh's (Moses) birth. Joseph's death 1445/1444 BCE or 1640 BCE or 1452 BCE and Mosheh's birth 1592 BCE or 1576 or 1393 BCE. All of this information shows the maximum amount of time that the Hebrews / Israelites were in slavery was 217 years, approximately or less and not 400 years as **Genesis 15:13-14** says. This is a big problem! We have the TRUTH or we have incorrect, misquoted, error or a big lie. We can believe the TRUTH or we can believe a lie or we can stay in our stupor. I will believe the TRUTH THAT and YAH IS NOT IN ERROR, but man's teaching is WRONG. I MAKE NO APOLOGY! Since YAH cannot lie, we have things coming to The United States right now. Why, because we are approaching the 400th year as YAH stated, HE will punish that nation, extreme cold, flooding, fires, sickness on every side, store closings, opioid crisis, etc. Sooner or later insurance companies will not recover from their losses (insolvent). WE ARE AT THE 400TH YEAR OF FREEDOM AS YAH STATES IN **GENESIS 15:13-14.**

P.S, I forgot blackface. YAH is showing how badly the non-colored people have treated Avram's true seeds. CHECK IT OUT YOURSELF AND TELL, WARN, DECLARE and ADVERTISE TO YOUR CONGREGATION, **WHAT IS GOING TO HAPPEN** and BE PREPARED FOR WHAT WILL HAPPEN TO **THE UNITED STATES OF AMERICA.** The nation of Israel are dark-skinned people and are not non-color people. Pa'al has dark skin (**Acts 21:38**). Mosheh has dark skin (**Exodus 4:6**). Miryam, Mosheh's sister, has dark skin (**Numbers 12:1-15**) A person of non-color can only produce that of non-color. The Hebrews/Israelites are still people of color, the so-called blacks, African-American, Negroes. WE ARE THE TRUE SEEDS OF Avram, The Hebrew (**Genesis 14:13**). Mosheh is a

Hebrew/Israelite/Levi. Mosheh is dark skin (**Exodus 4:6-8**) Since his hand turned white as leprosy and when he stuck his hand back into his bosom, it changed to his other flesh. Mosheh has dark skin as the Egyptians and Yoceph as the Yashar`e'liy. Pharoah 's daughter claimed Mosheh as her son. Mosheh' s farther, Amram, is a Hebrew; Kohath, Mosheh's grandfather is a Hebrew; Levi, Mosheh's great grandfather is a Hebrew; Yashar'el, Mosheh's great great grandfather is a Hebrew; Yitschaq, Mosheh's great great great grandfather is a Hebrew; Avraham, Mosheh's great great great great grandfather is a Hebrew. Hebrews are ALL people of color. You see we have been blinded by the teaching of non-colored people led by satan, the adversary of YAH. This is our bloodline We Are The My People in The Bible.

The letter i still exists today, so changing the j to i doesn't make sense. In the 1611 kjv version it was IESUS and in the version after that, it became Jesus, but the 'i' still exists today and this makes this weird or WRONG. There is no way a person of non-color can produce a person of color. So when you are preaching about Moses or JESUS (which is not HIS NAME), almost every person in the KJV being white or non-color, we are preaching and teaching a lie. You may say color doesn't matter. Then PREACH THE TRUTH since color doesn't matter because TRUTH DOES MATTER!

The church or the assembly of The Called Ones did not replace Israel or could not replace Israel, but the Church was grafted into Israel. CHRIST DIED to redeem us back to HIS FATHER, to become the NEW MAN OR NEW HUSBAND to get back HIS FIRST WIFE (Israel). YAH divorced (**Yirmeyahu 3:8**) ISRAEL, HIS FIRST WIFE. In the Old Covenant, **Deuteronomy 24:1-4** the old husband could NOT ever remarry his first wife even if he wanted her back. IT WAS FORBIDDEN! CHRIST had to die to become a new MAN or NEW HUSBAND to get HIS first wife back, which is Israel. HE BECAME A NEW MAN. The divorce created this situation. So, when CHRIST DIED, HE became a NEW MAN and ISRAEL also died and became a new bride or wife. And through CHRIST'S DEATH, we all became NEW! As Pa'al states in Romans 11, Israel shall be saved. Israel stumbled, but GOD(YAH) HAS NOT CAST AWAY HIS PEOPLE. YAH FORBID! The church was grafted into Israel. The church believes it has replaced Israel, but that is living in a fantasy world. To think YAH has forgotten who Israel is? The answer is inequitable NO! The church still refers to the **Hebrew** young men by their Babylonian name Shadrach, Meshach and Abednego. The church needs to refer to them by their Hebrew name Hannaniah, Mishael and Azariah. Why do preachers use their pagan name and not their

Hebrew names? The names' meanings are so opposite from their Hebrew names. The church still lies about CHRIST death and birth. CHRIST DIED on The Israelites Passover day. He was in the tomb for three days and three nights. The church preaches the tradition of men and not YAH'S Words. "Oh HE died on friday afternoon and rose early sunday morning. THIS IS A BIG FABLE, STORY,INCORRECT, ERRONEOUS INFORMATION AND MISREPRESENTATIVE OF THE TRUTH IN OTHER WORDS IT IS A BIG FAT LIE! And this preaching grieves THE RUACH'S Heart to HIS SOUL for men to spread false information and for others to be led down the wrong road. **Matthew 12:40** states as Jonah was in the belly of the whale three days and three nights, so shall the son of man be in the heart of the grave and there is no way that CHRIST DIED on friday evening and rose early sunday morning is 3 days and 3 nights. THIS IS A LIE ACCORDING TO Matthew 12:40. Who do you believe? According to the scripture, we make THE WORD OF YAH A LIE; Thereby did GOD LIE? But we do know GOD CANNOT LIE. So man is a liar according to THE WORD OF YAH. IF YAH HAD LIED;THEN WHY ARE WE STILL HERE? Heaven and earth would pass away. Man says CHRIST was born on CHRISTmass day. All lamb are born in the springtime and not in the wintertime. Ask Google. CHRIST's announcement of HIS conception was the six month of Israelite calendar and you go back three months and we will have the springtime. CHRIST WAS THE PASSOVER LAMB for THE FATHER. Passover was on the fourteenth day of Nisan and that day fluctuated from year to year just like the Fourth of July. So quit preaching lies and tell your congregation The TRUTH or face judgment of your deception for your position, power and money for THE DECEPTION. STUDY AND RIGHTLY DIVIDE THE WORD OF TRUTH! Preacher/ Pastor PREACH and teach THE WORD OF YAH according to the scriptures and not the tradition of false men teaching (**Yesha`yahu 40:8, 55:11, Matthew 24:35, Mark 13:31, Luke 21:33**).

Sincerely, your BROTHER IN CHRIST, THE SON OF
THE ELOHIYM (YAH THE FATHER)

Carl L Jones

Letter 4

All my life, I have been taught and informed that the name JESUS is THE SON OF THE FATHER. I was also informed that JESUS and Joshua meant the same, Salvation or deliverance. A thought came to me several years ago; Why are Jesus and Joshua names spelled so differently and not the same as Carl and Charles. Carl and Charles mean the same "manly". Carl and Charles are spelled differently as you can see, but Carl is derived from Charles. So then why is Jesus and Joshua spelled so differently? In the 1611 KJV, there is no letter "j" in that version. In the 1611 KJV the name Jesus did not exist; It was IESUS. LOGICALLY SPEAKING, why change a name to JESUS just because you add an j to the english language? IT IS NOT LOGICAL TO CHANGE A NAME because an alphabet is added to the language?The "i" still exists today; The "j" was not added till AD 1524. THIS DOES NOT MAKE ANY LOGICAL SENSE AT ALL! You add an alphabet and your name changes. This is so NOT LOGICAL! So why not call THE SON OF THE FATHER THE LIVING ELOHIYM (YAH THE FATHER) (PSALM 68:4) BY HIS HEBREW NAME?

YAHUSHA is a combination of two names

YAHUAH is THE FATHER'S name

YESHUAH means Salvation

YAHUSHA means The FATHER'S Salvation

YAHUSHA DIED for several reasons and not just to redeem man back to ELOHIYM.

Yahuchanon 11:48 *"If we let HIM alone, all men will believe on HIM: and the Romans shall come and take away both our place and nation."* YAHUSHA was killed for religious, political and economic reasons. HAMASHIACH was making HIS name known throughout the land. YAHUSHA was feeding the poor, healing the sick physical and spirit of man, turning water into wine, opening the eyes of the blind, opening the deaf ears, healing the handicap and raising the dead from the tomb. He was awakening the masses' hearts. The religious leaders were taking notice and they were afraid of the foreseeable future of the Romans taking their money, lands, position and power away from them. Look at what the verse says about our place (position and economy) and nation (land). All this was in danger if ELOHIYM THE SON LIVED and HE had to end with HIS DEATH on the cross and HE arose at the end of the third day. Also, HIS DEATH was determined before the foundation of the world was established.

The second reason YAHUSHA HA'MASHIACH had to die was because HE was THE PASSOVER LAMB that takes away the sin of the world. **Yahuchanon 1:29** declares, *"Behold THE LAMB YAHUAH which takes away the sin of the world."* YAHUSHA died as many lamb died on Passover Day, which is a high Sabbath Day. **Yahuchanon 19:31**. During Passover Day, many lamb died that day in the evening because ELOHIYM established that in **Exodus 12.** ELOHIYM ORCHESTRATED THE DATE and THE TIME OF EVERYTHING we read. There is a time for all things and the timing of HIS DEATH, THE SON OF ELOHIYM was SPECTACULAR. IT WAS TREMENDOUSLY ACCURATE. IT WAS RIGHT ON TIME. It was placed on the specific date to occur at a specific time. Look at it. The Pecach or Passover had to fall on a special day for **Matthew 12:40** to occur. To pull a time for HIS SON TO spend three days and three nights in the tomb to be born the right time and HIS DEATH FELL ON the PERFECT PASSOVER Day to fall when it did was amazing in the first month of Nisan on the fourteenth day at evening three days and three nights. HIS WORD IS ABOVE HIS NAME TRULY. It was established by ELOHIYM'S WORD and HIS WORD must be fulfilled. The REDEMPTION LAMB was for the entire world. **Hebrews 9:22** states without the shedding of blood, there is no redemption of SIN. Man/Israel were REQUIRED to bring sacrifice for their sins that they had committed. They brought this sacrifice to the high priest and the Levites. THIS WAS THE LAW! When YAHUSHA DIED, who were there to place HA'MASHIACH on the CROSS The Israelites (religious leaders and the Israelites in the crowd Miryam the mother of YAHUSHA, Mary Magdalene, Yahuchanon and others) and the Gentiles (other nations) the Roman soldiers who and the religious leaders urging the crowd and who whipped THE SON OF ELOHIYM and man's sin were forgiven to those who believe. We are no longer required to bring a blood sacrifice for our sins because ADONAI YAHUSHA HA'MASHIACH was whipped, crowned with thorns, spitted upon, beard pulled, hit upside the head, an illegal trial, mocked, nailed hands and feet to the cross, speared in the side, told a man on the cross thou shalt be with me in paradise and he died and was laid in a tomb wrapped in a clean linen cloth and raise from the tomb with all power so that we may believe and live with HIM forever! In other words, man was required to bring a blemishless sacrifice, a perfect sacrifice before THE FATHER AND YAHUSHA WAS THAT PERFECT sin offering. ELOHIYM GAVE HIMSELF AS THE PERFECT OFFERING (as HE said in **Genesis 22:8** *"My son ELOHIYM will provide HIMSELF a lamb for a burnt offering."*) so man ELOHIYM could have the perfect union together again as in the beginning as Yitschaq said in **Yasher 22:44-45** *"As YAHUAH lives, the ELOHIYM of my father Avraham, if YAHUAH should say unto my father, "Take now your son Yitschaq and bring him up an offering before ME. I would not refrain but I would joyfully accede to it" And YAHUAH heard the word that Yitschaq spoke to Yishma`el, and it seemed good in the sight of YAHUAH, and he thought to try Avraham in this matter.*

When Ad-am, the first man, sinned and was spiritually separated from ELOHIYM. This was death. The death of YAHUSHA and HIS resurrection; We now are able to join back to ELOHIYM'S fellowship. As in THE WORD OF YAHUSHA, ***"IT IS FINISHED!"***

HALLELUJAH! We don't have stress, we don't have to work to receive salvation because THE MESSIAH completes the guilt and shame of death and now we have forgiveness eternal because we are **SAVED**. And now all we have to do is believe what YAHUSHA DID and we are saved. How long? It is not based on my works but YAH's WORKS. YAHUAH RIGHTEOUSNESS and my righteousness. Just as long as you believe YAHUSHA died and rose again, thou are saved because we are in The FATHER's Mighty Hands and those are some mighty strong HANDS! I AM SAVED! WHAT ABOUT YOU? One question: Can a drowning man save himself from drowning; and you are struggling trying everything in your power to save yourself? Yes or No. Every effort you take and you are still drowning; Can you save yourself? I will say no because he is drowning and taking on more water into your lungs. And it is just one more moment you are sinking to the bottom and your lungs are filled with water. This man needs help. We are that DROWNING person and we need help from HA'MASHIACH always because we can never, no, not ever save ourselves because our righteousness is as a FILTHY rag (**Yesha`yahu 64:6**) What is a filthy rag? One that we use to wipe our butt and the other is a woman uses for her monthly commitment. Do you see how FILTHY we are compared to ELOHIYM? JUST PLAIN FILTHY AND NASTY individuals! BUT ELOHIYM has MADE THE WAY and has shown us HIS GRACE. GOD 'S REDEMPTION AT CHRIST EXPENSE.

Third and final reason is YAHUSHA had to die because ELOHIYM had to obtain HIS wife back, which is Israel. ELOHIYM divorced Israel. HE removed His Hand of protection and shrugged off HIS wife's plea of mercy. **Yirmeyahu 3:8** says, *"And I saw, when for all the cause whereby backsliding Israel committed adultery I had put her away, and given her a bill of divorce; yet her treacherous sister Judah feared not, but went and played the harlot also."* ELOHIYM divorced ISRAEL, and according to the law, the first husband is unable to obtain his first wife back NO MATTER WHAT. IT WAS AGAINST THE LAW. There was no provision in the law where the first husband could obtain his wife back. It would defile the land. SO ELOHIYM CREATES A NEW MAN (LAW) AND NOT BREAK THE LAW HE CREATED. ELOHIYM HAS TO OBEY HIS OWN WORD ALSO OR HEAVEN AND EARTH WOULD PASS AWAY, AND HE CREATED A NEW LAW. ELOHIYM had to become a new man to get HIS FIRST WIFE BACK (**Deuteronomy 24:1-4**). HE became a new man because they did not recognize HIM after the resurrection **Luke 24:13-18 and Yahuchanon 20:14.** These are my two witnesses that did not recognize HIM because HE had become a new man and now see this as face value and just don't try to reject this knowledge as some will.

So when YAHUSHA DIED AND ROSE again, HE (ELOHIYM) became a new man; Thereby, the old man is dead. He became a new man (husband). The old man has died and the new man arose and the old wife died and the new wife arose with the new man. The new man can now marry his new wife and there is no longer defilement in the land. So we have a NEW HUSBAND and NEW WIFE JOINED TOGETHER AGAIN and FOREVER.

HALLELU(**JAH**) **Psalm 68:4!**

Church leaders today will not or do not realize what the TRUTH IS or refuse to expound the TRUTH for various reasons. What reasons? MONEY, being ostracized, losing their congregation, just going along to get along, ignorance, being laid back, not caring and so on. Knowing that judgment will be done. There is no way around this and you and I will see THE SON OF ELOHIYM in judgment because HE IS THE JUDGE (**Yahuchanon 5:22**). Church leaders are preaching Easter which has nothing to do with THE SON OF ELOHIYM. The word "Easter" is in KJV once and in another bible called The Cepher, it is Pecach, which is Passover instead of Easter, so the KJV got it wrong; thereby, it is translated incorrect, false and misleading, YAHUSHA DIED ON Passover day, the High Sabbath Day, which is the fourteenth day of Nisan and that day fluctuate every year just like the fourth of july. If they PREACH anything else, it would be fabricating THE TRUTH, which is THE WORD OF ELOHIYM **Yahuchanon 17:17.** You are a bastard to the truth of YAH Holy Words. THE WORD OF ELOHIYM SAYS THREE DAYS AND THREE NIGHTS **Matthew 12:40.** If you can count. If YAHUSHA died at three o'clock on Friday and rose early Sunday morning, how many days and nights is that? Did ELOHIYM make a mistake or did ELOHIYM LIE or is the preacher telling the TRUTH or telling a lie or did the preacher make a mistake? Who do you believe? I KNOW ELOHIYM CANNOT LIE. Why? Because we are still here **Mark 13:31, Luke 21:33.** Most will go in their own mind-set because there is nothing you can write to convince them any other way just like the **Pharisees.**

Pastors and teachers who have elected to reject The Word of ELOHIYM have become bastards to that word of truth and not acknowledge what they had learned was, in fact, error and not truth. They celebrate so-called religious days like easter or ashtoreth. The word easter is disguised to deceive us. And we are so stuck in men's tradition that we go along not to buck this corrupt system. Preachers do not know or study ELOHIYM Words, but are misleading the flock of ELOHIYM because pastors are just stewards and you are convinced they would not mislead YAH's People. Pastors are just stewards and do not own anyone. It is YAHUSHA'S assembly who are the called out ones. THE SON OF ELOHIYM is the Head and not the steward. The stewards were appointed to lead those congregations only. Easter was placed in the KJV and not translated. This was a device of satan to cause confusion among YAHUSHA People. You should know why you are celebrating something because the resurrection of THE SON OF ELOHIYM has nothing whatsoever to do with a pagan holiday. Do you think THE RESURRECTION has anything to do with easter bunny or easter eggs? THINK ABOUT THAT and question in your mind why you are doing what you are doing. We have mixed paganism with The RESURRECTION. Pagan holidays and HOLY DAYS don't mix as man wants it to. The world has been conditioned to accept The Mark of The Beast. And you should know this.

Letter 5

Dear Pastor Kevin Anthony Powell,

I missed the fellowship we had also, but I had to move on because of a philosophy change. This will be my last written words to you. I got tired of hearing that we are Christians when I know we are NOT. You believe that we (the people of color) are Christians. Just saying you are Christians doesn't make it so because the KKK is a Christian group and I sure don't want to be associated with them. I no longer subscribe to that belief that we are Christians. We are not Christians, but we are Hebrews by ethnicity and nationality. I profess we are THE SONS AND DAUGHTERS OF JACOB (YA`AQOV) direct descendants. What my thoughts are THE SON OF GOD (ELOHIYM THE FATHER, THE SON, AND THE HOLY SPIRIT) DIED FOR MAN TO BRING US back into unity with HIM. As (John) Yahuchanon the baptizer told us in **John 1:29,** THE LAMB OF GOD WHICH TAKES AWAY THE SIN OFTHE WORLD.

The KJV has taken the majority of Hebrew names Reuven, Yahudah, Diynah, Asher, Yoceph, Yisshakar, Leviy, Naphtaliy and not translated them but transposed them into some form into an English version in which King James could read and understand and this has been ignorantly surpassed down through all these generations and we have been brainwashed to believe this description of what we have been taught wrong. My belief is WHAT THE CHRIST DID NOT CHANGE, BUT HOW I am labeled has. We have been brainwashed to believe a lie or the deception of satan, that we are not "the my people" in the KJV. HAS GOD, HAS GOD, HAS GOD, HAS GOD cast away HIS people? The answer as Pa'al said will be definitely NO! If you went to France, would your name be changed ? No!

The name JESUS is not Hebrew, but English. JESUS and Joshua's name means the same deliverer/salvation. HIS Hebrew name is YAHUSHA, which means THE FATHER'S SALVATION. His name is a combination of two words YAHUAH (THE FATHER'S name) and YESHUAH (meaning Salvation). So we have THE FATHER'S SALVATION. **Psalm 68:4** says *"Sing unto ELOHIYM, sing praises to HIS name: extol HIM that rides upon the heavens by HIS name YAH."* In the KJV, it has JAH, but we say HIS every time we say The word HALLELU**JAH**. And the "j" is pronounced with a "y" sound instead of a j sound. This is so strange, a j is pronounced with a "y" sound. In the 1611 KJV, there were no j but i instead. So we would have IAH, whereas today, we have a j and the i was pronounced with a "y" sound.

The Bible says, *"Study to show thyself approved unto **GOD**, a workman that needeth not to be ashamed, rightly dividing **THE WORD OF TRUTH**"* **2 Timothy 2:15. Proverbs 15:28a** declares, *"The heart of the righteous studies to answer."* I may sound like a crazy person, but that's alright because I am crazy for CHRIST. YAHUSHA states in **Yahuchanon (John) 10;16** *and other sheep **I have**, which are **NOT** of this **fold.**"* The other sheep is those that accept HIM as Savior, but HE was talking to this fold. Who is this fold? ISRAEL. And the other sheep are those that commit their lives to CHRIST. (**Zechariah**) Zakaryahu 2:11 says *"And many nations shall be joined to EL-YAHUAH in that day, and shall be **my people**: and I will dwell in the midst of you, and you shall know that YAHUAH TSEVA'OTH has sent me."*

The KJV has wording as THE LORD which stills exists in England today. We have Lord so in so that the word "Lord" is still used by England today as a nobility title, so it really does little to identify THE FATHER, THE CREATOR, THE GREAT I AM as HE SAID IN THE PSALM "JAH" is HIS NAME. CHRIST died for all of mankind's sins. HE was on the cross, HE CRIED TO HIS FATHER ABBA, HE was in the tomb three days and three nights as the scripture says. HE didn't die on a friday because if HE had died on a friday, **Matthew 12:40** WOULD NOT BE CORRECT BUT WOULD BE INHERENTLY WRONG. YAH CANNOT LIE, but man has certainly lied and preached this lie to those that have not let THE HOLY SPIRIT interpret the holy scripture. You may say it doesn't matter, but in correctness of the scriptures, it does. All these years believing the Roman Catholic doctrine of lies that Good Friday exists in which it DOES NOT EXIST, just another LIE that has been perpetuate and taught by those in the GOD pulpits throughout this earth to an unlearned PEOPLE of YAH, whom they depended upon to tell THE TRUTH of THE WORD INSTEAD OF MISINFORMATION and misrepresent YAH WORDS. And GOD'S PEOPLE refused to questioned these leaders, these stewards of GOD'S PEOPLE because of reverend or respect (no man deserves this type of reverence, where they can't be called into question into what they are proclaiming to be truth; we can question ELOHIYM, but we can't question a man proclaiming supposedly what is truth or not to start trouble just to get along or whatever the reason is, but the day of reckoning is coming when these leaders will be before YAHUSHA to give HIM an account of their stewardship before HIM. The word Bishop as Pa'al taught about is not one of the titles issued by THE MESSIAH. **Ephesians 4:11** *And HE gave some, apostles; and some, prophets; and some, evangelists; and some, pastors and teachers;* We don't see Bishop here. The word bishop is a chess piece; it is NOT a title assigned by HIM. Where did Pa'al get this ideal? If you look at the concordance it is simply pastor/teacher and to think some people called themselves Bishop.

The Bible was written by Hebrew men led by the inspiration of THE LIVING, EXCELLENT, ALL-WISE HOLY SPIRIT **THE RUACH HA'QODESH.** The Bible is mostly about Hebrew men and women. We have been brainwashed to have believed a fabricated information and misrepresentation of fact by those who know the truth that we are THE MY PEOPLE in the Bible. I will become a martyr. How do I know this? I was told this years ago by an Angelic being verbally like you and I having a conversation. And now I see why! HalleluJAH. I am writing my death warrant because those in charge do not want this information out what is in this book, but I am NOW ready to give My Life for ADONAI YAHUSHA HA'MASHIACH because HIS cause is worthy so that HIS people can come out of their blindness. You see people don't see as I see but this earth is coming to an end and the majority of people are not aware, but this earth is ending. And I had a prophet speak this truth to me years ago and now I am seeing the fulfillment of those words before my very eyes. You can always doubt a man's words, but don't doubt that man's experiences. You see, I have not only been called, but I have also been chosen at this time to deliver this message WE ARE THE PEOPLE IN THE BIBLE AND CHRIST (HA'MASHIACH) IS COMING BACK.

We are in the last days. Everything seems to be at peace at this very time. Or did you hear GOD talking saturday, november 30, 2019, about 3:00 p.m.? The news is reporting the economy is good, and we believe Lester Holt, David Muir, Norah O'Donnell, but it is all a deception or cover-up because they are simply reading from a piece of paper and they are getting paid to promote seemingly truth, which is a lie. But it is like a woman in a $300.00 make-up job. It is just a cover-up to deceive us. The total chaos is coming soon. The USA is $22,000,000,000,000 trillion dollars in the hole, in debt, banks will soon be closed with all our money in them (someone told me "They can't do that" and I said "Wanna bet") and this can be done by the president of the USA declaring an executive order of MARTIAL LAW. People unable to access their bank accounts. The Federal Reserve Bank is a private bank that has shareholders. It is NOT a federal bank that is just a name, nothing more. Now what do you think? No food, no water, no salary, people on the street (unable to pay your mortgage loan then you are homeless), can't buy gas for cars, no electricity, no gas for your stove, then the chips are waiting for those who want to eat and sleep in a house etc. We are in this period where this economy will crash; and guess what? We will have destruction everywhere. The USA will see its destruction as YAH HAS SAID, but those that believe YAHUAH WILL BE SAFE. WHY, because safety is in YAHUAH HANDS **Proverbs 21:31b, 29:25b, 30:5b.** This time is coming. THE WORLD WILL BE IN A TOTAL AND COMPLETE CHAOS. Martial law will be activated, hopelessness, FEMA DEATH CAMPS! And WHO WILL BE IN CHARGE the man of sin. The saints will be gone before this calamity occurs. And those left will be gone in snap.

I have always wondered how my physical death would happen and now I know because YAH has shown me THE TRUTH of HIS WORD. We are THE PEOPLE IN THE BIBLE.

YAH has given me insight, not boasting at all, but I wish I could have lived a normal life, but it was never for me because YAH had other plans. You see, I have nothing at all to boast about. Period. You see, physical death is not pleasant but pain for me and my loved ones. For it was by the GRACE AND MERCY OF YAHUAH AND YAHUSHA AND RUACH HA'QODESH that I am still breathing on this earth and not in hell, smelling the stink and the darkness of hell. Pa'al never states he was a christian. We find the word "Christian(s)" three times in the

New Testament **Acts 11:26 Acts 26:28** and **1 Peter 4:16. In Acts 11:26** and **1 Peter 4:16,** the word was translated or transposed from the word Mashiachiym, meaning Christian, but in

Acts 26:28 It is Netseriy translated or transposed which is Nazareth the adopted hometown of MESSIAH. So as you read there is nothing about this verse that is referring to Mashiachiym. So this word is loosely Christian. YAH LOVES JACOB (YA'AQOV) which is Israel and his grandfather is Avraham. We can take the red pill and wake up or we can take the blue pill and stay asleep and never wake up. I am not expecting an answer from you. I am just giving you information that you can accept or reject. You have the ability to reject this or study. That is up to you. But CHRIST is coming back for ISRAEL only and there will be one shepherd and one fold Israel only. As Pa'al states, the church (the called out ones) have been grafted into Israel.

Pa'al never states he was a christian. He stated I am **1]** Israelite **2]** Benjaminites **3]** Hebrew of Hebrews **Phillipians 3:5, 2 Corinthians 11:22.** Their skin tone was not so-called white, but colored because a white person **CANNOT** GET WHITER! Mosheh **Exodus 4:6-7,** Miryam **Numbers 12,** Naaman **2 Kings 5:27,** Pa'al **Acts 21:38.** The Roman guard thought Pa'al was an Egyptian. The disease Michael Jackson has been called vitiligo and that is a cover-up. What if the doctors called it by its original name **LEPROSY! What would people think then?** All of this CONFUSION by those who interpreted THE WORD OF YAH THROUGH white eyes, thinking that Mosheh, Yoceph and all of THE ISRAELITES and GOD THE SON ARE WHITES. Man open your eyes and see the deceit and the cunning. This fraudulent information can no longer go out. Guess what, church leaders refused to recognize that we are the My People of The Bible. As Pa'al asked in the book of Romans has GOD cast off HIS PEOPLE? Don't be like the unlearned man in **(Isaiah) Yesha'yahu 29:12-13.** THE WORD IS given to him to read, but because of his inability to read; he has an inability to understand what is before him. You may say color doesn't matter, but it does. Why are we always harassed by white people called and labeled as n _ _ _ _ r. It does matter. If your poop was black, would it matter? Have you ever eaten a green orange or eaten a green banana? Of course you would because color doesn't matter lol! So please don't say the color "Color doesn't matter" because in fact it DOES matter in this life. There was a poll and the majority of whites said they WOULD NOT follow a SAVIOR of COLOR! This is how bad this is. I guess you would want a world with no color?

This little boy went to heaven and he asked his dad, "Why did he see all these N _ _ _ _ _s in heaven." This little boy was taught by his racist white dad that GOD is white. I am no longer using the label christian, but Hebrew like Pa'al. Christian is a label, but our nation or our identity is **Hebrew**, not African American, Negro, colored and certainity not n _ _ _ _ _. In the Bible, some identify with Christ, Peter, Paul and so on, but Pa'al states I follow Christ. I FOLLOW THE MESSIAH. We are a lost nation. A white person can only produce a white seed. So since Mosheh is a man of color and not white, his lineage has to **to be people of color also.** **THIS IS NATURAL BIOLOGY.** Can a bird mate with a dog and produce dogs? Can a grape seed produce an orange? So by nature, a white man cannot produce a person of color. **NO WAY POSSIBLE.** So when Mosheh stuck his hand in his bosom and it turned white like leprosy and he placed his hand back into the bosom and brought it back out again, it was as his other flesh. A white man cannot get whiter. **Exodus 4:6-7** son, Amram the father Kohath the grandfather, Levi the great grandfather, (Ya`aqov) Israel the great-great grandfather,

Yitschaq the great-great-great grandfather and Avraham the great-great-great-great grandfather and the rest of the line Terah, Nahor, Serug, reu, Peleg, Eber, Salah, Arphaxad, Shem, and Noach. **These ARE MEN OF COLOR and not white.** Let us put things into the right and correct perspective and not into the wrong white perspective as we have been taught by the white man pulpit. **TRUTH** and **HALLELUJAH. We are The True Israelites, The men, women and children of our father Avram The Hebrew (Genesis 14:13). Amein.**

Psalm 77:15 You have with your arm redeemed **your people**, the sons of Ya`aqov and Yoceph. Celah. ELOHIYM STATES I CHANGE NOT! **Romans 11:29** states``The *gifts and **calling** of YAH are without repentance.* The word repentance means **IRREVOCABLE.** In other words it can't change. **IT IS SET IN MARBLE! IT CAN'T BE BUDGED.** What is calling? Name, call, was called,surname or to call. What did **YAH** call us in **Psalm 77:15**

You have with your arm redeemed **your people**, the sons of Ya`aqov and Yoceph. We are HIS PEOPLE. So you can still go by the christian label, but I was born a **HEBREW** and I will die a Hebrew in YAHUAH. Amein! We are "The My People " in The Bible. I am ready for death because of this information. **"I WILL DIE FOR MY SOUL IS SET FREE."** Amein, the Hebrew spelling. This is why the english translation has screwed up things because you got people saying amen and then saying awomen so MUCH CONFLICTED and confusion. If the translators had left it alone we would not have this type of confusion.

We know KJV is an english text. And we know that there are translation errors; It is not 100 percent correct, but we do know YAH cannot lie because The Word says heaven and earth would pass away if one jot was not fulfilled, but The Word of YAH ENDURES through forever and forever. Amein.

Psalm 77:15, Psalm 105:6 Psalm 147:19-20

The first name in English; The second is the Hebrew name Paul Pa'al, Peter Kepha, Abram Avram, David David, Jesus YAHUSHA, John Yahuchanon, Joseph Yoceph, Jacob Ya`aqov, Judah Yahudah, Matthew Mattithyahu, Moses Mosheh, Aaron Aharaon, Israel Yashar`el, Issac Yitschaq, Rebekah Rivqah.

Do you see why they were covering up?

So I am not concerned about death, for death will happen for me, but **YAHUAH** is **MY SHIELD! HALLELUJAH Proverbs 30:5.**

Every WORD of GOD is pure; HE is a shield unto them that put their trust in HIM. And ALL PRAISES TO THE GOD OF THE HEBREWS **Exodus 3:18**

The meaning of Hebrew = Door to the House of first or Doors to the House of the Beginning.

Letter 6

DOES THE TRUTH MATTER? YES or NO. PLEASE KEEP READING. Since you are the leader, THE SHEPHERD of this congregation, I'm writing this to you so you can pass this on to your congregation. Please PASS IT ON TO YOUR CONGREGATION. You are the watchman over this congregation. The time of CHRIST'S COMING is soon. THE WORD OF GOD IS THE TRUTH, AND HIS WORD MUST BE FULFILLED as HE has stated. It seems like a fairytale, but it is true. If HIS Words are nor fulfilled, then heaven and earth will pass away as HE states since GOD CANNOT LIE HIS WORDS WILL BE FULFILLED. It is INEVITABLE. Do we actually take THE CREATOR at HIS WORD? Most of the time, we would YES, but do we really actually think what THE CREATOR said HE will do? Now that is the question we have to know for ourselves. In other words, do we believe if what THE CREATOR says is true? Let that question cure or mediate in your being for a few precious moments. Do you believe that the men of Yashar`el marched around Jericho without saying a word and on the seventh day they holler and YAH brought the walls down? And they cross the Red Sea on dry land and I am not going to ask you to dwell on the fact that HE made twelve roads through the Red Sea as it says in **Yasher 81:38.** Many of you may have trouble with the one road on dry land. You see THE MY PEOPLE IN THE BIBLE are under THE PROTECTION of YAH! Do you believe what has happened? I BELIEVE WHAT THE CREATOR SAYS, HE WILL DO IT AND COMPLETE HIS WORD. Many people do not believe there is A CREATOR IN THE FORM of THE FATHER THE SON AND THE RUACH HA'QODESH (ELOHIYM) and if you believe there is whatever you are going through HE IS. HE CREATED everything you see. Do we believe Jonah was in the whale belly for three nights and three days? Do you believe Hananiah, Mishael and Azariah went into the fiery furnace? Did Daniy'el sleep among the hungry lions? Was HIS SON born to a virgin? Do we believe GOD's SON was three nights and three days in the tomb?

Now to The MEAT of why I am writing this to you. THE CREATOR said that of surety to Avram that his seed would spend 400 years in affliction. So if (since) we believe all of the above, **Genesis 15:13-14** has <u>NOT</u> been FULFILLED as of YET as we have been led to believe, but it will be real SOON. Many feel it was FULFILLED by verse in Exodus 12:40, but if you examine those verses, look at the key words afflicted: Genesis says 400 years and Exodus says sojourning 430 years. Affliction and sojourning do not even mean the same. We have made a big mistake; believing a lie. I was myself caught in this lie until further study. But GOD CAN COUNT. There is an older version than the KJV that is called The Septuagint and it says in **Exodus 12:40**, *"And the sojourning of the children of Israel, while they sojourned in the land of Egypt and the land of Chanaan, four hundred and thirty years."* As you have read, The KJV left out 5 (five) words! WORDS left out OR even changed in a <u>sentence, paragraph or book</u> will **CHANGE** how the brain will <u>PROCESS</u> the NEW INFORMATION it has obtained. Now was this intentional? Who knows? But it has been part of the deception and now we have been enlightened by The TRUTH. This is one of the mistakes that has blinded us and the movie *The Ten Commandments* and also the non-color religious leaders, pastors, teachers, the popes and so on. We have been blindsided by satan and men working for the devil to hide The TRUTH from our eyes.

The first slaves were brought into this United Staes on THOSE FILTHY and NASTY slave ships on august 19, 1619, so we are in that period.

As many of you know the Gregorian calendar is days off, but YAH said four hundred years so it will be a four hundred years period. We can choose not to believe YAH, but I believe YAH. Our calendar is off, but YAH knows the correct time. Our teachers and pastors have gotten information from those that have the truth, but refused to expose the TRUTH to keep us in darkness, but THE CREATOR is opening up the eyes of HIS PEOPLE TO THE TRUTH OF THE BIBLE! <u>WE ARE THE PEOPLE IN THE BIBLE!</u> Our forefathers came on those nasty and filthy slave ships **Deuteronomy 28:68 i**nto the United States.

The book of **Genesis** states THE CREATOR WILL judge that nation (The United States) and we shall go out (Exodus) with great substance. You see it does not say nations, but nation. This is singular and not plural. Non-color people have been taught that Jesus/ YAHUSHA look like them which is certainly WRONG, but The SAVIOR GAVE HIS LIFE FOR ALL MEN! There will still be punishment because what comes out of YAH'S mouth can not be void. It has to happen just as my people were shipped into slavery as HE said.

CHAPTER 31

—— ❧ ——

Writings The True Facts

The perspective of this world system is seeing things in the wrong view. The philosophy of this world is funk-up. We are told this and that and we refuse to believe what is in front of our eyes. The sun and the moon are in front of our eyes, but we believe what man says that the sun is 93,000,000 million miles away and the moon is 250,000 miles away, but they are in the arch of the sky. How can we have a solar or lunar eclipse and how big is the sun? People are labeled incorrectly. Black people have been labeled black and we are not but the majority of us are brown skin. Mexicans have been labeled brown and are not brown. And people from India and some of them are darker than me. This is totally wrong and where is this stinking thinking coming from? If you look at me I am not black, but my skin tone is brown! A man labeled as white is not! The Mexicans are not just brown but both brown and non-melanated. Why or how did this happen? Why have so-called white people labeled themselves as white in which in fact they are non-melanated. This matrix or this world system gave them this opportunity because so-called white people have status under this godless world system. People who are labeled black have no status or recognition in this system. Two documents reverend in the USA

1] The Declaration of Independence says "ALL men are created equal" 2] The Constitution of The USA has labeled a person of my skin tone as 3/5th of a man. These documents contradict one another. And this is the reason we the people of color (The Hebrews) are treated as we are, but I WILL DECLARED THE DAY OF RECKONING is coming for the Hebrews because THE CREATOR sees all that has happened to us and as HE told Avraham cursed are those that curse you and blessed are those that blessed you. So, keep what you are doing because one day it will come and you will receive what you gave out for THE CREATOR sees what you have done or even what is in your heart.

This satan world is coming to an end and what will you have to say because all will give an account and where will your end be because you could have been born in my shoes, but you were born in your body and what did you do for your fellow man? Did you just pray and move on? Did you stop to think how? Did you give thanks because it could be you? Did you help when you could or did you talk or gossip about that person? Only you will give an answer on your judgment day. But this world system presented to you is ungrateful. Listen, we all come from two people. We came from one source and HE Created two people and from those two is what we have today. satan's house has influenced this system, but man agreed to this corrupted system and this is why we have a world full of confusion. We are so afraid of a virus that people who have KNOWN each other for years no longer shake hands or hugs because of a virus. Or are we so afraid of a virus we can't see? Does THE CREATOR have your protection? You feel a vaccine and a mask is your protection? Even Lysol said it kills 99.9% of viruses and bacteria. If you take that number that is 1/10% (one tenth of a percentage). Do you know what 1/10% is? Of course you DON'T because if you did you wouldn't be so uptight about things. What does **Genesis 15:13-14** say? You are afraid. These doctors, satanism and scientists got you so winded up about a virus. I am so fed up with this damnable satanic worldly system. Listen people Lysol says it kill 99.9%, 99.9%, 99.9%, 99.9%,99.9% and 99.9%, but that number could be 99.99%, 99.999%, 99.9999%, 99.99999%, 99.999999%, 99.9999999% which means that 1/10% could be 1/100%,1/1000%, 1/100000%,1/1000000%, 1/10000000% or 1/100000000%. In math this number will go into infinity. **DO YOU SEE WHAT I MEAN? DO YOU SEE WHAT I MEAN?** The percentage could go to infinity and you are masking up like crazy. Driving ALONE with a mask on huh. Driving Alone with a mask on! **DO YOU BELIEVE THERE IS A CREATOR?** Have you gone to church in vain? **PHYSICAL DEATH IS GOING TO OCCUR.** Physical death for those left behind is very devastating, but the sun will revolve around the earth and will come up in the morning. You can't **STOP** physical death but eternal death (separation) is possible. All you had to do is BELIEVE in WHAT THE SON did on the cross and believe HE arose again, but many are TRAPPED IN THIS WORLD SYSTEM of disbelief. This Matrix! We have accumulated physical wealth, but soul wealth no. We have clothes in every closet in the house. We have storage full and nowhere to put anything, but our spiritual closet is empty and full of spider webs. We are flat broke, thinking we live on this forsaken planet called earth. Earth the heart of THE CREATOR. Exchange the h and put it the front earth and you will have heart and put the h at the end and you will earth. So THE CREATOR put HIS HEART in earth. And where did HE place man in HIS Heart? Here on earth HIS Heart. Can you deny it? Where would you place someone that scorn your heart? Think about or meditate on that please. Yes you can because of your world view because you don't believe there is a CREATOR who created all you see. You deny HIS power. HE created things, the way HE wanted them, but HE also created a way out, but you refused HIS way. You say I will do good, but your righteousness is like a filthy rag. What is a filthy rag? A man wiping his hands on a towel after he has worked on a car all day and that rags has all of the oil on it and your righteousness is as that rags and you put those rags in your mouth or a rag that you blow that mucous out of your nose. This is your righteousness. FILTHY! We who know and serve THE CREATOR who know you, so we give our trust, your life to HIM because HE has a place for you in HIS Kingdom. A place of rest and peace for you in HIS Kingdom. A place of rest and peace with no struggles, come and get your rest because HE is awaiting for you and forgiveness is yours. For all you have to do is believe. You see, you think that dime and quarter is silver, but it is no longer silver, but imaginary because now it is just silver plated monopoly money. Come to THE CREATOR HE is wanting you, but HE won't force you. You have the opportunity, but time will soon end for you and then eternal life or eternal death. I have given you time for you to think. THE CREATOR is not a million miles away. HE is in your presence NOW. So receive this word and just believe because HE IS. COME NOW because HE is on your very lips. So believe HE IS and that is all HE asks and HE will come in and you will be with HIM through all eternity because this earth is coming to an end.

(Revelation)Chizayon 21:1

(Isaiah)Yesha`yahu 51:6, 65:17, 66:22

(John)Yahuchanon 10:16

(Enoch) Chanok 18:15, 93:17

(Zephaniah)Tsephanyahu 3:8e-9

(2 Peter)Kepha Sheniy 3:13

(Jubilees) Yovheliym 23:18

(Matthew) Mattithyahu 24:35

(Psalm)Tehilliym 148:6

So come before the last breath, leave your body before it is too late for there are but two places **ETERNAL REST** or **ETERNAL DESTRUCTION.** You have a choice before the last breath escapes your body, but once you take your last breath you will have made your choice and "I have no other choice, but to give you what you wanted, but to be eternally away from THE CREATOR. This is the choice you made. So I AM giving you your choice." This world philosophy has screwed with the way people think and have caused all of this confusion, But The CREATOR is coming for HIS People. As Yoceph was looking at his brothers and he knew them, but his brothers did not know him because all they saw were just Egyptians, people of color. This is the confusion and man says the earth rotates around the sun even though Joshua said "sun stand still" and not earth stand still. Who is right, GOD or man? But many will deny this but who has been a liar? Man says mask up and come and get your injections and now your booster whereas YAH has given man an immune system to fight things that attack the body. Whereas YAH said breath in oxygen and exhale carbon monoxide. Where is the virus? Is the virus in your body? Can you see the virus? Since the virus is so small that you can't see it and your arm or legs have holes and your head you can't see the holes which means the virus can penetrate that area of your body. Don't you sweat? THE CREATOR has created a human immune system and it does its job excellent as long as you do that which is right. You must eat and drink healthy. You can make the system not function properly by doing something that is not correct. Vitamin D is very IMPORTANT. In other words SUNLIGHT baby SUNLIGHT very important and water, fruits, vegetables, greens, nuts, seeds and movement. If you treat the system right you will be alright. You can not expect the house to clean itself, you have to work and your body is your house. You can't let someone come in and cleanse your house. You should do this. In other words do yourself some good and respect your house. And keep the pipes in your house cleared out. If you treat the system right, you will be alright. It is like the system in your house. You don't put the wrong things down the pipes of your house and expect it to function properly do you? Put a rag in that system and see what happens? So treat this system proper. Remember because someone is watching over you. Because this world will end and where will your end be?

THINGS AGAINST CORONA

1. Corona is 666 The beast system number is 666

   A) The word corona has 6 letters

   B) Each letter has a value

      C=3, O=15, R=18, O=15, N=14, A=1

      3+15+18+15+14+1= 66

   C) 6 Letters + 66 value of all the letters and we have **666** the beast number

2. Our children do not have to wear a mask, but adults do

   What type of mindset has did done to our children

3. The INCONSISTENCIES of when to wear a mask

4. Is the virus airborne

5. My Human Immune System that YAH made for man

6. Lysol says it kills 99.9% which is 1/10% of a percentage

7. No one can tell me where the virus is?

8. My DNA (Deoxyribonucleic acid) is difference from people of non colored

9. Not Afraid because after physical death I will be with MY CREATOR forever and ever

10. **Proverbs 21:31, 29:25b, 30:5b**

11. It is real, but a virus a virus

    A) Does man have patents on these viruses

    B) Why have a patent on a virus

12. What are the ingredients in these vaccines? We have the ingredients for breads and deodorants; Right on the package.

    A) Why not?

13. YAHUAH IS MY SHIELD AND PROTECTOR

    A) Like Avraham in the furnace

    B) Daniel in the hungry lion dens

    C) Hananiah, Mishael and Azariah in the fiery furnace

Many of you AIN'T believing this because you have been beguiled to believe this world system and not to believe YAH. Look at the movie The Matrix, they never realized they were not in the real world until they were awakened. WAKE UP and quit sleeping and wash your eyes and look into this world system on how it has strayed away from what THE CREATOR has said.

You see, the 400 years did not happen in Egypt as we have been **TAUGHT**, but it happened in spiritual Egypt (The United States of America). The People of GOD as **Exodus 1:8-11** says only went into slavery after Yoceph's death and there is not 400 years after Yoceph's death and Mosheh's birth. Josephus states that The People of GOD were only in slavery maybe 215 years and not 400 years as some think it to be. Genesis states as record 400 years of affliction. The information in **Exodus 12:40** and **Genesis 15:13-14** has **BEEN** totally misunderstood and misinterpreted all these years, but those are our teachers. **Exodus 12:40** says 430 years and not 400 years, but we never THINK to question this, but we just go on and if you study you will see that words are left out of this verse. I am going to ask you "**Can GOD count?**" The one who made the universe. "Can HE count?" Yes or No? So, since HE can count our stinking thinking, our interpretation of HIS words is then incorrect and so horrendously mistaken.

Genesis 15:13-14 says 400 years of affliction. **Exodus 12:40** has the word sojourn in it. And sojourn and affliction does not mean the same or are you going to say yes they could mean the same. Then stay in your blind state because GOD will not be mocked. **Genesis 15:13-14** says 400 years of affliction. The first slaves came to Jamestown in august of 1619 and the 400 years of affliction end in 2019. 2019-1619=400. We are now awaiting for The Exodus. Look at what this nation is going through as **Genesis** says deeper in debts, police officers are NOW being punished for what they use to get away with, extreme cold and population diminishing.

The KJV which many people rely on has left out five words or more according to The **Septuagint Bible** and **The Cepher Bible**.

KJV Exodus 12:40 says, *"Now the sojourning of the children of Israel, who dwelt in Egypt was four hundred and thirty year.*

The Septuagint Exodus 12:40 says *'And the sojourning of the children of Israel, while they sojourned in the land of Egypt, and the land of chanaan, was four hundred and thirty years."*

The Cepher Bible Exodus 12:40 says, *"Now the sojourning of the children of Yashar'el, who dwelt in the land of Mitsrayim, and in the land of Kena`an they and their fathers, was four hundred and thirty years."*

And when words are left out this changes the meaning of the statement. As you can read and see KJV left out words which should be there to get the right interpretation of prophecies that have been said and just maybe we would have thought another way, but then this will not deviate some people mind they still rely on what they have been told. Question was the slave bible different from the slave master bible? The answer to that question is yes.

Avram was 75 years old when he went to (Canaan) Kena`an land. Avram had no child until Yitschaq (Issac) 25 years later. Yitschaq had (Jacob) Ya`aqov when he turned 60 years later. 25+60=85 years in Kena`an land. Yashar'el/Ya`aqov enters Egypt when he was 130 of age **Genesis 47:9.**

25+60+130=215years in Kena`an

Yashar'el died in Egypt <u>17 years</u> later **Genesis 47:28**. Yashar'el is 91 years older than Yoceph. Yoceph died at 110 year old and that is 54 years later after his father Yashar'el died. 17+54= 71. Mosheh was born and basically was in Egypt for 40 years. 71+40=111. Mosheh was gone for 40 years 111+40=151. 215-151=64.

A) 25+60+130=215 years
B) 17+54+64+40+40= 215 years

215 in Kena`an +215 years in Egypt=430 years As stated in The Septuagint and The Cepher Bibles **Exodus 12:40**

DESPAIR

As I lay the tears of despair well up in my eyes, but I realize you are there and YOU Yourself despaired once upon this earth when things seem as though Your FATHER seems to have forsaken You and You cried out "It is Finished" So now I cry out. It is Finished! I know You are there so I cry out HALLELUJAH to Your glory because I know you are there with all of your glory I say HALLELUJAH to YAHUAH WHO IS THE GREAT I AM that I AM because HE has set me on a task to tell the world you are coming again. And I want to thank you. It seems as though it is lonely, but you validate my pain and my frustration with your tears toward Your despair for man because you died on the cross and after 3 days and 3 nights You arose again, but man still REFUSES to believe so this despair of those who won't believe we pray they turn to you and not fall for the plan of your enemy but the hopelessness of man you see but what can you do more? Your tears of despair and one day you will call us home and man will get what he wants. ELOHIYM is now gone and has left man to the devices of man/satan The Adversary. Man returns to YAH. For it will get to a point where it will be out of YAH'S Hands because of HIS Word. YAH cannot cross HIS word. And you will suffer the consequences of your actions and your bitter ways. For it is my Hope that you turn around, but I can't go past MY Word. So despair and hopelessness is in your heart. I am hurting, but the joy of LOVE uplift me and I will remove my presence from those who refused and you will get what you want. Bye Bye Bye pain and now joy forever for those whom I have called will be with me both now and forever bye and HALLELUJAH forever

CHAPTER 32

Three Fifth of a man

The Declaration of Independence and The United States Constitution are two different documents, but both hold great weights and regard to this country. The ideal of freedom and independence. The Declaration of Independence declares all men are CREATED EQUAL, but The United States Constitution declares I am just 3/5th of a man, but The Declaration of Independence declares <u>All</u> men are created equal except in the eyes of justice and and the eyes of The United States Constitution. These documents are reverent with conflicting WORDS. Anytime there is conflict, that conflict has to be RESOLVED. If THE confliction is NOT RESOLVED, then we will have conflict as it is today. Look at the conditions of today between brothers. We ALL came from two people Ad-am and Chuah. I am declared 3/5th of a man or my right are less than a dog when it is under the knee of a white cop. According to The United States Constitution Rosa Parks had to ride in the back of the bus because The United States Constitution declares her as 3/5th, but The Declaration of Independence declares ALL men are created equal. Because of 3/5th of a man the 1850 slave act declared on september 18, 1850 I am not equal, but 3/5th of a man. You see I have been abandoned by the statement of **"All" men** are created equal by The United States Constitution when it declares I am 3/5th of a man, but only when you finally can see past the 3/5th of a man when this statement declares "All men are equal become true. When you see in your heart "We are all men" not just 3/5th of a man then this statement becomes TRUTH. Only until then can the statement of "ALL MEN" are created equal by desires and equities of the law then it becomes true. The words 3/5th **MUST** be removed physically and from the conscience from The United States Constitution because of the 3/5th of a man, the police are allowed to shoot me anytime without penalty because of

3/5th of a man. The white man is allowed to lynch me, but The Declaration of Independence declares "All men are created equal", but The United States Constitution declares I am 3/5th of a man. Abolish the word 3/5th in The United States Constitution by declaring 3/5th of a man is removed because "I AM A MAN". I am not a black man, but a man with brown skin. I am a man from the land of Eden and not from Africa. I am a man declared by THE ONE that made me. I am a man created in the very image of THE CREATOR of all men and HIS name is YAH.

Racial profiling because I am considered by The United States Constitution 3/5th of a man, but The Declaration of Independence says "All men are created equal." 3/5th of a man's voting rights are infringed. 3/5th of a man I am profiled driving, walking, shopping, moving and eating. Because 3/5th of a man Greenwood happened. Because 3/5th of a man police ineptness is happening. Because 3/5th of a man I AM STRIPPED OF ALL CIVIL LIBERTIES. The United States Constitution says I am 3/5th of a man and guess what it is in your HEART THIS NATION OF EVIL AND HATE because you see me not as a man, but a threat to your sinful heart but YAH HAS DECLARED I AM A MAN AND I WILL SEE PEACE BUT YOU WILL SEE HIS DARKNESS. Greenwood happened because I am 3/5th of a man. Because I am 3/5th of a man I can die because of not using a turn signal or courtesy lamp. Because I am 3/5th of a man I am put in a stranglehold and put under the knee because of the 3/5th of a man. I am shot in my own house by a so-called mistake because I am 3/5th of a man. A person in a blue uniform will shoot me through the window of my home in which I have every right under heaven to protect myself. Because I am 3/5th of a man a person in a blue uniform can pull me over for having a air fresheners hanging in my car and then shoot me by a person who has been working on the force for twenty-six years and TRAINING and supposedly mixed up a taser from her service gun. I am more than 3/5th of a man? Do I not bleed like you? Do I not eat food? Do I love my family? Will my son see how you have taken an innocent Man? A man who will no longer be able to give his sons and daughters hugs and no longer to say to his sons and daughters *"I love you"* because you don't consider me to be a man, but less than the dog you have at your home. Do you not see or know that THE FATHER sees what is going on? And HE will revenge my loss of life upon your head, but The Bible says, You will reap what you sow and you will reap more than what you sow and also what The Bible says it is better for you to place a millstone around your neck and then drown yourself than to hurt HIS little ones or have you not read

The Bible says that HE will blessed those that blessed Avraham seeds and cursed them that cursed Avraham seed? Remember, you will be taken into judgment by the person who lived in what you called the middle east; THE GOD of The Hebrew. Your theology devils have thought and pictures HIM as your skin tone and you are so far what is true. You have been taught by misleading and misrepresented teachers of untruth and because you followed that wrong teaching. You are so far off the wrong because THE GOD of what is THE GOD (ELOHIYM) of THE HEBREW PEOPLE. Check the record for yourself. For teachers and you will go into judgment for yourself and you will not stand on someone else's word, but you will stand on your own accord and what will you have to say for yourself? Your teacher won't be able to qualify you. Because you will stand before ME YAHUSHA HA'MASHIACH THE CREATOR of what is and your record will I have because I see all. I know your very thoughts, I know your heart and what you say will be from your very heart because you will open your heart and your thoughts and what will you say because you were led by wrong information, but your thoughts were formed by those you associate with. So now MY Peace will no longer be with you, but a certain darkness because you considered my servant 3/5th of a man not knowing My sons and daughters brothers and sisters are **SEEDS** of Avraham and thereby under The Avraham's Covenant of grace Amein.

Since, The Declaration of Independence is sooo very reverent by The United States of America and it has THE word "All". The word all is not exclusive but inclusive. The Declaration of Independence is a written contract that ALL means ALL. All = THE WHOLE AMOUNT or quantity of, every, the whole number. All leave nothing. It excludes no one. Everyone is included. So this word ALL leaves nothing out. It includes ALL and this The Declaration of Independence is by all accounts a written contract and it has not been fulfilled by The Constitution of The United States of America because **I AM COUNTED AS 3/5th OF A MAN.** So, thereby payment **MUST BE MET** by this country which exclude us the 3/5th of a man which should have been met by the word **ALL**. Words are so very important. Even The Bible says that there is power in the tongue, life or death. Choose life. The meaning of words is very important. Most people may not feel like this, but THE CREATOR said HIS WORD is greater than HIS NAME, but The Constitution of The United States of America speaks and writes words in which it has NO intentions of fulfilling the meaning The Declaration of Independence word **ALL men are created equal** in the eyes of a so-called white man. I am 3/5th of a man because my skin is brown, but **THE CREATOR** put me

THIS MAN in brown skin. So because of what THE CREATOR has done I deserved to be 3/5th of a man? Did I put myself in this brown skin? Did I not think as a man? Do I bleed as a man? Do I not have 4 fingers and a thumb? Do I not sit on the commode as a man? Do I not hungry? Do I do the things of a man? What is the difference in me being labeled 3/5th of a man? Is it just because of my skin tone that I am hated? All I want as a man is peace, security, wisdom, a place and income and the company of person to enclose me in their arms. This is all I need to be me because THE CREATOR has made me a man because one day HE will call me away from this earth to await on the new earth to be made and I will forever be with THE CREATOR because HE has always seen me as a man and those that that hate me because of my brown skin you will be before THE MESSIAH and you will see wooly hair and brown skin and what will you do or say?Because you have judged me because of my brown skin and the judgment of eternity life is out of your hand because now you are looking at THE CREATOR with brown skin. Like India Arie and Eric Benet, oh that brown skin.

But I forgot the authors of The Declaration of Independence were so-called white men that excludes ALL brown skin people. You see they were just thinking of themselves because one even had GOD'S People The Hebrew he claimed he owned! And Senator Mitch McConnell said African-American voted just like Americans. That is why we are still considered 3/5th of a man because these so-called white people don't consider us as men!

CHAPTER 33

KJV (King James Version)

A lot of people, not all, feel as though the KJV is the authorized WORD OF GOD, but it has led to a false sense of security. We have The Old Testament and The New Testament. The New Testament was translated from a Greek version and not Hebrew, but the Greek in which it has caused a diversion in me, but generally The Old Testament is translated from Hebrew. And so we get a general knowledge. I was reading and tears began to form in my eyes for what I see as errors. Whether these errors were intentional or unintentional, I DON'T know but error anyway. These are my observances.

1] The 1611 KJV did NOT have any names that start with the letter j. The letter j was not formed until 1524. So it would have been the King Iames Version and not the King James Version. So the name Jesus was Iesus, Joseph it was Ioseph, Joshua it was Ioshua, Judah it was Iudah and so on. You can download the 1611 KJV.

2] The KJV converted the majority of names into some type of english. Like in the tv series "*Roots*". The slave owner had Kunta Kinte tied down and whipped until he said said his english name Toby. Jacob's name in Hebrew is Ya`aqov. Even if you sound the name phonetically it is strange, cob is kub whereas Jacob is jay-kuhb. Issac's name in Hebrew is Yitschaq. Eve's name in Hebrew is Chuah. Abram's name in Hebrew is Avram. Noah's name in Hebrew is Noach, Ham's name in Hebrew is Cham. Cain's name in Hebrew is Qayin. Abel's name in Hebrew is H'avel. David's name in Hebrew is David. Esau's name in Hebrew is Esau. Samuel's name in Hebrew is Shemu'el. And the exchanging of names goes on. Even the name Lord is still used today by the English system and the word Bishop is used but that is a chess piece and not a title given by YAHUSHA. **Ephesians 4:11** *"And He gave some, apostles; and some, prophets; and some, evangelists; and some, pastors and teachers;"*

Now does beating a person to accept a name change means anything? Is it that serious? It must be serious to hide the True People of YAHUAH!

3] The KJV left off words in the scriptures also. In **The KJV Exodus 12:40-41** *"Now the sojourning of the children of Israel, who dwelt in Egypt, was four hundred and thirty years. And it came to pass at the end of the four hundred and thirty years, even the selfsame day it came to pass, that all the hosts of the LORD went out from the land of Egypt."*

The Cepher Bible Exodus 12:40-41 *"Now the sohourning of the children of Yashar'el, who dwelt in the land of Mitsrayim, and in the land of Kena`an, they and their fathers, was four hundred and thirty years. And it came to pass at the end of the four hundred and thirty years, even the selfsame day it came to pass, that all the host of YAHUAH went out from the land of Mitsrayim.*

In The Complete Works of Josephus page 107 *"they left Egypt in the month Xanthicus, on the fifteenth day of the lunar month; four hundred and thirty years after our forefather Abraham came into Canaan, but two hundred and fifteen years only after Jacob removed into Egypt.*

The Septuagint Bible Exodus 12:40-41 *"And the sojourning of the children of Israel whole they sojourned in the land of Egypt and the land of Chanaan, was four hundred and thirty years. And it came to pass after the four hundred and thirty years, all the forces of the Lord came forth out of the land of Egypt by night.*

So, I have presented to you four versions of information and the KJV left words And in the land of Canaan they and their fathers. **Does leaving out words in a paragraph or sentence change the meaning?**

4] The KJV also left words out when it was transferred to the New Testament from the Old Testament which would change the meaning also. When The MESSIAH was in the temple **Mathew 21:13** it says *"It is written, My House shall be called The House of prayer, but ye have made it a den of thieves."*

How passionate was The MESSIAH when HE said those words. The first part of that scriptures came out of **Isaiah 56:7** and it says *"for mine house shall be called a house of prayer for all people."* **Now do these two words change the thought of this sentence? Yes or No.**

Romans 1:17, Hebrews 10:38, Galatians 3:11 all say *"The just shall live by faith.",* but there is one word left out also in which I feel it **CHANGES** the dramatic effect on the way we think about things. **Habakkuk 2:4** says, ``*but the just shall live by **HIS** faith."* It left out the word his. Which to me is very important. To some people it is not important, but to me it is just that simple. What if I told you I was going to my home, but I meant I am going to my hometown. Do these statements mean the same thing? No they don't. Now his is not capitalized, but it is a small case, but it has nothing to do with a man at, but to THE CREATOR. How do I come with this information because I am led by THE RUACH. Man does NOT have enough faith at all. Let me explain why I came to this conclusion. We don't have enough faith, but we must always depend on THE CREATOR. THE CREATOR said if you have faith **the size of a mustard seed Matthew 17:20** *"And YAHUSHA said unto them, Because of your unbelief: for amein I say unto you, If ye have belief as a grain of mustard seed, ye shall say unto this mountain, remove hence to yonder place; and it shall remove; nothing shall be impossible unto you."* You can move mountain. Nothing will be impossible for you. Have you moved any mountain? Yes or No? So when words are left out, the thought, the thinking, the concept, the misused, bad ideals are concreted, orchestrated, in our thinking in which we become deformed in the way things should be. In other words our thinking has been funk-up. We are thinking this way and it should be this way. And it is man who has confused us with their inherent interpretation of YAHUAH words. I am here to give you the red pill to awaken your thinking. **Proverbs 16:33 The very essence is happening because of HIM.** And this deformity (our thinking is deformed) corrupt our way of life because we have been believe a certain way because we have been eating wrong in which our body inclined to follow a wrong pattern of corrupt stinking thinking in which this has go on for eon of ages with this malfunctional stinking thinking in which it has corrupted generation after generation of corrupt molded habits which lead us down the wrong road of inbreeding lies in our lives in which we can not conformed to the right way of thinking because this corruption of our mind in which we are blinded of THE TRUTH in which ELOHIYM wants to remove, but we have been led by this corrupt way of thinking and we feed junk to our children and they in turn feed it to their children and we got people with clog way of thinking unable to unload the corruption that has fulfilled their body mind and soul that ELOHIYM sees the only way is to destroy those that are led by the corruption of their mind and to lead a new way of thinking to those that will accept truth because of his words he cannot force you, but try to put his words into the mind that are not corrupt with this way the world think, but he will one day destroy those and their corrupt ways of following this world system of bowing down to the beast this world system and set us free who will one day leave us to The NEW Heavens and the new earth with no sin and no remembrance of the old world because he has change all things to make them new. For it is by HIS Faith and Not mine faith.

5] Many celebrate easter which is an old pagan god of astaroth or astarte or asteroth. This word was changed from the Hebrew word Pecach. Pecach is Hebrew for Passover. Many will say it is because MASHIACH came from the tomb early sunday morning. All of these lies. The Bible says three days and three nights and pastors who have not studied YAH'S words keep on telling these fables. **Matthew 12:40** says *"For as Yonah was three days and three nights in the fish's belly; so shall the SON of Ad-am be three days and three nights in the heart of the earth."*

And HE was called by Yahuchanon the lamb of YAHUAH **Yahuchanon 1:29.** But we go along with this culture that The SON of GOD died on friday and rose early sunday morning. So this day is quite contrary to the word, but preachers and teachers of MY Word refuse to listen and one day I will see you standing before me and **what will you say?**

6] Many celebrate christ-mass which is a pagan holiday. And the way you pronounce it with the t silence. Leaving out the cross. Bringing in trees and decorating in which it was against the law because as Jeremiah says and idol **Yirmeyahu 10:3-5** *"For the customs of the people are vain: for one cuts a tree out the forest, the work of hands of the workman, with the axe. They deck it with silver and with gold; they fasten it with nails and with hammers, that it move not. They are upright as the palm tree, but speak not: they must needs be borne, because they cannot go. Be not afraid of them; for they cannot do evil, neither also is it them to do good."* We have been misled into our stinking thinking, but this corruption will end. I used to do as you, but my eyes were opened. This day is supposed to be about The SON of God's birth date but that is so wrong. His conception took place in The Hebrew calendar month, which is the sixth month called of Elul. This is the gregorian calendar between august and september. Now when you go back three months that would be on the Hebrew calendar it is the month of Sivan, which falls in the springtime of the gregorian calendar of may and june. Man has deceived us again and december 25th is bogus holiday and the word holiday from two words to make one word and those to words are **HOLY DAYS and there is nothing about celebrating chrismus as we do.**

7] The word christian is misleading also for the following reasons:

A] You see the name Christ is a title which means anointed one in Greek and Since HE was not Greek, but Hebrew nationality. Thereby the name Jesus is Greek and not Hebrew and the title Christ is Greek and not Hebrew. And hereby lies the problem with the word christian. The Hebrew name for anointed one is Messiah which is what is used in The Old Testament and to say you are a christian this is not Hebrew. The word Christian means a follower of Christ, but since HE was not Greek, but a Hebrew. So then we should say **I am anointed** and not christian to be correct. And it was spelled MESSIAS in The New Testament. And to get technical it would be HA'MASHIACH which is HIS true title name meaning **anointed one**.

B] You will find the word christian(s) three times in The New Testament. **1) Acts 11:26 2) Acts 26:28 3) 1 Kepha 4:16** but like I have said before KJV converted the true words and changed it before it. **Acts 11:26** The word was Mashiachiym which means anointed ones.

Acts 26:28 It was Netseriy which is The MESSIAH adopted hometown. **1 Kepha 4:16** It was Mashiachiy which means Anointed One. So we have presented you with information and now you can inquire about THE TRUTH of what you have been told. Hey Christians why do you wear a cross? Did other people die on a cross also? Did HIS death have any significance? YES, but it meant nothing **WITHOUT THE RESURRECTION.** Without HIS Death there would be no resurrection and without HIS death there would be no resurrection. So HIS DEATH and RESURRECTION are both very important. So, why don't you wear a picture of HIS tomb and HIS cross.

8] Man says the sun is 93,000,000 million away from earth. This is what we have been taught all our lives and scientists are still displaying this information as truth. Earth is ELOHIYM heart.

The Bible say in **Genesis 1:17-18,** *"And ELOHIYM set them in the expanse of the heavens to give light upon the earth, And to rule over the day and over the night, and to divide the light from the darkness: ELOHIYM saw that it was good."*

I have read this, I don't know how many times, but I have never looked at the definition of the word firmament. According to Merriam Webster's Collegiate Dictionary tenth edition it says The vault of the sky is the firmament. The Strong's Exhaustive Concordance of the Bible says H7549, the visible arch of the sky. Who will you believe? So is the sun 93,000,000 million miles away from earth? GOD set the sun and the moon in the arch of the sky as you can read. I ask again who will believe man or GOD? In the book of **Enoch 78:1-3** It says *"The names of the sun are these: one **Aryares**, the other **Tomas** The moon has four names.*

The first is **Asonya**; *the second,* **Elba**; *the third,* **Benase**; *and the fourth,* **Erae**. *These are the two great luminaries, whose orbs are as the orbs of heaven, and the dimensions of both are equal.* **Enoch 72:47**, says *"Its light is seven times brighter than that of the moon, but the dimensions of both are equal."* **Enoch 69:28** says, *"By this oath the sun and the moon complete their progress, never swerving from the command to them forever and ever."* So the sun is not 93,000,000 million away as has been concluded by a simple mind man, but it is in the arch of the sky because ELOHIYM set the sun and the moon to revolve around the earth and not for the earth to revolve around the sun. This has been a delusion given to man by satan's house to deceive man. This is why we have the words sunrise and sunset. The sun rises always in the east and sets in the west because the earth is stationary. The earth doesn't move. **(Joshua) Yahusha 10:12-13**, *"Then spoke Yahusha to YAHUAH in the day when YAHUAH delivered up the Emoriym before the children of Yashar'el, and he said in the sight of Yashar'el, Sun, stand still upon Giv`on; and you, Moon, in the valley of Ayalon. And the sun stood still, and the moon stayed, until the people had avenged themselves upon their enemies. Is not this written in the Cepher of Yashar? So the sun stood still in the midst of heaven, and hastened not to come about a whole day."* So the sun and moon stood still and YAHUAH hearkened unto the voice of a man. So we are under a delusion to believe anything else, but as **(John)Yahuchanon 17:17b** says *"Thy WORD is truth."* **1 Chronicles 16:30** says, *"the world also shall be stable, that it be not moved."* **Psalm 93:1** says, *"the world also is stablished, that it cannot be moved."* **Psalm 96:10** says, *"the world also, shall be established that it shall not be moved:"*

Psalm 104:5 says, *"Who laid the foundations of the earth that it should not be removed forever."*

So the earth does not revolve as we have been told because Yahusha did not say earth stand still, but said sun stand still and YAH listened and heard Yahusha and the sun stood still. Many people will think I am off center that I should believe man, but I believe the universe as we see it was created in six days and six nights because ELOHIYM rested on the seventh day from all HE had created. The sun and the moon are in the vault, the arch or firmament as The Bible says. Many of you believe these men that do not believe there is a CREATOR.

9] The non-melanin people feel the people of the bible The People of GOD are non-melanin. We have to have a standard. Look at the statues of the Egyptians; these people have broad noses; people of color. This was all determined by the one that made men. This world has people with melanin in their skin tone or with very little melanin in their DNA. Melanin determines your eye color and skin tone and your hair and the texture. The more melanin in your DNA the darker your skin will be. THE CREATOR determines this. You have no determination who your father and mother will be and it was not by chance, but determined by The CREATOR. This was foreknown **Romans 8: 29, 11:2, Acts 2:23, 1 Peter 1:2, Ephesians 1:5, 11.**

So, Yoceph is standing before his brothers; Re'uven, Shim`on, Leviy, Yahudah, Dan, Naphtaliy, Gad, Asher, Yisshakar, and Zevulun and Yoceph recognized his brothers, but all of his brothers just saw Egyptians people of melanin or melanated skin tone not black people. You see we have been blinded by a delusion. Non-melanin see a man and say I am black. Why? You see, my true skin tone is brown. Is a Hershey's bar black? A Hershey's bar is dark brown, but this world would say I am black and they would label my grandson Landon as black and he is much lighter than me and one of my ex-wife who is lighter than Landon is also listen as black. So our stinking thinking has been corrupted again by this world system by putting the incorrect label on a skin color in which there was absolutely nothing I could do about that because I did not create me but I am created by THE CREATOR who designed all that is period. **Acts 21:38** The Roman guard thought Pa'al to be an Egyptian. So Pa'al is a person of color because he looks like the Egyptians. Pa'al states in **Phillipians 3:5** he is 1] An Israelites 2] Benjaminite 3] Hebrew. So The People of Color with melanin in their skin tone are The True People of GOD. The Israelites are people of color. The Benjaminites are people of color. The Hebrews are people of color. Avraham in **Genesis 14:13** says, *"And there came one that had escaped, and told Avram the Hebrew."* Yitschaq, Ya`aqov (Israel) and his twelve sons and one daughter all Hebrews people of color Re'uven, Shim`on, Leviy, Yahudha, Dan, Napthaliy, Gad, Asher, Yisshakar, Yoceph, Zevulun, Diynah, Binyamiyn. So the blessings and the curses are passed down to the children and the seeds of Avraham the father of the children of Yashar'el. So when you The United States of America is calling yourself blessing Israel you are not blessing Israel, you were not because WE THE PEOPLE OF GOD are in your own backyard as **Hebrew 11:25** says, *"Choosing rather to suffer affliction with the people of YAHUAH."* You see we are The People of YAHUAH. We are The People of YAHUAH in the americas who you non-melanin people have dislike and dismissed and you will receive the curses of Avraham because THE WORD does not dis rebuke your ignorance of your teachers and preachers who **REFUSED** to accept and admit MY WORD of TRUTH and RIGHTEOUSNESS.

10] **The KJV** says in **Mark 14:3,** *"And being in Bethany in the house of Simon **the leper**, a He sat meat, there came a woman having an alabaster box of ointment of spikenard very precious; and she brake the box and poured it on HIS Head."*

The Cepher Bible says in **Marqus 14:3,** *"And being in Bethany in the house of Shim`on **the jar maker**, as HE sat to eat, there came a woman having an alabaster box of ointment of spikenard very precious; and she broke the box, and poured it on HIS Head."*

The KJV verse referred to Simon as a leper. The Cepher Bible says Shim`on is a jar maker and not a leper. Which verse is correct? Is Simon or Shim`on a leper or jar maker? I shall make my case because Shim`on was a jar maker and not a leper. These are the facts to prove Shim`on was not a leper but a jar maker. **1]** Lepers could not be around people because they were defiled and they had to be put out of their society and once they became cleanse they had to go before the priest. **2]** Remember what MESSIAH said to the ten lepers **(Luke) Luqas 7:11-17.** Why is this person in his house? Lepers were put out of their home. **3]** There was no indication that he asked The MESSIAH to heal him. **4]** This was a translation error. It should be a jar maker and not leper. Lepers were put out of their household because Miryam and not Mary Martha and El`azar lived in this house also because Yahudah Iyshqiryot (Judas the one who betrayed The MESSIAH). The KJV says in the present states ``Simon the leper". Nowhere in this bible does it even <u>assume</u> that The Messiah heals him. It simply says Simon the leper invited The Messiah into his house. So if he is leper would the Hebrews/Israelites disobey the law? Miryam in the **Numbers 12** was put out of the camp. **2 Kings 5:27** Gehazi the leper and his seed forever. **Matthew 8:3** *"his leprosy was cleansed",* but nowhere does it say Simon the leper was healed, but HE (THE MESSIAH) sat at meat (eating) and a woman came in. Shim`on talked about this woman **Matthew 26:6, Mark 14:3, Luke 7:37** And if he was a leper he had no business talking about this woman.

Leviticus declares lepers were put out and could come back once they become cleanse. So this verse is incorrectly transcribed. The Cepher Bible says Shim`on the jar maker and because the word leper has been engraved, ingrained, embedded, informed, misinterpreted, and just plain wrong by what The KJV has saying the authorized word of God and there are mistakes in that Bible and we fail to realize this because we have been so indoctrinated by leaders who are not aware, but also refuse to believe that this could be wrong. For so many years we just read and never question what we are reading. For so many years we have been deceived by those we trust to declare the truth but the sheeples will just fall in line with the wrong shepherd. We ass-u-me this as truth and it is once again a false narrative that we believe to be true and it is once again a false narrative that we believe to be true but in fact error. In other words the liar has inputted untruth into that which is so misleading. We are sucker punched with that is misleading us from truth, but this what we have because we stop and accept a false narrative. I have read this so many times, but I just overlooked and never thought or had the inkling to simply ask a question to simply ask a question is this truth. Sometimes our eyes get so slumber we fall to sleep and one day The CREATOR opens our eyes so that we may see the truth because HE has a plan and He will open our slumber eyes to HIS truth and righteousness when it is time. So Shim`on was a jar maker and not a leper as it says in the Cepher Bible and not the KJV. **Leviticus 13:45, 14:2-3, 45, 22:4. 2 Chronicles 26:21** says, *"And Uzziyahu the king was a leper unto the day of his death, and dwelt in a several house, being a leper; for he was cut off from the house of YAHUAH: and Yotham his son was over the king's house, judging the people of the land."* The word **several** in Strong Concordance H2669 is *hopsut or hospital or H1004 a house, dungeon, winter house, prison,* In other words he was taken out of his kingship because of leprosy. **So do you think Shim`on was a leper?**

11] Many have said or mentioned "I want the patience and faith of Job (Iyov Hebrew name)."

I have even said this and YAH hears us and HE knows exactly what we need and when we need it because The testing is because of YAHUAH. Do we really know or realize what Job went through? Job lost all of his children in one day. Ten funerals in one day. Can you imagine losing all of your children in one day? Job lost the respect of his wife. Job had very sore boils from the crown of his head to the soles of his feet. Can you imagine the pain he was in and how he looked? His friends did not recognize him. Job's closest friends accused him of something that was not in his situation. All of his friends hurled outlandish accusations. Job lost all of his wealth. Now do you want Job's faith?

Now on this are living by your faith or you living by HIS faith. We have been misled because our faith is not strong enough. **Romans 1:17** says The just shall live by faith, but it should have said The just shall live by his faith. **Habakkuk 2:4** *by his faith.* A lot of confusion because "his" is left out. Please don't leave out "his" because that HAS NOTHING TO DO with a man, but ELOHIYM. What do I say this is because THE MESSIAH said that if you have faith the size of a mustard seed you can move a mountain. Have you moved a mountain? Many will disagree, but is this what the word says or did The MESSIAH lie to us. So if you have faith the size of a mustard seed you can say to that mountain move, because in all of your experiences you can't. So "his" was left out creating all kinds of mistaken thinking and preaching. Preachers prostituting the gospel by manipulating The WORD of ELOHIYM and many preachers are getting their just rewards here on this earth. For it it is by HIS faith and not by faith that we should live! HalleluJAH!

13] The end. Many people believe not that the earth is going to end, but The Bible make it so clearly it will **Revelation 21:1, Isaiah 51:6, 65:17, 66:22, Enoch 93:17, Hebrew 2:5, 2 Peter 3:13, Matthew 24:35, Psalm 148:6** each of these verses point to a conclusion as the psalmist writes. YAH has made a decree and HE will bring about an end in which those that believe what THE SON of ELOHIYM did will escape this destruction. In the last book of The Bible ELOHIYM THE SON addresses Yahuchanon about the last events that will happen. There is not a chance of these things from happening and it doesn't matter how much money you have you will not be able to escape this punishment. It doesn't matter who your parents are; you will not be able to escape. A meteorite will hit earth. **Revelation 8:10-11**. Large hailstones weighing 75 to 100 lbs will hit earth. Can you imagine hail stones that size? **Revelation 16:21.** The sun going dark **Revelation 8:12, 9:2.** Locusts stinging you because you refused to accept what THE SON did on the cross? **Revelation 9:3** Not being able to buy or sell because you refused to take the mark or you refused to worship someone or could not praise a name?

Revelation 13:16-17. If you can't buy, you can't eat? How long can you go without food in your body? You want to be able to work unless you take the mark. Answer these questions of how long will you last before you will take the mark or worship that name of the beast in the end time. There is a way to escape and that is to accept what THE SON of ELOHIYM did on the cross for man because as Isaiah said It is a prayer house for all.

14] The KJV left out certain books it should have retained because Yasher or Jasher give us more details about Avram's life and Mosheh's life especially. Hananiah, Mishael and Azariah were aware of Avram going into Nimrod's furnace. And Mosheh's different names by The Hebrew people. **Yasher 68:25-31** These are Mosheh's Hebrew names **1]** Amram his father called him Chabar. **2]** Yokeved his mother called him Yechuthiy'el **3]** Miryam his sister called him Yered **4]** Aharon his brother called him Aviy Zanuch **5]** Qohath his grandfather called him Abigdor **6]** The nurse called his Aviy Sokoh **7]** All of Yashar'el called him Shema`yahu.

A lot of us fail to realize it, but Mosheh is his Egyptian name given by Pharaoh's daughter and The promises YAHUAH had made toward **Avraham seeds Yasher 35:12,"** *And ELOHIYM saw all his works, and swore unto, and promised him that he would deliver his sons and <u>all</u> his seed from every trouble that would befall them, because he had this thing, and through his love to his ELOHIYM stifled his compassion for his child."*

You have to get into things to study something, you have to investigate and ask questions please because you can not pour water into a closed mouth. Who do you ask? I am glad you asked. You ask questions to The FATHER first and He will lead you where to go. It may not be right then, but be patient because HE will answer. But keep at it. A.S.K. Keep **A**sking, Keep **S**eeking and Keep **K**nocking. **K**eep **E**veryday **E**very moment **P**rays or **P**raise before YAHUAH why HE is looking at you!

15] The KJV says **Psalm 8:5** "*For thou hast made him a little lower than angels, and hast crowned him with glory and honour.*"

The Cepher Bible says **Psalm 8:5** *"For you have made him a little lower than ELOHIYM, and have crowned him with glory and honour."*

The KJV says this and The Cepher says that; which is correct? I am going to say The Cepher because of what YAHUAH states in **Genesis 1:26** And ELOHIYM said, Let us make man in our image, after our likeness: **Genesis 1:27** So, ELOHIYM created man in his own image; in the image of ELOHIYM created him; male and female created he them. In the book of **Exodus 3:14** He said I Am THAT I AM. YAHUSHA said in **Yahuchanon 8:58** He said I AM. So the man ELOHIYM is a replica of HIM and we have been saying A-dom, but in the dictionary it is like this Ad-am. If you read that we are saying add am. ELOHIYM made another one like himself and just looked at the imagination of a man. Always trying to outdo HIS ABBA (DAD). And this maybe why the angels revolted against YAH because of envy and jealousy for we were made a little bit lower than ELOHIYM.

CHAPTER 34

---✦---

Natural Born Citizen

Article 2 Section 1 of the Constitution of The United States

It states No person except a <u>natural born Citizen</u>, or a <u>Citizen of The United States</u>, at time of the Adoption of this Constitution, shall be eligible to the Office of President;

Now there are two citizens, one a <u>natural born citizen</u> and a <u>citizen of The United States</u>. Are you naturally born or a Citizen of The United States? What is the difference? We have to ask questions? Why is this not on any document? All I have ever seen in any form is "Are you a United States Citizen." Why is this? What are they (the one in charge of this system) hiding? What are they not telling us? I am leery of when people hide information and I am also leery of the statement U S citizen; When it should read exactly as it is written in The Constitution of The United States. You see, your CITIZENSHIP is more important than we think. Citizen is first and not behind the U.S., but the way these documents are presented to us it says U.S. first and then citizen is secondary. Are we to bow down to this system of conglomerate of **CORPORATIONS**? Doesn't this make you think. I see this matrix as cunning, but the majority are not dumbfounded but just go along with this system. System what are you hiding? A citizen of The United States is one born in Washington District of Columbia or one of the territories of The United States. If you are born outside The District of Columbia, you are not a U.S. Citizen or Citizen of The United States, **you are a natural born citizen**! This term is in The Constitution of The United States. So if you were born in one of the fifty states you are a NATURAL BORN CITIZEN and are not, no way a U.S. Citizen as this system want you to believe and thereby you are not ties to those law as a natural born citizen because THE CREATOR has given you inalienable rights that

NO MAN can take from you because they were GOD given and only HE has the rights to take those away from man. Man wants to replace GOD, but we don't have the power to do so because all glory belongs to YAHUAH THE MIGHTY LIVING GOD THE EHAYAH ASHER EHAYAH I AM THAT I AM.

So since you were born in Texas, Tennessee, Mississippi, California, New York, Connecticut, Nevada, Oregon, Washington, Montana, North Dakota, South Dakota, New Jersey,

Rhode Island, Alaska, Hawaii, Idaho, Missouri, Florida, Georgia, North Carolina,

South Carolina, Kentucky, New Mexico, Arkansas, Kansas, Iowa, Michigan, Illinois, Delaware, Maine, Arizona, Alabama, Wyoming, Utah, Louisiana, Minnesota, Maryland, Oklahoma, Wiscousin, Indiana, Ohio, West Virginia, Virginia, New Hampshire, Masshuchetts, Virginia, Vermont, Pennsylvania, and Nebraska you are natural born citizen and you are a citizen of The United States or a U.S. citizen. If you don't believe me ask the person in charge why NATURAL CITIZEN is nowhere found on any document? When you seek a passport or credit card, what is the question you are asked or what is on the form? The contract or The Constitution placed two types of citizenship that is written on the piece of paper as the legal document or contract that this nation put into effect to be governed by. There is one word with two letters which establish or substantiate this **TRUTH** in The Constitution of The United States and it is **"OR".**

The meaning of or is *"used as a function word to **INDICATE** an alternative. What is an alternative?* Alternative a proposition or situation offering a choice between two or more things, offering or expressing a choice. So thereby you CANNOT BE a natural born citizen and citizen of The United States because of the word or. It is impossible to be both because of the two letters word or. So what are they HIDING? They have HIDDEN this from our eyes as the movie "Eyes Wide Shut." The word "or" setup, creates, binding, establishes, irrevocable, indissoluble, conclusive, unalterable and unbreakable the difference between a natural born citizen and citizen of The United States. The Constitution is by law a contract, a legal and binding document and by putting the word "or" in it this distinguishes the two citizens as established THE LAW of this document. This is like the signature on a bank check, if your check signature have "or" on it, it requires one signature, but it if says "and" then both signatures MUST BE ON THE signature line (the so-called line because it is not a line but it is words that are so small you think it is aline). So the constitution which is by all courts considered a legal document, distinguishes a natural born citizen and the citizen of the United States. So I asked and most will say "no" it doesn't make a difference. If you agree it doesn't make a difference then let this go, but if your eyes are open and you agree, then ask the question "Why did they who wrote The Constitution placed the word "or" between *natural born* and *citizen of The United States?* Words have meaning and they are placed together for a specific purpose. So, what is the difference between a natural born citizen and citizen of the United States? You see we have been deceived by those in charge and the cover has been placed over our heads so that we won't discover their dirty deeds. Amein.

For we that are not born in the District of Columbia are Natural Born Citizens. And according to lawful law this makes a difference, but we have been deceived by our leaders who will be before The CREATOR and asking, pleading and begging for mercy! And if you will further notice the United States is second to the word citizen so thereby none of us ARE U.S. Citizen, why because as in the Bible the greater emphasis is placed in the first position and the second has less emphasis. So when the word citizen is placed first that is the GREATER emphasis or the greater value. So thereby the word citizen is of greater value than the United States like in The Bible when it says Esau and Jacob; Esau was born first and had the greater right and Jacob had the inheritance of the second born. Jacob would get one-third of his father's material wealth whereas Esau would receive a greater portion, but spiritually this was reversed. Anyway we have placed so much authority or priority on the word United States when the priority should be the citizen as the constitution says; for none of the people in The United States are **NOT** United States Citizen, you are either a Citizen of the United States or as the majority that are born in the continental of The United States: We DECLARE we are in fact **NATURAL BORN CITIZEN** and not U.S. citizen as this system want us to aggressive agree too for The TRUTH has been hidden from us. So we totally disagree with this system no matter what documents we have signed stating we are United States citizens. We declare by THIS statement we are **NATURAL BORN CITIZEN** as stated by **THE LEGAL LAW ABIDING LIVING DOCUMENT of THE CONSTITUTION of THE UNITED STATES of AMERICA** and no other law can legally override The Constitution of The United States of America. The Constitution is legal and everything else is illegal because this is the legal binding document that was declared by this system of government on July 4, 1776 because as it says in the preamble; We the people of The United States, in order to form a more perfect Union establish Justice, insure domestic Tranquility provide for the common defence, promote the general Welfare, and secure the Blessings of Liberty to ourselves and our Posterity (future generations), do ordain and establish this constitution for The United States of America.

This is what this country was formed for. So let us declare our Natural Born citizenship. Open your eyes for we have been blindsided by those operating in this system who are not operating under The Constitution of The United States of America, but under UCC which is Uniform Commercial Code because these systems opposite each other as The Bible says you cannot serve two masters! **What do you see?**

CHAPTER 35

God's Perspective Versus MAN's Perspective

Man thinks he knows more than HIS CREATOR and some men don't acknowledge THE CREATOR. WRONG STINKING THINKING WILL GET SENT TO HELL!

1] Man says the sun is 93,000,000 million miles away from earth. Is that true or false? In the book of **Genesis 1:16-17** GOD placed the sun and the moon in the firmament or expanse of the sky. What and where is the firmament or expanse of the sky? The expanse is the arch of the sky. And we see the sun everyday when it is not cloudy. So from GOD'S perspective the sun is not 93,000,000 million miles from earth. Then that led to a question man; How big is the sun? I see from GOD'S perspective it can't be that big. In the book of Enoch **78:3** the sun and the moon are equal in dimension. And this is why we can have solar and lunar eclipses. **Enoch 72:47** says the sun is seven times brighter than the moon.

2] Does the sun rotate around the earth or does the earth rotate around the sun? Man says the earth rotates around the sun. **Joshua 10:13** says Joshua asked YAHUAH for the sun to stand still and the moon to stand still. So, the sun rotates around the earth and we have these words sunrise and sunset which is true. The earth is stationary **Psalm 104:5** says, *"Who laid the foundations of the earth that it should not be removed forever."* So as you can read, what man says is not true. The sun is not the center of this universe. Just look into the sky each day and you will notice, what I notice, the sun in the arch of the sky.

3] YAHUAH called the land Eden and not Africa. Man named the continent Africa (after the Roman general name Scipio Africanus, who conquered the land), but **Genesis 2:8** says," *And YAHUAH ELOHIYM planted a garden eastward in Eden."* So as you can see and read, man changed things around again. To the majority may feel it is what man says, but it is what YAH says that matters. There is a program that shows wildlife called the land Eden as should be. The Moors called it Alkebulan meaning "mother of mankind."

4] Man says take the vaccine, but YAH created in man an immune system which man will compromise this immune system in which YAHUAH has created for times such as these. Man always wants to take GOD or YAH out and replace what HE has done with his own philosophy. Man wants to become god and replace what YAH has already created. Just like at the tower of Babel. YAH allowed man to build, but at the end man was upended and dethroned and defeated because YAH is all knowing and HE knows where and when man shall end since he doesn't turn to HIM. So if you take this vaccine there may be matters that will surface in the future because people **TRUST** their doctors instead of YAH. **2 Chronicles 16:12** says *"And Aca in the thirty and ninth year of his reign was diseased in his feet, until his disease he sought not to YAHUAH, but to the physicians."* You can go to your physicians but seek YAHUAH first and always because HE may want you to the doctors so HE can bring the doctors to the knowledge of HIM. **Hoshea 4:6** says, *"My people are destroyed for a lack of knowledge"* and part b of that verse which is critical says *"because you have rejected the knowledge."* You fail because you rejected the very knowledge that could have saved you from what you are going through. Many will say "I don't know the ingredients to this or that"; but the ingredients are listed on the package somewhere are they not? But the ingredients of this vaccine are NOT listed at all. And you are putting those ingredients inside your body and you don't know what they are? You see THE ONLY PERSON I TRUST is YAHUAH. I am just inquiring.

It does matter who side you are on with these perspectives because one is true and the other one is a lie. One question: who side are you with? Are you going to take GOD'S side or you going to side with a man and all his errors? Has The FDA (Food and Drug Administration) had any drugs recalled? There are but two opinions. Is GOD lying or is man lying? It is impossible to have two truths on the same question. Someone has to be telling the truth and the other side is lying. Who do you think is lying, GOD or man? These are your choices and you cannot choose both. You have the choice of one over the other, but you can't say man is right and GOD is right because someone is lying. Man said to stay indoors from the sun, but Vitamin D is excellent for the body. It is my hope you chose GOD as I have decided to follow GOD and forever be on HIS Side.

5] Man also said The MESSIAH died on friday. Friday is not in The Bible and HE arose on a sunday morning and sunday is not in The Bible. **Matthew 12:40** says three days and three nights. Friday night to sunday morning that would mean **Matthew 12:40** is wrong. That would mean The Word of GOD is a lie, but GOD said heaven and earth would pass away if HIS word is not fulfilled which HE THE MESSIAH did not died on friday, but to fulfilled HIS Word HE died earlier in the week because in the book of John declared HE was THE LAMB OF GOD. HE was the passover's lamb for the entire world. So from GOD's perspective it was on the fourth day of the week at night (it would be wednesday night) that HE was slain and was laid in the tomb and resurrected at the end of Israelites Shabbath at 6:01 pm. Is anything too hard for YAH?

6] Man's perspective is trying to change time and this is why man's calendar starts in the winter and ends in the winter, but GOD starts HIS calendar in the springtime. YAHUAH told Mosheh in **Exodus 12:2** this shall be the first month for you. YAHUAH calendar starts in the springtime and ends in the winter. So the Hebrew calendar is spring, summer, fall and winter but man's calendar starts in the winter, spring, summer, fall and winter. **Who is Right?**

7] Men celebrate holidays by reveling, but Israelites give their time to YAHUAH to praise HIM. And these days were called HOLY DAYS. Two words with a different meaning and mind set.

8] Man has established land titles on every piece of property, but where did this come from? Who established land titles? Why were land titles established? Because who has the title to this earth?

9] The 400 years of slavery for us who are Eden-American ended in august 2019. It was not back in ancient Egypt, but this strange land that YAH brought our foreparents as it says in the book of Genesis. The enslavement in Egypt was no more than 215 years because there is NOT 400 years between Yoceph's death and the Exodus of Mosheh. We have been misled by lies told by pastors all over this earth and The Exodus will soon happen because that nation as it says in Genesis is being punished. Just look at the national debt in which it will no not ever be paid back. The amount of debt is insurmountable. If you take all the rich people's money, it would not make a dent in the national debt.

10] We have been labeled wrong. We have been labeled wronged. For we are not black because if you look in a crayola box and you look at the color black, does that match your color? The answer is No! We are various shades of color and Hispanic or Mexican-American who are labeled brown are for the most part NOT brown, but non-melanin. Who put these labels on people? Look at yourself and answer the question, are you black? And when I see us saying I am black I just shake my head. Some people may say, "It doesn't matter." But I say" Truth always matters." I guess people like being lied to. Why can't you just accept the plain truth of what is before your very eyes instead of walking around with an open blindfold. So I can tell you that 1+1=6? So, can I say this is true? Why not because if it is true for me and not you. Who is right? So we have to have a standard of what truth is.

11] The SON of YAH name is not Jesus because in the 1611 KIV it was Iesus. The letter J was not formed until 1524. Names in the 1611 KIV that started with an I were changed in 1633 KJV except a very few because it would have looked strange such as Isaac or Isaiah. Can you see what I am referring to? What if Isaac was changed to Jsaac or Isaiah to Jsaiah. A person in 1524 for some particular reason put a backward hook on the letter i and created a j. Why was this done? I can't answer, but it happened to change people's way of thinking to whitewash The TRUTH. All I am trying to do is to present to you information of what has been hidden from your eyes because what should be our desire is to discover the truth and be removed from the lies from this society. Let me ask you a question. Do you like being lied to? Yes or No? That is all I ask. If you like being lied to then take the blue pill and stay in your fantasy world. Your world of sleep or take the red pill and awake to truth.

12] This calendar is messed up because it has been manipulated, handled,or controlled like a tool. New year day, easter, halloween, christmas (chrismuss) and good friday are all pagan's holidays. Easter has NOTHING TO DO WITH The MESSIAH'S Death or Resurrection because the word was wrongly translated or inputted. It was Pecach or Passover. THE MESSIAH did NOT die on good friday because The Scriptures say 3 days and 3 nights and not a friday because it destroys the truth. The MESSIAH was not born on december 25th, but HE was born in the springtime. HE was conceived in the fall. New Year's Day is celebrated WRONG by man. Men say the new year starts in the wintertime, but The Hebrew New Year starts on the new moon on march 2nd. Easter is to the goddess ashtoreth a paganess god. Halloween is a celebration to the dead, witchcraft, devils and all evil. And no one can escape from hell.

13] Heaven is not our final destination. Heaven is a transitory period because as you can read in **Revelation 21:3** says" *And I heard a great voice out of heaven saying, Behold, the tabernacles of YAHUAH is with men, and he will tabernacle with them, and they shall be his people, and YAHUAH himself shall be with them, and be their ELOHIYM.*"

YAHUAH is going to renew, recreate Heaven and earth and we will reside with HIM forever. So heaven is not our final destination, but earth. Because The Psalmist The earth is YAHUAH and the fullness thereof. YAHUAH made the earth for himself. **Revelation 21:1-3** says this, read and understand that YAHUAH will recreate and HE will reside with men in peace forever

14] The true Hebrews are people with melanin in their skin tone. Yoceph was looking at his brothers and he recognized them, but all of his brothers saw were just Egyptians and the Egyptians came from Cham's side and Shem's side were the Hebrews. Pa'al in **Acts 21:38** was thought to be an Egyptian. Mosheh in **Exodus 4:6-8** placed his hand into his bosom and it changed to leprosy and it was white and he placed it back into his bosom and it changed to his other flesh. A man that does not have dark skin cannot become lighter that would be against nature. Miryam Mosheh's sister was turn leprosy because of her condemnation of her brother.

(Sometimes we need to stay in our lane. In other words mind your own business, Don't you try to be YAHUAH). Gehazi and his seed were cursed with leprosy forever because of his greed.

So does this matter 1] Truth 2] The promises for The True My People of The Bible.

15] Men and Women who say "I have never been married" or "I will never get married again." or "I have only been married once." Is this what The Bible says? Man or woman say I need a ring, stand in front of a preacher and have a license (a piece of paper). Is this marriage to you and the majority of people will say YES. This is man perspective right? YAH look at marriage as this; When a man and woman join their body together YAHUAH consider that marriage. You see we have been looking at it from man point of view and not from GOD point of view. What perspective should we be looking from GOD or man? And this is my last point.

Yahuchanon 4:16-18, "*YAHUSHA said unto her, Go, call your man, and come hither. The woman answered and said, I have no man. YAHUSHA said unto her, You have well said, I*

have no man: For you have had five men; and he whom you now have is not your man: in that said you truly."

1] This woman states she has no man **2]** she has been with five men *3]* the man she is with now is not her

The KJV used the term husband and wife. The word husband and wife are legal terminology. Husband and Wife is man's perspective and not GOD's perspective and we should always look from GOD'S perspective because man's perspective is in error from GOD. GOD'S perspective is when a man and a woman come together as one. So are you engaging in sex with different women? Are you engaging with sex with different men? Are you still a virgin? If not your first man you laid with is your man. Are you still with the first woman you laid with? If not your first woman you laid with is your woman? This is why when you lay around with different people committing adultery and fornication. And the majority will disagree with this, but I am just reading what is written and guess what I did not write this and this is why we have a SAVIOR because thinking of sex with a person is adultery **Matthew 5:27-30.**

SUMMARY

This life is a mess! This matrix or world system is holding men and women in bondage. This system hides the true information and gives out lies so everyone succumbs to the hold of this presence's darkness. Men's minds have been deleted from the truth and all of this system sees is corruption of what THE FATHER has allowed to go on but one day this darkness will vanish because light outshine darkness. We have The bastards which give out the wrong information to the sheeples and the sheeple swallow all of the crude, this present system gives it. I say this because you have bastards teaching filthy words to GOD'S people. They are to speak truth, but the only thing they give is a speck of truth and the people's eyes are not open to THE FATHER'S TRUTH. Their eyes are lain with sin and the toxicity of this present darkness. The darkness does not allow them to see The TRUTH just like the movie "The Matrix." People's minds are gone accepting that which is untrue and their eyes so laid with sin and slumber that they can't open their eyes because the weight is too much. People are going in their way not knowing the way they go will end. People in the matrix are hooked up to a machine feeding the system not knowing they are feeding a system that does not care about them. This system dilutes our sense of reality. For we **THINK** we are living in the true system, but we are not living in reality, but a simulation of reality. The people in the matrix were living, but they were attached to the system that was using them as electric current or power. This system is the same. We are attached from reality because this system will end and it will be an abrupt ending and you will wake up to a living and eternal hell of an existent that you would wish would end, but you have awaken to the reality that you waste all of your energy on the lust of life, the lust of take and eternity to realize what happened and NOW you have no way of escape because it is too late. You have all of the photographs of looking so called pretty, but it was all an illusion. You thought about what you did by yourself. This system, this matrix makes me **SICK** and I would like to throw up but I have come to realize that the god of this world in whom you were trying to please has your every thought. The coloring of your hair. The color of your lips and long fingernails. The arching of your eyebrows. The elongated nails and the heels all for **WHAT**? Now you see you forgot about THE SON, but This matrix wouldn't allow you to know HIM. All you could see was "**I did it ALL.**" No referral of THE FATHER. It is all about me. The matrix trick you into thinking you were somebody, but in reality it was not you and you gave all THE credit to yourself and not THE ONE that gave you air to breath and FOOD to eat and money and job and most of all your senses (common, taste, hearing, seeing, touch, smelling, feeling, blood running through your body) of being. You gave it all to yourself. You see it was not you, but THE CREATOR that should get all of THE GLORY. So as you read, you have been deceived because all of the time THE CREATOR **LOOKS** out for your safety and not yourself. You are so lost, so foolish to think that you sing better than THE CREATOR, who gave you your voice. Oh how foolish we have fallen, when we think we can do anything, anything better than THE CREATOR. Oh how often do you give thanks?

This matrix has us thinking that money we have is real, but it is counterfeit. Counterfeit is to make something that we think is real. Look at the money we have. Paper money is misleading and now digital money also. We use the same paper and place different number values on the same paper. In other words a $50.00 bill **IS** the same paper as the $20.00 dollars bill. No different. A digital currency can be wiped out in a moment. According to The Constitution of The United States it is not legal tender. I don't care what The Federal Reserve places on that piece of paper that can be burned to keep you warmed. Silver coins are no longer silver. Silver coins produced today have other metals in them. Unless it says 99.99% and that is a real silver coin. So, **WHY does this matrix put ridges around a quarter or a dime or fifty cents or silver dollars when they are no longer silver?** If you have real silver dollars it is way worth more than a dollar! Silver coins have not been produced since 1964. What is counterfeit? Since it is not real, but fake. The ridges are there to deceive people. Making it seem real. This is to get our minds away from **TRUTH!** Anything not true is a lie and if you don't like the lie then what about the word fake. Does it make you feel better? Do you like having fakeness in your life? Would you like for your woman to have fake boobs, hair, booty or lips? Would you like for your man to have a fake pipe (male apparatus)? **WAKE UP PEOPLE!** We are living a world of fake reality. This is not reality, but The Twilight

Zone. This reality is in your mind only and your mind is leading you down a road of eternal DESTRUCTION. We have grapes and watermelon seedless. Is this supposed to be real? All of these are against HIS design. Fruits are SUPPOSED to have seeds and man has designed seedless. Man has also decided to grow meat in the lab. Mad scientists I say and you are going to eat meat from a lab?

President John Fitzgerald Kennedy was assassinated, Why? There may be numerous reasons, but I submit he was assassinated for not these two reasons alone **1]** He did not want to go into Vietnam, but the war machine corporations saw their way to make a huge sum of money. They didn't care how many sons lost their lives for their greed or how it destroyed a family. **2]** He had written **executive order 11110** to issue silver certificates, which would have taken us from under the federal reserve notes. The federal reserve notes according to the The Constitution of The United States are not legal. Many people don't realize that The Federal Reserve System prints up NOTES. The word note as according to law means debt. The UCC (Uniform Commercial Code) makes money order, check, bank card, paper money etc so-called legal form of currency because The Constitution says silver and gold to pay ALL debts. So thereby these things as mentioned before are not constitutional legally, but before we accept this. Our mind has always been deceived not to this truth, but what you have been told to believe as truth. If you have been told to believe the truth. If you don't believe me, look at the line where you sign your name on a check. That line has to be magnified and you will see not a line, but these words ``AUTHORIZED SIGNATURE." Is it a line or is it NOT a line? You see we have been conditioned and feed garbage and the old line garbage in and garbage out (gigo). Many people label themselves as color white or black or brown, but in reality many sees a person that is labeled as negro, african-american or black which is oh soooo very wrong. You see I have been called ni_ _ _r, negro, african-american or black. The word negro comes from spanish which means black. Mexican-American have been labeled brown. People say african-american also wrong. If you have black shoes or black belt or black pants or black coat etc and look at my skin or any other person called black and then say that person is black and Mexican-American for the most part I have seen are not brown just as those that have been labeled white are not white. **WAKE UP PEOPLE!** This deception has gone on far too long. There you ass-u-me the power, but THE CREATOR will take over; and where can you run? Africa is wrong because YAH said in **Genesis 2:8** that HE planted a garden eastward in Eden. Eden not Africa. The name Africa probably came from a roman general name Scipio Africanus or Leo Africanus, but YAH in HIS Word called it Eden. So we have been deceived for such a long time. We are living in a world that is full of misconception and untrue. It is like a person who grew up living in the mud and didn't realize he is not to live in the mud, but to dine with kings and queens.

Preachers teach The MESSIAH died on friday and rose early sunday morning which if you read **Matthew 12:40** says "For as Jonah was three days and three nights in the fish's belly; so shall the Son of Adam be three days and three nights in the heart of the earth." And from friday @6pm to early sunday morning is **NOT** 3 days and 3 nights, but we continue to support these liars and their non biblical fantasy. Tithes and offerings please. It is not supposed to be in the church. Tithes and offerings have nothing to do with church. Pastors and teachers own jets and million dollar mansions and own sports cars. Why? How dare you and you preacher of The Word, oh how you fool the sheeples and you pastor the people of GOD and this chaotic mess goes on just like when The MESSIAH whipped the money changers out of HIS FATHER'S House.

The MESSIAH is only coming back for Israel only **Yahuchanon 10:16** says And other sheep I have which are not of this fold. Key words in this scripture are "other sheep" and ``this fold." The words this fold is talking about Israel and the other sheep are those in the church. So read this verse and get the idea that The MESSIAH is coming for Israel because HE also said there will be one fold and YAHUAH loves Israel. Israel's correct spelling is Yashar'el which means upright. So HE is only coming for them that are **UPRIGHT.** So how can you become **UPRIGHT? Believing** that The MESSIAH YAHUSHA HA'MASHIACH died for your sins and arose again and believe and admit you are a sinner and make confession with your mouth and heart and thou shall live eternity with THE CREATOR. Do I have to be immersed in water to be saved? Was the thief on the cross with The MESSIAH immersed in water? Water immersion is because you are saved, so if you can be immersed, get immersed.

Many believe the sun is 93,000,000 million miles away from earth even though you can look right into the sky and see it before your very eyes. Pull off those blinders. You believe this because this is what you were told by a man (scientists, teachers, professors) have told us and you believe these men. But **Genesis 1:17** And ELOHIYM set them in the firmament of the heavens to give light upon the earth. **He set them** the sun and the moon. The book of **Enoch** states **78:3** The dimensions of both are equal. **Enoch 72:47** The dimensions of both are equal. This is why we can have a total eclipse. The sun and the moon are in the firmament and not millions of miles away, but we would rather believe the point of a man than to take the Word of THE ONE who places them where they are. We refuse THE CREATOR TRUTH. They are both the same sizes.

The earth does not revolve around the sun, but the sun revolves around the earth. **Joshua 10:12-13**, Joshua asked YAHUAH in front of Yashar'el sun and moon stand still and YAHUAH listened to Joshua and the sun and moon stood still in the midst of the heaven, but many won't believe this, but we will believe those who think this universe was created by the big bang theory who doesn't believe that there is A CREATOR, A MIGHTY GOD, THE EHAYAH ASHER EHAYAH, THE GREAT I AM THAT I AM. The GREAT I AM where HE IS SELF EXISTENCE. Do you think the earth revolves around the sun? I know THE CREATOR exists because I have been in HIS very presence or essence in the place HE resides. You see we are in this matrix, but everyone who challenges this matrix is killed off. Do you believe this? Have you actually open your eyes and see I am not black, but my skin tone is brown. Who labeled us who have brown skin as black and who labeled Mexican-American as brown when the majority are like the people who have little melanin in their dna? We have been called black, negro or african-american. CAN YOU OPEN YOUR EYES and see the truth or you still see what the matrix has told you as truth and once you know the truth then you are set free because we are all just mere men created by ELOHIYM. There is GOD, angels and man. GOD ELOHIYM [FATHER SON HOLY SPIRIT]. Angel [Warriors, Demons fallen entity]. Man [Man Woman Child (boy, girl)].

This earth is going to be destroyed, replaced, done away with, renewed by a glorious new earth. You have seen these Movies: **2012, Deep Impact, Knowing, Armageddon and Greenland.** Every one of these movies has some truth in them, but man is saved in the end except **Knowing** (The earth was replaced, but there were people saved from this destruction. Saved by The Watchers). All of these movies are referring to the destruction of this earth. If you don't believe please believe because this is going to happen. Read the following verses

Isaiah 51:6, 65:17, 66:22 Revelation 21:1, Hebrews 2:5, 2 Peter 3:13, Matthew 24:35, Enoch 93:17, Psalm 148:6b.

Psalm 148:6b He has made a decree which shall not pass. All which THE CREATOR has said will come to pass. There is no maybe or probability, but shall and will for THE CREATOR is THE VERY of Existence in Eternity right now. HE sees all and what HE said it will do. Read **Isaiah 55:11** *"So shall my word be that goes forth out of my mouth; it shall not* *return unto me void, but it shall accomplish that which I please and it shall prosper in the thing whereto I sent it."*

So you can doubt what is written, but be assured it will become **TRUTH**. For we are living in the last days for YAH has warned this evil generation. Women and men don't sanity their bodies. One woman said "She sucks off every player on a professional basketball team in a single night." Men will go and put their manhood into another man butt. We have **L-G-B-T-Q-I-A** [Lesbian, Gay, Bisexual, Transsexual, Questioning or Queer, Intersex, Asexual, Agender, Ally (two spirit)]. What are you going to say before HIM, THE ONE that created you? You can date whoever you want, but **WE** will answer to HIM, who created **US.** Then what? Man or this system or this world, this matrix is always trying to adjust themselves away from what YAH has said. HE [YAH] made man and woman and sin has perverted this world system. YAH said you are going to sweat, but man says antiperspirant. So as you can see MAN says something again what THE CREATOR says. Sin has flipped things around in this world that has created things around in this world that has created a disaster of YAH'S creation. This earth does not belong to man, but YAH created this earth for man used and man has totally destroyed earth. This earth is YAH'S Heart. Put the h at the end of heart and you will have earth, but man refused to abide.

Man wants to control things his way. Man seeks to think he can owe someone. Can I really own someone? Can I take control of your body? Man creates suffocating taxes. The masses are trying to owe. Can I go here and there and be a free man? No, can I not be tied to a particular country without a passport or license or identification with just my name. Man can be so ridiculous. How easy is it to produce another identification? An id that is so real that it is important when forgers can forge fraudulent papers. So we are people of the world.

Many are using vaccines and masks as their safety net. Please read **Proverbs 21:31b, 29:25, 30:5, Iyov(Job) 5:11-15, 21-22.** Our safety is in YAH'S hands if we trust **in HIM.** Even when death occurs (death will occur) we will forever be with HIM. We will live forever on this earth because this is totally out of our control. And many people are not prepared for what is going to occur. Physical death will happen. So prepare. Buy some insurance. Make your arrangements. My funeral is all paid up and I know like Iyov, MY REDEEMER is ADONAI YAHUSHA HA'MASHIACH LIVES ON HIGH. Read **Iyov (Job) 14:5, 12:10.** For my end has been determined by THE GREAT I AM.

In this matrix today we are following the principles and teaching and thoughts of people who do not believe THERE IS A GOD, THE CREATOR of Heaven and earth. So I ask you a question "Why are you following the teachings, the thoughts, the philosophies, the principles of someone THAT DOES NOT BELIEVE THE CREATOR exist believers? Because it sounds good or reasonable (from a man's point of view), but is it true? Why are you not trusting and believing THE CREATOR? This sounds like in the times of Nimrod when he tried to kill Avram. Read **Yasher 12:1-70** Listen man you cannot stop YAHUAH because what HE says will be done.

White america terror group the KKK is not ever stop by the police. They have never ever been stopped. Maybe because they are in and controlling this force? I wondered who led the Tulsa's Massacre. Melanin people are stopped for hanging air freshener over the mirror, not using a turn signal and killed. Walking down the streets and being stopped because I have never seen you walking this way and then asked for identification. This racist hypocritical society that has deem us a threat and the threat is the non-melanin society. And President Joe Biden has the nerve to talk about China abuse. The United States DON'T DARE point your fingers at another country when YOU have treated people with melanin in their skin tone worse than the family dog in your house. You (non-melanin) society sees us as a threat because you breath these lies on your televisions every single day and when something is deem as a danger every single day, every hour, every minute, every second of everyday it becomes true in your eyes, but this matrix has got you deceived to believe the lie, but this lie seems true in your sight because you have been condition not to believe truth, but the lie that seem truth, but it is sooo very far from TRUTH that you can no longer wean yourself from this lie because you have accepted the lie as truth and now you cannot accept truth because you have been feed lies all your life and this garbage has created rottenness in your indwelling part and all you sees, feels is the lie you have accepted as truth all of your life and you have no way of accepting truth because all you have seen was this picture or ideal or thought that has provoked you in all of your mind to accept as truth and the filth of that information you have no way, but to accept what is before your eyes as truth. Wake up people because you are going into a deep sleep, a delta sleep from which you cannot ever wake up because you have been taught this pattern all of your life and the TRUTH is not in your life, but you have no way to escape because you have been on this roller coast of lies for sooo long that it has grown and nourish by your forefathers of generations for far to long. That it can't be overturned so you stick to the web of lies, but you refuse to look at the truth when Mosheh stuck his hand in his bosom and brought it out and it turned much lighter than his other flesh and you know you cannot become lighter because that is against nature. You know this, but you refuse to believe TRUTH. Wake up people. The "My People In The Bible" **ARE THE PEOPLE WITH MELANIN IN THEIR SKIN TONE,** but you still refused to believe this is truth because of what lies has been presented to you in your path and to believe that The MESSIAH who was born in The Land of Eden to Hebrew parents, who has melanin in HIS skin tone continue to believe that and when you pass from this body and end up on the other side, then your eyes will be opened to truth! Basically what I am saying is, it is like a person that has been used to a flip phone and has been dependent on that flip phone and they start using a smartphone and can't get used to the smartphone and they revert back to the flip phone.

In this system or this Matrix uses words that have a different meaning than from reality, the thinking, the concepts are totally different from that which is real. White is the opposite of black. Indeed when this matrix has labeled people these definitions are in the very front of our mind. When you have labeled me incorrectly and by labeling me incorrectly I am then screwed in the deep forest of the mind of the person looking at me. And THIS label has been instilled in the thinking of people for over four hundred years. This thought has been engrained and embedded in their thinking for all these years and passed from generations to generations and this stinking thinking has been enclosed with a prejudiced thinking and I am not even CONSIDER a man, but a beast. Many people will say I am black, but in reality my color is brown. So their thinking has been enthroned with wrong thinking. What is one reason that I have been labeled black is because The Office of Management Budget Directive 15 says so and this has been the norm of the so-called white society, who think they are white because they feel as though they are right. Look at The 16th Chapel in the Vatican these images have been implied as correct, but in actuality, it is so very WRONG. Look what history has taught this society. Wrong information has been in this society and it has led people with the wrong ideological ideas all these years. Like I said garbage in and garbage out, but this matrix doesn't see it as this. Whosoever **WROTE** those words, their thinking is all screwed up because they weren't influenced with the truth. A pig was designed to live in the mud, but a duck was not, but if that duck grew up with pigs, that duck would live in the mud because the duck wouldn't know any better. The melanin in my skin cell determines my skin color, in which this matrix says black, but in reality I AM BROWN and NOT BLACK. I AM the

"**MY PEOPLE**" in The Bible. A Hebrew designed by THE CREATOR. You see this matrix is crooked and those who are running this matrix are crooked and those who are running this matrix [the agents, the elites] know THE TRUTH, but these agents are letting the peons thinks they know, but they will all end in the pit and fiery furnace of eternity because there is no way to escape of what THE CREATOR has said that will happen for there will be a new Heaven and new earth. People there will be no excuse if your name is not found in the book of life, you will forever be on an eternal death of doom and despair hoping for an end, but it goes on and on never ending, but an eternity of being destitute of want, destitute of any hope or release and eternity of gloom, hoping and wishing for a reprieve, but this reprieve or hope is now eternity lost or doom and gloom because you had your opportunity, but you lost that chance and NOW you are hoping for another opportunity that you will never ever hope to receive and now all you have is eternal disgrace and hopelessness for eternity. What is this like? It is like a bird flying from point a to point b grabbing one grain of sand from the east coast going to the west coast and delivering that grain of sand and flying to grab another grain of sand. And you thought this life was bad? Just think of what you have right now? Are you listening to or getting information from someone who does not believe in a CREATOR? Be careful because their unbelief could have you going down the road of destruction because of what they base their information on. This could be tied to this matrix or this world system, which is based on teaching on this world system. This system which swayes you away from THE CREATOR that it does not think A CREATOR exists.

The name Jesus is not Hebrew, but Greek. The name Jesus did not come into existence until 1633. In the 1611 KIV there was no name that started with the letter J. In the 1611 KIV (KJV) it was Iesus. Thereby since The MESSIAH was born to a Hebrew's mother over 2000 years ago, HIS name had to be something else. Miryam was HIS mother name and not Mary. I was led to The Cepher Bible and The Cepher Bible converted the name back to their original Hebrew name. The MESSIAH name is YAHUSHA HA'MASHIACH. HA'MASHIACH means anointed ones and YAHUSHA is a combination of two names. THE FATHER name is YAHUAH and the word Yeshuah means salvation. We have the name YAHUSHA which means

THE FATHER'S SALVATION. Whereas the name Jesus only means deliverer. So as you can read the name Jesus is insufficient. Where is The FATHER in this name? The name Jesus is close to the Greek supreme god zeus. You see Yeshuah [salvation] is all

THE FATHER'S Plan of salvation, THE GREAT EHAYAH ASHER EHAYAH [THE GREAT I AM THAT I AM] SELF EXISTENCE.

We have been deceived by this matrix in so many ways. In The Constitution of The United States it mentions these words about The President of the United States qualification. He can be a natural born citizen or citizen of the United States [Article 2 section 1]. The key word here is "or". Or meaning is used to link alternatives. Or is not the same as and, it is a differentiation. So, there is a difference between a natural born citizen and a citizen of United States, but no one is given an option unless you are aware and I guarantee because the way we have been taught that the majority of people are not aware of this because the word natural born is not place on any documents you see or sign. We just checked the box United States Citizen. Our body has been sold by an illicit organization for bondage. The word actually is citizen of the United States and not United States Citizen. It has been flipped and being flipped changes its meaning. People born in Washington D.C. Puerto, Virgin Islands, American Samoa, and Guam are citizens of The United States. If you are born in the fifty states you are natural born and not a citizen of The United States. Why do I say this is because you and I have been duped by this matrix to give up our right as natural born citizens as a person to be ruled not by a man but self. Why has this system done this? This is the question we need to ask because we have given up our rights, our body (sold) to be ruled by thugs in the highest order. I hope this opens your eyes and just asks questions.

This matrix has turned us against THE CREATOR to get us to turn again THE CREATOR to believe false information. Many believe the earth rotates around the sun, but in the tenth chapter of Joshua, Joshua said the sun stood still and YAH listened and ordered the sun and the moon to stand still and if the earth rotates around the sun, why didn't Joshua ask the earth to stand still? And if you believe in GOD and GOD stands the sun and the sun does stop. The sun rotates around the earth and this is why we have the words sunrise and sunset. The sun is not 93,000,000 million miles away from earth! And the sun is not the center of the universe. YAH placed the sun and the moon in the firmament or expanse. What is the firmament? The firmament is the arch of the sky. **Genesis 1:17** says ELOHIYM set THEM, where in the arch of the sky. The book of **Enoch** states the sun and the moon are same dimension **69:28**

72:47 and **78:3.** This Is my reasoning. People who say the opposite of this don't believe what THE CREATOR has declared. And those who profess anything else are spreading false and misleading information. And false information getting us to believe their lies. So, since the sun and the moon are the same size and this is why we have an eclipse and not the lies they (the one sprouting this false information) want you to be led by.

We believe that YAH started HIS calendar in the springtime and not the wintertime. This is the matrix system to start in the wintertime. This is the matrix system calendar winter, spring, summer, fall and winter. But YAH told Mosheh in **Exodus 12:2** that this shall be your beginning. YAH'S calendar is spring, summer, fall and spring. This is the true calendar and not the gregorian calendar which is a false calendar.

The MESSIAH did not die on a good friday and if anyone believes this false information, they don't believe **Matthew 12:40**. **Matthew 12:40** says 3 days and 3 nights. Let me ask you a question, Can GOD count? Do you think HE would mislead you? We have been misled so badly. We would rather believe a lie than to seek truth. If THE MESSIAH died on friday then **Matthew 12:40** is a lie and if anyone believes that he or she is a bastard to that word. THE MESSIAH died on wednesday and was laid in the tomb by 6pm on <u>wednesday nite</u> **one night, one day** <u>thursday</u>, **two night** <u>thursday night</u>, **two day** <u>friday</u>, **three night** <u>friday night</u> and **three day** <u>saturday.</u> **Matthew 12:40** is only right according to this scenario. The Israelites day starts in the evening as it says in Genesis as YAH said. So if you preach HE died on friday at 3pm and rose early sunday morning, where is the other night and the other days. What many people missed is the Hebrews/Israelites had twelve Shabbath periods. When The MESSIAH died this was a high Shabbath day **Yahuchanon 19:31. Who is telling the truth YAH or man?** I am going to tell you to believe YAH and not this matrix because this matrix will leave you down the road of devastation, destruction and condemnation.

The MESSIAH was NOT born in the winter. The MESSIAH was born in the springtime. I asked google this, when are lambs born? The first time Google stated in the springtime.

Luqas 1:26 The angel Gavriy'el made the announcement in the to Miryam in the sixth month of the Hebrew calendar which is Elul, which is to the gregorian calendar of august and september and you go back three months and we have the month of Sivan, which is the gregorian calendar of may june and not december and we have springtime and not wintertime. Do you see the deception? Who are you going to believe? So, quit going into debt to buy a so-called christmas gift because you are celebrating a pagan holiday which has nothing to do with The MESSIAH'S birth, but in reference to Nimrod's resurrection through his child. This is a pagan holiday. Look who is leading this holiday; satan/santa same letters. Just open your eyes.

Many believe Pa'al was a christian, but nowhere does Pa'al never ever express or profess that he was a christian. Pa'al professed he was a believer, but as I have said before The New Testament was transcribed from Greek and not Hebrew. So the words would be Greek and not Hebrew. The Hebrew word for anointed would be MASHIACH or MESSIAH. Pa'al was Binyamin, Hebrew and Israelite, but he followed MASHIACH. Pa'al saw MASHIACH on the Damascus road and Pa'al was thought to be an Egyptian by the Roman guard because he has melanin in his skin cell. A person labeled as white by the matrix CANNOT become whiter? This is against nature.

How did we in The United States get these categories? **1]** Look at the OMB (Office of Management and Budget) directives Number 15 has made this decision. Who is this group make-up? This group needs to meet again because this group has designated we who have melanin in our skin tone totally wrong and those in the middle east as white. You see people in this group are called white and are not white by skin tone and those listed as black are not black. You see people who look at me and say black, but my skin tone is the same as some of the people from Egypt, Iran, Iraq, India,and Mexico. I am listed black, but according to directive 15, they are white. This matrix has made an error. Do you realize how degrading this is? The injustice of designation. Look at the definition of black and whte. Psychologically this is a disadvantage that should not be. And this office has done this; knowing this. It was done grievously because the law has grievously treated us that has been labeled as black has downright, low down and dirty is aware of this condition it would do. This stinks up to heaven and it will one day be overturned and pay back will be given. For the crime they have treated THE TRUE PEOPLE OF GOD will be given back to them who has done it and they will receive more than what they have given out and will have eternal rewards. You see they [the one that point this out] always mention the jewish holocaust, but the real holocaust was when our foreparents were kidnapped and placed on those stinking slave ships which was the promise from THE CREATOR, The knowledge of HIM, our names have been taken away, our language, our clothes, our food, and our culture, we were forced to forget our homeland and whipped to submit to a man who treated us so outrighteousness our men were told to stripped and these so-called white men took advantage of that man and stuck his penis in another man back hole and rape our mothers, but soon his reign will be over and he will forever regret his actions, but it is too late for he will forever remember what he did to us, but there will be no grace and the OMB need to remove the designation because no other group has the designation of black and white. They have the designation of their countries like Iran, India etc. And those who refuse to hear this grievance will one day hear the echo of their voice into the eternal darkness and fire of the lake of fire. Amein When I hear the word black people I cringed every time because my eyes have been opened to **TRUTH.** When you say or check a block that says black or African-American you have done what this matrix wants. The word black has no legal rights in this damnable system. You have instantly surrendered your status in this worldly system because you are not black. Your and my skin tone range from the lightest color (like those we call white) to the deepest brown. Is a Hershey's bar black? Compare your skin tone to the color black, but the mask has been foolishly placed on our eyes to accept that we are black, but in actuality we are not black. Your skin tone is determined by how much degree of melanin is in your skin tone. Wake up people, wake up, quit sleeping because this matrix doesn't want you to awake, but to stay mindless and numb to the TRUTH. If you look at your picture when you were young, you will see your hair is black and your skin tone is not black, but the majority of us are a shade of brown and not black. This hell of a system does not want you to wake up, but to stay in your numbness state and to accept what the system is puking out toxic waste of information. Wake up people and realize the truth. **YOU ARE NOT BLACK!** So how did we get here? For our foreparents were kidnapped from The Land of Eden and placed in bondage. Placing a person in bondage takes away all of their mindset to be on the right course. Many of you will refuse to accept this truth because your senses are blinded by your sense of belonging to this system of waste. Wake up people and come to TRUTH and be free from this system and change your mind and be set free from this evil system run by the one who was cast out of heaven. Who changed his estate because he fell out from THE FATHER'S abode never to be able to return to his estate of heavenly glory. 2] The OMB Directive 15 states American Indian, Alaskan Native, Asian Pacific Islander, Black, Hispanic and White. If you look you will see Black and White. Why does this list Black and White? There are no Black people or White people. This is totally wrong. This doesn't make sense, but this has been legally designed as such. Words have an effect. Words are so very important. Words can uplift and words can bring you down. Once that word is out there is no way you can suck it back into your lips. It is out and it is out forever So **QUIT** using the term <u>black</u> to identify yourself. Use **HEBREW** as your nation and there is no such thing as race because in The Bible it is nations.

So melanin women quit trying to emulate that non-melanin woman. Wear your own hair and quit getting those straight hair wigs, YAH made your hair and many of you are NOT satisfied with your hair! Just as Chuah (I will eat this fruit). Do you think Miryam would have followed the Egyptian? Notice what I did not say. I know many of you will disagree with this, but this is what I have observed. I did not say not to wash it, but don't buy a straight hair wig that is not your natural style. Like I said before, many of you would be pissed if a non-melanin woman were to put on a wig that looks like your original hair. There is an old saying you become what you see. What do you see on television everyday? You see commercials with non-melanin hair every single day and you are trying to emulate what you see. WAKE UP! Listen, YAH has made your hair the way HE wanted it. And what are you doing? YAH said it is not good for the man to be alone and YAH formed you from the bone from the man's side. He formed every part of you including your hair and HE was very specific in this design of you. Many of you would ask your man and he is afraid to tell you the truth because right now as you are reading this you are pissed, but I am giving you the truth. Who made you? But what I discovered in this life, women like being lied to, but I am trying to inform you that YAH gave you your hair the way HE made you for we did not make yourself. So appreciate what you have and give YAH all the HALLELUJAH. Barak, Yadah, Hallal, Towdah, Shabach, Zamar, Tehillah And now Amein.

You have one strike against you because of how you have been designated by having the wrong skin tone (the thought of the matrix) that we had nothing to do with you and I have been designated as a child of THE MOST HIGH GOD, THE CREATOR, THE GREAT I AM THAT I AM, EHAYAH ASHER EHAYAH. Since we were from THE CREATOR very **THOUGHTS** to go through what we have experienced. You see we did not create ourselves, but we were created as such. It was NOT by our choice, but it was designed and HIS design. And HIS Design was not by chance, but it was given a very precise thought to be so! So, since we were designed by THE CREATOR FOR HIS PURPOSE. So endure what you are going through because it was specifically designed for you. So on judgment day you won't have any regret because THE CREATOR created you specifically for what you are going through. Most people will not accept this because you feel it is what you think and what you do, but where do your thoughts come from? We can't do anything unless THE CREATOR allows it period. Do you think you set the alarm clock without the brain functioning properly? First calculate this statement. The movements of your body are all in play, but somebody's soul and spirit has left their body and they are with THE CREATOR or so very far from THE CREATOR. YAH has allowed us to live. So give thanks to THE CREATOR. Do you think Yoceph or Pa'al desired to go through what they went through? Do you think Yonah desired to go to Nineveh through the belly of a fish? Do you think THE MESSIAH desired to be separated from HIS FATHER? So think, are you not specifically designed for yourself? Are we in charge of our lives or is THE CREATOR in charge? So, whatever happens to you YAH is looking at you! Iyov 34:21 says *"For HIS Eyes are upon the ways of man and HE sees all his goings."*

And you think you can escape?

The WORD of YAH has to be COMPLETED. Once out it can't return void. It will be fulfilled! The coming destruction is coming and prayer won't help.

CONCLUSION

In Conclusion; It was my attempt to give you what I have learned and what I was given by YAH. I am just a servant of YAHUAH. We have been given information by preachers who are to declare GOD'S TRUTH, but they have missing information (or it is missing or they failed to give it out?) they are not declaring. I have used information from the KJV Bible the 1611 KIV or KJV, The Septuagint Bible, The Cepher Bible, The Strong's Exhaustive Concordance, Merriam Webster's Collegiate Dictionary and The New Complete Works of Josephus and **THE RUACH HA'QODESH. Everyone gets their information from a source.** This information is passed down by our eyes, witnesses, orally, by hearing or published on papers through books. NO ONE was at the beginning, but THE CREATOR, Everything there is because of HIM. We have to ask questions and listen because like the old saying g.i.g.o." garbage in and garbage out because if you are given bad instructions and if you follow those instructions you will be lost and this applies to everything in our life. Want to bake a cake, follow the instructions and you won't go astray, but you say "I am going my course." It may be alright but then it could be a horrendous mistake. And some mistakes you don't want to pay for. You said," I did this before and nothing happened;" but every situation is not the same. This time it could be a horrendous mistake and saying "I am sorry may not fix this mistake. A person on a podcast taking shots and smoking marijuana and at the end starting driving. This person ran over a police officer and now this person is saying "I am sooo sorry." Well the police officer is dead. The police officer can't come back to their spouse or children, but now you were talking all type of trash and did something **STUPID,** but we have all done something stupid. So what is the lesson? Make sure you have good information and follow those instructions because I am so sorry won't fix this situation. In other words, this life that we have will end. So make sure your information you have will not lead you on the road of eternal destruction because you have the information that lead you to eternal life or do you have the information that lead you to eternal doom, eternal darkness and eternal destruction because eternal darkness is as a bird grabbing one grain of sand and flying back and forth from one shore all way across the country and flying back and forth. This is what awaits you and it will never end and forever you will be doomed forever because of wrong information that you were informed of. Be sure of the information you have because you could be doomed because this earth will be renewed and how will you get to this renewed earth? I am sure I will forever be with ELOHIYM [THE FATHER, THE SON, THE RUACH HA'QODESH]. And now I conclude my writing and to all of THE BELOVED of ADONAI YAHUSHA HA'MASHIACH I will see you on the other side of Yardan. Because this earth will end as it says. Where will you be when this happens? For example, I was talking to a classmate and she offered me some cocaine and this was back in 1986 and I turned her down because I knew this basketball player who just got drafted and never played one game because he never awakened from that hit of cocaine. Information absorbed and information followed and information learned. So be careful of what information you follow.

THE END

This book is the accumulation of years of study of my life and experiences, teachings, learning, and studies. The BIBLE says study to show thyself approved to GOD (ELOHIYM). This book began because of what men have been taught preaching that JESUS died on a friday and rose from the grave early sunday morning. According to **Matthew 12:40**, *"For as Jonah was three days and three nights in the whale's belly; so shall the Son of man be three days and three nights in the heart of the earth."* So when preachers preach Jesus died on friday and rose early sunday morning, I realize this to be INHERENTLY WRONG and grievously mistaken as the TRUTH and not according to what is written in the word of YAH. Can YAHUAH count? It is my hope those who will read this book will open their eyes to the truth of YAH. What is the truth? John 17;17b says "THY WORD IS TRUTH." PERIOD. We face so many challenges in interpreting THE WORD OF YAH, but its meaning is the truth. THE RUACH HA'QODESH has given it the correct meaning or will. Just ask. We need to just listen up to THE HOLY SPIRIT. Let THE HOLY SPIRIT walk you in all of HIS WAYS. Be led by the truth and not by men's false or false preachers, telling you a lie or a deception, but believe YAH. Merchants will sell us a lie as long as they get their green dollars. The easter bunny, good friday, santa claus, palm sunday and christmas tree and all these lies. These white masters everyday refused to succumb to the truth that the Hebrew slaves were coming to the Americas that this was the real holocaust. Yes, I said holocaust because the number lost this journey no man knows.

Our forefathers were treated worse than animals. Stinking flesh chain up to one another, not being able to freely move, not being to bathe and brush their teeth, dying on the slave ships and being thrown overboard and fed to the sharks, not being to wipe their booties from the dung and pissing on themselves, women menstruating on themselves, having diseases, having babies on those ships, being chained to one another on this long hot journey, being forced to eat, raping our women and sometimes the men. And once we came into America, we were sold, children separated from fathers and mothers. We were placed in holes and hung up like animals and beaten within an inch for not taking the slave master name he gave us. We were not allowed to read and learn the language, for it was against the law and if we were caught learning to read, the penalty was severed.

We ARE THE TRUE NATION OF ISRAEL. As YAH told Avram, your seeds shall be in a strange land for four hundred years and I Will exodus them out of that strange land and I will punish that nation. The four hundred years have ended and the exodus is near. The other sheep that are not of this fold will also be exodus. And Let The People of YAH say Amein!

At the end of this life, we will all be judged by YAHUSHA **John 5:22** says," *For THE FATHER judgeth no man, but hath committed ALL judgment unto the Son.*

INFORMATION

THE 1611 KIV OR KJV

Psalm 68:1-5

1. Let his enemies be scattered: let them also that hate him, flee before him.
2. As smoke is driuen away, so drive them away: as waxe melteth before the fire, so let the wicked perish at the presence of GOD.
3. But let the righteous be glad: let them reioyce before God, yea let them exceedingly reioyce.
4. Sing vnto God, sing praises to his Name: extoll him that rideth vpon the heavens, by his name Iah, and reioyce before him.
5. A father of the fatherlesse, and a iudge of the widows, is God in his holy.

Matthew

16. And Iacob begate Ioseph the husband of Mary, of whom was borne Iesus, who is called Christ.
17. So all the generations from Abraham to Dauid, are fourteene generations: and from Dauid vntill the carrying away into Babylon, are fourteene generations: and from the carrying away into Babylon vnto Christ, are fourteene generations.
18. Now the birth of Iesus Christ was on this wise: When as his mother Mary was espoused to Ioseph (before they came together) shee was found with childe of the holy Ghost

SAME FATHER AND FOUR
DIFFERENT MOTHERS

Jacob Ya`aqov   **Israel Yashar'el**

The twelve tribes of Yashar'el

English	**Mothers**	**Hebrew**
Reuben	Leah	Re'uven
Simeon	Leah	Shim`on
Levi	Leah	Leviy
Judah	Leah	Yahudah
Dan	Bilhah	Dan
Naphtali	Bilhah	Naphtaliy
Gad	Zilpah	Gad
Asher	Zilpah	Asher
Zebulon	Leah	Zevulun
Dinah	Leah	Diynah
Joseph	Rachel	Yoceph
Benjamin	Rachel	Binyamiyn

PROOF OF THE 400 YEARS DID NOT HAPPEN IN EGYPT

Sources	Matthew McGee	Dan Roth
Joseph's death	1640 BC	1672 BC
Mosheh's birth	1576 BC	1608 BC

I have used two sources which show The Hebrew/Israelites were not in affliction for four hundred years. Genesis 15:13-14 said 400 years of affliction. Do you think GOD lied? This affliction is happening here in The United States and this is why we are having all of this troubles and YAHUAH words have to be fulfilled and prayer will not void HIS Words. There shall be more troubles. So, remember what is written. Can YAH lie?

MOSHEH'S FAMILY LINE

---◦⁓◦---

Avraham Great Great Great Great Grandfather
Hebrew Genesis 14:13

Yitschaq Great Great Great Grandfather
Hebrew

Ya`aqov Great Great Grandfather
Hebrew

Leviy Great Grandfather
Hebrew

Qohath Grandfather
Hebrew

Amram Father
Hebrew

Mosheh Son
Hebrew **Exodus 4:6-8**

These are men of color because a person that is called white cannot become whiter. Mosheh's skin was turned white.

THE HEBREW CALENDAR

<u>NISAN</u>	Mar-Apr	30 days
<u>IYAR</u>	Apr-May	29 days
<u>SIVAN</u>	May-Jun	30
<u>TAMMUZ</u>	Jun-Jul	29
<u>AB</u>	Jul-Aug	29
<u>ELUL</u>	Aug-Sept	29
<u>TISHRI</u>	Sept-Oct	30
<u>HESHVAN</u>	Oct-Nov	29/30
<u>CHISLEV</u>	Nov-Dec	29
<u>TEVET</u>	Dec-Jan	30
<u>SHEVET</u>	Jan-Feb	30
<u>ADAR</u>	Feb-Mar	29/30

The Messiah's conception was announced in <u>the sixth month</u> by the angel Gabriel Luke/ Luqas 1:36. The sixth month is Elul. so, the child (MESSIAH) was born in the month of Sivan which is in the springtime. The Hebrew/Israelites were always to celebrate The Passover which is in the first month on the 14th day of Nisan Exodus 12:1-6.

The MESSIAH was The Passover's lamb. So he died on the 14th day of Nisan as the Passover's lamb.

ABOUT ME

— ❧ —

My name is Carl L Jones. I have been saved since I was twelve years old. I have had tough times, easy times, spiritual highs and spiritual lows. My faith in ELOHIYM has not faltered. I have six children. I have worked for SBC, GTE, Verizon and WalMart. I have been associated with the Methodist Church, Church of The Living GOD, Church of CHRIST, The Called Fellowship, Community First Baptist Church and The Church of GOD In CHRIST. The pastors in my life have been Pastor Davis of Mount Olives Baptist Church, in Corsicana, Texas (who immersed me in water); Pastor Travis B. Cannon, Evangelist Temple Church of GOD in CHRIST, Dallas, Texas; Pastor C. H. Gerald of Community First Baptist Church, Dallas, Texas; and Pastor Kevin A. Powell of The Called Fellowship, Dallas, Texas. I would like to give my thanks and appreciation.

I would also like to thank each pastor for all that I have obtained from them.

I would like to thank the following: my Dad L.B. Jones; mother, Mary Jones; my children; my Aunt Sister; Uncle Joe; my first Cousin Kenneth Martin; Pastor Tony Evans of Oak Cliff Bible Fellowship; Pastor Bob George of People to People Ministry in Farmer Branch, Texas; Pastor Paul Sheppard of Enduring Truth in California; Pastor Rickie Rush of The Inspiring Body of Christ; Pastor Corby Bush of Greater Harvest Church; Evangelist Dixon; Evangelist Richard White aka Mr Clean; Evangelist Mother Board; Bob George of People to People Ministries; These pastors and evangelists has been instrumental in my walk with HA'MASHIACH. And I would very much like to thank the Evangelist (I can't remember his name) who told me years ago to accept and believe you are **"saved"** because at that time I was struggling with whether I was saved or not. From that point on, I accepted the fact that I am saved and GOD has worked on me because HE had a specific purpose for me. I would love to give thanks for Sunday School. It was through Sunday School that I became a student of The Word of GOD. We are trying to save this earth, but as The Bible says this earth will be replaced or renewed or reset. In other words it can't be saved, period. Why, because YAH said it. Since YAH stated that heaven and earth would pass away, if not HE lied. So if it doesn't happen YAH has lied, but since HE has stated it, it has to happen. Baby, it is going to happen. RESET! It may seem strange to you, living your life, but look at what we are doing? Greenhouse effect, polluted water, polluted oceans, food supply contaminated, we are in so muuuuucccchhhh debt $24,000,000,000,000 trillion dollars etc. Remember this has to be paid back. We need a reset. So be ye ready when all of a sudden mother nature goes off. The MESSIAH is coming back.

I was led by THE RUACH to write this book to get YOU to think ABOUT This WORLD SYSTEM we live in CALLED THE MATRIX. So ? everything you have been taught, PLEASE! I am NOW finished and NOW I drop THE MIC! Now Pass it on!

WHAT IS YOUR ESCAPE PLAN?

— ✌ —

What do YOU know?

Are <u>YOU ASSURED</u> OF THE PATH
YOU ARE GOING?

WHERE WILL YOU
BE
AT THE END?

HOW WILL YOU
GET TO THIS
NEW EARTH?

WILL WHEN THIS HAPPENS?
ONLY **<u>GOD</u>** KNOWS!

ARE
YOU
READY?

AND

YOU SAY

FOR

WHAT

This earth will be destroyed!

This is what I KNOW!

MAKE YOUR ESCAPE

PLAN

NOW!

First witness

Revelation 21:

And I saw a new heaven and a new earth: For the first heaven and the first earth were passed away;and there was no more.

OLD EARTH
DESTROYED BY FIRE!

Second witness

Isaiah 65:17 For, behold, I created new heavens and a new earth: and the former shall not be remembered, nor come into mind.

NEW EARTH
GLORIOUS!
PEACEFUL @ REST!

Questions

1. WHO IS YAH?

2. WHERE IS YAH?

3. DO YOU BELIEVE IN THE ONE GOD?[FATHER SON AND HOLY SPIRIT]

4. DOES YAH HAVE SAYINGS?

5. IS THERE ACTUALLY A PLACE CALLED HEAVEN[WHERE YAH RESIDES]

6. WHAT DOES YAH SAY?

7. WHERE IS HEAVEN LOCATED?

8. HOW DO YOU GET TO HEAVEN?

9. DO YOU WANT TO RESIDE IN HEAVEN?

10. WILL YOU RESIDE IN THIS PLACE CALLED HEAVEN?

11. IS THERE A ONE WORLD SYSTEM COMING (TO BE RULED BY THE MAN OF SIN, SATANIC CONTROLLED)?

12. DID YOU KNOW THAT THIS WORLD IS COMING TOWARD ITS END?

13. IS THIS WORLD COMING TO AN END?

14. WHERE WILL YOU SPEND ETERNITY?

15. ARE YOU WILLING TO DIE (PHYSICALLY) FOR YOUR BELIEF?

16. WHERE WILL YOU SPEND ETERNITY?

17. WILL THERE BE A NEW HEAVEN AND A NEW EARTH?

18. DOES YAH MEAN WHAT HE SAYS?

19. IS THE WORD OF YAH TRUE?

Isaiah 57:15

MY LIFE FOR YAHUSHA HA'MASHIACH Ministry.

FOOTNOTES

—— ✑ ——

1. "GOD", *Encyclopedia Americana* 2001, Volume 12, page 835.

2. "Deism", *Encyclopedia Americana* 2001, Volume 8, page 644.

3. "Passover", *Britannica Encyclopedia* 2002, Volume 9 page 188

4. "Moon",*Britannica Encyclopedia* 2002, Volume 19 page 434

5. "Jewish Calendar" *The Criswell Study Bible*, Thomas Nelson Publisher

6. "Calendar" *Encyclopedia Americana* 1999, Volume 5, page 187-188.

7. "Webster" *Third New International Dictionary Unabridged* Copyright 1993: The Merriam-Webster Inc. Publishers.

8. "Webster's II New Riverside University Dictionary 18984: The Riverside Publishing Company ISBN 0-39-33957-x

9. "Melanin", Wikipedia

10. "The Letter J" Wikipedia

WHAT IS THIS BOOK ABOUT

—✦—

What this book is about is the failed communication (the lies) of this matrix to the public about the truth of this matrix in which we live. We have been deceived by misinformation believing what we have been taught all our life. The leader of this misinformation is being led by the god of this world and men have joined in his court for money, fame and the threat of death. So it was my endeavor to contradict what man has given information that is supposed to be truth but in reality it is false, but we have been led to believe it is TRUTH. One truth that man has published is that the sun is the center of this universe and that it is 93,000,000 million away from this earth and all you have to do is look at the sky and see it is in firmament as Genesis says and ask the question is that 93,000,000 miles away from earth and the earth does not the rotates around the sun, but the sun rotates around the earth and the earth is stationary and the earth does not move. And we celebrate good friday, but THE MESSIAH did not die on a friday as told by men (preachers), but was in the tomb three days and three nights as Mattithyahu 12:40 says and that the true MY People of YAH are we who has melanin in our skin tone and that we are not black but different shades of color. The MESSIAH was born into a Hebrew's family and thereby making HIS nationality Hebrew and HIS true name is not Jesus (which is Greek) but YAHUSHA which is HIS Hebrew name because HE has a dark color in HIS skin tone. The My People are Hebrew and would have Hebrew names and not English names such as Jacob, Issac, John, Matthew, Luke, Peter but would have Hebrew names like Ya`aqov, Yitschaq, Yahuchanon, Mattithyahu, Luqas, Kepha etc. If MY People are called by my name. The FATHER name is **YAH** as HalleluJAH

Psalm 68:4. You see we have been misled to believe not truth, but lies. The people of americas are **"THE MY PEOPLE OF THE BIBLE!"**